Bankruptcy & Distressed Restructurings

Analytical Issues and Investment Opportunities

Bankruptcy & Distressed Restructurings

Analytical Issues and Investment Opportunities

Edited by **Edward I. Altman**

BeardBooks

Washington, DC

Library of Congress Cataloging-in-Publication Data

Bankruptcy & distressed restructurings : analytical issues and investment
    opportunities / edited by Edward I. Altman.
        p.   cm.
    Originally published: New York : New York University Salomon
Center, Leonard N. Stern School of business : Homewood, Ill. :
Business One Irwin, c1993.
    Papers from a conference held March 1991 under the joint
sponsorship of the New York University Salomon Center and a number
of interested corporate contributors.
    Includes bibliographical references.
    ISBN 1-893122-00-X (paper)
    1. Corporate reorganizations—United States—Congresses.
2. Bankruptcy—United States—Congresses. I. Altman, Edward I.,
1941–   . II. Title: Bankruptcy and distressed restructurings.
KF1544.A75B36   1998
346.7307'8—dc21   98-35632
                                              CIP

Printed in the United States of America

PREFACE AND OVERVIEW

In today's vulnerable and volatile business climate, corporate bankruptcy and Chapter 11 reorganization are common occurrences among U.S. corporations of all sizes and in all sectors. No longer are our larger entities immune to corporate distress, failure, and defaults on their outstanding indebtedness. The uniqueness of corporate "death" in the United States has many fascinating by-products. The market for distressed firms' debt and equity securities has captured the interest and imagination of the investment community like never before. And this trend in corporate distress analysis has not escaped the scrutiny and interest of academic scholars in corporate finance, financial markets, economics, and law.

With these factors in mind, we organized a conference on Bankruptcy and Distressed Restructurings in March 1991 under the joint sponsorship of the New York University Salomon Center and a number of interested corporate contributors. The conference brought together the academic and practitioner communities to study and discuss corporate distressed restructurings and bankruptcies for the first time in a meaningful and comprehensive way. We were impressed to find a substantial number of theoretical and empirical investigations by academics on the general subject of corporate distress. Such topics as the determinants of successful distressed exchange issues and Chapter 11 proceedings, bankruptcy and liquidation costs and their impact on corporate values, investment opportunities in distressed and defaulted securities, management and competitor behavior related to distress, and an evaluation of investor priorities and market efficiencies were analyzed in detail.

A number of academic papers analyzed the conceptual and empirical aspect of corporate restructurings—both distressed and not. The papers in Session #1 analyzed out-of-court distressed exchanges and compared their expected and actual performance with formal Chapter 11 reorganizations. Jensen argued for the efficiency of these private transactions that obviate the need for more drastic bankruptcy filings. To some extent the private distressed exchange arrangement has been replaced by the so-called pre-packaged Chapter 11 bankruptcy.

Gilson, John, and Lang investigate the firm characteristics and capital structure features that distinguish a successful out-of-court distressed restructuring from an unsuccessful one. Brown, James, and Mooradian also analyze out-of-court arrangements in terms of how they are structured and why they might fail. These involve asymmetric information of different stakeholders about the firm's prospects and holdout problems when public debtholders are involved. Their analysis leads to predictions about how stock prices will respond to the announcement of a debt restructuring. Betker, Franks, and Torous examine, in a later session, a related area analyzing whether stockholders are better off when a firm is restructured privately.

Our first key-issue panel, moderated by Gerald Buccino, a turnaround specialist, analyzed the management and the valuation of distressed firms (i) at the point of a highly leveraged restructuring, e.g., LBOs; (ii) during the post-restructuring period; and (iii) after distress sets in and even bankruptcy is declared. Altman and Smith link classic capital structure theories with the recent successes and failures of highly leveraged restructurings. They postulate about and examine a simple but critical ingredient in successful highly leveraged transactions—the ability to pay down a significant proportion of the new debt very soon after the restructuring. Michael Price, a Heine Securities, Inc., money manager of considerable success and experience, discussed (not in this volume) both active and passive strategies involved with investing in distressed and defaulted securities.

Our next session focused on various aspects of the bankruptcy process with particular emphasis on the costs of financial distress to the debtor. Weiss analyzes 37 firms that reorganized under the new (post-1978) Bankruptcy Code in order to assess their direct, out-of-pocket costs and any violations of priority of claims in the process. He finds very small direct costs, about 3 percent of total firm value, which is consistent with prior studies which looked at bankruptcies prior to the new Code's enactment. He also finds that the absolute priority of claims is violated in the vast majority of cases, although secured creditors' claims are upheld in all but a few cases. Johnson, Wolfe, and Lynch next assess the impact on shareholders of a successful reorganization under the Code versus a liquidation. Finally, Lang and Stulz assess the conflicting effects of bankruptcy announcements on competitors of the bankruptcy firm. They find that a bankruptcy declaration has a small but rather reliable negative effect on common stock values. This implies that the contagion effect slightly dominates the competitive effects—the latter of which should favor competitors on the news of the bankruptcy. They also assess the impact of firm size on the two different announcement effects.

Our second key-issue panel focused on an increasingly important dimension of distressed firm investments. While the trading in distressed and defaulting firms' public debt has been a popular investment strategy for quite some time, the trading in private debt, both bank and trade claims, is a relatively new and exciting arena. Dennis Dolan and his colleagues from Salomon Brothers present a primer on the highly leveraged transaction loans (HLTs) market and argue for the attractive return potential on the estimated $800 billion HLT market—only a small portion of which is currently available for transactions.

Martin Fridson, Director of High Yield Debt Research at Merrill Lynch & Co., presents a more cautious appraisal of the emerging secondary market in distressed bank loans. He is particularly concerned about potential regulatory influence on the market and surveys six broad regulatory areas. For example, the issue of recourse arrangements and their impact on calculating regulatory capital for banks is explored with respect to this emerging market.

In Part Four of the volume, a number of academic researchers discuss strategic issues for distressed firms and their claimants/investors. Karen Wruck assesses distressed firms' organizational efficiency. She finds evidence that financial distress has benefits as well as costs, and that the financial and ownership structures affect net bankruptcy costs.

Stuart Gilson presents two papers on corporate governance issues of distressed firms. Changes in management strategies, efficiencies, indeed the very turnover of managerial personnel itself, have implications for the assessment of bankruptcy costs. His study presents new evidence on these and related topics such as how ownership of distressed company residual claims (e.g., equity) changes as debt is renegotiated. Incentives for recontracting out of default instead of bankruptcy is a recurring theme of research in Gilson's as well as a number of other papers in this volume. One conclusion reached is that managers' default related costs losses are significant.

Eberhart et al. analyze the so-called absolute priority (APR) doctrine—a very important issue in distressed firm analysis. They find that, despite this "doctrine," bankruptcy proceedings are leaving shareholders and junior creditors with valuable assets even when senior claimants receive only partial settlements. They hypothesize that the high frequency and magnitude of these violations of absolute priority should be reflected in security prices. Their research shows that, on average, 7.6 percent of the total firm value is paid out to junior claimants in excess of what is necessary under APR. Indeed, they find violations of APR in 23 of the 30 cases examined. And firm equity values, measured subsequent to the bankruptcy announcement, do reflect those "excess" amounts.

Papers by Franks, Torous, and Betker, and Franks and Torous analyze the institutional features of Chapter 11 bankruptcies and compare this process with privately restructured arrangements. They find that the formal-legal Chapter 11 process is complex, lengthy and costly, adding substantially to the costs of bankruptcy. This is consistent with several of the other conceptual and empirical studies discussed in this volume. Like Eberhart et al., they find many violations of absolute priority and assert that they occur due to the bargaining process and the fact that stockholder-oriented managements can preserve firm value.

The pricing of risky equity is also investigated by these authors. They extend the earlier work of Gilson, John, and Lang, discussed above, which found statistically significant higher abnormal returns out of bankruptcy than in. On the contrary, Betker et al. find only marginally predictive ability as to which firms will be able to avoid the Chapter 11 process. Finally, the benefits of the Chapter 11 process are presented as arguments to mitigate the preconceived notion that private, out-of-court arrangements are almost always preferable to formal proceedings.

The final paper in this volume is presented by the editor to explore a number of important new trends in the bankruptcy-reorganization environment. One of these new developments, the "prepackaged Chapter 11," involves a sufficient number and amount of claimants (½ and ⅔, respectively) agreeing on a plan of reorganization followed by the actual bankruptcy petition. This arrangement can achieve the benefits of both an out-of-court settlement and the less stringent voting requirements of Chapter 11 proceedings. In many ways, it is a substitute for a less formal distressed restructuring which has become less advantageous due to some recent tax legislation and bankruptcy court decisions.

Another new occurrence involves fraudulent conveyance legal claims by creditors who assert that a highly leveraged transaction, e.g., an LBO, caused the firm's insolvency which eventually led to a default and losses to creditors. Typical defendants to these legal actions are the senior creditors, old shareholders, and/or advisors to the original transaction. The paper explores the legal, economic, and empirical issues involved in these claims.

Finally, we examine an increasingly common financing source for bankrupt firms—the debtor-in-possession (DIP) loan. Many large firms, particularly retailers, have a critical need for working capital soon after a Chapter 11 petition. The DIP loan, which usually provides a super-priority as well as a secured status to the lender, is now a popular source of financing for many debtors. The paper explores the conceptual as well as practical advantages of this loan-type for the lender as well as the debtor.

There were a number of practitioner participants at our conference who did not present self-authored papers but who contributed a great deal to the important information flow that the New York University Salomon Center strives for in all of its conferences. We particularly want to thank Michael Cook (Skadden, Arps, Slate, Meagher & Flom), Joseph Donohue (J. P. Morgan & Co.), Peter Geraghty (NMB Postbank Groep), Lawrence King (Wachtell, Lipton, Rosen & Katz and NYU), Michael F. Price (Heine Securities), and Michael C. Singer (BDS Securities) for their insightful comments. Finally, our gratitude to the important perspectives presented by two prominent bankruptcy judges, the Honorable Judges Conrad B. Duberstein and Howard Schwartzberg.

We were extremely fortunate to have the enthusiastic and generous support of a number of sponsors for the conference, including Buccino & Associates, Merrill Lynch & Co., NMB Postbank Groep N.V., R. D. Smith & Co. (now BDS Securities), Salomon Brothers, and Skadden, Arps, Slate, Meagher & Flom. This support not only helped to cover our administrative expenses but also went to sponsor additional research in the area of distressed firm analysis and related topics.

A final word on the superb administrative talents of Mary Jaffier of the NYU Salomon Center, not only for the smooth running of the conference but for the preparation of this volume. Jim Cozby also deserves a great deal of credit for the preparation of this volume.

Edward I. Altman
Max L. Heine Professor of Finance
Managing Director, Fixed Income
   & Credit Markets
NYU Salomon Center
March 1992

CONTENTS

PART ONE

DISTRESSED RESTRUCTURINGS

CHAPTER 1

CORPORATE CONTROL AND THE POLITICS OF FINANCE

Michael C. Jensen

The U.S. market for corporate control reached the height of its activity and influence in the last years of the 1980s. Among their many accomplishments, mergers and acquisitions, LBOs, and other leveraged restructurings of the past decade sharply reduced the effectiveness of size as a deterrent to takeover. The steady increase in the size of the deals throughout the 1980s culminated in the $25 billion buyout of RJR-Nabisco in 1989 by KKR, a partnership with fewer than 30 professionals.

The effect of such transactions was to transfer control over vast corporate resources—often trapped in mature industries or uneconomic conglomerates—to those prepared to pay large premiums to use those resources more efficiently. In some cases, the acquirers functioned as agents rather than principals, selling part or all of the assets they acquired to others. In many cases, the acquirers were unaffiliated individual investors (labeled "raiders" by those opposed to the transfer of control) rather than to other large public corporations. The increased asset sales, enlarged payouts, and

Michael C. Jensen is Edsel Bryant Ford Professor of Business Administration at the Harvard Business School. In 1973, he founded the *Journal of Financial Economics* of which he now serves as managing editor.

The author appreciates the research assistance of Brian Barry, Susan Brumfield, and Steve-Anna Stephens, editorial and substantive comments and help from Don Chew and Karen Wruck, and research support provided by the Division of Research of the Harvard Business School.

Reprinted with permission from the *Journal of Applied Corporate Finance* (Summer 1991).

heavy use of debt to finance such takeovers led to a large-scale return of equity capital to shareholders.

The consequence of this control activity has been a pronounced trend toward smaller, more focused, more efficient—and in many cases private—corporations.[1] And while capital and resources were being forced out of our largest companies throughout the 1980s, the small- to medium-sized U.S. corporate sector was experiencing vigorous growth in employment and capital spending. At the same time our capital markets were bringing about this massive transfer of corporate resources, the U.S. economy was experiencing a 92-month expansion and record-high percentages of people employed.

The resulting transfer of control from corporate managers to increasingly active investors has aroused enormous controversy. The strongest opposition has come from groups whose power and influence have been challenged by corporate restructuring: notably, the Business Roundtable (the voice of managers of large corporations), organized labor, and politicians whose ties to wealth and power were being weakened. The media, always responsive to popular opinion even as they help shape it, have succeeded in reinvigorating the American populist tradition of hostility to Wall Street "financiers." The current controversy pitting Main Street against Wall Street has been wrought to a pitch that recalls the intensity of the 1930s. Newspapers, books, and magazines have obliged the public's desire for villains by furnishing unflattering detailed accounts of the private doings of those branded "corporate raiders."

Barbarians at the Gate, for example, the best-selling account of the RJR-Nabisco transaction, is perhaps best described as an attempt to expose the greed and chicanery that goes into the making of some Wall Street deals. And, on that score, the book is effective (though it's worth noting that, amidst the general destruction of reputations, the principals of KKR and most of the Drexel team come across as professional and principled). But what also emerges from the 500-plus pages—though the authors seem to fail to grasp its import—is clear evidence of corporate-wide inefficiencies at RJR-Nabisco, including massive waste of corporate "free cash flow," that would allow KKR to pay existing stockholders $12 billion over the previous market value for the right to bring about change.

And now that over two years have passed since that control change, KKR has defied skeptics not only by managing the company's huge debt load, but also by creating another $5 billion in value (providing the original LBO warrant and equity holders with a compound annual rate of return of 59 percent), extracting about $6 billion in capital through asset sales, and bringing the company public again.[2] In the process, it has also paid off almost $13 billion of the original $29 billion in debt (without, according to KKR, any losses to note or bond holders). Thus, the consequences to date of the RJR buyout for all investors, buying as well as selling, appear to be a remarkable $17 billion in added value.[3]

For economists and management scientists concerned about corporate efficiency, the RJR story is deeply disturbing. What troubles us is not so much the millions of dollars spent on sports celebrities and airplanes—or the greed and unprofessional behavior of several leading investment bankers— but rather the waste of billions in unproductive capital expenditures and organizational inefficiencies.[4] Viewed in this light—although, here again, the authors don't seem aware of what they have discovered—*Barbarians* is testimony to the massive failure of the internal control system led by RJR's board of directors. As former SEC Commissioner Joseph Grundfest has put it, the real "barbarians" in this book were *inside* the gates.[5]

Moreover, the fact that Ross Johnson, RJR's CEO, could be held up by *Fortune* as a model corporate leader only months before the buyout[6] attests to the difficulty of detecting even such gross inefficiencies and thus suggests that organizational inefficiencies of this magnitude may extend well beyond RJR. Although parts of corporate American may be guilty of under-investing—as the media continually assert—there is little doubt that many of our largest U.S. companies have grossly *over*invested, whether in desperate attempts to maintain sales and earnings in mature or declining businesses or by diversifying outside of their core businesses. Many of our best-known companies—GM, IBM, Xerox, and Kodak come to mind most readily— have wasted vast amounts of resources over the last decade or so. The chronic overinvestment and overstaffing of such companies reflect the wide-spread failure of our corporate internal control systems. And it is this funda-mental control problem that gave rise to the corporate restructuring movement of the 1980s.

The Media and the Academy.   But the role of takeovers and LBOs in curbing corporate inefficiency is not the story told by our mass media. When media accounts manage to raise their focus above the "morality play" craved by the public to consider broader issues of economic efficiency and competitiveness, the message is invariably the same: Leveraged restructurings are eroding the competitive strength of U.S. corporations by forcing cutbacks in employment, R&D, and capital investment. The journal-istic method of inquiry is the investigation of selected cases, a process potentially subject to "selection bias." And the typical journalistic product is a series of anecdotes—stories that almost invariably carry with them a strong emotive appeal for the "victims" of control changes, with little or no attention paid to long-run efficiency effects.[7]

Using very different methods and language, academic economists have subjected corporate control activity to intensive study. And the research contradicts the popular rhetoric. Indeed, I know of no area in economics today where the divergence between popular belief and the evidence from scholarly research is so great.

The most careful academic research strongly suggests that takeovers—along with leveraged restructurings prompted by the threat of takeover—have generated large gains for shareholders and for the economy as a whole. My estimates indicate that over the 14-year period from 1976 to 1990, the $1.8 trillion of corporate control transactions—that is, mergers, tender offers, divestitures, and LBOs—created over $650 billion in value for selling-firm shareholders.[8] And this estimate includes neither the gains to the buyers in such transactions nor the value of efficiency improvements by companies pressured by control market activity into reforming without a visible control transaction.

Some of the shareholder gains in highly leveraged transactions (HLTs) have come at the expense of bondholders, banks, and other creditors who financed the deals. But the amount of such losses is not likely to exceed $50 billion; a current best estimate would probably run around $25 billion.[9] (To put this number into perspective, IBM alone has seen its equity value fall by $25 billion in the past six months.)[10] And thus far, there is no reliable evidence that any appreciable part of the remaining $600 billion or so of net gains to stockholders has come at the expense of other corporate "stakeholders" such as employees, suppliers, and the IRS.[11]

The well-documented increases in shareholder value have been largely dismissed by journalists and other critics of restructuring as "paper gains" having little bearing on the long-term vitality and competitiveness of American business. Some even point to such gains as evidence of a "short-term" orientation that is said to be destroying American business.

For financial economists, however, theory and evidence suggest that as long as such value increases are not arising from pure transfers from other parties to the corporate "contract," they are reliable predictors of increases in corporate operating efficiency. And, as I discuss later in this chapter, research on LBOs has indeed produced direct evidence of such efficiencies; moreover, macroeconomic data now reveal a dramatic improvement in the health and productivity of American industry during the 1980s.

The Present.   In the past two years, restructuring transactions have come to a virtual standstill, and there are few signs today of a well-functioning corporate control market. Total M&A transactions fell 56 percent from a peak of $247 billion in 1988 to $108 billion in 1990; and this decline has accelerated through the first six months of 1991.

Widespread S&L failures (along with some failures of commercial banks and insurance companies) and a number of highly publicized cases of troubled HLTs have combined with the criminalization of securities law disclosure violations and the high-profile RICO and insider trading prosecutions to create a highly charged political climate.[12] Such political forces have produced a major re-regulation of our financial markets. The political origin of such regulatory initiatives is revealed by the fact that bad real estate loans dwarf junk bond losses and bad HLT loans as contributors to the current weakness of our financial institutions.[13]

With the eclipse of the new issue market for junk bonds, the application of HLT rules to commercial bank lending,[14] and new restrictions on insurance companies,[15] funding for large highly leveraged transactions has all but disappeared. Even if financing were available, court decisions (including those authorizing the use of poison pills and defensive ESOP plans) and state antitakeover and control shareholder amendments have significantly increased the difficulty of making a successful hostile offer.

As a result, takeovers today are likely to revert to the pattern of the 1960s and the 1970s, when large companies used takeovers of other companies to build corporate "empires." The recent AT&T acquisition of NCR is an example. And if the past is a reliable guide, many such acquisitions are likely to end up destroying value and reducing corporate efficiency.

Contracting Problems Compounded by Politics. As prices were bid up to more competitive levels in the second half of the 1980s, the markets "overshot." Contracting problems between the promoters of HLTs and the suppliers of capital, as I will argue later, led to too many overpriced deals. In this sense, the financial press is right in attributing *part* of the current conditions in our debt and takeover markets to too many unsound transactions. Such transactions, especially those completed after 1985, were overpriced by their promoters and, as a consequence, overleveraged (and it is important to keep this order of causality in mind).

But it is also clear that intense political pressures to curb the corporate control market have greatly compounded the problems cause by this "contracting failure." However genuine and justified their concern about our deposit insurance funds, the reactions of Congress, the courts, and regulators to losses (which, again, are predominantly the result of real estate, not HLT, loans) have sharply restricted the availability of capital to noninvestment grade companies, thereby significantly increasing the rate of corporate defaults. They have also limited the ability of financially troubled companies to reorganize outside of court, thus ensuring that most defaulted companies wind up in bankruptcy. All of this, in my view, has contributed significantly to the current weakness of the economy.[16]

In this chapter, I have seven major aims.

First, I review new macroeconomic evidence on changes in productivity in American manufacturing that is dramatically inconsistent with popular claims that corporate control transactions were crippling the industrial economy in the 1980s.

Second, I show how the restructuring movement of the 1980s reflected the reemergence of active investors in the United States—a group that had been essentially dormant since the 1930s. In so doing, I argue that much of this leveraged restructuring activity addressed a fundamental problem facing many large, mature public companies: the conflict between management and shareholders over control of corporate "free cash flow."

Third, I summarize my conception of "LBO associations" as new organizational forms—structures that overcome the deficiencies of large public conglomerates. I also discuss the similarity between LBO associations and Japanese business financing networks known as *keiretsu*.

Fourth, I extend this overseas comparison by summarizing my argument that the highly leveraged financial structures of the 1980s should lead to the "privatization" of bankruptcy (i.e., out-of-court reorganization) that characterizes Japanese practice in reorganizing troubled companies.

Fifth, I present a theory of "boom-bust" cycles in venture markets that explains how private contracting problems combined with the political interference mentioned above to bring about financial distress in many of the leveraged transactions put together in the latter half of the 1980s.

Sixth, I argue that misguided changes in the tax and regulatory codes and in bankruptcy court decisions have blocked the normal economic incentives for creditors to come to agreement outside of Chapter 11, thus almost putting an end to out-of-court reorganizations. The consequence has been an increase in the costs of financial distress, and a sharp rise in the number of Chapter 11 filings.

Seventh and last, I propose a set of changes in the Chapter 11 process designed to correct the gross inefficiencies built into the current process. Rather than attempting to preserve the control of current management and extend the life of organizations (in some cases, without economic justification), my proposals reflect the thinking of academic economists and lawyers about how to reduce the costs of financial distress and thus maximize the total value of the firm to all investors.

NEW INSIGHTS FROM MACROECONOMIC DATA

In addition to the continuing stream of scholarly work documenting efficiency gains by LBO companies, productivity gains are also visible in the aggregate data. As summarized in the top two panels of Figure 1-1, the pattern of productivity and unit labor costs in the U.S. manufacturing sector over the period 1950–1989 is inconsistent with popular characterizations of the 1980s as the decade of the dismantling of American industry. Beginning in 1982, there was a dramatic increase in the productivity of the manufacturing sector (see panel A)—a turnaround unmatched in the last 40 years. In panel B, we see a striking reversal of the steady increase in unit labor costs—a reversal also unmatched in the last 40 years.[17]

Such cost reductions and efficiency gains have not come at the expense of labor generally (although *organized* labor has certainly seen its influence wane). As show in Panels C, D, and E, there has been a rise in total employment and hours worked since the end of the 1981–82 recession; hourly compensation has continued to rise since 1982 (although at a somewhat slower rate than before); and percentage unemployment has fallen dramatically since 1982.

The Effect on Capital Investment.   Critics of leveraged restructuring also claim that corporate capital investment was a casualty of the M&A activity of the 1980s. But, as shown in Panel F, after a pause in 1982, capital growth in the manufacturing sector has continued to rise—although, again, at a slower rate than previously. This pattern is consistent with my "free cash flow" argument that corporate restructuring was a response to excessive capital in many sectors of American industry. The pattern also suggests that, although capital was being squeezed out of the low-growth manufacturing sector by the payouts of cash and substitution of debt for equity, it was being recycled back into the economy. Some of that capital was transferred to smaller companies, including large inflows to the venture capital market. At the same time, the resulting organizational changes and efficiency gains at larger companies have provided the basis for renewed capital spending.[18]

The Effect of R&D.   Another persistent objection to the control market is that it reduces valuable R&D expenditures. But, as shown in Figure 1–2, while M&A activity was rising sharply after the 1982 recession (until

FIGURE 1–1
Trends in Manufacturing, 1950–1989

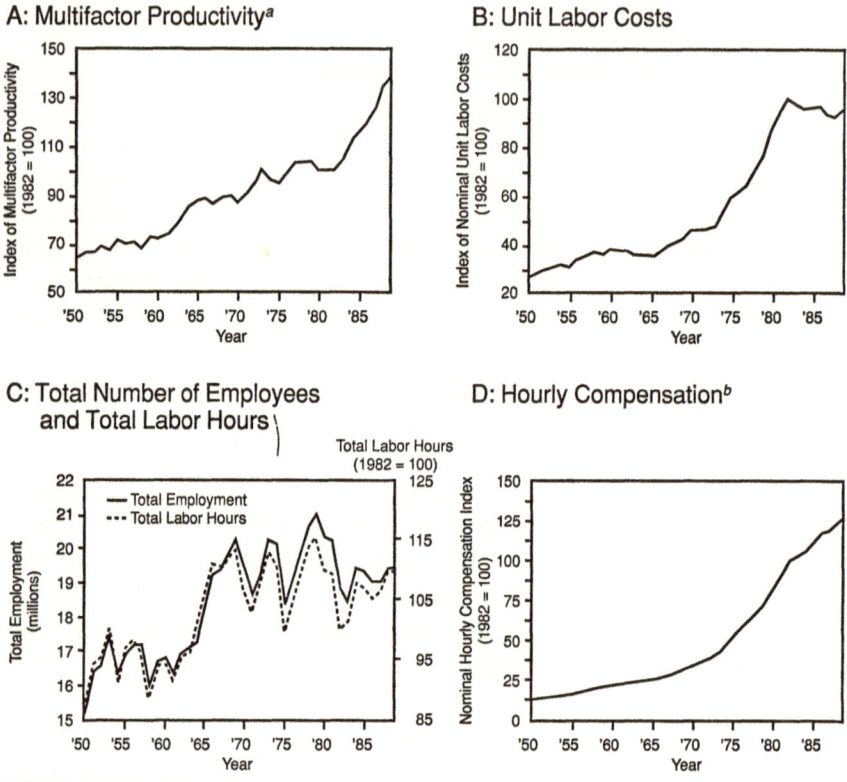

A: Multifactor Productivity[a]

B: Unit Labor Costs

C: Total Number of Employees
and Total Labor Hours

D: Hourly Compensation[b]

plummeting in 1990), real R&D expenditures were reaching new highs in each year of the period from 1975 to 1990. R&D also rose from 1.8 percent to 3.4 percent of sales during this period.[19]

In short, although the macro data do not establish control market activity as a *cause* of the dramatic productivity improvements, they provide no support for the popular outcry against the workings of the corporate control market.[20]

The Costs of Restructuring (and the Alternative to Takeovers)

There is no doubt that the corporate restructuring movement resulted in changes painful to many individuals. With the shrinkage of some compa-

FIGURE 1–1, concluded

E: Unemployment Rate

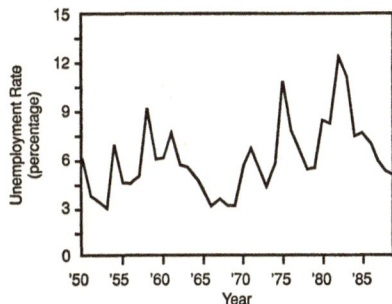

F: Capital Inputs

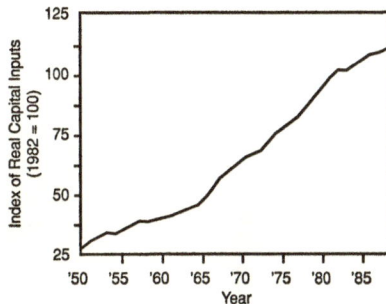

[a] Multifactor productivity is real output per unit of combined capital and labor.
[b] Hourly compensation includes wages and salaries, supplements, employer payments for social security, and other employer-financed benefit plans.

Sources: **Panels A and F**—Bureau of Labor Statistics, "Multifactor Productivity, 1988 and 1989," Table 3. **Panels B and D**—Bureau of Labor Statistics, "International Comparisons of Manufacturing Productivity and Labor Cost Trends, 1989" (July 1990), USDL #90-383, Table 2. **Panel C**—Bureau of Labor Statistics, "Employment and Earnings," supplement obtained from Office of Employment and Unemployment; Bureau of Labor Statitistics, "International Comparisons of Manufacturing Productivity and Labor Cost Trends, 1989" (July 1990), USDL #90-383, Table 2. **Panel E**—Bureau of Labor Statistics, "Labor Force Statistics Derived from the Population Survey, 1948-1987" (August 1988), Bulletin 2307, Table A-35; Bureau of Labor Statistics, "Employment and Earnings, January 1990," Table 11.

nies, there has been loss of jobs among top management and corporate staff, though not among blue collar workers as a group.[21] Much of the contraction resulting from takeovers is fundamentally a reflection of larger economic forces—forces that dictate that changes be made if resources are to be used efficiently and industrial decline is to be halted. Hostile takeovers typically achieve quickly—and thus, I would argue, with considerably lower social costs—the same end brought about in more protracted fashion by intense competition in product markets.[22]

Consider the current plight of our auto industry. Few industries have experienced as severe a retrenchment as the one this industry went through in the 1977–1982 period—and will surely have to experience in the future.[23] It is precisely the auto industry's past immunity to takeover and major restructuring, along with government protection from foreign competitors, that is responsible for the extent of its present requirement to downsize. Had normal economic forces like competition, failure, and takeover been al-

FIGURE 1–2
M&A Activity versus Industry R&D Expenditures, 1975–1990

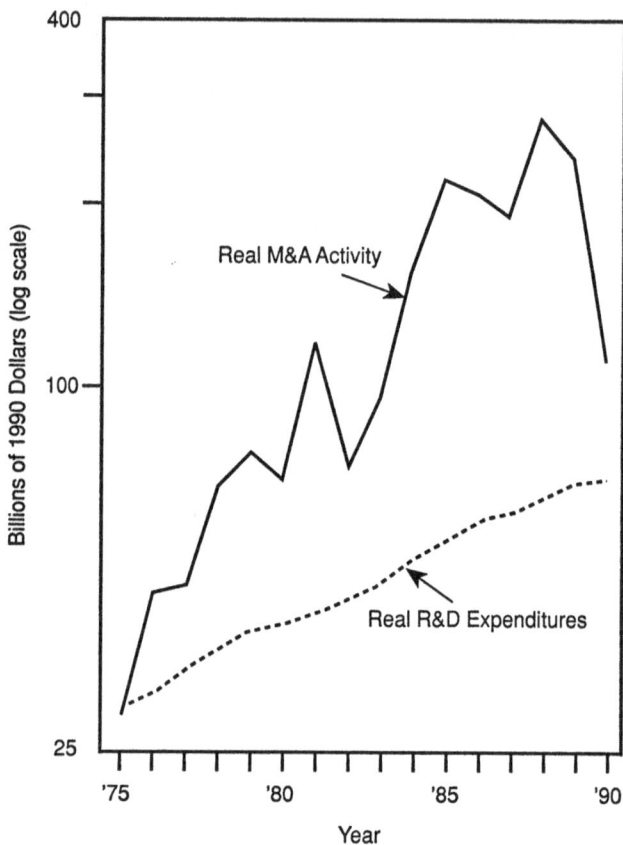

Source: Business Week, "R&D Scoreboard," annual; and Merrill Lynch, *Mergerstat Review, 1990,* fig. 5.

lowed to operate, the massive contraction still required to restore competitiveness to our automobile industry would have been largely behind us today, and the social costs and dislocations would have been far smaller. The devastated economies of Eastern and Central Europe today are vivid examples of what happens when state protection prevents normal economic forces, including failure, from moving resources from lower- to higher-valued uses.

While change imposes costs on some individuals, such costs are outweighed by the benefits to the general economy. At the end of the 1970s, when the Dow Jones average was around 900, Lester Thurow complained that one of the principal shortcomings of a "mixed" economy like ours was its inability to "disinvest"—that is, to move capital out of declining industries and into vital ones.[24] But this forced "disinvestment," I would argue, is the primary accomplishment of the wave of restructurings we saw in the 1980s. Such restructuring, as I argue in the next section, reflected the efforts of a new breed of "active" investors to prevent management from wasting resources by reinvesting cash flow in mature, low-return businesses with excess capacity. This is why restructuring activity was concentrated in industries such as oil, tobacco, tires, food processing, retailing, publishing, broadcasting, forest products, commodity chemicals, and financial services.

THE RETURN OF ACTIVE INVESTORS

Over the last 50 years, institutional investors and financial institutions have been driven out of their former role as active investors. By "active investor" I mean one who holds large equity and/or debt positions and actually monitors management, sits on boards, is sometimes involved in dismissing management, is often closely involved in the strategic direction of the company, and, on occasion, even manages. That description fits people like Warren Buffet, Carl Icahn, Sir James Goldsmith, the Pritzkers, and Kohlberg, Kravis, and Roberts (KKR).

Before the mid-1930s, investment banks and commercial banks played a much more important role on boards of directors, monitoring management and occasionally engineering changes in management. At the peak of their activities, J. P. Morgan and several of his partners served on boards of directors and played a major role in the strategic direction of many firms.[25]

The diminished role of banks in corporate governance and strategy over the past 50 years is the result of a number of factors. Among the most important are laws passed in the 1930s that increased the costs of being actively involved in the strategic direction of a company while also holding large amounts of its debt or equity.[26] Such regulations, together with today's strongly pro-management and chronically inefficient proxy mechanism,[27] do much to explain why money managers do not serve on boards today and seldom think of getting involved in the strategy of their portfolio companies.

The restrictive laws of the 1930s were passed after an outbreak of populist attacks on the investment banking and financial community. During the formative years of the SEC, then-chairman William O. Douglas shocked Wall Street investment bankers with the following statement:

> [T]he banker [should and will be] restricted to…underwriting or selling. Insofar as management [and] formulation of industrial policies [are concerned]…the banker will be superseded. The financial power which he has exercised in the past over such processes will pass into other hands.[28]

As Mark Roe interprets Douglas's statement, "Main Street America did not want to be controlled by Wall Street. Congress responded to Main Street, not Wall Street; laws discouraging and prohibiting control resulted."[29]

The consequence of these political forces over the past 50 years has been to leave managers increasingly unmonitored. At present, when the U.S. institutions that own more than 40 percent of all U.S. corporate equity become dissatisfied with management, they have few options other than to sell their shares. Moreover, managers' complaints about the churning of financial institutions' portfolios ring hollow: most prefer churning to a system in which those institutions would actually have direct power to correct a management problem. Few CEOs today like the idea of having institutions with substantial stock ownership sitting on the corporate board. That would bring about the monitoring of managerial activities by people who bear part of the wealth consequences of managerial mistakes and who are not beholden to the CEO for their directorships.

After financial institution monitors left the scene in the post-1940 period, many managers came to believe that their companies belonged to them and that stockholders were merely one of many "stakeholders" the firm had to serve.[30] The growth of this "managerialist" attitude also coincided with a 10-fold reduction in the percentage equity ownership of the CEOs of our largest companies—from roughly 3 percent in 1937 to less than .03 percent today.[31] U.S. companies, to be sure, also became much larger (even in inflation-adjusted dollars) over this period; but while management equity ownership was falling by a factor of 10, average company size increased by only about three to four times. The consequence, as Adolph Berle warned us back in the 1930s, is that for almost 50 years we experienced a widening of the divide between ownership and control in our largest public companies.

Why Corporations Should Maximize Value. Financial economists have long understood that the fundamental aim of our corporations ought to be the maximization of their "long-run" value.[32] The critical role of the value-maximizing rule is to provide guidance to decision makers evaluating trade-offs of resources at different points in time. (Extended to incorporate the effects of uncertainty, this rule is the essence of modern capital theory.) When Congress and the courts begin to interfere with this primary mandate, they lose sight of what creates value and raises the standard of living in our society. It is precisely by allowing corporations to concentrate on that aim that the long-run interests of all other stakeholders—employees, creditors, suppliers, taxpayers, and so forth—are ultimately best served.[33] Again, the poverty of Eastern and Central Europe today is largely the consequence of eliminating all pressure, or incentive, to maximize the value of business enterprise.

Value-maximizing does not mean that stockholders are an especially deserving group, or that corporate stakeholders other than stockholders should be ignored in management's decision making. Even the most aggressive maximizer of stockholder wealth must care about other constituencies such as employees, customers, suppliers, and local communities. Maximizing value, in fact, means allocating corporate resources (to the point where marginal costs equal marginal benefits) among all groups or interests that affect firm value. Value-maximizing decision making devotes resources to members of each important corporate constituency to improve the terms on which they contract with the company, to maintain the firm's reputation. In this sense, there is no conflict between management's service to its stockholders and to other corporate stakeholders.

The Increase in Agency Costs. The banning of financial institutions from fulfilling their critically important monitoring role has resulted in major corporate inefficiencies. The increase in "agency costs"[34] after the 1930s—loosely speaking, the loss in value resulting from the separation between ownership and control in widely held public corporations—appears to have taken a sharp rise in the mid to late 1960s when a substantial part of corporate America launched diversification programs that led to the assembly of conglomerates. We now know this course was unproductive, and it has been in large part reversed over the past 10 years.[35]

It is ironic, moreover, that while most attacks on takeovers have been directed at unaffiliated entrepreneurs such as Icahn and Goldsmith, it is the diversifying acquisitions by our largest corporations such as DuPont, Exxon, R. J. Reynolds, Goodyear, and U.S. Steel that have proven to be the least productive. Given the evidence attesting to the waste caused by corporate diversification, the criticism directed at the KKR buyout of RJR-Nabisco (a transaction that has led to renewed focus) seems misplaced, especially given the lack of controversy surrounding the recent AT&T takeover of NCR. This misdirected criticism of takeover entrepreneurs ("raiders"), while sparing corporate conglomerators, lays bare the political origins of the opposition.

The fact that takeover and restructuring premiums regularly average about 50 percent indicates that managers have been able to destroy up to a third of the value of the organizations they lead before facing serious threat of displacement.[36] This destruction of value generates large profit opportunities. In response to such opportunities, we have seen the rise of new kinds of institutions whose principal purpose has been to recapture that lost value. Along with the takeover specialists have come others such as the family funds (owned by the Bass Brothers, the Pritzkers, and the Bronfmans), Warren Buffet's Berkshire Hathaway, and Lazard Frères's Corporate Partners Fund—institutions that have discovered ways to bear the costs associated with insider status while being active in the strategic direction of the firm. These new institutions purchase substantial interests in (or entire) companies and play an active role in them. They often *are* the boards of directors. Because of their significant ownership interest, such institutional directors have far stronger incentives to monitor management than the typical outside directors of our public companies.

THE LBO ASSOCIATION: A NEW ORGANIZATIONAL FORM

LBO associations such as KKR, Clayton & Dubilier, and Forstmann-Little represent new organizational forms—in effect, a new model of general management. The diversity of the businesses owned by these LBO partnerships make such organizations look like conventional corporate conglomerates. But such conglomerates, the result of the rush to diversify in the 1960s and 1970s, have generally been overcome by their own internal organizational failures. During the height of the restructuring activity in the 1980s, they were routinely broken up and indirectly replaced by LBO associations that have solved the internal problems of the typical conglomerate.

LBO associations generate large increases in efficiency. They are generally run by partnerships instead of the headquarters office in the typical large, multibusiness diversified corporation. These partnerships perform the monitoring and peak coordination function with a staff numbering in the tens of people, and replace the typical corporate headquarters staff of hundreds or thousands.

But while the new LBO associations may look like conventional conglomerates, they have a fundamental affinity with Japanese groups for firms called *keiretsu*. LBO partnerships play a dual funding and oversight role that is similar in many ways to that of the main banks in the Japanese keiretsu. Like the main banks, which typically hold significant equity stakes in their corporate borrowers, the leaders of the LBO partnerships hold substantial amounts of equity in their companies and control access to the rest of the capital. Further like the Japanese banks, the LBO partners are actively involved in the monitoring and strategic direction of these firms.

Unlike the typical conglomerate (or the keiretsu, for that matter), the operating heads of the individual business units comprising the typical LBO association also have substantial equity ownership—ownership that gives them a pay-to-performance sensitivity that, on average, is 20 times greater than that experienced by the average corporate CEO.[37] Moreover, the managing partners in the LBO associations—which is really the proper comparison with the CEOs of conglomerates—have an even larger pay-for-performance as a result of their 20 percent override on the value created in the company.

LBO business unit heads also have far less bureaucracy to deal with, and far more decision-making freedom, in running their businesses. In effect, the LBO association substitutes incentives provided by compensation and ownership plans for the direct monitoring and often centralized decision making in the typical corporate bureaucracy. The compensation and ownership plans make the rewards to managers highly sensitive to the performance of their business units, something that rarely occurs in major corporations.

Also important, the contractual relationship between the partnership headquarters and the suppliers of capital to the buyout funds is very different from that between the corporate headquarters and stockholders in the diversified firm. The buyout funds are organized as limited partnerships in which the managers of the partnership headquarters are the general partners. Unlike the diversified firm, the contract with the limited partners denies partnership headquarters the right to transfer cash or other resources from one LBO business unit to another. Instead, cash payouts from each LBO business unit must be paid out directly to the limited partners of the buyout funds. This reduces the waste of free cash flow that is so prevalent in diversified corporations.[38]

The Evidence on LBOs

Financial economists studying LBOs have produced substantial evidence documenting gains in operating efficiency as well as increases in stockholder value.

Stockholder Gains.   As would be expected in a competitive corporate control market, the gains to selling stockholders in LBOs have been roughly comparable to shareholder gains from takeovers. Estimates of the average premium over market two months prior to the buyout range from 40 percent to 50 percent.[39] For buyouts that came back public or were otherwise sold or valued, the total value (adjusted for market movements) increased 96 percent from two months before the buyout to the final sale about three years after the buyout. These gains were divided roughly equally between the pre- and postbuyout investors.[40] The median net-of-market return on the postbuyout equity alone was approximately 785 percent.[41]

Increases in Operating Efficiency.   In addition to the studies of value changes, studies examining the operating performance of large samples of LBOs after the buyout have found real increases in productivity. The Kaplan study cited above finds average increases in annual operating earnings of 42 percent from the year prior to the buyout to the third year after the buyout, and increases of 25 percent when adjusted for industry and business cycle trends. He also finds 96 percent increases in cash flow in the same period (80 percent increases after adjustment for industry and business cycle trends).

The Bottom Line.   In a review paper published in 1990, my Harvard colleague Krishna Palepu summarized the findings of more than two dozen studies of LBOs and their effects as follows:

- Stockholders of firms undergoing LBOs earn substantial returns from the transactions.
- Company productivity and operating performance improve substantially in the years immediately following a buyout. The improvements are a result of the changes in financial and management structure associated with the buyout. There is little evidence of a decline in employment levels or average wage rates of blue-collar workers after a buyout, suggesting that the postbuyout cash-flow improvements are not the result of widespread wealth transfer from workers.
- Although some prebuyout bondholders suffer losses at the buyout, these losses account for a very small fraction of the total gains to prebuyout shareholders.

- Buyouts give companies increased depreciation and interest tax shields which account for some of the equity gains from these transactions. Buyouts also increase tax revenues to the U.S. Treasury in several ways, however, and the net effect of LBOs on aggregate tax revenues is likely to be positive.
- LBOs appear to have two opposing effects on firm risk. Although the leverage increase associated with the buyout increases financial risk, the changes in the organizational structure and strategy appear to reduce business risk. The net result is that LBO investors bear significantly lower risk than comparable levered investments in public corporations.[42]

THE PRIVATIZATION OF BANKRUPTCY

The high leverage associated with LBOs and other HLTs—notwithstanding its benefits as a monitoring and incentive device,[43] and the related reductions in business risk just cited—was bound to increase the probability of companies getting into financial trouble. Indeed, when testifying before the House on LBOs in February 1989, I expressed surprise at how few mistakes we had witnessed in a revolution in business practice as great as that occurring over the last decade.[44] At that time, fewer than 30 of some 1,500 going-private transactions completed since 1979 had gone into formal bankruptcy. Since then, of course, the number of HLTs in default or bankruptcy has risen sharply.

As I also pointed out in my testimony, the costs of dealing with corporate insolvency could be expected—barring unforeseen changes in capital market regulations and the bankruptcy courts—to be much smaller in the new world of high leverage ratios than they have been historically. The reason for my prediction has much to do with the fact that the HLTs that get into trouble today are likely to be fundamentally different from the traditional corporate bankrupts of the past. In contrast to the traditionally low-levered firms that end up eating through their large equity bases and becoming candidates for liquidation, today's troubled HLTs are likely to be fundamentally profitable companies generating large positive (pre-interest) cash flows. And, given our costly and cumbersome court-supervised bankruptcy process (a subject I return to later), it seems clear that far more of this operating value can be preserved by privately resolving conflicts among the firm's claimants rather than filing under Chapter 11.[45]

Because of these stronger incentives to preserve value in the new leverage model, I argued that a different set of institutional arrangements were arising to substitute for the usual bankruptcy process. In short, I predicted that the reorganization process would be "privatized."[46]

Extending the Japanese Parallel. As mentioned above, the funding and governance of companies by LBO associations are strikingly similar to many of the practices of Japanese keiretsu. And this similarity also extends to their practice in reorganizing troubled companies. Japanese companies make intensive use of leverage, far more so than their American counterparts; and Japanese banks appear to allow companies to go into bankruptcy only when it is economic to liquidate them—that is, only when the firm is more valuable dead than alive. As leader of the consortium of banks lending to any firms, the Japanese main bank takes responsibility for evaluating the economic viability of an insolvent firm, and for planning its recovery—including the infusion of new capital and top-level managerial manpower (often drawn from the bank itself). Other members of the lending consortium commonly follow the lead of the main bank and contribute additional funding, if required, to the reorganization effort. The main bank bonds its role by making the largest commitment of funds to the effort.[47]

Reorganization in the 1980s. Similar practices appear to be the norm in the American LBO community. (In fact, the recent restructuring of RJR's balance sheet together with a new equity infusion is a nice illustration of this process.) The combination of debt and equity claims held by Japanese banks had an American analog in the "strip financing" techniques commonly observed in the early LBOs. The practice of strip financing—wherein roughly proportional "strips" of all securities in the capital structure were held by most of the claimants—reduces the conflicts of interest among classes of claimants that inevitably arise in troubled companies.[48] The intensity of such conflicts—which, as I will argue later, are aggravated by our system—are contributing to the current costs of workouts and bankruptcies.

The stronger incentives created by high leverage to manage the insolvency process more efficiently were also reflected in the extremely low frequency with which LBOs actually entered bankruptcy in the first half of the 1980s, as well as the general experience of troubled companies at that time. For example, 91 (or 47 percent) of the 192 NYSE and ASE companies that defaulted during the period 1980–86 were reorganized privately.[49] Some assert that the early success of LBOs was ensured by the bull market of the middle 1980s. The story was not that simple, however, because during the late 1970s and the first half of the 1980s, major sectors of the economy experienced bad times, and buyouts occurred in many of these sectors.

We now know that LBOs frequently got into trouble in the early 1980s. But instead of entering formal bankruptcy, they were typically reorganized in a short period of time (several months was common), often under new management, and at apparently lower cost than would occur in the courts. Drexel Burnham Lambert, which underwrote much of the high-yield bond offerings throughout the 1980s, also transformed the 3(a)9 exchange offer into a valuable innovation in the workout and reorganization process. The available evidence indicates, moreover, that the direct costs of exchange offers are only about 10 percent of those in the average Chapter 11 of comparable size.[50] Such innovation is to be expected when there are such large efficiency gains to be realized from new reorganization and recontracting procedures.

Moreover, I warned in my House testimony (in February 1989) that serious problems would result among Drexel's clients if regulators hampered its ability to handle reorganizations and workouts. Drexel's position in the high-yield bond market gave it a unique ability to perform this function and no substitute was likely to emerge soon.

Today, of course, Drexel is gone. And, though I seem to have been right about the consequences of Drexel's demise, my predictions about the continuing privatization of bankruptcy could not have been more wrong. What I failed to anticipate were major new regulatory initiatives, a critical change in the tax code, and a misguided bankruptcy court decision that together are forcing many troubled companies into Chapter 11.

CONTRACT FAILURE IN VENTURE MARKETS

Judging from press reports, academic case studies of failed transactions,[51] and a recent study of 119 large LBOs by Steven Kaplan and Jeremy Stein, it now seems clear that more of the transactions completed in recent years have been overpriced and, as a result of the overpricing, overleveraged. According to Kaplan and Stein, of the 66 large LBOs (greater than $100 million in value) completed during the period 1986 to 1988, 18 have defaulted and 7 have filed for bankruptcy. In contrast, only 4 of the 53 large LBOs completed during 1980–85 have defaulted and 3 filed for bankruptcy.[52] The question troubling economists is this: Are there *systematic* factors that would account for the high concentration of default among deals transacted in the latter stages of the leveraged restructuring movement?

I believe there have been two major factors contributing to problems in the market for highly leveraged transactions. First, the HLT market experienced a "contracting failure"—one that gives rise to the boom-and-bust cycles common in venture markets such as real estate development, oil and gas drilling, and the venture capital market. Second, major changes in the regulatory and legal environment have greatly compounded the problems arising from this contract failure by reducing the ability of companies to refinance their existing debt and, when necessary, to reorganize claims efficiently. Such flexibility is essential to the privatization of bankruptcy I described earlier. By increasing the cost of high leverage, significantly restructuring companies' ability to adjust their capital structures, and interfering with the private workout process, regulatory intervention has substantially increased both the frequency and the costs of financial distress and bankruptcy. (In this sense, as I argue later, the regulatory attack on high leverage has become a self-fulfilling prophecy.)

Boom and Bust

My explanation for the boom-and-bust cycles in venture markets—one which applies in particular to the LBO market—centers on a misalignment of incentives between dealmakers and the creditors and investors they bring together. I call this misalignment a *contracting* failure because it can be corrected (without government intervention) by the private parties entering into the arrangements. I call it a *failure* because corrections seem to take too long to appear and the mistakes repeat themselves too often to be consistent with our theory of rational investors.

As explained above, *after* the deal has been completed, the general structure of LBOs provides strong incentives to the relevant parties to maximize value. I refer in particular to the governance structure of the LBO partnership, the 20 percent override received by the LBO general partners as well as their cash investment in the LBO equity, management incentive contracts with high pay-for-performance sensitivity, the control effect of high leverage, constraints on the cross-subsidization of one LBO by another, and the large percentage equity holdings of managers made possible by high leverage.

The contracting failure that concerns me is the tendency for venture markets to evolve in a way that fails to provide incentives for the dealmakers to select and promote *only* deals that are worth more than they cost. Such a misalignment of incentives goes far in explaining not only why LBOs and other HLTs became overpriced, but also why other activities like real estate, venture capital, and oil and gas well drilling go through boom-and-bust cycles.

The Case of LBOs. In the earlier years of the LBO movement, the partnerships that promoted the LBOs put up significantly more equity capital than they did in the latter part of the 1980s. They were forced to do so by the novelty of the transactions and investors' understandable resistance to the unknown. But, as the initial deals succeeded and equity returns were reported to be in excess of 100 percent per year, investment capital began to flow into the industry.

In the next stage of this process, both limited partners and suppliers of debt capital demanded and received more of the equity, thus reducing the dealmaker's commitment of both capital and back-end stake in the success of the transaction. Further distorting the incentives of dealmakers, the flood of capital into LBO funds allowed the dealmakers to command "front-end-loaded" fees simply for closing the transactions.[53] Such fees, which often substituted for the actual commitment of equity capital, combined with the convention of the 20 percent override (which amounts in practice to a free warrant on the outcome of the venture), enabled dealmakers both to profit up front and to hold a residual interest while shifting virtually all downside risk to the creditors and limited partners.[54]

Such an arrangement, whereby dealmakers are effectively being paid for "doing" deals, ensures that too many deals will be done. In such situations, it pays dealmakers who do not value their reputations (or have no reputation to protect) to do deals that they know (or should know) cost more than the value they are expected to produce. Although this arrangement cannot be sustained indefinitely because of the losses it's bound to generate, the several-year information lag revealing the profitability of the deals allows it to continue for some time. During this time, dealmakers can earn fees on bad deals.

As the information on high returns continues to make itself known, and the market continues to mature, the probability of failure also rises because new and inexperienced dealmakers (who thus have less reputational capital at stake) enter the market; the supply of attractive deals thus begins to shrink and prices are bid up to competitive levels. Under these circumstances, the market is likely to overshoot and bidders are more likely to overpay. As a direct consequence, limited partners and creditors—both of whom must rely to some extent on the reputation and assurances of the dealmaker—are more likely to experience losses. In this situation, the "go/no-go" decision effectively falls back on the suppliers of credit, who are generally not able to obtain the necessary information at reasonable cost to make good decisions.[55]

What, then, corrects this contracting failure and restores the market to equilibrium? As losses begin to appear, investors pull back, yields rise sharply—and with them the cost of high leverage. The reputations of many dealmakers are tarnished, and the whole activity becomes tainted. In the meantime, however, some LBO specialist firms—especially well-established dealmakers such as KKR, Clayton & Dubilier, Forstmann-Little, and others—continue to have a strong interest in maintaining their reputational capital. Such firms, even if they have fallen to the temptation of front-end-loaded structures, will work hard to salvage troubled deals and to minimize losses to their investment partners.

In contrast, many of the newer players entering the market have considerably less to lose from walking away from a bad deal. The perceived potential reward to breaking into the market with a big success often far outweighs the risk of loss—provided you don't have to commit the firm's capital. The Revco and Fruehauf failures provide good examples of this problem; and so do the bankruptcies following Interco's leveraged restructuring and Campeau's acquisitions of Allied and Federated.[56] It is interesting that none of these deals was sponsored (or promoted, in the Interco and Campeau cases) by established LBO partnerships; rather they were all either sponsored or promoted by nonpartnership newcomers eager to enter the business.

Incentives to overpay in highly levered transactions were also exaggerated by another set of conflicts of interest. In some of these transactions, the substantial amounts paid to the current managers for their old stock far exceeded their investment in the equity of the newly levered company. Such large up-front distributions almost surely encouraged them—especially if their jobs were also being threatened by a hostile offer—to go along with deals whose expected returns were not commensurate with the risks.

In effect, if not by conscious intent, the investment bankers structured deals that *paid* the managers to abandon their normal caution so that the deals could get done and the fees collected. Again, Revco, Interco, and Campeau provide illustrative examples. In each of these cases, there was no LBO partnership with a long-run reputation to protect. The investment bankers that promoted the deals invested no net money of their own and took out substantial fees. And, in the cases of Revco and Interco, the managers were paid substantial sums to do the deals.[57]

COMPOUNDING THE PROBLEMS BY REGULATION AND NEW BARRIERS TO WORKOUTS

After almost a decade of progressive deregulation across many sectors of American industry, we are now experiencing "re-regulation" of our financial markets. Much of the S&L industry has effectively been nationalized. Drexel Burnham Lambert, one of the prime movers in the leveraged restructuring movement, has been destroyed. And, with the proliferation of poison pills, state antitakeover laws, and growing legal support for the "just say no" defense, the one vigorous market for corporate control is now largely dormant.

As suggested earlier, the regulatory measures designed to purge our credit markets of "speculative excesses" have greatly added to the current difficulties in our HLT markets. When regulators began to step in during the summer of 1989, there were already signs of a normal correction as participants began to realize that the LBO market had overshot the "efficient margin." There was already under way a return to larger equity commitments, less debt, lower prices, lower projected growth rates, and lower bank fees.[58] In the absence of most regulatory intervention, these fundamentally self-correcting processes would have disciplined participants in the venture and credit markets, thereby providing the basis for renewed activity at sustainable prices.

Unfortunately, however, the flurry of legislative and regulatory initiatives provoked by real estate losses overrode such normal market correctives and created a "downward spiral" in prices (and business activity generally). The S&L legislation (FIRREA),[59] HLT regulations, and much tightened oversight by banking regulators depressed high-yield bond prices further, raised the cost of high leverage, and made adjustments to overleveraged capital structures all the more difficult. In so doing, such regulations have caused nonprice rationing of credit, along with a sharp constriction of its availability to middle market and small firms.[60] They have also reduced the flexibility of lenders to work with highly leveraged companies who cannot meet lending covenants or current debt service payments. These changes, coming on top of the departure of Drexel, the principal market maker, have caused a sharp increase in defaults. Indeed, 19 defaults among the Kaplan and Stein sample of 119 large LBOs have occurred since the beginning of 1989; only three in that sample defaulted prior to that time.

Problems with Workouts. Compounding the problem with losses and defaults is surely not what most Congressmen and regulators intended when they enacted such policy shifts. In addition to the "political" objections to the control market I have cited earlier, much of the impetus for the new rules and regulations undoubtedly came from legitimate concern about the protection of deposit insurance funds and the soundness of our financial institutions.[61] But I can think of no such charitable explanation to account for the barriers to private workouts recently thrown up by bankruptcy judges and tax authorities.

As stated earlier, a major means of reorganizing distressed companies in the 1980s was the 3(a)9 exchange offer employed by Drexel during the early 1980s. Such a technique, even in the absence of Drexel, should have been useful for accomplishing out-of-court settlements under current conditions. In January 1990, however, Judge Burton Lifland ruled in the LTV case that bondholders who participate in exchange offers thereby reduce the value of their claim in bankruptcy to the market value of the claim accepted. Because such market values are typically well below face value, bondholders today are not likely to tender their bonds into an offer if there is any serious chance the firm will later file Chapter 11. This ruling, together with tax penalties imposed in 1990 by Congress on reorganizations outside the bankruptcy court,[62] has caused exchange offers to slow to a trickle, and bankruptcies to rise sharply. For example, only two of the 119 LBOs in the Kaplan and Stein study entered bankruptcy prior to 1989. Since then, eight more have followed.

In sum, our political, regulatory, and legal system has produced a set of policy changes that are frustrating instead of encouraging the normal market adjustment process that was under way in 1989. Indeed, from an economist's perspective, such changes seem virtually the opposite of what is necessary to promote the efficient reorganization of troubled companies, an expansion in the availability of debt capital, and a general return to growth. By drying up traditional credit sources, regulation has sharply increased the cost of debt and thus increased the number of defaults. At the same time, other changes have interfered with the private workout process, thus ensuring that many of those defaults will turn into bankruptcies. All this might not be so troubling, except that the rulings and practices of our bankruptcy courts are making the Chapter 11 process seemingly ever more costly, adding to the waste of resources.

A PROPOSAL FOR REFORMING THE BANKRUPTCY PROCESS

The function of the bankruptcy courts is to enforce contracts between the firm and its creditors and to provide a formal process for breaking such contracts when they cannot be fulfilled and when private parties cannot resolve their conflicts outside of court. In addition, bankruptcy courts resolve ambiguities about the size, legitimacy, and priority of claims. Unfortunately, the U.S. bankruptcy system seems to be fundamentally flawed. It is expensive,[63] it exacerbates conflicts among different classes of creditors, and it often takes years to resolve individual cases. As a result of such delays, much of the operating value of businesses can be destroyed.[64]

Much of the problem stems from the following two fundamental premises underlying the revised (1978) U.S. Bankruptcy Code: (1) reorganization is strongly preferred to liquidation (and current management should be given ample opportunity to lead that reorganization); and (2) the restructuring of the firm's contractual claims should, whenever possible, be *completely* voluntary. In practice, a majority in number (representing at least two thirds of the value) of any class of claimants deemed to be impaired[65] must approve a reorganization. Judges have the power to "cram down" a settlement on a class of creditors without their approval, but they seldom do it. Reflecting the pro-debtor bias in the code, the managers of the firm are effectively given the sole right to propose a plan for 120 days after the filing. Bankruptcy judges also regularly approve multiple extensions of this exclusivity period.[66] As I will argue later, these features of the code give rise to chronic inefficiencies.

Absolute Priority: Theory versus Practice

In thinking about what we want the bankruptcy system to accomplish and how it might be improved, it is important to distinguish between the different conditions of firms filing for Chapter 11. I find it useful to classify these companies into the following four categories:

1. Companies with profitable operations but the "wrong" capital structures—that is, cases in which the promised time path of

payments to claimants does not match the availability of cash flow to make those payments, and a rearrangement of the timing will allow all payments to be made.

2. Companies with profitable operations whose value is being maximized under the current management team, but whose total firm value for reasons now beyond management's control is below the value of total liabilities. In such cases, regardless how payments on those liabilities are reordered through time, their total face value cannot be covered.

3. Companies with potentially profitable, but poorly managed, operations that could meet their total obligations provided the firm's operating strategy (or the management team) were changed (and perhaps the timing of payments reordered as well).

4. Companies that cannot meet their contractual obligations and whose liquidation value exceeds their going concern value.

In principle (and setting aside for now the problem of investor uncertainty about which of these categories fits a given company), the broad outlines of the bankruptcy process should be very simple.

For companies falling into case 1—fundamentally profitable firms with the wrong capital structure—the solution is simply to rearrange the timing of the payments through a voluntary financial restructuring in the capital markets. And if such private restructurings are not practicable—because of regulatory constraints on lenders, tax problems, or holdouts—then a simple, low-cost reorganization of the claims in bankruptcy court (using, if possible, the new "prepackaged bankruptcy" format)[67] should be able to provide complete value to all claimholders.

In case 2—the well-managed firm in which the maximum total firm value is less than the total claims held by creditors—the company can be reorganized by creating a new capital structure and distributing those claims to each of the claimants, giving value equal to 100 percent of each of the claims until total firm value is exhausted. The last class of claimants to be paid would not in general receive full payment, but would receive mostly equity claims on the new entity. This solution follows what is called *absolute priority*.

Case 3—the case in which the firm's operating strategy is wrong— would involve a change in the operating strategy (and/or management) of the firm together with a new capital structure and a distribution in accordance with absolute priority.

Case 4—in which the firm is worth more dead than alive—calls for the liquidation of the firm's assets and distribution of the proceeds according to the absolute priority rule.

In practice, court-supervised solutions to financial distress seldom bear any relation to these conceptual solutions. A study by Larry Weiss of 37 bankruptcies administered under the 1978 code finds that actual solutions violate the contractually agreed-upon priority rules in almost 80 percent of the cases.[68] Equityholders and lower priority claimants routinely receive partial payment on their claims even though more senior claimants are not fully paid. In two particularly flagrant cases, equityholders retained 100 percent of the equity while unsecured creditors received only 37 and 60 percent of their claims.

As suggested earlier, such priority violations are virtually guaranteed when the courts (1) routinely allow the current management team to remain in place and (2) require reorganization plans to receive the approval of all impaired creditor classes. Through these practices, the courts give management and junior creditors a major lever—in practice, the threat of dragging out the proceedings and thereby adding substantially to the legal and opportunity costs—which they use to expropriate value from more senior claimants.

The Consequences of Failing to Enforce Strict Priority

Current court practices—especially the failure to enforce absolute priority and to limit the period of management's monopoly rights to propose a restructuring to 120 days—are very difficult to justify on efficiency grounds.[69] I can see no argument for violating the contractually agreed-upon priority of valid claims.[70,71] Consistent and widespread violations of absolute priority will generate large inefficiencies in the economy. And they will do it in two principal ways.

First, the larger the deviations from strict priority the system tolerates, the harder the junior creditors will push to expropriate value from the senior claimants. This means more intractable, longer, and more costly conflicts among claimholders. Such conflicts prolong the length and increase the costs of bankruptcy; in so doing, they reduce the value of debtor firms.

But the effect of such violations is not limited to troubled companies in reorganization. Of greater consequence, large and frequent deviations from strict priority will interfere with voluntary contracting and specialization in bearing default risk. This will raise the corporate cost of capital (especially for those smaller and riskier firms that generated much of the economic gains of the 1980s). Senior creditors accustomed to seeing their claims violated will increasingly refuse to allow junior claimants into the capital structure. And when junior claimants are allowed, senior creditors will refuse to lend to all but the highest rated credits. In the extreme, such a development would reduce all claimants to the same status, which in turn would dictate that the capital structures of all companies with significant default risk would become the equivalent of 100 percent equity.

Given the risk-bearing and control benefits of debt financing, the costs to the economy in the form of increased inefficiencies from thus restricting debt would likely be enormous. As suggested, it would also substantially raise the cost of capital to American firms, especially smaller ones. A significant increase in the "cost of capital" may not sound consequential; but, as demonstrated by the plight of noninvestment grade companies during the current credit crunch, a higher cost of capital means not only fewer leveraged control transactions, but less corporate capital investment, fewer jobs, and reduced growth for the economy as a whole.

The Information Problem (and the Role of Auctions in Solving It)

One of the major, and heretofore unrecognized, reasons for the intractability of intercreditor conflicts is the "information problem" aggravated—if not actually *created*—by our current bankruptcy system.[72] In outlining solutions for the four different classes of bankruptcies listed above, I made the assumption that all claimants have reliable information about the firm's prospects and that their assessments of the value of the reorganized and restructured firm are identical. In practice, of course, there is tremendous uncertainty about the value of the reorganized company. Adding to this uncertainty, there are few, if any, incentives in the current process for interested parties to provide unbiased estimates of the true value of the firm.

To see the issue clearly, let us ignore the optimal capital structure problem and assume the firm's claimants will be paid entirely in common stock in the unlevered reorganized firm.[73] Senior claimants have incentives to underestimate the value of the firm so they will be awarded a larger fraction of the equity. Equityholders have incentives to overestimate the value so they will retain a larger fraction. Junior claimants have more complicated incentives, depending on whether their claim is clearly "in the money" (in which case their incentives are identical to senior creditors') or "out of the money" (in which their position is much like the equityholders').

Current managers want to retain control, which means they are likely to resist valuable changes in firm strategy (especially if they have no significant equity stake) that would also reduce the probability of their retaining their jobs. The bankruptcy judges—those effectively charged with solving this "information problem"—have neither the information nor the expertise to assess the firm's value.

One way to solve the information and incentive problem would be to allow any party—outsiders as well as current claimants—to make an all-cash bid for the control rights to the company. At the close of the auction, the highest bidder would *immediately* assume control of the company and its operations. The current managers could themselves bid, or they could bid as part of an investor group (including creditors). The investor groups themselves, by bidding for the services of, or deliberately excluding, the current management team, would thus be forced to ascertain whether the managers were valuable to the reorganization of the business or were, instead, a continuing part of the problem. The firm's new capital structure, moreover, would be in the hands of the bidding groups; and, in determining how they raised the funds, they would be subjected to the market test.

Such an auction process would also do much to reduce the problem of biased information produced by our current system. It would do so by forcing current equityholders attempting to preserve control to back *with their own money* their (otherwise biased) estimates of firm value—or at least to find outside investors willing to back those estimates. The same requirement would apply to creditors, who frequently claim to be able to create more value than the settlement being worked out in the voluntary process.

In such an auction system, the role of the bankruptcy court would be sharply narrowed. After investing the proceeds from the auction of the firm in riskless securities, the court would then proceed with the allocation of that value among claimholders. All claims would accrue interest at the riskless rate, thereby limiting the bias for junior claimants to drag out the proceedings. After determining the legitimacy and priority of claims, the court would then distribute the auction proceeds in *strict accordance with absolute priority*. In contrast to the reality of our Chapter 11 process, the court allocation process (with funds held in a riskless portfolio) could proceed at its own pace without concern that firm value was being eroded by management distractions or uncertainty among employees, customers, or suppliers about the future of the firm.

The auction process would thus have two major advantages over the current system. First, it would separate the task of assessing the firm's value from that of dividing that value among creditors and equityholders, effectively assigning the first to capital markets and the second to the courts. Second, it would shelter the value of the firm's operations from the destructive conflicts among creditors and equityholders over the division of firm value—conflicts that make the current formal bankruptcy process so inefficient.

The auction process would also effectively take the control rights to the firm out of the hands of the court (which effectively delegates them to managers in most bankruptcies) and transfer them to the highest bidder in the market. In so doing, it would also take the court out of the awkward position of having to decide whether current management should be replaced and having to "second guess" the business judgment of professional managers.[74]

CONCLUSIONS: WHERE WE ARE HEADED

Given the current political climate, we are almost certain to see further regulation of our capital markets in the attempt to prevent active investors from playing a major role in corporate governance. Bank and insurance company financing for highly leveraged transactions is now almost unavailable; and even when it is, it is expensive and available in much smaller amounts than previously.

In emasculating the market for corporate control, regulators will continue to remove the discipline imposed by the new institutional monitors on corporate management. The consequence is likely to be a sharp decline in the productivity and competitiveness of our corporations in the 1990s and beyond. It could well mean a return to the economic stagnation of the 1970s, a period in which corporate returns on capital fell well below investors' cost of capital—and in which inflation-adjusted stockholder returns were thus substantially negative.

In the short run, we are also facing capital shortages for small- to medium-sized companies—those that created most of the growth in the 1980s. Denying credit to such companies has two serious consequences. First, it has contributed significantly to the recent recession and is now slowing our recovery from it. Second, and perhaps even more important, by removing a major source of competition for large firms, a credit crunch will remove another important discipline that acts to limit inefficiencies in our largest companies.

In the absence of a well-functioning control market and vigorous competition from small U.S. firms, the major remaining source of discipline on corporate management is the pressure exerted by international product markets. Provided we can resist the appeals to shield our companies from global competition by means of quotas and restrictive tariffs—regulations that continue to allow our largest steel and auto companies to remain high-cost producers—the pressure now exerted on corporate management by the globalization of product markets is likely to be the most powerful force for productivity increases. Barring overseas competition, the only other disciplines on corporate management are our current system of internal monitoring by corporate boards of directors and, as a last resort—and the worst of all possible choices—government intervention.

The evidence of the last 40 years indicates, to me at least, that the conventional model of internal management control supervised by outside directors has generally failed as an effective control mechanism in our public corporations. As stated earlier, it is not likely to work well in the case of mature companies with large cash flow and few good investment opportunities. There are certainly companies that have reformed without any tangible threat of takeover or without a crisis in the product markets. For example, the case of General Mills is one that has been well documented by my colleague, Gordon Donaldson;[75] and General Electric's restructuring and reorganization under Jack Welch has been spectacular. But, in the vast majority of cases, unless management and the board have a large ownership stake, major *voluntary* reversals in corporate strategy (such as selling or shutting down a major business) are highly unlikely to come about without pressure from capital or product markets.

In the absence of capital market pressure, international competition is most likely to bring about necessary change. But, given the incentives and ability of U.S. companies to use the political process to insulate themselves from overseas competitors as well as from the control market, I predict that finding new ways to improve existing internal corporate controls will become an issue of great urgency in the decade ahead of us—one that will attract the attention of politicians, regulators, institutional investors, as well as management scientists. Coming to a resolution of this issue will be difficult and contentious, but the consequences of failing to restore effective corporate control mean we must not fail.

NOTES

1. For supporting evidence, see Sanjai Bhagat, Andre Shleifer, and Robert W. Vishny, "Hostile Takeovers in the 1980s: The Return to Corporate Specialization," *Brookings Papers: on Economics Activity Microeconomics 1990,* pp. 1–84; Steven N. Kaplan, "The Effects of Management Buyouts on Operating Performance and Value," *Journal of Financial Economics,* Vol. 24, No. 2 (October 1989), pp. 217–54; and Robert Comment and Gregg Jarrell, "Corporate Focus and Stock Returns" (Bradley Policy Research Center working paper MR 91-01, May 1991).

2. The equity gains are based on RJR-Nabisco's July 15, 1991, stock and warrant prices of $11.50 each. The original LBO investors contributed about $3.2 billion in equity ($1.5 billion initially on 2/9/89 and $1.7 billion in the restructuring on 7/16/90); as of 7/15/91, the total value of this equity had grown to $7.3 billion. The new public equity purchased for cash or exchanged for debt in March and April of 1991 totaled $2.0 billion; and the total value of this equity had increased to $2.8 billion as of 7/15/91.

3. Given these conclusive indications of success, it seems ironic that one of the most recent journalist attempts to capitalize on the antagonism to corporate restructuring, Sarah Bartlett's *The Money Machine* (New York: Warner Books, 1991), should describe the RJR deal as "the deal...people regard as most symptomatic of the excesses on Wall Street." "RJR-Nabisco was not a departure," she goes on to say, "it was the culmination of a process that had gone badly out of control." (p. 237)

4. As revealed in the book, John Greeniaus, head of Johnson's baking unit, told KKR that if "the earnings of this group go up 15 or 20 percent...I'd be in trouble." His charter was to spend the excess cash in his Nabisco division to limit earnings in order to produce moderate but smoothly rising profits—a strategy that would mask the potential profitability of the business. [See Bryan Burrough and John Helyar, *Barbarians at the Gate* (New York: Harper & Row, 1990), pp. 370–71.]

   The Wall Street Journal reported that Greeniaus told them that the company was "looking frantically for ways to spend its tobacco cash," including a $2.8 billion plant modernization program that was expected to produce pre-tax returns of only 5 percent. (Peter Waldman, "New RJR Chief Faces a Daunting Challenge at Debt-Heavy Firm," *The Wall Street Journal,* March 14, 1989, p. A1:6.

5. Joseph Grundfest, "Just Vote No or Just Don't Vote," Stanford Law School working paper (1990).

6. Bill Saporito, "The Tough Cookie at RJR-Nabisco," *Fortune* (July 18, 1988).

7. To compound the problem of selection bias, such journalistic accounts often contain inaccurate, or at best misleading, reporting of the facts. Jude Wanniski, editor of the *MediaGuide* (and a former *Wall Street Journal* reporter) calls attention to such reporting in his comments on a *Wall Street Journal* article on the 1986 Safeway LBO that, ironically, was awarded a Pulitzer Prize for "explanatory journalism" (Susan Faludi, "The Reckoning: Safeway LBO Yields Vast Profits but Extracts a Heavy Human Toll," *The Wall Street Journal,* May 16, 1990). As Wanniski comments, "This was not business reporting, nor was it a human interest story. This was pure and simple propaganda, the work of an ideologue using the *Journal*'s front page to propagate a specific opinion about how corporate America should conduct its affairs." Jude Wanniski, *Financial World* (December 11, 1990), p. 13.

8. Measured in 1990 dollars. Measured in nominal dollars, the total value of transactions and total gains were $1,239 billion and $443 billion, respectively.
9. As reported by the Salomon Brothers High Yield Research Group (*Original Issue High-Yield Default Study—1990 Summary*, January 28, 1991), as of the end of 1990, the face value of defaulted publicly placed or registered privately placed high-yield bonds in the period 1978–90 was roughly $35 billion (about $20 billion of which entered bankruptcy). Given that recovery rates historically average about 40 percent, actual losses may well be below $20 billion. Not all of these bonds were used to finance control transactions, but I use the total to obtain an upper-bound estimate of losses.

   Although the authorities have not released the totals of HLT loans and losses, bankers have told me privately that such losses are likely to be well below $10 billion.
10. More precisely, between February 19, 1991 (before announcing two consecutive declines in quarterly earnings), and July 17, 1991 (the time of this writing).
11. A 1989 study by Laura Stiglin, Steven Kaplan, and myself demonstrates that, contrary to popular assertions, LBO transactions result in increased tax revenues to the U.S. Treasury—increases that average about 60 percent per annum on a permanent basis under the 1986 IRS code (Michael C. Jensen, Steven Kaplan, and Laura Stiglin, "Effects of LBOs on Tax Revenues of the U.S. Treasury," *Tax Notes,* Vol. 42, No. 6 (February 6, 1989), pp. 727–33).

   The data presented by a study of pension fund reversions reveal that only about one percent of the premiums paid in all takeovers can be explained by reversions of pension plans in the target firms (although the authors of the study do not present this calculation themselves) (Jeffrey Pontiff, Andre Shleifer, and Michael S. Weisbach, "Reversions of Excess Pension Assets after Takeovers," *Rand Journal of Economics,* Vol. 21, No. 4 (Winter 1990), pp. 600–13).

   Joshua Rosett, analyzing over 5,000 union contracts in over 1,000 listed companies in the period 1973 to 1987, shows that less than 2 percent of the takeover premiums can be explained by reductions in union wages in the first six years after the change in control. Pushing the estimation period out to 18 years after the change in control increases the percentage to only 5.4 percent of the premium. For hostile takeovers only, union wages *increase* by 3 and 6 percent for the two time intervals, respectively. [Joshua G. Rosett, "Do Union Wealth Concessions Explain Takeover Premiums? The Evidence on Contract Wages," *Journal of Financial Economics,* Vol. 27, No. 1 (September 1990), pp. 263–82.]
12. Many of the most visible of these prosecutions by U.S. Attorney Giuliani have now been either dropped for lack of a case or reversed. The only RICO conviction, Princeton/Newport, has been reversed (although other securities law violations have been upheld), and so too the GAF, Mulheren, and Chestman cases. Only one major conviction of that era remains (Paul Bilzerian) and it is under appeal. The guilty pleas often obtained under threat of RICO prosecution, of course, remain.

   For a brief discussion of pressures from Congress on the SEC to bring down investment bankers, arbs, and junk bonds, see Glenn Yago, "The Credit Crunch: A Regulatory Squeeze on Growth Capital," *Journal of Applied Corporate Finance,* Spring 1991, pp. 99–100.
13. The more fundamental cause of problems among banks is excess capacity caused by regulation and restrictions on takeovers of financial institutions. For elaboration of

this point, see note 61 below.

14. See Creighton Meland, "Clarifying the New Guidelines for Highly Leveraged Transactions" (unpublished manuscript, Lathan and Watkins, 1990).

15. See "NAIC (National Association of Insurance Companies) Policy Regarding Insurance Companies," Merrill Lynch Fixed-Income Research, June 12, 1990.

16. See the "Middle Market Roundtable" as well as the five articles on the credit crunch in *Journal of Applied Corporate Finance,* Spring 1991.

17. Interestingly, the Japanese economy experienced a similar turnaround in the growth of per unit labor costs almost a decade earlier than the United States.

18. Safeway, for example, went through an LBO in 1986 and sold half its stores. It has since come back public and has also launched a record five-year $3.2 billion capital program focused on store remodeling and new store construction.

19. The discrepancy between the data and the impression left by critics turns on a confusion between the level and the rate of increase of R&D spending. While achieving record levels, R&D spending grew more slowly in the late 1980s.

    In a study of 600 acquisitions of U.S. manufacturing firms during 1976–85, Bronwyn Hall found that acquired firms did not have higher R&D expenditures (as a fraction of sales) than firms in the same industry that were not acquired. Also, she found that "firms involved in mergers showed no difference in their pre- and postmerger R&D performance over those not so involved." See "The Effect of Takeover Activity on Corporate Research and Development," Chapter 3 in Alan Auerbach (ed.), *Corporate Takeovers: Cause and Consequences,* University of Chicago Press, 1988. In two recent papers, "The Impact of Corporate Restructuring on Industrial Research and Development," *Brookings Papers on Economic Activity, Microeconomics 1990,* pp. 85–124, and "Corporate Restructuring and Investment Horizons," University of California, Berkeley, unpublished manuscript, December 1990, Hall finds little relation between mergers, control changes, and LBOs and R&D expenditures, but finds a negative effect of leveraged restructurings on R&D.

    A study by the Office of the Chief Economist at the SEC ("Institutional Ownership, Tender Offers, and Long-Term Investments," 4/19/85) also concludes: (1) increased institutional stock holdings are not associated with increased takeovers of firms; (2) increased institutional holdings are not associated with decreases in R&D expenditures; (3) firms with high research and development expenditures are not more vulnerable to takeovers; and (4) stock prices respond positively to announcements of increases in R&D expenditures.

20. I have been unable to find references to the sources of data that have formed the bases for the critics' conclusions. Other sectors show somewhat lower rates of growth of productivity than does manufacturing, but I have been unable to find any significant evidence of declines in the aggregate data to support the claims of critics.

21. In their study of 20,000 plants involving control changes, Frank Lichtenberg and Donald Siegal found that changes in control reduce white collar employment in nonproduction facilities but do not reduce blue collar or R&D employees. They also found significant increases in total factor productivity after both acquisitions and LBOs. For a summary of this work, see Frank Lichtenberg and Donald Siegal, "The Effect of Control Changes on the Productivity of U.S. Manufacturing Plants," *Journal of Applied Corporate Finance* (Summer 1989), pp. 60–67.

22. On rare occasions, the internal control systems manage to accomplish significant change without the threat of product or capital markets. General Mills is an example. In a case study of General Mills, Gordon Donaldson describes the company's decade-long restructuring—a very gradual adjustment process that was finally successful in reversing a disastrous diversification strategy. [See Gordon Donaldson, "Voluntary Restructuring: The Case of General Mills," *Journal of Financial Economics,* Vol. 27, No. 1 (September 1990).]

Donaldson raises the possibility that such a gradual adjustment process has lower social costs than the abrupt change enforced by dramatic restructurings or takeovers. I believe a careful estimate of the social waste associated with keeping people unemployed or underemployed (while still on the payroll) and the wasteful utilization of assets over a decade-long period makes the year-long adjustment following a takeover or LBO a far lower-cost social strategy.

23. From 1977–82, total employment fell by 336,000 from its high of over 1,000,000 in 1977. From 1982 to 1989, when the industry succeeded in gaining protection by means of import quotas, industry profits increased and employment in the industry rose to almost 840,000 even as U.S. automakers were losing significant market shares.

24. Lester Thurow, *The Zero-Sum Society* (Basic Books, 1980), p. 81.

25. See Vincent Carosso, *Investment Banking in America: A History* (Harvard University Press, 1970).

26. For example, the Glass-Steagall Act significantly restricted commercial bank equity holdings as well as bank involvement in the reorganization of companies in which they have substantial debt holdings. In addition, the 1940 Investment Company Act put restrictions on the maximum holdings of investment funds. [See Mark Roe, "Political and Legal Restraints on Ownership and Control of Public Companies," *Journal of Financial Economics,* Vol. 27, No. 1 (September 1990), pp. 7–42; and Joseph Grundfest, "Subordination of American Capital," *Journal of Financial Economics,* Vol. 27, No. 1 (September 1990), pp. 89–117.]

27. For a historical account of the evolution of our proxy system into its current form, see John Pound, "Proxy Voting and the SEC: Investor Protection Versus Market Efficiency," *Journal of Financial Economics,* Vol. 28, No. 2 (October 1991), pp. 241–86.

Bernard Black, formerly of the legal staff of the SEC, concludes his analysis of proxy regulation as follows: "In fact, institutional shareholders are hobbled by a complex web of legal rules that make it difficult, expensive, and legally risky to own large percentage stakes or undertake joint efforts. Legal obstacles are especially great for shareholder efforts to nominate and elect directors, even to a minority of board seats. The proxy rules, in particular, help shareholders in some ways, but mostly hinder shareholder efforts to nominate and elect directors."

See Bernard Black, "Shareholder Passivity Reexamined," *Michigan Law Review* (December 1990), p. 523.

28. As cited in Roe (1990), p. 8, cited in note 26.

29. Extending Roe's analysis of the influence of politics on finance, former SEC Commissioner Joseph Grundfest analyzes the process through which politicians take advantage of the agency problems between managers and shareholders to transfer wealth to favored constituencies (particularly managers, who are one of the most powerful constituencies in the process) through the securities regulation process. See

Grundfest (1990), cited in note 26.

30. This view is expressed in the Business Roundtable's March 1990 report, *Corporate Governance and American Competitiveness*. That statement, moreover, is significantly different from a statement it issued 12 years earlier, which emphasized accountability to shareholders alone. For a discussion of this "retreat" from shareholder accountability, see Robert Monks and Nell Minow, *Power and Accountability* (Harper Collins, 1991), pp. 81–84.

31. Michael C. Jensen and Kevin J. Murphy, "CEO Incentives: It's Not How Much You Pay, But How," *Harvard Business Review*, Vol. 90, No. 3 (May/June 1990), pp. 138–53.

32. I put "long-run" in quotes because financial economists do not distinguish between current and "long-run" values. Virtually all credible evidence that we have suggests the market is willing to and capable of taking the long view of a corporation's prospects. It does of course make errors, but the evidence indicates that, without inside information, it is almost impossible for investors to tell whether those errors are positive or negative at any given time.

33. Value maximizing is socially optimal assuming there are not externalities or monopoly power. Externalities are the impositions of costs (or conferring of benefits) by one party on others in which the acting party does not bear the costs (or have the opportunity) to charge for the benefits. The pollution of air and water, without tax penalties or compensation to those affected, are examples.

34. Agency costs, more generally, reflect management's natural predisposition to growth rather than profitability and the incentives they face to expand their firms beyond the size that maximizes shareholder wealth. [See Gordon Donaldson, *Managing Corporate Wealth* (Praeger, 1984).]

    Corporate growth is also associated with increases in the level of management compensation. One of the better-documented propositions in compensation theory is that, for every 10 percent increase in the size of the company, the CEO's compensation goes up by 3 percent. [G. Baker, M. Jensen, and K. Murphy, "Compensation and Incentives," *Journal of Finance* (July 1988).] Also, the tendency of companies to reward middle managers through promotion rather than year-to-year bonuses also creates an organizational bias toward growth. Only growth can supply the new positions that such promotion-based reward systems require. [See George Baker, "Pay-for-Performance for Middle Managers: Causes and Consequences," *Journal of Applied Corporate Finance* (Fall 1990), pp. 50–61.]

35. See Comment and Jarrell (1991), cited in note 1. See also Michael Porter, "From Competitive Advantage to Corporate Strategy," *Harvard Business Review* (May-June 1987).

36. A 50 percent premium that recovers the previous value of the firm means that 33 percent of the previous value was destroyed (50 / 150 = .33).

37. Kaplan (1989), cited in note 1, documents that the median CEO receives $64 per $1,000 change in shareholder wealth from his 6.4 percent equity interest alone. By contrast, Kevin Murphy and I find that the average CEO in the Forbes 1000 receives total pay (including salary, bonus, deferred compensation, stock options, and equity) that changes by only about $3.25 for every $1,000 change in stockholder value. [See Jensen and Murphy (1990), cited in note 31.]

In their clinical study of the 1986 OM Scott LBO from ITT, George Baker and Karen Wruck show that after the buyout, in addition to a substantial equity stake, Scott's managers were subject to an annual cash bonus plan that increased the average payouts from 3 to 6 times. [See "Organizational Changes and Value Creation in Leveraged Buyouts," *Journal of Financial Economics,* Vol. 25 (1989).]

38. For a survey of research on the economic effects of LBOs, see Krishna Palepu, "Consequences of Leveraged Buyouts," *Journal of Financial Economics,* Vol. 27 (1990) and the references therein.
39. Ibid.
40. Kaplan (1989), cited in note 1.
41. Average total buyout fees amounted to 5.5 percent of the equity two months prior to the buyout proposal.
42. Krishna Palepu (1990), pp. 260–61, cited in note 39.
43. See Jensen (1986), cited in note 38. See also Karen Wruck, "Financial Distress, Reorganization, and Organizational Efficiency," *Journal of Financial Economics,* Vol. 27 (1990).
44. Michael C. Jensen, "The Effect of LBOs and Corporate Debt on the Economy," remarks before the Subcommittee on Telecommunications and Finance, U.S. House of Representatives Hearings on Leveraged Buyouts (Washington, DC, February 22, 1989).
45. Bankruptcy, however, does have special advantages in some cases; for example, in retailing, trade credit is crucial to continuation of the business and it is difficult to negotiate privately with hundreds or thousands of trade suppliers.
46. See my article, "Active Investors, LBOs, and the Privatization of Bankruptcy," *Journal of Applied Corporate Finance* (Spring 1989). My argument was anticipated in part by Robert Haugen and Lemma Senbet in their article, "The Insignificance of Bankruptcy Costs to the Theory of Optimal Capital Structure," *Journal of Finance,* Vol. 33 (1978), pp. 383–93.
47. For a more detailed discussion, see Carl Kester, "Japanese Corporate Governance and the Conservation of Value in Financial Distress," *Journal of Applied Corporate Finance,* Vol. 4, No. 2 (Summer 1991).

As I have argued earlier, however, even as our system has begun to look more like the Japanese, the Japanese economy is undergoing changes that are reducing the role of large active investors and thus making their system resemble ours. With the progressive development of U.S.-like capital markets, Japanese managers have been able to loosen the controls once exercised by the banks. So successful have they been in bypassing banks that the top third of Japanese companies are no longer net bank borrowers. As a result of their past success in product market competition, Japanese companies are not "flooded" with free cash flow. Their competitive position today reminds me of the position of American companies in the late 1960s. And, like their U.S. counterparts in the 1960s, Japanese companies today appear to be in the process of creating conglomerates.

My prediction is that, unless unmonitored Japanese managers prove to be much more capable than American executives at managing large, sprawling organization, the Japanese economy is likely to produce a large number of those conglomerates that U.S. capital markets have spent the last 10 years trying to pull apart. And if I am right, then Japan is likely to experience its own leveraged restructuring movement. [See Michael C. Jensen, "Eclipse of the Public Corporation," *Harvard Business Review,* Vol. 89, No. 5 (September-October 1989), pp. 61–74.]

48. For a discussion of strip financing, see Michael C. Jensen, "Takeovers: Their Causes and Consequences," *Journal of Economic Perspectives,* Vol. 2, No. 1 (Winter 1988).

49. See Stuart Gilson's article in *Journal of Applied Corporate Finance,* Vol. 4, No. 2. Wruck (1990), pp. 425–26, cited in note 43, using data obtained privately from Stuart Gilson, reports that only 51 percent of all 381 firms performing in the lowest 5 percent of the NYSE and ASE defaulted in the period 1978–87. It seems likely that many of these companies avoided default by means of private reorganizations.

50. See Stuart Gilson's article in *Journal of Applied Corporate Finance,* Vol. 4, No. 2. See also Stuart Gilson, Kose John, and Larry Lang, "Troubled Debt Restructurings: An Empirical Study of Private Reorganization of Companies in Default," *Journal of Financial Economics,* Vol. 27, No. 2 (September 1990).

51. See Wruck's study of Revco in this issue. See also Steven N. Kaplan, "Campeau's Acquisition of Federated: Value Destroyed or Value Added," *Journal of Financial Economics,* Vol. 25, No. 2 (December 1989), pp. 191–212.

52. See Steven N. Kaplan and Jeremy Stein, "The Evolution of Buyout Pricing and Financial Structure in the 1980s," unpublished manuscript, University of Chicago, April 1991.

53. Kaplan and Stein (1991), cited in note 52, find that, in the 53 large LBOs done prior to 1986, total fees amounted to 2.7 percent of the purchase price of the equity. By contrast, in the 66 large LBOs completed between 1986 and 1988, total fees rose to 4.9 percent of the purchase price of the equity.

54. Venture capital organizations are structured similarly. See William Sahlman, "The Structure and Governance of Venture Capital Organizations," *Journal of Financial Economics,* Vol. 27, No. 2 (September 1990). Some contracts with limited partners help reduce these incentives by making the sharing rule cumulative on all deals funded by the partnership. Under these contracts the dealmaker can't avoid the losses as easily.

55. The decision making by suppliers of credit may also be distorted by their own "agency problems." Commercial lenders, for example, were often rewarded principally for loan and fee generation, which in turn arose from the efforts of banks to retain market share by underpricing loans in an industry troubled by chronic excess capacity. High-yield bond mutual fund managers, to the extent they are paid on the basis of funds under management, also have some incentive to gamble on uneconomic deals rather than return funds to subscribers. For an exposition of such agency problems, see Martin S. Fridson, "Agency Costs: Past and Future," Merrill Lynch *Extra Credit* (June 1991). For a related theory of cycles founded on information lags, not incentives, see DeLong, Shleifer, Summers, and Waldmore, "Positive Feedback Investment Strategies and Destablizing Rational Speculations," *Journal of Finance* (June 1990).

56. Interestingly, the Campeau acquisitions of Allied and Federated and the leveraged restructuring of Interco were all promoted by the same non-LBO partnership investment bank. See Kaplan (1989), cited in note 51.

57. See Wruck's discussion of Revco in *Journal of Applied Corporate Finance,* Vol. 4, No. 2. In the case of the Interco restructuring, Interco's managers owned $12.5 million

in equity prior to the deal (1.15%). They were paid $15.8 million in cash, $13.3 million in debt in the restructured company, and ended up with 4.14 percent of the equity (a trivial amount relative to normal standards) with only a $7.9 million total value (Interco May 1989 proxy statement). For a critical review of the price-setting process, see George Anders and Francine Schwadel, "Costly Advice: Wall Streeters Helped Interco Defeat Raiders But at a Heavy Price," *The Wall Street Journal* (July 11, 1990).

58. See Kaplan and Stein (1991), cited in note 52.

59. The Financial Institutions Reform, Recovery and Enforcement Act, passed in the summer of 1989, which banned the purchase and effectively banned the holding of high-yield bonds by thrifts.

60. See the "Middle Market Roundtable," as well as the five articles on the credit crunch in *Journal of Applied Corporate Finance,* Vol. 4, No. 2.

61. There are admittedly complex economic and political forces at work today that make it difficult for regulators to formulate policy. But, in their obsession with protecting the deposit insurance funds, regulators are responding to symptoms while ignoring the fundamental cause of the problems in our S&L and banking systems. With over 12,000 commercial banks, the banking system has substantial excess capacity and is inefficiently organized. It seems unlikely that the new bank reforms now being entertained by Congress will allow for the orderly exit and radical restructuring of the industry that is needed to restore profitability. An active market for corporate control has not been allowed to function in this industry; and it seems doubtful it will be allowed to do so in the future. In the absence of takeovers, the most likely exit route will be through bankruptcies, forced mergers, and liquidations in response to losses caused by the intense competition in the financial products markets. Without the capital markets to aid in the exit of resources, we can expect individual banks to struggle to add to their capital base to ensure that, when the music stops, they will be one of the survivors. This process, by increasing capacity in an industry that already has to shrink, has led and will continue to lead to substantial waste of scarce resources.

62. Under the Revenue Reconciliation Act of 1990, when new bonds issued in an exchange offer have lower interest rates, the firm must realize taxable income on the exchange. Such exchanges, tax-exempt prior to the Act, are now tax-exempt only if issued in bankruptcy.

63. Frank Easterbrook, however, has pointed out that the direct costs of bankruptcy are lower than the direct costs of taking a company public. See "Is Corporate Bankruptcy Efficient," *Journal of Financial Economics,* Vol. 27, No. 2 (September 1991). No one has as yet obtained a good estimate of the indirect costs of bankruptcy, but, as illustrated in the Eastern Airlines case, they can be substantial.

64. Judge Lifland of the New York bankruptcy court wasted at least hundreds of millions of dollars of creditors' and society's resources by allowing Eastern Airlines to continue to operate in an industry flooded with excess capacity and in the face of extremely hostile unions (who prevented a potential sale of the airline and were rumored to want to destroy it). According to Eastern itself, on March 31, 1989, the company had sufficient assets ($3.7 billion) to repay fully its $3.4 billion in liabilities at the time of its bankruptcy filing in 1989. In March of 1990, a year later, management proposed a plan to pay creditors 48 cents on the dollar (or about $1.7 billion), but then backed out of it. The last plan rejected by creditors proposed payment of 25 cents on

the dollar. The actual payout is projected to be about 10 cents on the dollar, thus producing total losses of about $3 billion. This $3 billion reduction in the value of Eastern's assets while in Chapter 11 illustrates the cost of our current bankruptcy process.

65. In the sense that the plan doesn't promise to pay them what they would get in a straight liquidation under Chapter 7 of the code.

66. This is what Judge Lifland did in the Eastern case. Consistent with these policies, he just approved (in June 1991) the *eighth* extension of Lomas Financial Corporation's manager's sole right to propose a plan for reorganization. Such extensions are especially problematical in cases where the managers' strategy has been responsible for the firm's financial difficulties. But it is very difficult, of course, for a judge to make this judgment when he or she has little or no prior knowledge of, or experience with, the company or the industry.

67. For a discussion of this technique—which amounts to a hybrid between private workout and bankruptcy—see John McConnell and Henri Servaes, "The Economics of Pre-packaged Bankruptcy," *Journal of Applied Corporate Finance*, Vol. 4, No. 2.

68. Assuming the courts determine impairment correctly. See Lawrence A. Weiss, "Bankruptcy Resolution: Director Costs and Violation of Priority of Claims," *Journal of Financial Economics*, Vol. 27, No. 2 (September 1990).

69. For a sophisticated attempt to justify the efficiency of the current system, see Easterbrook (1990), cited in note 63.

70. As Leonard Rosen (noted bankruptcy counsel and senior partner of Wachtell, Lipton, Rosen & Katz) comments in the Roundtable in *Journal of Applied Corporate Finance*, Vol. 4, No. 2, subordinated claimants have shown considerable ingenuity in devising new theories to justify the violation of the priority of the contracts they signed. One that is now popular and is apparently used frequently as a bargaining threat is "fraudulent conveyance." Under this theory, which has yet to be widely accepted by the courts, the argument goes that the banks' secured claims should be subordinated to all others because they loaned money to an LBO or other levered transaction in which they earned fees—all the while knowing that the new entity was insolvent.

This argument makes little economic sense for two reasons: (1) the banks are putting large amounts of their own capital at risk in the deal (unlike the investment bankers who receive large fees and frequently play a large role in promoting the deal); and (2) the subordinated debt holders are put in the position of denying that they had information in the prospectus revealing that the transaction was highly levered and risky, and that they were being paid a risk premium for accepting this risk.

While there can be legitimate cases of fraud in which assets are bled from a firm in a leveraged transaction and the new owners end up owning only a shell, the beneficiaries of such fraud are those old shareholders and bondholders who collected the proceeds, not the banks or others who put large amounts of money into the new entity. The theory seems designed to transfer wealth from the banks simply because they are on the scene at the time of the bankruptcy litigation.

Widespread acceptance of the theory of fraudulent conveyance would be another important and unwise step in forbidding banks, bondholders, insurance companies, and individuals from engaging in the specialization of bearing default risk in transactions that had any positive probability of ending up in bankruptcy court.

71. Another argument used to justify deviations from strict priority is based on "equitable subordination." The principle of equitable subordination in American law seriously hinders the efficient resolution of financial distress. It does so by prohibiting banks from working closely with financially distressed companies to whom they have loaned money.

    The Japanese system works exactly the opposite. Indeed it is considered a moral obligation of the company's main bank to play a major role in working with the managers of a financially distressed client to resolve the problem. And this historically has frequently involved placing bank personnel in positions of major responsibility in the client firm. Nissan, for example, was run for years by an alumnus of the Industrial Bank of Japan after IBJ helped it get out of its financial difficulties.

72. Karen Wruck analyzes this generally unrecognized problem in her recent *Journal of Financial Economics* paper [see Wruck (1990), cited in note 43] and in her clinical study of the Revco LBO in *Journal of Applied Corporate Finance*, Vol. 4, No. 2.

73. Or that the claimants will all receive a proportionate strip of all claims in the new capital structure.

74. In fact, the beneficial effects of an auction are sometimes obtained even in our current system. Some companies—Fruehauf, for example—have resolved financial distress privately by sale of all or a major part of the assets to others. And some firms have been purchased out of bankruptcy: A. H. Robins was purchased by American Home Products. But current procedures give managers significant veto power over such offers. The $925 million bid by the Bass Group for Revco in bankruptcy was reportedly blocked, in part, by resistance from management.

    For additional analysis of an auction system, see Douglas G. Baird, "The Uneasy Case for Corporate Reorganizations," *Journal of Legal Studies* (January 1986), pp. 127–47.

    For useful discussion of the current legal maze facing acquirers of bankrupt companies, see Mark D. Brodsky and Joel B. Zwiebel, "Chapter 11 Acquisitions: Payoffs for Patience," *Mergers & Acquisitions* (September-October 1990), pp. 47–53.

75. See Donaldson (1990), cited in note 22.

CHAPTER 2

FIRM VALUATION AND CORPORATE LEVERAGED RESTRUCTURINGS

Edward I. Altman
Roy C. Smith

INTRODUCTION

The concept of corporate value, and how to maximize it, will be one of the key elements in the dynamics of corporate activity in the next decade. While always central to the field of finance, corporate valuation issues have never been more relevant than today. This is so because of the massive organizational changes that took place in the U.S. in the 1980s and the almost certain explosion in corporate governance and capital structure issues in Europe in the 1990s. And new texts and articles are being written, extolling the virtues of value enhancing techniques, e.g., Copeland, Koller, and Murrin (1990).

The purpose of this chapter is to examine valuation, not from the standpoint of specific techniques and procedures, but from the perspective

Edward I. Altman is Max L. Heine Professor of Finance and Professor of Finance & International Business, Leonard N. Stern School of Business, New York University, and Limited Partner, Goldman, Sachs & Co.

The authors would like to thank Professor Yakov Amihud for his thoughtful comments and Professor J. Fred Weston for his encouragement. An earlier version of this paper was presented at a conference on "The Valuation of Firms: An International Comparison," Luigi Bocconi University, Milano Italy, October 12, 1990. A version of this paper concentrating on Europe was published as "Highly Leveraged Restructurings: A Valid Role for Europe" in the *Journal of International Securities Markets*, Fall 1991.

of the firm's capital structure. We analyze capital structure issues within the context of massive changes brought about by leveraged restructurings, particularly leveraged buyouts. In doing so, we also address the venerable query in corporate finance—does debt matter and is there an optimal capital structure?

Our inquiry follows a decade of extraordinary activity in mergers and acquisitions in the United States. The transaction values of these restructurings rose as exceptionally high acquisition prices were offered due to the competitive interaction of numerous buyout funds and other sources. In turn, the debt amounts and proportions in the merged firms' capital structures also rose to levels never before seen in corporate America. Hence, both values and bankruptcy risks escalated.

We will show that these high values can, in most cases, be sustained only if the levels of debt and distress risk are reduced very quickly after the initial restructuring. If this is not achieved, similar transactions will not be successful in attracting capital from the markets. In the case of leveraged restructurings which prove to be unsuccessful, debt levels will still be reduced through distressed exchange arrangements or, failing that, through Chapter 11 bankruptcy reorganizations. If all of these fail, the firm's assets will need to be liquidated. In these latter distressed situations, corporate values will decline sharply to levels significantly lower than if the firm had been able to reduce its debt as planned within a short time after the restructuring.

We will first examine classical and modified financial theories dealing with corporate valuation in terms of debt policy. These theories can, in our opinion, help to explain not only why leveraged restructurings can change the valuation of firms, sometimes substantially, but also why these restructurings have met with the full spectrum of results, from great success to dismal failure, in the United States during the 1980s. In so doing, we hope to provide some insights into successful capital structure changes for future transactions.

CORPORATE RESTRUCTURINGS—DEFINITIONS, OBJECTIVES, AND EXAMPLES

A corporate restructuring is any substantial change in a firm's asset portfolio or capital structure. Its objectives are usually to increase value to the owners, both old and new, by improving operating efficiency, exploiting debt capacity, and/or redeploying assets. In some cases, the objective is less strategic, in an operating sense, and not necessarily value maximizing, being directed simply to effect a change in corporate control or to defend against a loss of control, i.e., to preserve "independence." Independence of operation has long been important to boards of directors or principal shareholders of some corporations, who have been accustomed to rule their firm's actions without full regard for the rights of public shareholders or in fear of being taken over against their will. In addition, senior management has often professed a goal to be independent of the influence that large lenders may exert on the operations of the firm.

CORPORATE RESTRUCTURINGS

Mergers and Acquisitions

The United States has gone through at least four distinct cycles of M&A activity. The latest one, in the 1980s, involved large corporate financial restructurings, often resulting in acquisition of control by another industrial or a non-industrial firm. Though this cycle has been completed in the United States, the forces behind it have been manifest somewhat in Europe, which has recently seen its first major M&A movement. This movement is primarily a result of an overdue need for industrial restructurings and other influences. European merger and acquisition activity began after the 1985 EC Commission's announcement of a single European market objective to be achieved by 1992. Reduced barriers to cross-national firm mergers were the result of newly found confidence that deregulated, private sector markets could result in improved corporate performance compared to previous national income and protectionist policies. For more details on economic restructuring in Europe, see Smith and Walter (1990) and Altman and Smith (1991).

Leveraged Restructurings

Corporations have also tried to increase value to shareholders by massive changes in leverage. These restructurings are mainly in the form of leveraged recapitalizations or leveraged buyouts. The former involves some type of debt for equity swap and the latter involves management either acting alone or as a partner with a third-party investment firm, purchasing all of the outstanding common stock so that the firm effectively becomes a private entity. The vehicle to buy back the equity is leverage—hence the name leveraged buyout. We will explore this mechanism in much greater depth after discussing the evolution of financial theory in valuation analysis and its relationship with a firm's capital structure.

Before we try to reconcile the financial theories, discussed below, with current corporate financial practice, it will be beneficial to define and discuss what has come to be known as the leveraged restructuring movement of the 1980s, particularly the late 1980s. The objectives of corporate restructurings are usually to do one or more of the following in order to **increase the value of the firm**—however one chooses to define value:

- Redeploy assets to change the mix of the business
- Exploit leverage and other financial opportunities
- Improve operational efficiency

These objectives can be achieved by one or more of the following restructurings:

- Acquiring other companies or businesses
- Divesting businesses or assets owned
- Leveraged buyouts
- Recapitalizations—i.e., stock repurchases or swaps of debt for equity
- Major organizational, leadership, or corporate policy changes

Leveraged Management Buyouts

A number of new techniques for increasing the value of firms were developed in the United States in the 1980s, usually involving several of the steps outlined above. The most visible, in many aspects, was the LBO in which control of a company was acquired in the market through a takeover bid, usually at a substantial premium over the market price of the shares (estimated at about 46% by Kaplan (1989) for LBOs in the early and mid-1980s and growing to even a greater premium for the LBOs of the late 1980s). Often, the transaction was bitterly opposed by existing directors and managements if they were not part of the takeover team. As the premium grew, the new equity team had to rely more and more on borrowed capital from banks and the public. This resulted in a number of leverage excesses.

Management buyouts (MBOs) have been around for many years, both in the United States and Europe. The early transactions essentially involved the senior management of a publicly held company "buying out" all the outstanding shares and "taking the firm private." A significant amount of the financing for the buyout was provided primarily by commercial bank loans with the balance coming from the managers' equity investment. The transaction was a leveraged one but the size of the firm and the consequent amount of financing were relatively small. The resulting capital structure, while heavily leveraged, was quite simple with essentially one class of debt.

The type of firm most suitable to a management buyout was, and still is, one with a relatively stable and predictable cash flow sufficient to easily repay the fixed costs from the additional interest and principal on the debt. The major motivation behind the buyout is that management will now directly benefit from their own efforts and reap the firm's profits in the form of equity returns, instead of a fixed or semi-fixed salary earned as managers. Indeed, it is often argued that the manager-owner will work more efficiently due to the added incentives built into ownership and control.

The leveraged MBO differs from the MBO by the larger size and greater complexity of the transaction and the inclusion of a significant second ownership interest. Indeed, this second party, usually in the form of an investment company or partnership, provides and acquires the bulk of the equity capital, with at most 10–15% going to management. The greater complexity involves several layers of debtholders (some with deferred as well as current-pay interest payments as well as equity participation features) and also several types of equity capital (preferred and common stock, sometimes including equity warrants and options).

A typical capital structure of a large LMBO in the United States in the 1987–1988 period is shown in Exhibit 2–1. Note that the senior debt from banks and insurance companies provided a maximum of 60% of the transaction value and amounted to about two thirds of the total debt financing. These creditors were not willing to provide 100% of the debt financing, since the amounts came to be so large and the perceived risk greater. Indeed, many of these buyouts were greater than $1 billion with the largest, by far, being the $25 billion RJR Nabisco buyout in 1989.

Below the senior debt was the subordinated current-paying debt, i.e., when interest payments commenced immediately. The primary innovation here was that this debt was, in many instances, sold directly to the public markets as part of the growing "junk bond" issuance. This debt is also known as "mezzanine" financing since its priority is below the "balcony," i.e., senior debt, and above the "orchestra," i.e., equity financing. After 1986, the subordinated debt came mainly from publicly placed "junk" bonds. About 25–30% of the transaction price was provided by this source.

EXHIBIT 2–1
Selected Capital Structures

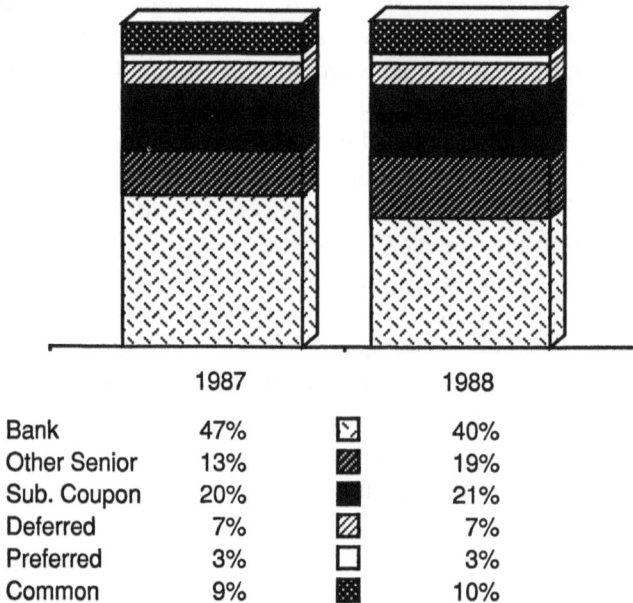

	1987		1988
Bank	47%	◨	40%
Other Senior	13%	▨	19%
Sub. Coupon	20%	■	21%
Deferred	7%	▨	7%
Preferred	3%	☐	3%
Common	9%	▦	10%

Several new variants of subordinated debt were introduced in the late 1980s in order to reduce the initial cash interest payment burden of the transaction. These involved deferred payment interest bonds (DIBs) and payment-in-kind (PIKs) bonds. The latter paid whatever the coupon stated, not in interest but in additional bonds, so the liability and future interest payments grew over time.[1]

The Role of Subordinated Debt and Equity

The subordinated debt in these restructurings played a pivotal role. Usually included as debt by those interested in total firm valuation, subordinate cash-pay and non-cash-pay debt nonetheless provided an important equity-like "cushion" from the standpoint of potential senior creditors. But, unlike the preferred stock financed mergers of the 1960s, subordinated debt provided important tax benefits, i.e., the "constructive equity" nature of low level debt.

Finally, below the multi-layered debt structure came the preferred and equity financing, over 85% owned by the investment company with the residual owned by management. Despite this small percentage ownership for management, the sheer magnitude of the transactions could lead to extremely high returns to all of the equity owners—if the restructuring was successful.

SUCCESSFUL AND UNSUCCESSFUL LBOs

A successful LBO from the standpoint of all parties concerned, including the old and new debt and equity holders, is one that:
- Results in relatively quick and successful repayments to the debt-holders
- "Cashes out" within 3–7 years so that the equity holders recoup their investment and earn substantial profits.
- Does not cause any significant economic disruption of the acquired company, e.g., unemployment resulting in some political reaction.

Operating efficiencies and asset sales (if necessary) can provide sufficient cash to the firm to repay a large portion of the senior debt, within two years. After this period, even the increasing debt burden from the deferred interest junk bonds can be met without difficulty. If, however, earnings and cash flows are disappointing and asset sales are unsuccessful, then distress can set in and the LBO will, in many cases, fail.[2]

To "cash out" means that the firm is sold or recapitalized, either in part or as a whole, or the LBO goes public again by selling shares in the open market. In the case of partial firm sales, proceeds were often paid out to the new owners and debt refinanced, usually over a longer maturity period. Exhibit 2–2 lists statistics on the average large-firm LBOs that took place in the period 1980-1986, and in 1988. The former period was prior to the leverage excesses of 1987–1989 that resulted in many failures. Note that the average premium paid to the original selling shareholders was 46% in the earlier period, resulting in average incremental debt of $400 million on a $524 million transaction. The initial debt/equity ratio was about 6:1. Successful LBOs netted the new owner returns of about 250% over 3–5 years.

With respect to the leverage excesses and inflated prices paid in 1988, results in Exhibit 2–2 show how the average premium rose to about 74% from the earlier 46% and the average cash flow multiplier rose to almost 12

EXHIBIT 2–2
Average Historical LBO Experience Based on Sample of 76 LBOs in 1980-1986[a] and 64 LBOs in 1988[b]—($ Millions)

	1980–86	1988
Prebuyout Value of Equity	$360	$1,023
Average Buyout Purchase Price	$524	$1,783
Average Gain To Prebuyout Shareholders	46%	74%
Equity as a Percent of Total Capital	15%	12%
Debt as a Percent of Total Capital	85%	88%
Debt/Equity Ratio	5.8:1	7.3:1
Incremental Debt	$400	$1,570
Post Buyout Sale of Firm	$750[c]	n.a.
Post Buyout Gain from Sale (50%)	$250[c]	n.a.
Return to New Equity Owners (Total)	250%[c]	n.a.
Cash Flow Multiplier (Earnings after Taxes before Depreciation, Amortization and Deferred Taxes)	6–8X[b]	12X

[a] From S. Kaplan, "Management Buyouts: Evidence on Taxes as a Source of Value," *Journal of Finance* (1989), p. 616.
[b] Compiled by the authors from data supplied by Merrill Lynch *Capital Markets*.
[c] Based on 46 completed LBOs.

times from the 6–8 times of the earlier period. Finally, the average size of larger firm transactions grew from $500 million to $1.8 billion in a relatively short period. The use of subordinated debt as tax deductible "equity" helped to spark this dramatic increase.

The average post buyout sale of the 1980-1986 deals resulted in a $750 million payment; or a $250 million (50%) post buyout gain from the sale. The actual gain to the equity holders was magnified, of course, as a result of the large amounts of leverage employed. Since their investment was only $100 million, the return on equity was 250% over an average period of 3–4 years. Clearly, these are examples of how value was increased via the LBO.

A very recent example of a successful LMBO was the sale of the budget motel company, Motel 6, to the French-based hotel giant Accor S.A. Motel 6 was bought by the largest LBO firm, Kohlberg, Kravis and Roberts, (KKR) in 1985 for $125 million. Its sale for $1.3 billion in 1990 gives KKR and its partners a return of more than five times their original equity investment. The original purchase involved a cost of $881 million, financed with the $125 million in equity and $756 million in debt—a debt equity ratio of

6:1. One year after the buyout, KKR sold nearly half of its common equity units to the public and began repaying the debt. As will be shown next, value can be increased via the buyout-restructuring route, especially if the enormous debt incurred is reduced quickly.

LINKING CAPITAL STRUCTURE THEORY WITH LEVERAGED RESTRUCTURINGS

The relationship between a firm's capital structure and its true valuation has interested financial theorists for over forty years, but it was the works of Modigliani and Miller (M&M) in 1958 and 1963 that catapulted the subject to center stage in the finance literature. In their classic 1958 article, M&M argued that the relationship between a firm's debt and equity had absolutely no impact on its overall value; the only variables that determined firm value were its future earning power (encompassed in expected cash flows) and the business risk-return class of the firm. In other words, how the firm packaged its financing had no material impact on value or the firm's overall weighted average cost of capital (WACC). Value was determined by what businesses a company was in and how well its managers ran it—nothing else. Their conclusion is represented by the horizontal line V in Exhibit 2–3. [Note that these representations, and those found in Exhibits 2–4 to 2–6, are fairly standard, e.g., see Brigham and Gapenski (1991).]

Even though this theory rested upon a set of unrealistic assumptions, (many of which were addressed in footnotes to their original (1958) article), and some rather simplistic empirical tests, the theory caused an immediate and strong response from the academic community.[3] A number of "traditionalists" opposed M&M's ideas; for example, Durand (1959) argued that the amount of debt did matter and that therefore there was an optimal debt/equity ratio represented by the minimum point on the WACC schedule in Exhibit 2–4. It was felt that a firm could lower its WACC, and at the same time increase its value (V_L), by adding a judicious amount of debt. The relatively low after-tax cost of debt $[K_d(1 - T)]$ would bring down the overall cost despite the higher and rising cost of equity (K_e). At some point, however, the combination of increasing costs of debt and equity would begin to raise the overall cost (its capitalization rate) and lower the firm's value. And some empirical tests, notably by Weston (1963), showed that leverage did indeed impact the firm's overall cost of capital. Two and a half

EXHIBIT 2–3
Original M&M Theory

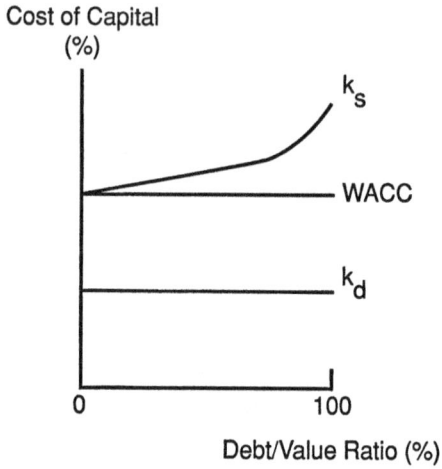

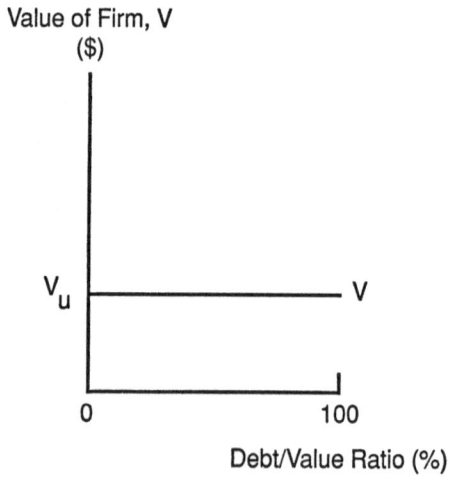

Cost of Capital
(%)

k_s

WACC

k_d

0   100

Debt/Value Ratio (%)

Value of Firm, V
($)

V_u V

0   100

Debt/Value Ratio (%)

EXHIBIT 2–4
Effects of Leverage: Traditional Approach

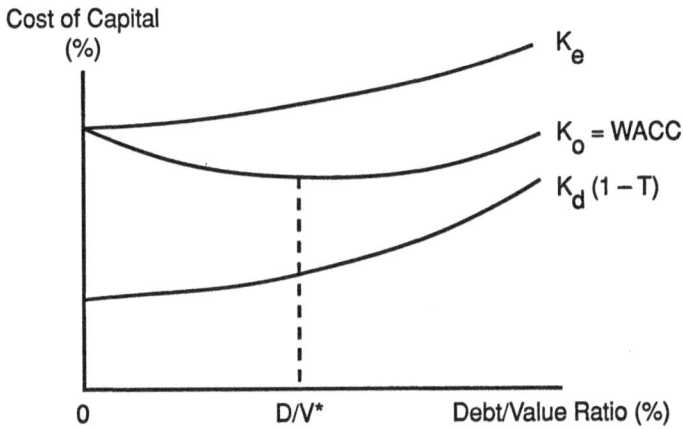

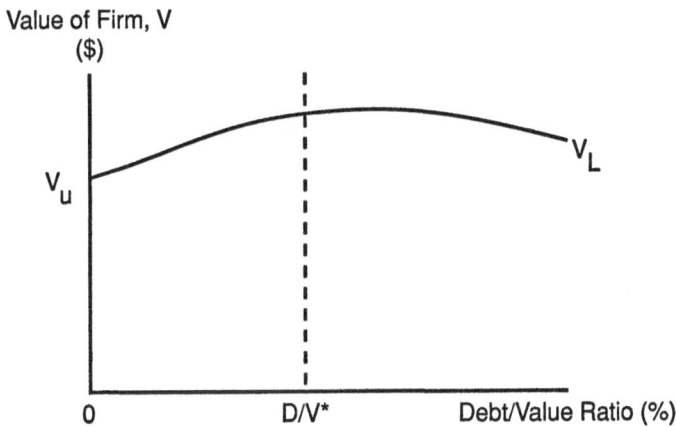

K_e = Cost of Equity Capital
K_d = Cost of Debt Capital
K_o = Weighted Average Cost of Capital
T = Corporate Tax Rate
V_u = Value of Unleveraged Firm
V_L = Value of Leveraged Firm

decades later, Weston (1989) reflected on the M&M capital structure controversy.

In 1963, M&M published a correction article which stated that they had underestimated the important contribution to firm value from the tax subsidy on debt interest payments. They reasoned that a firm could indeed lower its capitalization rate and increase its value by adding debt and receiving a "bonus" equal to TD (the tax rate times the amount of debt) (Exhibit 2–5). And it appeared that this increasing value of the leveraged firm (V_L) was evident *regardless* of the amount of debt. Could this have been the seminal work that guided the leveraged buyout movement that emerged in the United States over 20 years later?[4] We will return to this question at a later point.

Finally, a combination of renewed traditional theory and some new concepts dealing with financial distress costs (or bankruptcy costs) and "agency" conflicts added both rigorous new theory and empirical tests to support the traditional view of an optimal capital structure which was not 100% debt. It was argued that as a firm's leverage increases, the probability of bankruptcy also increases and if the costs of bankruptcy are significant, then a firm's value will fall when the marginal increase in the expected value of financial distress costs is greater than the increase in the expected value of the tax benefits from debt. The overall cost of capital will rise beyond some optimum leverage proportion and the firm's value will fall.

Altman (1984) measured the costs of bankruptcy, not only in terms of the direct out-of-pocket costs to lawyers, accountants, etc. and the lost opportunities due to management's diversion from running the business, but the indirect costs as well. Indirect costs were defined as those lost sales and profits caused by customers choosing not to deal with a firm which was a high potential bankrupt as well as increased costs of doing business (e.g., higher debt costs and poorer terms with suppliers) while in a financially vulnerable condition. He found that while the direct costs were consistent with Warner's (1977) earlier results, the indirect costs were quite significant.

Agency effects, first articulated by Jensen and Meckling (1976), argued that due to conflicts between debt and equity stockholders, indeed also between holders of different classes of debt (Bulow & Shoven, 1978), a firm incurred real costs as the threat of bankruptcy grew. On the other hand, many have argued that the highly leveraged LBO, transforming the "manager-only" to a "manager-owner," has positive agency benefits by removing some manager-owner conflicts of interest.

EXHIBIT 2–5
Effects of Leverage: MM with Taxes

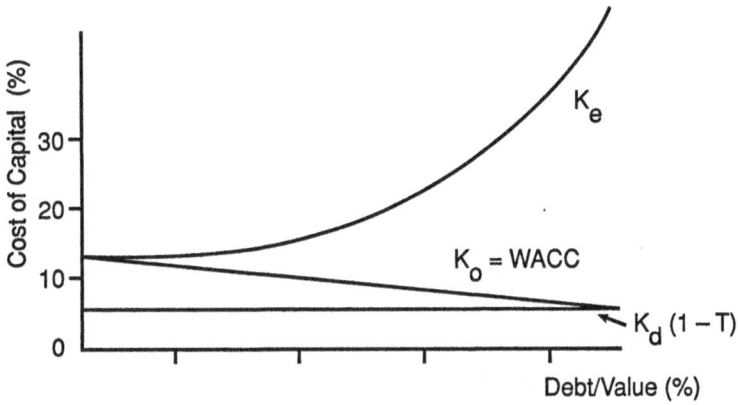

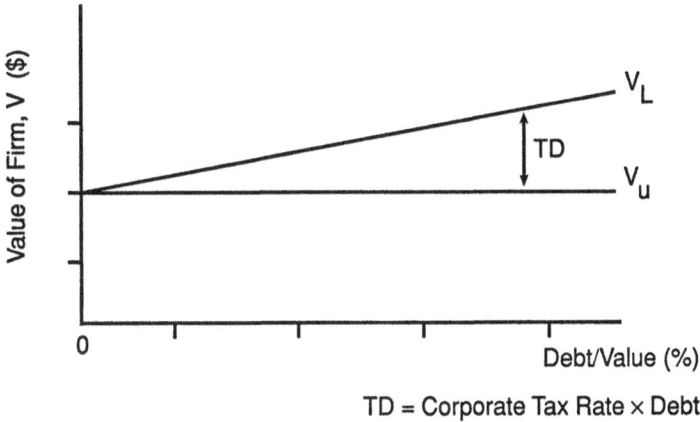

TD = Corporate Tax Rate × Debt

Exhibit 2–6 shows that financial distress and agency costs are the major factors accounting for the difference between the so-called pure MM value of the firm with the tax subsidy and the revised traditionalist value of the firm. The net result is an optimum point on the debt/value axis (D^*), at which the firm's value is maximized.

DELEVERAGING—THE TREND FOR THE 1990s?

As we postulated, a successful highly leveraged restructured firm must reduce its debt substantially and usually within a short time after the restructuring transaction. The consequences of not achieving this deleveraging are apparent both in theory (Exhibit 2–6) and in our observance of the substantial increase in highly leveraged, high priced, LBO distressed situations of the 1980s and the consequent increase in defaults. Exhibit 2–7 shows that through the first eleven months of 1990, junk bond defaults mounted to $16.5 billion, resulting in a default rate of 7.8% (the rate for the entire year was 8.74%). This default rate is substantially higher than the weighted average default rate of 3.2% for the period 1978 to 1989. Losses from the recent defaults, most but not all of which were the result of restructurings, also increased due to the lower lender recovery rates, i.e., lower prices just after default. The average recovery in 1990 was about 26%, compared to about 35% for the five-year period 1985–1989 and 40% for most of the history of defaults.

Deleveraging can be either voluntary or not—the latter can result from forced distressed exchange issues whereby the creditors of a distressed firm

EXHIBIT 2–6
Net Effects of Leverage on the Value of the Firm

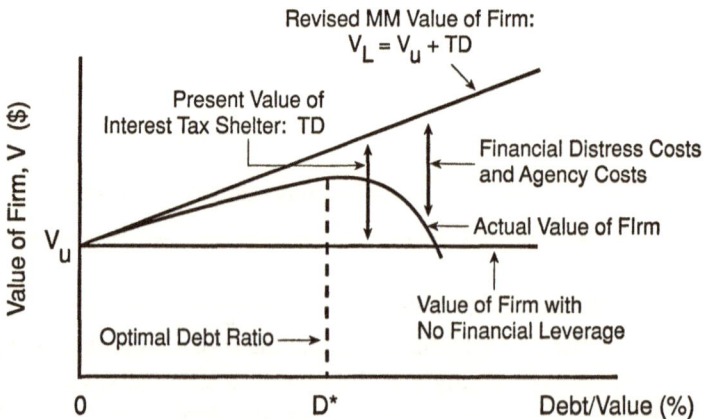

EXHIBIT 2-7
Historical Default Rate—Low Rated, Straight Debt Only, 1978–90 ($ Millions)

Year	Par Value Outstanding	Par Value Default	Default Rate (%)
1990[a]	$210,000	$16,480.00	7.848%
1989	201,000	8,110.30	4.035
1988	159,223	3,944.20	2.477
1987	136,952	7,485.50[b]	5.466[b]
1986	92,985	3,155.76	3.394
1985	59,078	992.10	1.679
1984	41,700	344.16	0.825
1983	28,233	301.08	1.066
1982	18,536	577.34	3.115
1981	17,362	27.00	0.156
1980	15,126	224.11	1.482
1979	10,675	20.00	0.187
1978	9,401	118.90	1.265

Arithmetic Average Default Rate, 1970–1989 2.485%
Arithmetic Average Default Rate, 1978–1989 2.096%
Arithmetic Average Default Rate, 1983–1989 2.706%

Weighted Average Default Rate, 1970–1989 3.179%
Weighted Average Default Rate, 1978–1989 3.201%
Weighted Average Default Rate, 1983–1989 3.383%

[a] Through December 1, 1990
[b] $1,841.7 million without Texaco, Inc., Texaco Capital, and Texaco Capital N.V. The default rate without these is 1.345%.

agree to accept a package of new securities in lieu of the existing debt. Invariably, this package contains equity in the troubled firm. The ability for firms to effect an equity for debt swap before distress becomes apparent was severely hampered by the malaise in the equity markets, starting in the second half of 1990. Conditions improved markedly in 1991 as new equity issues soared. Deleveraging can also be prompted by the fear of a crisis situation especially prior to some "trigger" date such as an interest rate reset or cash-pay commencement date.

Some voluntary debt reductions have occurred from debt repurchases by firms with sufficient cash to take advantage of the significant reduction in bond prices of virtually all highly leveraged firms starting in the summer 1989. Deleveraging will continue from debt repurchasing and may expand even more rapidly when the equity markets rebound.

Two examples of major firm deleveraging efforts in the face of economic and financial uncertainties are the recent attempts by RJR Nabisco and Macy's—both large LBOs of the late 1980s. RJR Nabisco, bought by KKR in 1989, had already reduced debt by over $6.0 billion by mid-1990, but still found itself with about $20.0 billion of debt outstanding. RJR's recapitalization plan commenced in July 1990 with an additional $6.9 billion in debt reduction, featuring retirement of about $2.4 billion of publicly held "reset" notes, using a combination of cash and stock. While one might argue that the swap was prompted by the firm's perceived financial vulnerability, even so, its cash flow in 1990 was extremely positive permitting partial bond paybacks and other deleveraging actions. Indeed, debt repurchases continued into 1991, culminated by the upgrading of most of the RJR Nabisco debt to investment-grade status in December.

Macy's, an LBO with several large institutional stockholders, was attempting in 1990 to reduce its considerable debt burden. One strategic move was to reduce some of its $5.6 billion in debt through periodic repurchases financed by the sale of new convertible preferred stock to the public. The preferred stock sale was complemented by the sale of Macy's receivables and some real estate. These actions were precipitated primarily by the drastic reduction in market value of several of its outstanding debt issues and the perceived concern in the markets of the deterioration in credit quality of Macy's.

LEVERAGED RESTRUCTURING AND VALUE— THREE EXAMPLES

Case 1: Debt for Equity Swaps

We will explore a number of scenarios whereby a restructuring of the permanent capital can be shown to increase firm value. The first scenario involves a classic debt for equity exchange, or "swap," which is a type of leveraged recapitalization. Exhibit 2–8 illustrates a situation whereby a firm in a 40% tax bracket swaps $3,000 of its equity for new debt. Before the transaction, the firm had $2,000 in debt at a before-tax cost of 8.0% and $4,032 in equity—the latter based on a price/earnings ratio of 8 times after tax earnings of $504. The total value of the firm's securities was therefore $6,032 and the weighted-average cost of capital (WACC) was about 10.0%.[5]

EXHIBIT 2–8
Restructuring and Value
CASE 1: Leveraging Up (Debt for Equity Swap = $3,000)

	Before	After	Change (Return %)
EBIT	$1,000	$1,000	—
Debt (BV)	$2,000	$5,000	$3,000
(MV)	$2,000	$4,600	$2,600
Cost of Debt:			
Before Tax	8.0%	10.0%	2.0%
After Tax	4.8%	6.0%	1.2%
Tax Rate	40%	40%	—
Interest	$ 160	$ 460	$ 300
EAT	$ 504	$ 324	–$ 180
Cost of Equity	12.5%	14.3%	1.8%
Equity Multiplier	8X	7X	–1X
Equity Value	$4,032	$2,268 ($+3,000)	$1,236=31%
Total Firm Value	$6,032	$6,868	$ 836=14%
Cost of Capital	10.0%	8.7%	–1.3%

After the swap, the cost of debt rises to, say, 10%, as the debt/total value ratio increases from 33% to 67% and the equity multiplier falls to 7 times due to the higher financial risk. But, since debt is now a greater proportion of total capital, although its after-tax cost has increased from 4.8% to 6.0%, the WACC decreases to 8.7%. The new equity value is $2,268 (7 times earnings of $324), plus the $4,600 in debt raises the firm's total value by $836 to $6,868. This is a 14% increase.[6] Note that if the firm's increase in value was equal to the tax benefits from the additional debt, the increase would be $1,200 (.4 × 3,000) instead of $836. We are therefore implicitly assuming bankruptcy and agency costs of $364. This increase in value was depicted earlier in our theoretical discussion and shown in both Exhibit 2–4 (M&M with taxes) and Exhibit 2–5 (traditional approach). Indeed, the value to the old equity holder has increased 31%, even more than the 14% increase in firm value.[7]

In addition to the tax benefits inherent in a debt for equity swap, there is evidence that a company's exchange offer is interpreted by the market as a signal about future cash flows. Copeland and Lee (1990) examine data on exchanges covering the period 1962–1984 and find evidence consistent with the signalling hypothesis. They also find that leverage-increasing exchange offers result in decreases in systematic risk, increases in adjusted earnings, sales, and assets. Opposite results are found for leverage-decreasing exchange offers. We postulate that the vast majority of the firms in the Copeland and Lee sample had excess debt capacity—not found in many of the over leveraged firms in today's environment.

Case 2: LBO Restructuring

The second scenario involves the same initial condition as in Case 1, except now the swap is an extreme one with all of the equity purchased through an LBO and the public firm becomes privately owned. The purchase of $4,032 in equity is accomplished by offering the old shareholders a 40% premium, or $5,645 (recall that 40% was about the average LBO premium in the period 1983–1986). The cost is financed by 90% debt and 10% equity, increasing the total book value of debt from $2,000 to $8,048. The dollar equity investment is $565 (10% of the cost). Case 2 is illustrated in Exhibit 2–9.

After the buyout, the firm's cost of debt increases to, say, 11% (a 3% increase), which if publicly issued would no doubt be rated as a "junk" bond. The after-tax cost of debt rises from 4.8% to 6.6% and the old debt's value falls from $2,000 to $1,250. Due to the high debt amount and increased cost, the interest expense is now $719 ($160 on the old and $559 on the new debt) and net earnings drops to $169. Since this is now a highly leveraged private firm, the P/E approach cannot be used directly to value the equity or the entire firm, although an estimate of value can be made by using P/E ratios of comparable highly leveraged firms that are publicly traded. Instead, a commonly used firm valuation practice in highly leveraged companies is the cash flow multiplier approach.

A typical range of total firm value to cash flow during the 1983–1986 period of LBOs was from 6–8 times.[8] The firm in Case 2 has earnings before interest and taxes plus depreciation—sometimes referred to as EBITD—of $1,500. Assuming the more conservative multiplier of 6 times,

EXHIBIT 2–9
Restructuring and Value
CASE 2: LBO Financed by 90% Debt and 10% Equity

	Before	After	Change (Return %)
EBIT	$1,000	$1,000	—
Depreciation	$ 500	$ 500	—
Total Debt(BV)	$2,000	$7,080[a]	—
(MV)	$2,000	$6,330	$5,080
Cost of Debt:			
Before Tax	8.0%	11.0%	3.0%
After Tax	4.8%	6.6%	1.8%
Interest	$ 160	$ 719	$ 559
Tax Rate	40%	40%	—
EAT	$ 504	$ 169	$ 335
Equity Multiplier	8X	—	
EBITD Based Firm Multiplier	6X		
Equity Value	$4,032	$2,670	373%
(Investment = .10 × $5,645 = $565)			
Total Firm Value	$6,032	$9,000	$2,968 (49%)

[a] LBO Purchased at a 40% Equity Premium = $5,645, New Debt = $5,080

the total firm value is $9,000. Subtracting the market value of debt ($6,330) from total firm value results in an equity value of $2,670. Since the equity investment was only $565, the rather immediate returns to the new equity holders are estimated at 373%. Of course, at this point these returns are merely hypothetical. Total value of the firm also increases dramatically by 49% over the initial $6,032, reflecting the future benefits of the restructuring.

Note, we have not indicated any increase in EBITD from before to after—both are at $1,500. Most LBO and financial restructuring advocates, however, argue that a firm will usually become more efficient in its cost containment and productivity increases after it goes private. Indeed, Jensen (1989) argues for the "discipline-of-debt" as a positive motivation for increasing firm values—not to mention the tax benefits that we have seen in Cases 1 and 2. Evidence of sizeable increases in cash flow can be observed in several articles from Amihud (1989), especially Bull.

On the other hand, opponents of LBO restructurings argue that the enormous debt burden stifles new investment and puts the highly leveraged firm at a distinct long-term disadvantage vis-à-vis its less leveraged competitors. Further, optimistic forecasts of higher earnings and cash flows and successful asset sales do not always materialize and the suffocating amounts of debt cause perfectly good companies to falter. In faltering situations, both the new debt and equity holders will lose a significant proportion of their investment.

Case 3: Asset Sales and Debt Paydown

Our last restructuring scenario picks up where we left Case 2 and assumes that within a few years the firm sells 50% of its assets and uses all, or in another case only part, of the proceeds to repay or repurchase debt (see Exhibit 2–10).

Selling one half of its assets results in a 50% reduction in earnings and cash flow. We assume that these assets are sold for six times their cash flows (the same conservative multiplier as in our earlier assumption). This results in an asset sale cash generation of 50% of $9,000, or $4,500. These proceeds are used to pay down debt to a total of $2,580 from $7,080 (middle column of Exhibit 2–10).

Since debt is considerably reduced, we assume the cost of debt falls to 10% and earnings after interest and taxes rises to $194. The new interest cost is based on a blend of the original $2,000 in old debt of 8% and $580 of the debt issued by the LBO at 11%. The new cash flow of $750 is assigned a seven times multiplier since the financial markets are usually favorably impressed with successful asset sales and immediate debt paydown. The seven times multiple results in a new firm value of $5,250 (7 × $750) and an equity value of $2,435 ($5,250 − $2,815 debt). Hence, the new equity value is similar to the hypothetical equity value just after the LBO occurred. The LBO equity holder realizes a 331% return but the risk exposure is greatly reduced. This scenario of Case 3 shows a positive reaction to the chain of events surrounding the LBO.

A less positive scenario is depicted in the last column of Exhibit 2–10. Here the same asset sale takes place but only half of the proceeds are used to repurchase debt, i.e., .5($4,500) = $2,250. This reduces total debt to $4,830

EXHIBIT 2–10
Restructuring and Value
CASE 3: LBO Financed by 90% Debt with Subsequent Asset Sale
and Debt Paydown (50% of Assets Sold)

	Post LBO (From Case #2)	Sell Assets & 100% Debt Paydown	Sell Assets & 50% Debt Paydown
EBIT	$1,000	$ 500	$ 500
Depreciation	$ 500	$ 250	$ 250
Total Debt (BV)	$7,080	$2,580[a]	$4,830[b]
(MV)	$6,330	$2,815[a]	$5,050[b]
Cost of Debt:			
Before Tax	11.0%	10%	10.5%
After Tax	6.6%	6.0%	6.3%
Interest	$ 719	$ 324	$ 471
Tax Rate	40%	40%	40%
EAT	$ 169	$ 194	$ 17
Firm Multiplier (EBITD Based)	6X	7X	5X
Equity Value Withdrawal	$2,670	$2,435	−$1,300+$2,250
Total Value	$9,000	$5,250	$3,750
Debt/Total Value	70%	54%	135%

[a] $7,080 −.5 × $9,000 = $2,580; market value of debt increased by about 9%.
[b] $7,080 −.5 × $9,000 = $4,830; market value of debt increased by about 5%.

and we assume the cost of debt decreases but only to 10.5%.

Since only one half of the proceeds are used for debt reduction and earnings after taxes drop to $17, the new EBITD cash flow multiplier on the remaining operations is assumed to be five. This results in total firm value of $3,750 (5 × $750) and a negative equity of −$1,300. The LBO equity holders, total value and return are still positive, however, since half of the asset sales ($2,250) is added to their wealth. But the result is not as positive as the first asset-sale scenario with the higher debt paydown, i.e., a return on equity investment of 68% as compared to 330% in the 100% debt paydown scenario. Note the negative book equity situation and the 135% debt/value ratio in the lower paydown case.

In the scenarios we have illustrated, the result described is of course dependent on our assumptions—ones we think are fairly realistic. The end result, regardless of the multipliers selected, shows the impact that financial structure can have on firm valuation. And, with the exception of one case, all showed the positive effects of a leveraged restructuring on the value of the firm.

While positive results were common in the mid-1980s, the end result was not always so happy. In Appendix A, we chronicle the results of two leveraged buyouts that took place in 1986–1987. One, Borg Warner Corporation, seems to have worked out very well for everyone involved. The other, Fruehauf Corporation, did not work out as well, although it was not the disaster that several large LBOs (e.g., Revco, Jim Walter, Southland, Integrated Resources, National Gypsum, became in the late 1980s and early 1990s).

LINKING BACK TO FINANCIAL THEORY

As we observed in Exhibit 2–6, the value of an enterprise could be increased by an addition to debt and the present value of that increase in value was equal to TD (tax rate times the total amount of debt). Since an LBO is probably the extreme of a voluntary increase in debt, no doubt one of the motivations is to accrue these tax advantages. Hence, an ever-increasing debt/value ratio makes sense in a world of insignificant distress and agency costs. But these costs are not trivial, and the curve marked "Actual Value of Firm" falls after some optimum debt amount (D^*).

In an earlier paper (Altman, 1984), it was shown that a firm's optimum debt was where the expected bankruptcy (distress) costs were equal to the expected value of the tax benefits from debt; i.e.,

$$P_{B,t}\,(BCD_t + BCI_t) \cdot (PV)_t = (PV_t)\,T_c\,(Id_t) \cdot (1 - P_{B,t})$$

where:

$P_{B,t}$ = Probability of bankruptcy estimated in period t
BCD_t = Direct bankruptcy costs estimated in t

BCI_t = Indirect Bankruptcy costs estimated in t
T_c = Marginal tax bracket of the corporation
Id = Interest expenses from period t to infinity
PV_t = Present value adjustment to period t

Where the expected bankruptcy costs are lower than the expected tax benefits, increased leverage can be successfully undertaken. Altman reported (1984) that most firms in his sample of bankrupt companies had expected bankruptcy costs greater than expected tax benefits.

THE CONCEPT OF TEMPORARY DEBT

The bankruptcy cost/tax benefit tradeoff analysis rests on the assumption of fairly permanent, or at least long-term, debt. If, however, the initial burst of debt in an LBO is planned to be temporary, then the objective could, and in our opinion should, be to move back along the $V_L = V_u + TD$ function, in Exhibit 2–6, to an optimal amount of debt (approximately D^*). While the expected value of the tax benefits are probably lower at this point than further out on the line, the probability of bankruptcy is also considerably lower. In so doing, the owners of an LBO can reap the initial increase in value and sustain that increase until they cash out. The new debt holders will benefit either by having their debt repurchased within, say, two years (especially the senior debtholders) or continuing to receive the high yields on the subordinated debt (mezzanine or junk bonds) in highly leveraged restructurings.

If, however, the firm cannot move back successfully along the value line, then distress may grow to the point that the firm's value decreases sharply—perhaps to its liquidation value in extreme cases. This will occur when disappointing cash flows occur, lowering the unlevered value of the firm (V_u), and/or asset sales are disappointing or impossible (usually due to changed market conditions). Finally, another type of distress could occur when a seemingly healthy entity cannot refinance its existing debt. Theoretically, this should not occur as long as the intrinsic value of the assets exceed the debt burden. But difficult conditions in the debt and equity capital markets can prevent refinancings, even for reasonably healthy but highly leveraged firms. This was the case in 1990, as markets lost confidence in highly leveraged transactions, the new issue junk bond market in the United States dried up, banks were increasingly hesitant to refinance the highly leveraged transactions, and equity markets were performing poorly.

EMPIRICAL EVIDENCE ON SUCCESSFUL LBOs AND DEBT PAYDOWN

We are beginning to amass some empirical evidence on successful and unsuccessful LBOs. In a study carried out in cooperation with the Controller of Currency, Moore (1990) investigated a sample of 11 successful and 9 unsuccessful LBOs as to their three-year post-LBO experience on a number of performance variables. Unsuccessful LBOs are those which have failed, bonds have defaulted or a distressed exchange issue was completed. Successful LBOs are those which were still in operation without disturbance for at least three years after the LBO and were considered healthy by the Controller of Currency.

The average long-term debt/total assets (LTD/TA) ratio was 62.4% for the successful sample, just after the LBO. This ratio fell to 53.6%, 39.7%, 37.6%, and 49.4% in the four post-LBO years (Exhibit 2–11). The unsuccessful LBOs, on the other hand, had a lower (46.4%) LTD/TA at the time of LBO, but saw the ratio rise to 71.2% in the fourth year after. Hence, we observe evidence of the correlation between debt paydown and successful LBOs.

Admittedly, this is a small sample with a fair amount of variation, but the data seem quite compatible with our "temporary debt" thesis.

CONCLUSION

We have noted the increased importance of financial restructurings in corporate securities valuation. To the extent that different forms of financing, including subordinated debt, are available to firms to complement the traditional role played by banks, firm valuation can be raised by increasing the leverage in the capital structure. In the case of over-leveraged companies with significant risk of distress and/or default, the opposite tonic is called for, namely deleveraging to a less burdened capital structure. Thus, capital structure is shown to be one of the key variables in determining (and changing) corporate valuation.

Exhibit 2–11
Successful vs. Unsuccessful LBOs and Debt Paydown Experience
(Long-Term Debt/Total Assets Ratio)

Successful LBOs (%)

Obser-vation #	LBO -3	LBO -2	LBO -1	LBO YEAR	LBO +1	LBO +2	LBO +3	LBO +4
1		25.8	23.8	60.6	52.7	35.8	20.3	4.2
2	8.3	1.3	3.7	76.0	72.7	38.7	42.7	44.6
3				54.0	44.7	31.6	18.0	40.6
4					36.7	36.7	63.7	69.6
5	0.6	0.3	2.9	36.0	60.5			
6						38.5	26.4	52.2
7			2.2	59.8	59.3	56.9		
8	2.8	2.9	2.2	83.8	61.4	43.5	34.0	
9	30.4	45.1	34.5	49.5	62.6	58.3	82.0	85.0
10			9.7	64.2	44.5	27.7	31.1	
11				77.6	40.9	29.3	20.2	
Average	10.5	15.0	11.2	62.4	53.6	39.7	37.6	49.4
Number	4	5	7	9	10	10	9	6
Standard Deviation	11.8	17.7	11.8	14.2	10.9	10.0	20.6	25.2

Unsuccessful LBOs (%)

Obser-vation #	LBO -3	LBO -2	LBO -1	LBO YEAR	LBO +1	LBO +2	LBO +3	LBO +4
1		12.6	41.1	33.7	36.1	36.6	33.6	41.7
2			37.3	33.0	35.8	28.1	36.9	75.2
3	8.4	5.1	4.2	61.9	62.8	64.4	67.7	129.6
4				32.4	24.9	36.4	38.0	38.1
5	35.9	35.3	23.1	65.0				
6			21.3	41.1	34.2	46.1	64.1	
7			14.6	56.4	57.1	46.0	76.1	
8			19.5	43.9	49.6	57.0		
9	17.8	31.2	41.2	49.9	50.2			
Average	0.2	21.1	25.3	46.4	43.8	44.9	52.7	71.1
Number	3	4	8	9	8	7	6	4
Standard Deviation	11.3	12.5	12.5	11.8	12.1	11.6	16.9	36.7

Source: H. Moore, "Trends and Characteristics of Recent LBO Experience," NYU working paper, November 1990.

NOTES

1. Another innovation pioneered by U.S. investment banks was "reset" notes which "guaranteed" that the interest rate would be reset periodically so as to cause the bonds to sell at par value. This innovation, like so many of the others, ultimately operated adversely to the interests of the issuers as the junk bond market became more concerned with credit quality. Such innovations can increase the likelihood of credit problems in the future.
2. This occurred in 1989–90 to several of the large LMBOs and other highly leveraged transactions that resulted in critical bankruptcies and other distressed situations. These include the Campeau (Allied and Federated Stores) fiasco, Hillsborough Holdings, Southland, National Gypsum, and several others. In the United Kingdom, the Isosceles PLC buyout of Gateway Corporation is a current distressed situation due mainly to disappointing asset sales and smaller than forecasted reductions in debt.
3. Miller recently (1989) argued, however, that "the view that capital structure is literally irrelevant or that 'nothing matters' in corporate finance, though still sometimes attributed to us, is far from what we ever actually said about real-world applications of our theoretical propositions." One could infer that when M&M relax their restrictive assumptions—e.g., no taxes, perfect information about earnings prospects—they too agree as to the value-enhancing power of debt. Indeed, Miller's comment (1989) on the rise in junk bonds to help bring about leveraged restructurings was that he was puzzled why the use of such instruments took so long to develop.
4. Indeed, Dr. Modigliani was asked this very question soon after he had received the Nobel Prize in Economics and after the LBO boom had begun. He vehemently denied this, citing other factors that might lower a firm's value as leverage increased.
5. The WACC is equal to the sum of the component after-tax costs of debt and equity, each multiplied by the amount of each as a proportion of total capital; i.e., $10.0\% = .048\ (2000 / 6032) + .125\ (4032 / 6032)$.
6. The breakeven firm value point, comparing the before situation to after recapitalization, would manifest if the equity multiplier fell to about 4.4 times instead of 7.
7. Based on a 7 times P/E ratio, the new equity value is $2,268 ($7 \times \$324$) plus the $3,000 derived in the swap brings the total value of the old equity holder to $5,268—a 31% increase over $4,032.
8. Indeed, as the LBO movement in the United States heated up and exceptional profits were made, cash flow multipliers increased to 10–12 times and even higher.

APPENDIX A TO CHAPTER 2

TWO LEVERAGED MANAGEMENT BUYOUTS

The following discussion illustrates a relatively successful venture (Borg Warner) and one less successful (Fruehauf). Borg Warner, primarily a manufacturer of automotive components and accessories, was a classic LBO candidate with fairly stable and positive cash flows, a low debt level, and strong management. Despite a substantial profit margin, however, the firm's return on equity was relatively low (under 4.0%). Borg Warner was taken private in an LBO transaction in March 1987. The purchaser was Merrill Lynch Capital Partners, Inc., one of the leading LBO firms. Exhibit A–1 illustrates the Borg Warner situation just before, just after, 14 months after, and 26 months after the leveraged buyout took place.

The LBO was financed by a large infusion of over $3.6 billion in long term debt and an equity infusion of just $200 million. Total debt rose to $4.66 billion resulting in a debt/asset ratio of 92%.

The cost of debt, measured by the yield-to-maturity, rose from 8.55% on the existing 5½s of 1992 to 13.64%, an increase of over 5 percent, indicating its "fallen-angel"—junk bond status. A second issue of 8% bonds due in 1996 went from 8.11% to 14.69% over that same time span. The actual premium paid to the existing shareholders was a relatively low 24%, compared to the average of over 40% typical of LBOs in the mid-1980s and much below the premiums paid in the late 1980s. The cash flow, EBITDA (earnings before interest and taxes plus depreciation and amortization) multiplier was about 10 times. The company, therefore, was transferred from a conservatively financed company to a heavily leveraged one operating with an interest coverage ratio of 1.29 on continuing operations.

The buyout's progress was extremely positive with higher returns on a much smaller asset base, strong asset sales, and, most importantly, significant debt paydown. Long-term debt was reduced to $1.3 billion in 1988 and $926 million at the end of 1989—a reduction of over $2.3 billion within the first 14 months after the buyout and a continuing reduction thereafter. As a result, the cost of debt on the first debt issue noted above dropped to 10.85% in December 1988—a fall of about 2.8%. (The yield to maturity as of December 1989 was even lower at 9.46%). While its bond rating still reflected a junk bond, its yield was more consistent with an investment grade rating.

If the entire firm was liquidated or shares sold again to the public in December 1988, we estimate that its equity would have been worth from $893 million to $2,085 million depending upon the cash flow multiplier consistent with the value of the firm. For instance, an EBITDA multiple of 10—the multiplier paid for the LBO of Borg Warner by Merrill Lynch Capital Partners, would result in a total firm value of $2.980 billion as of 12/88 (EBITDA = $298 million). Multiples of 8 or 12 give the lower and upper figures ($2,384 and $3,576) for the total value as indicated in Exhibit A–1.

A total firm value of $2.980 billion as of December 1988 results in an equity value of $1.489 billion ($2.980 − total debt of $1.491 billion). The lower bound equity value of $893 million is somewhat above the value that the private owners estimated ($541 million).* This appeared at the time to have been a conservative estimate of the LBO's equity. One year later, a six-times multiplier would have resulted in an equity value consistent with its book value of $632 million. Cash flow multiples did certainly decline in 1989, although it is not clear what Borg Warner's would have been.

The Borg Warner LBO appears to be a success with an increase in profitability (from 6.2% return on assets to 7.0% and 8.7%), a reduction of the cost of debt capital and the amount of debt (discussed earlier), and an increase in equity value of at least 200%. This is an excellent example of the concept of "temporary debt," discussed earlier, as the key to a successful highly leveraged restructuring.

Of course, the final judgment on this LBO will not be known until either the firm is sold, new equity issued to the public, or, on a negative theme, a distressed situation develops. The outlook, however, is quite bright for just about everyone involved. An indicator of that is the fact that the Borg Warner Corporation 5% bonds, while Ba3/B+ rated, were selling at a relatively low yield (high price) of 11.5% in September 1990—almost three years after the buyout. The 8% bonds were selling at a 12.75% yield at this time. The latter bond is perhaps a better indicator of yield since there were still $100 million outstanding compared to only $3 million for the 5s of 1992.

Fruehauf Corporation

While Borg Warner is an example of a successful LBO, Fruehauf was a type of qualified failure. Restructured in December 1986, the manufacturer of truck trailers and automotive parts was bought for almost $750 million

---

*Derived from 1988 Borg Warner Corporation Annual Report.

EXHIBIT A–1
Pre- and Postbuyout Experience—Borg Warner Corporation ($Millions)

	Before Buyout (3/87)	Immediately after Buyout (9/87)	14 Months after Buyout (12/88)	26 Months after Buyout (12/89)	
EBIT	$315	$336	(177)[a] $187	$196	
Depreciation and Amortization	$143	$174	$111	$92	
EBITDA	$458	$510	$298	$314	
Cost of Debt					
(YTM) (5½s, '92)	8.55%	13.64%	10.85%	9.46%	
(8s, '96)	8.11%	14.69%	12.48%	12.02%	
Cost of LBO/EBIT(M1)	—	14.16X	—	—	
Cost of LBO/EBITD(M2)	—	10.02X	—	—	
EBIT/Interest	5.80X	1.29X[b]	1.00X	1.46X	
EBITD/Interest	8.20X	2.38X	1.47X	2.44X	
% Premium Paid Per Share	—	24%	—	—	
Total Assets	—	$5,386	$2,668	$2,252	
EBIT/Total Assets	—	6.2%	7.0%	8.7%	
Long-Term Debt	—	$3,642	$1,300	$926	
Total Debt	$395	$4,655	$1,491	$1,229	
Total Value (TV)	$3,987	$4,855	$2,385	$3,512	
			$2,980	$3,140	
			$3,576	$3,768	
Equity Value (TV − Debt)	$3,592	$200	$893	$1,283	
			$1,481	$1,911	
			$2,085	$2,539	
			vs. $541	$632	(Book Equity)

[a] $177 million from continuing operations and a 1.29 interest coverage.
[b] Equivalent to an EBITDA multiplier of six.

based on a cash flow multiple of 7.6 times and resulting in a 56% premium paid to the old shareholders. The acquisition was financed by an increase in debt of about $1.0 billion, of which $579 million was long-term (Exhibit A–2). The debt to asset ratio was 85%—fairly typical of LBOs in 1986. Immediately after the increase in debt, the yield-to-maturity on the existing 9¾s of 1996 increased from 9.8% to 13.1%—a sizeable rise of over 3%, although not as much as in the Borg Warner case.

The situation deteriorated within two years of the LBO due to a combination of factors including lower profitability, disappointing asset sales, and the consequent diminution in equity. EBIT dropped 74% to $18 million although fixed assets were reduced by just 9%. Return on assets also fell to just 1.10% from 2.88%. Interest coverage by earnings dropped to just 0.18

EXHIBIT A–2
Pre- and Postbuyout Experience—Fruehauf Corporation ($ in Millions)

	Before Buyout (11/86)	Immediately after Buyout (12/86)	2 Years after Buyout (12/88)
EBIT	$68.9	$68.9	$18.1
Depreciation	$96	$96	$106.6
EBITD	$165	$165	$124.6
Cost of Debt			
(YTM) (9¾s, '96)	9.79%	13.07%	14.25%
Cost of LBO/EBIT (M1)	—	18.47X	—
Cost of LBO/EBITD (M2)	—	7.61X	—
EBIT/Interest	0.86X	0.65X	0.18X
EBITD/Interest	2.05X	1.56X	1.23X
% Premium Paid Per Share	—	56%	—
EBIT/Total Assets	—	2.88%	1.10%
Fixed Assets	$582	$811	$736
Long-Term Debt	$544	$1,123	$710
Total Debt	$566	$1,553	$747
Total Value	$1,001	$1,835	$450
			$699
			$948
Equity Value			
(Common + Preferred)	$525	$283	–$297
		($25)[a]	–$48
			$201
			vs. $181 (Book)

[a] Common

times while cash flow coverage barely exceeded 1.0. The anticipated asset sales reduced fixed assets by less than $100 million and long-term debt was reduced by $400 million (37%). The high interest burden and low cash flow resulted in a cost of debt increase to 14.25%—over 1% higher than just after the LBO. Clearly, the LBO was in trouble.

As a result of Fruehauf's deterioration, we estimated the value of equity to be between –$297 million to a positive $201 million. This is based on firm multipliers on cash flow ($124.6 million) of 3.6–7.6 times. The latter was the multiplier paid for by the new owners. The lower multipliers were more likely although the book value of equity as of 12/88 was very close to the higher estimate of $201—i.e., $181 million.

As the situation developed, Fruehauf's problems resulted in a distressed exchange in 1989 of cash and securities to the debenture holders worth approximately 89¢ on the dollar. This was accomplished by a sale of the firm's assets and the assumption of its remaining liabilities by Varity Corporation. While sustaining a capital loss, this distressed LBO was spared the more dramatic loss typically found in a default or a severe distressed exchange, i.e., a recovery of only from 20–60% of par value after the default or exchange, depending upon the particular situation and the priority status of the debt. For a discussion of recoveries after default, see Altman (1990).

In the case of Fruehauf, it appears that the optimistic earnings forecast, not realized, was the prime reason for the problems that developed for the debtholders. Of secondary, but still considerable, importance was the relatively small reduction in debt.

REFERENCES

Altman, Edward, (1984), "A Further Empirical Investigation of the Bankruptcy Cost Question," *Journal of Finance,* (September).

Altman, Edward, (1990), "Investing in Distressed Securities: The Anatomy of Bankrupt Debt and Equities," *Altman Foothill Report,* (April) and *Distressed Securities: Analyzing and Evaluating Market Potential and Investment Risk,* Chicago: Probus Publishing, 1991.

Altman, Edward, and Roy Smith, (1991), "Highly Leveraged Restructurings: A Valid Role for Europe," *Journal of International Securities Markets* (Fall).

Amihud, Yakov, (1989), *Leveraged Management Buyouts: Causes and Consequences,* Homewood, IL: Dow Jones-Irwin.

Brigham, Eugene, and Luis Gapluski, (1991), *Financial Management: Theory and Practice* (6th ed.), Hinsdale, IL: Dryden, chapter 12.

Bulow, J., and J. Shoven, (1978), "The Bankruptcy Decision," *The Bell Journal of Economics* (Autumn).

Copeland, Thomas; T. Koller; and J. Murrin, (1990), *Valuation,* New York: John Wiley & Sons.

Copeland, Thomas, and W. H. Lee, (1990), "Exchange Offers and Stock Swaps— New Evidence," UCLA working paper.

Durand, David, (1959), "The Cost of Capital in an Imperfect Market: A Reply to Modigliani and Miller," *The American Economic Review* (June).

Jensen, Michael, (1989), "Eclipse of the Public Corporation," *Harvard Business Review* (September–October).

Jensen, M.; S. Kaplan; and L. Stiglin, (1989), "Effects of LBO's on Tax Revenues of the U.S. Treasury," in E. Altman (ed.), *The High-Yield Debt Market,* Homewood, IL: Dow Jones-Irwin.

Jensen, M., and W. Meckling, (1976), "Theory of the Firm: Managerial Behavior,

Agency Costs and Ownership Structure," *Journal of Financial Economics* (October).

KPMG—Peat Marwick, (1989), "Rapporto 'Mergers & Acquisitions'—Allegato— Operazioni MBO 1988-89," Milano, Italy.

Kaplan, Steven, (1989), "Management Buyouts: Evidence on Taxes as a Source of Value," *Journal of Finance* (September).

Miller, Merton, (1989), "The Modigliani-Miller Propositions after Thirty Years," *Journal of Applied Corporate Finance* (Spring).

Modigliani, Franco, and Merton Miller, (1958), "The Cost of Capital, Corporation Finance and the Theory of Investment," *American Economic Review* (June).

Modigliani, F., and M. Miller, (1963), "Corporate Income Taxes and the Cost of Capital; A Correction," *American Economic Review* (June).

Moore, Harvin, "Trends and Characteristics of Recent LBO Experience," NYU working paper (November 1990).

Smith, Roy, and Ingo Walter, (1990), "Economic Restructuring in Europe and the Market for Corporate Control," presented at Conference on Economic Restructuring in Europe, INSEAD and Stern School of Business, NYU (May and Fall).

Thompson, S.; M. Wright ; and K. Robbie, (1989), "Management Buyouts, Debt and Efficiency: Some Evidence from the U.K.," *Journal of Applied Corporate Finance* (Spring).

Warner, Jerald, (1977), "Bankruptcy Costs: Some Evidence," *Journal of Finance* (May).

Weston, J. Fred, (1963), "A Test of Cost of Capital Propositions," *Southern Economic Journal* (October).

Weston, J. Fred, (1989), "What MM Have Wrought," *Financial Management* (Summer).

CHAPTER 3

TROUBLED DEBT RESTRUCTURINGS: AN EMPIRICAL STUDY OF PRIVATE REORGANIZATION OF FIRMS IN DEFAULT

Stuart C. Gilson
Kose John
Larry H. P. Lang

INTRODUCTION

With the proliferation of leveraged buyouts (LBOs) and other highly leveraged transactions, there has been growing popular concern that the corporate sector is being burdened with too much debt. Much of this concern is founded in the belief that highly levered firms could default in large numbers in a major recession [*The Wall Street Journal*, 25 October 1988]. At issue is whether corporate default is costly, and whether, as recently suggested by Jensen (1989a, b), private contractual arrangements for resolving

Stuart C. Gilson is Assistant Professor of Business Administration at the Harvard Business School, Boston.

Kose John and Larry H. P. Lang are, respectively, Professor and Assistant Professor of Finance at Stern School of Business, New York University.

The authors would like to thank Edward Altman, Yakov Amihud, Sugato Bhattacharya, Keith Brown, Robert Bruner, T. Ronald Casper, Charles D'Ambrosio, Larry Dann, Oliver Hart, Gailen Hite, Max Holmes, Scott Lee, Gershon Mandelker, Scott Mason, Robert Merton, Wayne Mikkelson, Megan Partch,

Continued overleaf

default represent a viable (and less costly) alternative to the legal remedies provided by Chapter 11.

This study investigates the incentives of financially distressed firms to choose between private renegotiation and Chapter 11. We analyze the experience of 169 publicly traded companies that experienced severe financial distress during 1978–1987. Our investigation yields a number of insights into the corporate debt restructuring decision. In about half of all cases, financially distressed firms successfully restructure their debt outside of Chapter 11. Financial distress is more likely to be resolved through private renegotiation when more of the firm's assets are intangible, and relatively more debt is owed to banks; private renegotiation is less likely to succeed when there are more distinct classes of debt outstanding.

An analysis of common stock returns provides complementary evidence on firms' incentives to settle out of court. Abnormal stock-price performance suggests stockholders generally fare better under private renegotiation than bankruptcy. In advance of the outcome, the market appears to be able to identify which firms are more likely to succeed at restructuring their debt outside of Chapter 11.

Finally, we present detailed descriptive evidence on how debt is restructured outside of bankruptcy. Previous empirical research in corporate financial distress has dealt largely with formal reorganization in Chapter 11. Detailed case analyses of selected firms in our sample provide additional insights into firms' incentives to choose between private renegotiation and Chapter 11.

The study is organized as follows. Section 2 discusses firms' incentives to choose between private renegotiation and bankruptcy as alternative mechanisms for dealing with default. Section 3 describes the data and methodology. Section 4 presents the empirical analysis of troubled debt restructurings. Section 5 concludes with a summary of the results. The

---

Note continued

Ramesh Rao, Roy Smith, Chester Spatt, Gopala Vasudevan, and Richard West for their helpful comments. This paper is reprinted with permission from the *Journal of Financial Economics,* Vol. 27, No. 2 (October 1990). The authors are especially grateful to Michael Jensen (the editor) and Karen Wruck (the referee) for their thoughtful suggestions. This paper has also benefited from the comments of participants of the conference on "The Structure and Governance of Enterprise" at Harvard Business School, and seminars at Dartmouth College, Harvard Business School, the University of Oregon, and the University of Pittsburgh. The first author acknowledges support from the Division of Research at the Harvard Business School. The second author acknowledges support from the Yamaichi Faculty Fellowship and the Garn Institute of Finance.

appendix presents ten detailed case studies of firms that attempted to re-structure their debt privately.

CORPORATE DEFAULT AND DEBT RESTRUCTURING

A firm that must restructure the terms of its debt contracts to remedy or avoid default is faced with two choices; it can either file for bankruptcy, or attempt to renegotiate with its creditors privately in a "workout." The alternatives are similar in that relief from default is obtained when creditors consent to exchange their impaired claims for new securities in the firm. Sometimes this exchange is implicit, as when the terms of a debt contract are modified. If bankruptcy is the alternative to private renegotiation, then firms' incentives to settle with creditors out of court, and the settlement terms, will reflect the legal and institutional constraints of the bankruptcy process. The remainder of this section briefly describes relevant bankruptcy law, and identifies some important economic factors that affect the choice between bankruptcy and private debt renegotiation.

Rules and Procedures of Bankruptcy

For most companies, bankruptcy practices are governed by Chapter 11 of the U.S. Bankruptcy Code (henceforth, the "Code"). Filings under Chapter 11 are treated as corporate reorganizations, and the bankrupt firm is expected to continue as a going concern after leaving bankruptcy. To protect the firm from creditor harassment while it tries to reorganize, Chapter 11 imposes an automatic stay that prevents creditors from collecting on their debt or foreclosing on their collateral until the firm leaves bankruptcy.[1]

In Chapter 11, an exchange of securities is formally proposed in a reorganization plan. The plan assigns claimholders to various classes, and a separate exchange is proposed for each class. All claims placed within a given class must be substantially similar. Thus, for example, trade debt might be placed in one class, secured bank debt in another, and so forth, although finer partitioning of claims is possible.

The value of new securities distributed to any class is in principle determined by the absolute priority rule, under which each creditor class is compensated for the face value of its prebankruptcy claims only after all other classes designated as senior are paid in full. Franks and Torous (1989),

Eberhart et al. (1990), and Weiss (1990) show that significant deviations from absolute priority occur in practice. All three studies document cases where stockholders participate in a reorganization plan that provides for less than full payment of senior claims.

The filing firm, or debtor, has the exclusive right to propose the first plan. If this plan is not filed within 120 days of the initial Chapter 11 filing, or accepted by creditors within 60 additional days, any claimholder class can propose its own plan. Acceptance of the plan requires an affirmative vote by a majority (two thirds in value and one half in number) of the claimholders in each impaired class. To break deadlocks, the court can unilaterally impose or "cram down" the plan on dissenting classes if the plan is "fair and equitable"—that is, if the market value of new securities distributed to each class under the plan at least equals what the class would receive in a liquidation. In practice, cram-downs are extremely rare [Klee (1979)]. It is in the joint interest of all classes to avoid a cram-down, because application of the fair and equitable standard requires the court to determine the firm's liquidation value and going-concern value in a special hearing. These hearings are considered extremely time consuming and costly. Avoidance of cram-down also explains observed deviations from absolute priority, since classes that receive nothing under the plan (including stockholders) are deemed not to have accepted the plan, giving creditors an incentive to voluntarily relinquish part of their claims.

Chapter 11 also provides for the appointment of committees to represent the interests of certain claimholder classes before the court. Committees normally consist of the seven largest members of a particular class who are willing to serve, and are empowered to hire legal counsel and other professional help. Committees' operating expenses are paid out of the bankrupt firm's assets. Appointment of a committee of unsecured creditors is mandatory in Chapter 11 cases; additional committees can be appointed to represent other classes, including stockholders, at the discretion of the judge [DeNatale (1981)].

Determinants of the Choice Between Bankruptcy and Private Renegotiation

Whether financial distress is resolved through bankruptcy or private renegotiation depends on two factors. First, stockholders and creditors will collectively benefit from settling out of court when private renegotiation generates lower costs than bankruptcy. Under the lower-cost alternative, the resulting value of the firm will be higher, and the firm's claims can be restructured on terms that leave each of the original claimholders better off. Claimholders' incentives to settle privately will increase with the size of the potential cost savings from recontracting outside of Chapter 11. Second, the lower-cost alternative will be adopted only if claimholders can agree on how to share the cost savings. Attempts to settle privately are more likely to fail when individual creditors have stronger incentives to hold out for more favorable treatment under the debt restructuring plan.

The remainder of the section develops this simple economic model of the corporate debt restructuring decision, and derives empirical proxies for firms' incentives to restructure their debt privately.[2]

Relative Cost of Formal Bankruptcy versus Private Renegotiation

Although attempts have been made to measure the costs of Chapter 11 empirically [Warner (1977b), Ang et al. (1982), Altman (1984), Weiss (1990)], we currently know little about how these costs compare with the costs of private renegotiation. In analyzing the costs of financial distress, it has become common to distinguish between direct and indirect costs. Direct costs are out-of-pocket transactions costs (such as charges for legal and investment banking services). Indirect costs include all other costs related to the firm's bankruptcy or debt restructuring. For example, managers may forego profitable investment opportunities because they are distracted by dealings with creditors or the bankruptcy court. Indirect costs also include the value of managers' time spent in such dealings.

It is widely believed among practitioners that direct costs are significantly higher for bankruptcy than private renegotiation, because the procedural demands and legal complexity of Chapter 11 result in inflated lawyers' fees [Stein (1989)]. Formal legal motions must be drafted and argued before the bankruptcy judge at each step of the reorganization. An inordinate amount of time may be required to make any decision that lies outside the ordinary course of the firm's business.[3] When debt is restructured privately, legal costs are reduced because such decisions can be made more quickly. In addition, bankruptcy lawyers have an incentive to prolong the firm's stay in Chapter 11, because their compensation is treated as a priority claim, which entitles them to be paid before any of the firm's general unsecured creditors or shareholders. These arguments suggest that indirect costs (as measured by the expenditure of managers' time) are also higher for bankruptcy than for private renegotiation.

The relative cost disadvantage of bankruptcy is offset by two factors. First, the Code's automatic stay provision ameliorates the common pool problem inherent in distressed situations, by imposing a well-defined queuing order on creditors (who would otherwise rush to be first in line to collect payment on their debt and seize collateral). Such activity will be wasteful if it results in costly duplication of effort or creates additional distraction for management [Jackson (1986)].

Second, firms in Chapter 11 can grant new lenders super-priority status, or a security interest equal or senior to that of existing debt (also known as debtor-in-possession financing). In the absence of this provision, firm value could be reduced because stockholders have an incentive to underinvest in positive-NPV projects that enrich senior claimholders [Myers (1977), Smith and Warner (1979)]. In principle, an equivalent provision could be negotiated among creditors and stockholders privately; however, senior creditors would have to voluntarily consent to subordinate their claims. The option to grant new lenders super-priority status will be especially valuable for firms that are in need of short-term trade financing, and have few free assets to pledge as security.

Data limitations preclude direct measurement of relative recontracting costs [see *Data and Sample Selection*, p. 87, below]. In the following analysis, we assume that firms and creditors expect private renegotiation to be less costly than bankruptcy. Empirical justification for this assumption is provided in the fourth section [see *Results*, p. 90, below], although we recognize that bankruptcy will dominate private renegotiation for some firms. The importance of relative recontracting costs is assessed by relating the firm's choice of recontracting method (i.e., private or legal) to a variable that measures cross-sectional variation in this assumed cost difference.

Such a test requires us to discriminate among firms on the basis of their expected cost savings from settling privately. This forced us to exclude certain costs (for example, legal fees and management's time costs) for which we were unable to find suitable empirical proxies. The cost that we use to test our model is the destruction of going-concern value that occurs when assets are sold to pay down debt and remedy default [Jensen (1989a, b)]. This loss of value will be greater for intangible assets, and assets that generate firm-specific rents (e.g., growth opportunities, managerial firm-specific human capital, monopoly power, and operating synergies whose value depends on the firm's assets being kept together). If, as argued below, assets are more likely to be sold when debt is restructured in Chapter 11 rather than privately, then Chapter 11 will be relatively more costly for firms whose assets are more intangible or firm-specific. We measure the potential loss of going-concern value due to asset sales by the ratio of the firm's market value to the replacement cost of its assets; replacement cost approximates what the firm's assets could be sold for piecemeal. Firms with a higher market value/replacement cost ratio will be more likely to restructure their debt privately, because Chapter 11 is relatively more costly for such firms.

For several reasons, assets are more likely to be sold when debt is restructured in Chapter 11 rather than privately. First, automatic stay gives the debtor more power over the disposition of the firm's assets, by enjoining creditors from exercising their nonbankruptcy right to sue the firm and seize collateral. Asset sales that would normally be in violation of the firm's debt covenants will be allowed if the firm can convince the bankruptcy judge that such sales are necessary for the continued operation of the business.

Second, since the debtor can undermine the value of lenders' collateral and grant new lenders super-priority standing, fully secured lenders will in general prefer liquidation over reorganization. This may create additional pressure for asset sales in bankruptcy. In Chapter 11, creditors can initiate asset sales by "making a motion to sell assets" before the court. In addition, Chapter 11 cases can be converted into Chapter 7 liquidations. Although conversion to Chapter 7 occurs for only about 5% of the bankruptcies that we examine, other studies have found much higher rates of liquidation. For a sample of Chapter 11 filings in the Southern District of New York (including nonpublic firms), White (1989) finds that about one third end up either in Chapter 7 or as liquidating reorganizations.

Finally, purchasing assets from a financially distressed firm is less risky in Chapter 11, because asset sales are executed by a court order, and are thus free from legal challenge. In addition, assets that are purchased from an insolvent firm that subsequently files for Chapter 11 may have to be returned as a "voidable preference" or "fraudulent transfer." Given the costs incurred if an asset sale is later challenged or cancelled, potential purchasers of an asset will prefer to deal with firms in Chapter 11.

Factors Affecting Creditors' Willingness to Settle Outside of Chapter 11

Even if stockholders and creditors believe that their combined wealth will be higher if debt is restructured outside of Chapter 11, negotiations can break down if particular creditors hold out for more generous terms. The severity of the holdout problem will depend on the voting rules for determining acceptance of the plan, the number of creditors who participate in the plan, and the type of debt that is restructured (bank loans, publicly traded debt, etc.). In addition, creditors may withhold their consent from a restructuring plan if they dispute the value of the new securities being offered under the plan.

Adopting a debt restructuring plan outside of bankruptcy generally requires the unanimous consent of all creditors whose claims are in default. Impaired creditors who are excluded from the plan can accelerate payment of their claims, or force the firm into bankruptcy by filing an involuntary Chapter 11 petition. Cross-default provisions in the firm's debt contracts will increase the proportion of creditors who participate in the plan. Thus in a typical workout the potential holdout problem is quite severe because of the veto power held by individual creditors. This problem is less severe in Chapter 11, where approval for a reorganization plan is required only from a specified majority of the creditors in each class of claims, and dissenting classes can be forced to comply with the plan under the Code's cram-down provision.

We hypothesize that the holdout problem is more severe (and the probability of successful private renegotiation lower) when relatively more creditors are allowed to participate in the restructuring plan. An increase in the number of total votes to be cast increases the probability that at least one of the votes will be negative. Reasoning along similar lines, Smith and Warner (1979) conjecture that private renegotiation of debt will be easier when the debt is privately placed (and owed to fewer lenders). On the other hand, having fewer creditors could result in more frequent bargaining deadlocks, if smallness of numbers causes individual creditors to feel more powerful and perceive greater dollar benefits to holding out. When there are few creditors—as in any bilateral bargaining situation involving few buyers and sellers—mutually beneficial trades will not always take place. If a negotiated solution is not forthcoming, the only way to break the deadlock may be to file for bankruptcy.

A related consideration is the heterogeneity of the firm's financial claims, or the complexity of its capital structure. Firms with more complex capital structures are hypothesized to succeed less often at restructuring their debt privately. The more that creditors' claims differ in seniority rights, security, and other features, the more likely different claims are to be treated differently under any proposed restructuring plan (in the package of new securities offered to holders of each type of claim). As a result, there may be greater disagreement over whether the plan is equitable in its treatment of different claims. In practice, inter-creditor disputes are extremely common, even among creditors who hold the same general type of security (for example, members of a bank lending consortium).

Achieving a consensus among creditors outside of bankruptcy will also depend upon what type of debt is being restructured. The holdout problem is especially severe for publicly traded bonds. Under the Trust Indenture Act of 1939, firms are prohibited from changing any of the "core" terms of the bond indenture (the principal amount, interest rate, or stated maturity) unless every bondholder gives his/her consent. Although only a simple or two-thirds majority is generally required to change other covenants in the bond, amendment of the core terms is often critical to resolving financial distress.

As a result, restructuring of publicly traded debt almost always takes the form of an exchange offer. In return for tendering their old bonds, bondholders receive a package of new securities (often including some form of equity) that offers a lower cash payout. Since participation in the offer is voluntary, bondholders will have incentives to hold out if their individual tendering decision has little impact on whether the offer is successful; such incentives will be stronger when the bonds are more widely held. To encourage bondholders to tender, exchange offers are structured to penalize holdouts. The new bonds are generally more senior, and mature sooner, than the old bonds. In addition, holders can be asked to jointly tender their bonds and vote for the elimination of protective covenants in the old bonds; for this reason the success of an exchange offer is often conditional on a stipulated voting majority of bonds being tendered.

In our sample, publicly traded debt is always restructured through exchange offers. These offers are typically completed in under two months. This time can be further reduced if the firm qualifies under Section 3(a)(9) of the 1933 Securities Act for an exemption from ordinary registration requirements for any new securities issued under the offer. These so-called 3(a)(9) offers were pioneered by Drexel Burnham Lambert in the early 1980s. A company will generally qualify to make such an exchange if it is not paying anyone to solicit the exchange, and if both new and old securities involved in the offer have the same issuer. These offers can be made by any firm that qualifies, even if it is not financially distressed. Over the period 1981–1986, approximately 30% of the 184 offers for which Drexel served as advisor were made by financially distressed companies. Currently, virtually all exchange offers made by distressed companies are structured as 3(a)(9) offers.

Bankruptcy practitioners assert that attempts to settle outside of Chapter 11 are more likely to succeed when relatively less debt is owed to trade creditors, and more is owed to bank lenders. The holdout problem is particularly severe for trade debt because the number of trade creditors is often quite large, and their claims are relatively heterogeneous, precluding the use of exchange offers to restructure this debt in the same manner as publicly traded bonds. Securing a consensus among trade creditors is also thought to be more difficult because they tend to be "acrimonious" and "unsophisticated." By similar reasoning, private renegotiation is less likely to succeed when the firm has significant contingent liabilities, such as those arising from product liability suits, where individual tort claims can number in the tens of thousands. Bank lenders, in contrast, tend to be more sophisticated and fewer in number than other kinds of lenders, and are more amenable to settling outside of Chapter 11 [Stein (1989)]. Similar arguments would seem to apply to insurance companies that hold privately placed debt.

Finally, creditors' consent to a restructuring plan will be harder to obtain when there is greater asymmetry in the information used by stockholders and creditors to value the firm. Through their control over the supply of such information, stockholders have incentives to influence creditors' perception of firm value to gain more favorable terms in the restructuring plan. DeAngelo et al. (1990) present evidence that is consistent with financially distressed firms using accounting accruals to influence their negotiations with bank lenders. Since rational creditors are aware of stockholders' incentives to misstate the value of the firm, private renegotiation may fail because of the resulting "lemons" problem. In Chapter 11, stockholders have a much smaller information advantage over creditors. Firms are required to make extensive, regular disclosures of their financial and operating data to the court. Additional information is contained in the court testimony of expert witnesses and management, and creditors can exercise their "rights of discovery" to require additional disclosures from the debtor. Any continuing disputes over value can be arbitrated by the court.

We use three variables as proxies for the severity of the holdout problem. First, troubled debt is more likely to be restructured outside Chapter 11 when there are fewer creditors. Second, debt is more likely to be restructured privately when relatively more of the debt is privately held by banks and insurance companies. In addition to the reasons discussed above, bank and insurance company debt is hypothesized to have this effect because such debt reduces the amount of information asymmetry between stockholders and creditors. Since these lenders are generally few in number, they have stronger incentives to monitor the firm than other kinds of creditors. Also, privately placed debt typically includes more financial covenants than other types of debt; even when firms are fully in compliance with these covenants, more information is implicitly revealed about firms' financial and operating characteristics.

Finally, holdouts by junior creditors will be less common when the firm's market value is high in relation to the replacement cost of its assets. As discussed above [see *Relative cost of formal bankruptcy versus private renegotiation,* p. 81], more going-concern value is dissipated in bankruptcy than in private workouts when more of the firm's assets are sold in bankruptcy. Junior creditors' position in the absolute priority ranking ensures that they bear most of this cost, and they will offer less resistance to any proposed restructuring plan. Thus, firms with a higher market value/replacement cost ratio will be more likely to restructure their debt outside of Chapter 11.

"Prepackaged" Chapter 11

The preceding analysis is based on a simple dichotomy between bankruptcy and private renegotiation. However, the Code also permits firms to make a 'prepackaged' Chapter 11 filing, in which the bankruptcy petition and reorganization plan are filed together. Terms of the plan are negotiated in advance between the firm and its creditors, and a vote is taken almost immediately.[4] Prepackaged Chapter 11 is thus a hybrid of conventional bankruptcy and private renegotiation that incorporates certain features of each recontracting alternative. In practice, successful prepackaged filings are extremely rare. Although prepackaged filings can significantly reduce the time that firms spend in court, and obviate the need for costly creditors' committees, disputes involving the plan are still possible after filing. We were informed by a professional bankruptcy consultant that only 5% to 10% of the largest bankruptcies begin as prepackaged filings, and that fewer than half of these are successful (the original plan is accepted). Only one firm in the sample made a prepackaged Chapter 11 filing [see the case of Crystal Oil in the appendix]. The company spent a total of only three months in bankruptcy, compared with a median of eighteen months for all bankrupt firms in the sample.

DATA AND SAMPLE SELECTION

Although identifying bankrupt firms is fairly straightforward, there are few legal or institutional guideposts for deciding what constitutes a debt restructuring. In contrast to Chapter 11 cases, most debt restructurings do not have a well-defined beginning or ending date. Restructuring rarely begins or ends with a formal public announcement, and no special documents have to be filed with any government agency. Information about the restructuring disclosed in normal Securities and Exchange Commission (SEC) filings often lacks detail. Sometimes the same debt is restructured on a number of successive occasions, or different classes of debt are restructured concurrently as separate transactions.

This study uses the same sampling procedure and definition of a debt restructuring as Gilson (1989, 1990). This definition emphasizes the economic similarities between Chapter 11 and private renegotiation as alternative mechanisms for dealing with financial distress. A firm is financially distressed if it has insufficient cash flows to meet the payments on its debt. To avoid or remedy a default, the firm must reduce or defer the payments, or replace the debt with securities having residual rather than fixed payoffs. Consistent with this simple intuition, a debt restructuring is defined as a transaction in which an existing debt contract is replaced by a new contract, with one of the following consequences: (i) required interest or principal payments on the debt are reduced; (ii) the maturity of the debt is extended; or (iii) creditors are given equity securities (common stock or securities convertible into common stock). In addition, the restructuring must be undertaken in response to an anticipated or actual default. This last requirement ensures that the sample includes only restructurings that are undertaken by financially distressed firms. As reported later in Table 2–3, approximately two thirds of sampled firms that privately restructure their debt are in default at some point during their restructuring.[5]

A debt restructuring is assumed to take place over the interval defined by the first and last reference to the restructuring in *The Wall Street Journal (WSJ)*, unless more accurate dates are available from other sources. Event-study tests undertaken below measure stock returns in relation to these two dates. If a firm restructures its debt in several discrete periods, these are treated as a single restructuring transaction if less than a year separates adjoining periods. A debt restructuring plan is considered successful if the firm does not file for bankruptcy within a year of the last reference to the restructuring.[6] Consistent with the joint reorganization of claims under Chapter 11, concurrent restructuring of the firm's publicly traded and privately placed debt is treated as a single debt restructuring.

This study analyzes a sample of 169 exchange-listed companies that were in severe financial distress during 1978–1987; eighty firms privately restructured their debt, and 89 firms filed for Chapter 11. Selection of the sample was a two-step process. First, for a given year, firms listed on the New York and American Stock Exchanges were ranked by unadjusted common stock returns at year-end (cumulated over three years), and a stratum was formed consisting of those firms in the bottom five percent. Second, financially distressed firms within this stratum were identified by searching through the *WSJ Index* for any reference to a default, bankruptcy, or debt restructuring in each of the surrounding five years. This two-step procedure was repeated for each of the years 1979–1985, resulting in an initial stratified sample of 793 firm-years (447 firms). Under the assumption that extreme stock price declines reflect extreme declines in firms' cash flows, this sampling procedure replicates the sequence of actual events that lead to financial distress.

This sampling method has two principal advantages. First, since we are interested in contrasting private renegotiation and bankruptcy as alternative mechanisms for dealing with extreme financial distress, we want to exclude debt restructuring by nondistressed firms. For example, a highly levered but profitable firm may wish to amend certain terms in its debt to enable it to invest in a positive-NPV project. In our view, extreme negative stock returns are a relatively unambiguous indicator of poor financial performance. Inspection of the source documents reveals that 56% of firms in the sample explicitly restructured their debt to avoid bankruptcy. The remaining firms either received a going-concern qualification from their auditors during the restructuring, were in default, or experienced a change in control at the hands of creditors (as evidenced by a creditor-initiated senior management change or placement of stock with creditors).

A second advantage is that the sample contains a more representative cross-section of debt restructurings than if the search had been based on reported cases of default. The latter criterion would exclude firms that restructure their debt to avoid default; evidence reported in the next section suggests that such preemptive restructuring is fairly common. Similarly, a sample that consists of defaults reported by *Moody's* or *Standard and Poor's* would exclude firms that have no publicly traded debt; such firms make up 54% of the current sample. Potential biases inherent in the sampling procedure are discussed in the next section.

Information on debt restructuring plans and other relevant data are obtained from the *WSJ*, the *Moody's* manuals, the *Capital Changes Reporter*, and the *Q-File* directory of 10k reports and proxy statements. Additional data are obtained from the exchange offer circulars issued by firms that restructured their publicly traded bonds. The market value/replacement cost ratio is constructed using data from the COMPUSTAT data base, and is described in Lang et al. (1989). Because stock returns (and market values) of highly levered firms are extremely volatile, we use a three-year average of this variable in the empirical analysis. The bank debt ratio is defined as the book value of debt owed to banks and insurance companies divided by the book value of total liabilities. Eighty-five percent of all firms in the sample owe debt to banks, while only 11% owe debt to insurance companies; results are qualitatively the same when the numerator includes only bank debt. The number of creditors is approximated by the number of distinct classes of debt referenced in the long-term debt section of *Moody's*. Data used to construct these variables predate as closely as possible the start of the firm's debt restructuring or bankruptcy.

RESULTS

Sample Characteristics

Most of the debt restructuring activity in the sample is clustered in the years 1981–1985 [see Table 3–1]. This is consistent with the timing of the general economic recession of the early 1980s, when one would expect there to be relatively more reported cases of financial distress. Seventy-six percent of the debt restructurings in the sample begin in this period. Also indicated is the percentage of restructuring attempts that eventually fail, and end with a Chapter 11 filing. The sample is about evenly divided between successful and failed attempts. Except in the first and last years of the sample period (when the number of events is extremely small), there does not appear to be any time trend in the observed failure rate.

The frequency of events corresponding to the beginning and conclusion of debt restructurings is listed in Table 3–2. Separate figures are reported for successful and failed restructuring attempts. Primary sources used to identify these events include the *WSJ* and firms' 10k reports. Panel A of the table reveals that in a number of cases, negotiations took place prior to the starting date identified from public sources. Forty-seven initial references in fact pertain to the final resolution of a debt restructuring. We believe that we have come reasonably close to identifying the true starting dates for 90 firms (53% of the sample), where the initial event takes the form of either a default (52 firms) or an announcement that the firm has just commenced (or will shortly commence) restructuring its debt (38 firms). Of the 52 default

TABLE 3–1
Time Series of Corporate Debt Restructuring Activity, by Starting Date and Eventual Outcome of Restructuring[a]

Year	Number of Attempted Debt Restructurings	Percentage of Restructuring Attempts that End in Bankruptcy
1978	9	11.1
1979	8	50.0
1980	11	63.6
1981	18	66.7
1982	38	47.4
1983	28	46.4
1984	25	60.0
1985	20	60.0
1986	10	50.0
1987	2	100.0
Total	169	52.7

[a] Sample consists of 80 firms that successfully avoid bankruptcy by restructuring their debt out of court, and 89 firms that are unsuccessful in restructuring their debt and file under Chapter 11 of the U.S. Bankruptcy Code. The sample period is 1978–1987. A debt restructuring is defined as a transaction in which an existing debt contract is replaced by a new contract, with one of the following consequences: (i) required interest or principal payments on the debt are reduced, (ii) the maturity of the debt is extended, or (iii) creditors are given equity securities (common stock or securities convertible into common stock). All restructurings are undertaken in response to an anticipated or actual default. Sources used to determine firms' financial status include the *WSJ*, Commerce Clearing House's *Capital Changes Reporter*, the *Moody's* manuals, and the *Q-file* directory of annual 10k reports and proxy statements.

announcements, 34 refer to payment defaults and 18 to technical defaults on financial covenants. Over the course of a restructuring, firms can be associated with more than one event listed in panel A. Although a default normally allows the debtor a 30-day grace period before creditors can exercise their right to accelerate full payment of the debt, negotiations to restructure the debt are assumed to begin immediately after the firm defaults.

Panel B of Table 3–2 reports the frequency of events used to identify the conclusion of a debt restructuring. By definition, all 89 restructuring attempts that fail end with a Chapter 11 bankruptcy filing. Of the remaining 80 successful debt restructurings, for 44 firms it was possible to identify the date on which the restructuring agreement was formally consummated. For 13 firms there was no clear concluding date, only some final reference in the *WSJ* to a restructuring that was still in progress. For ten firms the restructuring concluded with the sale of new debt or equity securities, with the issue

Table 3–2
Frequency Distribution of Events Used to Identify the Beginning and Conclusion of 80 Successful and 89 Unsuccessful Attempts by Firms to Restructure Their Debt Privately to Avoid Bankruptcy[a]

	Outcome of Debt Restructuring Attempt	
	Successful	Unsuccessful
Panel A: Events that identify the beginning of debt restructuring		
Default	29	23
Final resolution of debt restructuring announced	20	27
Initial announcement of debt restructuring	18	20
Reference to a debt restructuring that is already in progress	11	16
Creditor-initiated senior management change	1	1
Firm receives a going-concern qualification from its auditors	1	0
Firm engages investment banker to lead debt restructuring	0	1
Senior management denies that bankruptcy is imminent	0	1
Panel B: Events that identify the conclusion of debt restructuring		
Restructuring agreement formally consummated	46	0
Last public reference to an ongoing restructuring in progress	13	0
Sale of equity or debt securities as part of restructuring plan	10	0
Merged into another company	4	0
Creditors receive equity securities under restructuring plan	4	0
Shareholder approval obtained for restructuring plan	3	0
Chapter 11 filing	0	89
Totals	80	89

[a] All transactions take place between 1978 and 1987. Figures in the table are based on information contained in the *Wall Street Journal*, the *Moody's* manuals, Commerce Clearing House's *Capital Changes Reporter*, and the *Q-file* directory of annual 10k reports and proxy statements. See Table 3–1, note *a*, for a definition of debt restructuring and bankruptcy.

proceeds used to help finance the restructuring. In four additional cases the restructuring ended with creditors receiving an equity interest in the firm, either directly or as a result of interest being paid in equity securities instead of cash.

Starting and ending dates for bankruptcy are generally better defined. Of the 89 firms in the sample that filed for Chapter 11, 42 leave bankruptcy when their reorganization plans are formally confirmed by the court. An additional ten firms are merged into nonbankrupt firms, and four are liquidated following the conversion of their cases to Chapter 7 proceedings. For the remaining 33 firms, either bankruptcy was still in progress at the time of this writing (eight firms), or it was not possible to determine precisely when or how the firm emerged from Chapter 11.

Some general attributes of the 80 successful debt restructurings in the sample are presented in Table 3–3. Reported default rates in panel A indicate whether any of the firm's outstanding debt is in default; data limitations preclude a finer breakdown by particular classes of debt (secured debt, trade debt, etc.). Although defaults on senior securities and related "material" events must be reported in the firm's 10k report, the amount and detail of disclosure vary significantly. For example, a firm is not required to report when it first started to restructure its debt, or that it has been in discussion with creditors concerning a possible default. A firm might disclose that it has restructured its "subordinated debt," without specifying how particular claims in this category have been restructured. A default may go unreported if the firm does not file its 10k report; filing omissions by financially distressed firms are fairly common [Gilson (1990)]. As well, firms and creditors exhibit a penchant for secrecy in these transactions. For example, the debt restructuring of Tiger International Inc. [included in the appendix] began when the *WSJ* reported that the firm unilaterally suspended payments on about half of its $1.8 billion in debt:

> Tiger said that a total of $350 million in interest and principal on its bank and institutional debt is scheduled for payment in 1983. But the company wouldn't disclose how much of the $350 million would be affected by its decision to "temporarily defer" debt service on $900 million of its total debt. Tiger also wouldn't disclose when specific payments were due on any of the $350 million. Asked for elaboration...a company spokeswoman said she didn't know whether the company had missed a deadline for any payments on the $900 million in debt.... Tiger's lenders, whom the company declined to identify, were informed of the decision at yesterday's meeting [*WSJ*, February 15, 1983, p. 5].

TABLE 3–3
Selected Attributes of 80 Successful Corporate Debt Restructurings
Undertaken to Avoid Bankruptcy Between 1978 and 1987 [a]

Attribute	Percentage of Sample
Panel A: Incidence of default during debt restructuring [b]	
Payment default	36.3
Technical default	21.3
Unspecified default	17.5
All defaults	66.3
Panel B: Stockholder approval for restructuring plan	
Approval for issuance of new common stock specified under plan	17.5
Approval of asset sales specified under plan	1.3
No stockholder approval required	81.2
Panel C: Type of debt restructured	
Bank debt (by firms that have bank debt outstanding)	90.0
Publicly traded debt (by firms that have publicly traded debt outstanding)	69.8

[a] See Table 3–1, note a, for a definition of debt restructuring and bankruptcy.
[b] A payment default is defined as a default on an interest or principal payment; included are cases where a firm unilaterally suspends payment on its debt, even though no default is formally declared by creditors. A technical default is defined as a default on a financial covenant in the firm's debt. Sources used to determine whether debt is in default include the *Moody's* manuals, Commerce Clearing House's *Capital Changes Reporter,* the *Q-file* directory of annual 10k reports and proxy statements, and Standard and Poor's *Bond Owner's Guide.*

Fifty-three firms (66.3% of the sample) were in default before successfully restructuring their debt. Since 29 of these restructurings begin with a default [see Table 3–2], 24 firms did not default until after entering negotiations with creditors to restructure their debt. In 51 firms (64% of the sample), no default occurred, or occurred after the debt restructuring began. Thus, firms often begin restructuring their debt before any actual default (or without any default occurring).

Explicit stockholder approval was required for only 18.8% of all restructuring plans that were adopted [panel B]. In most of these cases, approval was required to issue common stock under the plan, either as a requirement imposed by the firm's stock exchange, or because it was necessary to increase the number of authorized shares. For the remaining 81.2%

of all cases where such approval was not obtained, the possibility exists that adoption of these plans was not always in the best interests of stockholders. Where managers have the authority to accept or reject a restructuring plan, there is no assurance that they will make the decision that maximizes stockholders' wealth. Gilson (1989, 1990) finds that turnover of senior managers and directors is lower when firms restructure their debt outside of Chapter 11. Thus, managers could have incentives to settle with creditors on overly generous terms to secure their consent to a plan, even though stockholders would be better off in bankruptcy. Stock-return evidence presented below, however, suggests that the market on average reacts positively to events that increase the probability of successful private renegotiation, and negatively to events that increase the probability of bankruptcy. This suggests that potential agency conflicts between managers and stockholders are not a deciding factor in whether firms privately restructure or file for Chapter 11.

Finally, firms that restructure their debt privately sometimes restructure only a subset of their outstanding debt contracts [panel C]. Only 90.0% of firms in the sample with bank debt outstanding, and 69.8% of firms with publicly traded debt, actually restructure such debt. In contrast, Chapter 11 cases necessarily require participation by all impaired claimholder classes, which in practical terms generally means all of the firm's outstanding claims. This suggests that private renegotiation may be less costly than Chapter 11 if the firm is able to recontract only with those creditors whose claims are in default, thus conserving on transactions costs.

Table 3–4 summarizes the principal terms on which firms in the sample restructure their debt, based on the three criteria used to define a debt restructuring (that is, there must be either a reduction in interest or principal payments, an extension of the debt's maturity, or a distribution of equity securities to creditors). Since firms do not always disclose the exact terms on which debt is restructured, figures in the table represent lower bounds on the frequency with which these terms are actually incorporated in restructuring plans.

New equity securities are distributed to creditors in almost 74% of all successful restructurings. A similar percentage of restructurings results in a reduction in promised payments on the debt. The least common provision in these agreements is an extension of maturity. Different classes of debt also appear to be restructured on substantially different terms. Approximately 49% of bank debt restructurings provide for an extension of maturity, compared with only 6.7% of restructurings of publicly traded debt; this latter result is consistent with firms offering shorter-maturity debt in exchange

TABLE 3–4
Summary of Restructuring Terms for 80 Successful Corporate Debt Restructurings Undertaken Between 1978 and 1987, by General Class of Debt Restructured (Bank, Publicly Traded, and Other Debt).[a]

Restructuring terms	Percentage of Debt Within a Given Class Restructured on Specified Terms			Percentage of Firms that Restructure Any Debt on Specified Terms
	Bank	Public	Other	
Extension of maturity	48.6	6.7	25.0	48.8
Reduction of interest or principal	54.2	56.7	75.0	72.5
Distribution of equity securities	51.4	86.7	75.0	73.8
Percentage of firms that restructure debt in a given class	90.0	37.5	20.0	

[a] *Extension of maturity* includes deferral of promised interest or principal payments. *Reduction of interest or principal* includes foreigveness of overdue or future promised payments, in addition to reductions in the stated rate of interest. *Distribution of equity securities* includes distributions of common or preferred stock, as well as securities that can be converted into either class of stock (e.g., warrants and convertible bonds); also included are provisions in the debt contract that give firms the option to make payments either in cash or in equity securities. *Bank debt* includes debt owed to commercial banks and insurance companies. *Other debt* includes debt owed to suppliers, trade creditors, and other non-bank companies.

offers to discourage holdouts [see *Factors affecting creditors' willingness to settle outside of Chapter 11*, p. 83, above]. Although 51.4% of bank debt restructurings result in bank lenders receiving equity in the firm, holders of publicly traded debt are given equity securities 86.7% of the time. The latter difference is a likely consequence of various legal and regulatory factors that make it prohibitively costly for banks to hold large amounts of equity in publicly traded companies.

In particular, banks are constrained from holding significant blocks of stock in other firms by section 16 of the Glass-Steagall Act, the Bank Holding Company Act, and the Federal Reserve Board's Regulation Y, although temporary exceptions are granted when stock is obtained in a debt restructuring. In general, banks must divest their stockholdings after approximately two years, although extensions are possible. Second, creditors can be held legally liable to other claimholders if the firm's financial condition deteriorates subsequent to their assuming a controlling interest in the firm and exercising "undue influence" over its business [Douglas-Hamilton (1975), Smith and Warner (1979)]. A given percentage equity ownership in a firm might, for purposes of proving legal liability, be assumed to confer greater control on a small group of bank lenders than a dispersed group of public bondholders. Finally, a controlling shareholding in a firm could be construed as an "insider relationship," thus obliging banks to return any monetary consideration received from the firm as a "preference item" if it later files for bankruptcy. Banks may prefer to receive relatively less equity in a debt restructuring if they assess a high probability that the firm will subsequently become bankrupt.

The preceding simple classification of restructuring terms provides a general overview of how these deals are structured. Given the complexity and idiosyncratic nature of these transactions, some useful insights can also be gained by direct examination of individual cases. The appendix presents detailed case descriptions of ten debt restructurings in the sample. The cases are intended to be a representative cross-section of various restructuring plan types and outcomes. These case descriptions provide evidence that complements evidence presented in the next section, where we attempt to identify factors conducive to restructuring debt outside of Chapter 11.

Table 3–5 contrasts selected characteristics of firms by whether or not they successfully restructure their debt outside of Chapter 11. Firms that privately restructure their debt have a higher market value/replacement cost ratio and have relatively more bank debt than firms in Chapter 11. The means and medians of both variables are significantly different between subsamples at the 1% level of significance. Both differences are consistent with the theory developed in the second section above. Firms with a higher market value/replacement cost ratio are hypothesized to find bankruptcy more costly than private renegotiation, and to be less prone to holdouts by junior creditors. Firms with more bank debt outstanding can more easily renegotiate their debt because banks are more sophisticated and less numerous than other kinds of creditors, resulting in fewer holdouts.

The mean number of debt contracts (approximated by the number of entries in the long-term debt section of *Moody's*) is marginally higher for firms that restructure their debt privately, but the difference is not statistically significant, and the medians are identical. Alternatively, we define the standardized number of debt contracts as the number of contracts divided by the book value of total liabilities. This variable is significantly lower for

TABLE 3–5

Selected Firm and Debt Characteristics for 80 Firms that Successfully Restructure Their Debt Out of Court, and 89 Firms that Are Unsuccessful in Restructuring Their Debt and File under Chapter 11 of the U.S. Bankruptcy Code[a]

Characteristic	80 Successful Restructurings				89 Unsuccessful Restructurings				p-value of t-test[b] for Difference in:	
	Mean	Median	Min.	Max.	Mean	Median	Min.	Max.	Mean	Median
Market value/replacement cost ratio	0.83	0.65	0.23	2.92	0.61	0.56	0.20	1.75	0.01	0.01
Debt ÷ total liabilities (book values)										
(i) Bank debt	0.40	0.36	0.00	0.88	0.25	0.20	0.00	0.83	0.00	0.00
(ii) Public debt	0.13	0.02	0.00	0.66	0.08	0.00	0.00	0.61	0.08	0.08
(iii) Secured debt	0.14	0.00	0.00	0.82	0.12	0.00	0.00	0.70	0.51	0.91
(iv) Convertible debt	0.07	0.00	0.00	0.68	0.06	0.00	0.00	0.77	0.67	0.65
Number of debt contracts outstanding	7.0	5.0	1.0	28.0	6.0	5.0	1.0	31.0	0.22	0.18
Book value of total assets ($millions)	633	101	9	10,209	317	49	6	9,383	0.15	0.02
Number of shareholders (1,000s)	14	4	1	207	5	3	1	34	0.04	0.08
Number of employees (1,000s)	5	1	0	76	3	2	0	32	0.26	0.88
Total liabilities ÷ book value of assets	0.94	0.83	0.43	4.92	1.01	0.86	0.39	10.00	0.65	0.99
Long-term debt ÷ book value of assets	0.64	0.55	0.00	4.23	0.58	0.45	0.00	8.70	0.63	0.02
Prior 3-year common stock return (%)										
(i) unadjusted	−36.4	−50.3	−93.3	360.0	−48.6	−60.7	−98.0	179.3	0.17	0.04
(ii) less market return	−134.0	−142.0	−230.4	273.8	−147.7	−160.4	−249.9	62.0	0.15	0.05

| Length of debt restructuring attempt (months) | 15.4 | 11.0 | 1.0 | 72.0 | 8.1 | 3.0 | 1.0 | 42.0 | 0.00 | 0.00 |
| Length of bankruptcy proceedings after unsuccessful restructuring attempt (months) | — | — | — | 20.4 | 18.0 | 3.0 | 43.0 | — | — | |

[a] Beginning dates for attempted debt restructurings all take place between 1978 and 1987. See Table 2–1 for a definition of debt restructuring and bankruptcy. When applicable, figures are those that most closely predate the beginning of firms' debt restructuring or bankruptcy. Figures defined in terms of firms' assets and liabilities are all based on reported book values in the *Moody's* manuals. *Bank debt* includes outstanding liabilities to both commercial banks and insurance companies. The *market value/replacement cost ratio* equals the three-year average ratio of the market value of assets to their replacement value. The *number of debt contracts* equals the number of separate descriptive headings in the long-term debt section of the *Moody's* manuals. The *market return* is the equally weighted market portfolio return in the CRSP daily returns file.
[b] Wilcoxon rank sum test.

firms that restructure successfully; mean and median differences (not shown) are significant at the 2% and 7% levels, respectively. The standardized number of debt contracts, or the number of creditors per dollar of debt, is arguably a better proxy for creditors' incentives to hold out. Anecdotal evidence suggests that holdouts are relatively more common among smaller creditors, possibly because they have less wealth at risk if the restructuring attempt fails.

Firms that restructure their debt privately are also generally larger, as measured by the book value of assets and the number of shareholders and employees. Both mean and median book values of assets are higher for firms that restructure successfully, although only the difference in medians is statistically significant using a Wilcoxon rank-sum test (p-value of 0.02). Firm size may be a proxy for the number of creditors or the complexity of the firm's capital structure; the simple correlation between the book value of assets and the (nonstandardized) number of debt contracts is positive and significant (0.72, with a p-value of 0.00).

The two groups of firms are fairly similar in overall leverage (measured by the ratio of total liabilities or long-term debt to total assets), and mean stock-price performance (measured over the current and preceding two years). On the other hand, median unadjusted and net-of-market returns are significantly higher for the firms that restructure privately, according to a Wilcoxon rank-sum test for differences in medians (p-values of 0.04 and 0.05, respectively). A comparison of medians is probably more appropriate given the extreme nonnormality of the sample (drawn from the left-hand tail of the unconditional returns distribution). One explanation for this difference is that superior performance is associated with a smaller reduction in going-concern value, resulting in a higher market value/replacement cost ratio and increased incentives to renegotiate debt privately. Consistent with this posited relationship, the correlation between prior unadjusted stock returns and the market value/replacement cost ratio is positive and significant (0.19, with a p-value of 0.04).

Finally, firms that restructure their debt privately require an average of 15.4 months, and a median of 11 months, to complete the restructuring. Restructuring of publicly traded debt is completed in a much shorter time than restructuring of nontraded debt. The 30 exchange offers in the present sample take an average of 6.6 months to complete (not shown), compared with 15.9 months for all other debt; corresponding median times are two and 10.5 months. Differences in both means and medians are statistically significant using a t-test and Wilcoxon rank sum test (p-values of less than 0.01).

Firms that file for Chapter 11 spend an average of 8.1 (median of 3) months attempting to restructure their debt before seeking bankruptcy protection, and an average of 20.4 (median of 18) additional months in Chapter 11. In the present sample, Chapter 11 cases take significantly longer to complete than successful debt restructurings; differences in the mean and median number of months elapsed under each alternative are significantly different from zero (p-values of less than 0.01).

Direct Measurement of Debt Restructuring Costs

We argued in the second section [see p. 79 above] that relative restructuring costs are an important determinant of whether firms restructure their debt privately or in Chapter 11. Because firms are generally not required to disclose the total costs incurred in a private workout, explicit measurement of these costs is generally not possible. Only four firms in the present sample reported debt restructuring expenses in their 10k reports (and only for restructuring of publicly traded debt). Data on bankruptcy costs are available only at considerable expense, by direct examination of court records [Weiss (1990)].

It is possible, however, to estimate the direct costs of exchange offers for publicly traded debt. Firms must provide an estimate of offer-related costs in the exchange offer circular distributed to bondholders. We obtained the circulars for 26 of the 32 exchange offers in the sample (including two made by firms that ultimately went bankrupt). For 18 of these offers, the circular provided an estimate of out-of-pocket costs (including payments made to the exchange and information agent, and related legal, accounting, brokerage, and investment banking fees). Firms were omitted when only a subset of the offer's total costs were presented, to avoid biasing the cost estimates downward (several circulars reported only that certain costs would be of some "customary" amount; another circular contained only blank spaces where offer costs were to have been reported). Firms were also omitted if the investment bank that served as financial advisor to the offer was paid in warrants or common stock, unless a dollar estimate of the value of this payment was provided in the circular.

In economic terms, exchange-offer costs appear to be trivial [Table 3–6]. Mean and median exchange-offer costs as a percentage of the book value of assets prior to the offer are only 0.65% and 0.32%, respectively. In relation to the face amount of the debt involved in the exchange offer, the corresponding figures are 2.16% and 2.29%. These estimates do not include

TABLE 3–6
Direct Costs of Troubled Exchange Offers for Publicly Traded Debt[a]

	Mean	Median	Minimum	Maximum
Exchange offer costs ($1,000s)	799	424	200	2,500
Offer costs as a percentage of the book value of assets	0.65	0.32	0.01	3.40
Offer costs as a percentage of the face value of bonds restructured under offer	2.16	2.29	0.27	6.84

[a] Sample consists of 18 exchange offers undertaken between 1981 and 1988. Costs consist of compensation paid to the exchange and information agent, and all legal, accounting, brokerage, and investment banking fees incurred by the firm in connection with the offer. These 18 exchange offers represent all offers in the sample for which an estimate of total offer-related costs was disclosed in either the exchange offer circular or the firm's 10k report. Such documentation was obtained for 26 of the 32 exchange offers in the entire sample (two of which were undertaken by firms that ultimately filed for bankruptcy). The book value of assets and the face amount of debt are the figures that most closely predate the commencement of the offer.

any indirect costs of exchange offers, or the costs of restructuring nonpublic debt.

There is evidence that direct bankruptcy costs are also relatively small. Warner (1977b) reports that direct costs for a sample of 11 railroad bankruptcies from the period 1933–1955 represent, on average, 5.3% of firms' market value at the time of the bankruptcy filing. Ang et al. (1982) investigate a sample of 86 firms that filed for bankruptcy (and eventually liquidated) in the Western District of Oklahoma between 1963 and 1979. They report mean and median direct costs (as a percentage of total liquidation proceeds) of 7.5% and 1.7%, respectively. Weiss (1990) analyzes a sample of 37 New York- and American Stock Exchange-listed firms that filed for bankruptcy between 1980 and 1986, and finds that average direct costs are, on average, 2.9% of the book value of assets prior to filing.

Direct costs of exchange offers in our sample also exhibit economies of scale. Average offer costs decline with both the book value of assets and the face value of debt involved in the offer. The correlation between average costs and the book value of assets (not shown) is –0.42 (p-value of 0.08); the correlation between average costs and the face value of debt is –0.57 (p-value of 0.01). A statistically significant negative relation is also found when average costs are regressed against each deflator in ordinary least squares regressions. Economies of scale have previously been documented for direct bankruptcy costs [Warner (1977b), Ang et al. (1982)].

Prediction of Successful Private Renegotiation

This section presents a logit regression analysis that relates the probability of successful private renegotiation to our empirical proxies for relative bankruptcy costs and the magnitude of the potential holdout problem. The dependent variable equals 1 if a firm successfully restructures its debt without entering Chapter 11, and equals 0 if the restructuring attempt fails and the firm files for bankruptcy. Thus, a positive coefficient on an independent variable in the regressions implies that firms for which this variable takes on a higher value are more likely to settle with creditors privately. Our explanatory variables are the firm's market value/replacement cost ratio, the bank debt ratio, and the standardized number of debt contracts outstanding (scaled by the book value of total liabilities).

Four estimated specifications of the model are shown in Table 3–7; in the first, all three explanatory variables are included, and in the remaining three, the variables are included separately. In general, all three variables have significant explanatory power, and are consistent with the univariate comparisons made in Table 3–5. The estimated coefficient on the market value/replacement cost ratio is positive and highly significant in both the combined and univariate regressions (both coefficients have p-values of 0.01). The positive coefficient has two non-mutually-exclusive interpretations, since this ratio is a proxy for both relative recontracting costs and the magnitude of junior creditors' losses if the firm files for Chapter 11 (greater expected losses will increase creditors' willingness to settle privately). The logit regression tests do not allow us to distinguish between these two hypotheses.

The estimated coefficient on the bank debt ratio is positive and significant in both of the regressions in which it appears, although it is somewhat more significant when included separately (with a p-value of 0.00, versus 0.05 for the combined regression). The standardized number of debt contracts is negatively related to the probability of successful private renegotiation, although the estimated coefficient is only marginally significant when included in the combined regression (p-value of 0.12). When this variable appears alone, the estimated coefficient is negative and significant (p-value of 0.03). These results suggest that creditor holdouts are less common when relatively more debt is owed to banks, and there are fewer creditors.

TABLE 3–7
Logit Regressions Relating Firm Characteristics to Outcome of Debt Restructuring[a]

Independent variables	(1)	(2)	(3)	(4)
Intercept	−1.40[b]	−1.16[b]	−0.82[b]	0.21
	(0.01)	(0.01)	(0.00)	(0.33)
Market value/replacement cost ratio	1.51[b]	1.49[b]	—	—
	(0.01)	(0.01)		
Bank debt ratio	1.59[c]	—	2.20[b]	—
	(0.05)		(0.00)	
Number of debt contracts outstanding	−2.60	—	—	−2.91[c]
	(0.12)			(0.03)
Sample size	112	119	159	157
Model p-value	0.0012	0.0030	0.0005	0.0163
Pseudo R-square	0.051	0.026	0.026	0.013

[a] Sample consists of 80 firms that successfully avoided bankruptcy by restructuring their debt out of court, and 89 firms that were forced to seek protection under Chapter 11 of the U.S. Bankruptcy Code. All transactions take place between 1978 and 1987. The dependent variable equals 1 if a firm successfully restructures its debt out of court, and equals 0 if the restructuring attempt fails and the firm files for bankruptcy. Asymptotic p-values are shown in parentheses.

See Table 3–1 for a definition of debt restructuring and bankruptcy. Explanatory variables predate as closely as possible the start of each firm's debt restructuring or bankruptcy. The *market value/replacement cost ratio* equals the three-year average ratio of the market value of assets to their replacement value. The *bank debt ratio* equals the book value of debt owed to banks and insurance companies, divided by the book value of total liabilities. The *number of debt contracts outstanding* equals the number of distinct descriptive headings under the long-term debt section of the *Moody's* manuals, divided by the book value of total liabilities; to facilitate reporting in the table, the estimated coefficient on this variable is divided by 1,000.
[b] p-value ≤ 1%.
[c] p-value ≤ 5%.

The results in Table 2–7 hold with the addition of alternative explanatory variables. Earlier, we hypothesized that private renegotiation is less likely to succeed when relatively more debt is owed to trade creditors, because it is more difficult to obtain their unanimous consent to a restructuring plan. In addition, firms that are more reliant on trade credit may view Chapter 11 more favorably, because the Code's super-priority provision makes it easier to raise new working capital. As a proxy for the importance of trade credit, we use the ratio of accounts payable to total liabilities observed before restructuring activity begins. The trade debt ratio is negatively correlated with the bank debt ratio (not shown), and positively correlated with the standardized number of debt contracts (correlations are −0.29 and 0.31, respectively, with p-values of 0.00). It is insignificant in the regressions, however, whether included alone or in combination with other variables.

Although the estimated coefficients are consistent with the hypotheses developed in the second section, the overall explanatory power of the regressions is small. "Pseudo" R-squares [Madalla (1983)] calculated for each regression indicate that the logit regressions explain no more than about 5% of the total variation in the dependent variable, although model p-values are generally less than 1%. The lack of overall power may be due to the relatively small sample size and the use of cross-sectional data. In addition, a number of other economic factors that may be critical to the success of private renegotiation are either unsystematic or impossible to quantify (e.g., the relative bargaining abilities and personalities of the parties involved). This last consideration underlies the analysis of stock returns in the next section.

A final concern is that the logit results may be subject to two possible biases. First, our empirical tests assume that private renegotiation is less costly than bankruptcy. Although we do not presume this to be true for all firms, general support for this assumption is found in anecdotal accounts of the bankruptcy process [Stein (1989)], and in stock-return evidence presented in the next section. In addition, a bankruptcy filing represents the first public announcement of financial distress for only 27 firms in the sample [see Table 3–2]; for 14 of these firms the *WSJ* report of the filing refers to a previous failed restructuring attempt. Thus 92% of firms in the sample first attempted to settle privately with creditors. It can be shown that creditors and stockholders will never attempt to settle privately if bankruptcy is less costly (assuming full participation by all creditors).

A second possible source of bias is the use of a nonrandom sample to estimate the logit regressions. The coefficient estimates in Table 3–7 will be biased if the relative frequency of private restructuring and Chapter 11 in the sample differs from the population frequency [Manski and McFadden (1983)]. Since firms are sampled on extreme negative stock returns, these relative frequencies could differ if the probability of successful private renegotiation depends on prior stock-price performance. Prior stock returns are insignificant when added to the regressions, however, and the remaining coefficient estimates are qualitatively unchanged.

Evidence from Stock Returns

Ideally, claimholders' incentives to choose between private renegotiation and bankruptcy could be assessed directly by comparing the value of the securities distributed under each alternative to various claimholder classes (secured lenders, public bondholders, etc.). Although such direct comparisons are precluded by a lack of relevant price data, analysis of common stock returns provides some insights into what determines claimholders' incentives to settle privately.

Given evidence in the last section that certain firm characteristics can be used to predict whether attempted private renegotiation will be successful, we are interested in knowing whether the stock market also forms such a prediction. By examining abnormal stock returns around the initial announcement of a restructuring attempt, one can assess whether the market uses similar information to predict the likelihood of successful private renegotiation.

To investigate this possibility, we perform two related analyses of stock returns. First, we partition the sample by whether or not firms are ultimately successful in privately restructuring their debt. If the market is correct on average in predicting this outcome, we should observe a different stock-price reaction for the two subsamples. This approach imposes no prior contraints on the information set that the market uses in making its forecast. The same approach is used by Bradley et al. (1983) in analyzing target companies' stock-price performance following a failed tender offer. Second, we use cross-sectional regression analysis to relate announcement-day returns to variables that were used in the logit analysis to predict the success of private renegotiation. This approach implicitly constrains the market's information set to contain only some subset of these variables.

By analyzing cumulative stock returns over the entire restructuring interval, it is also possible to make certain inferences about relative recontracting costs. Positive cumulative abnormal returns for successful restructurings are consistent with the hypothesis that fewer total costs are incurred (firm value is higher) under private renegotiation than bankruptcy. This allows us to contrast the costs of private renegotiation and bankruptcy without having to measure these costs directly. Baldwin and Mason (1983) undertake a similar analysis of the debt restructuring of Massey Ferguson [included in the current sample].

Stock returns observed around the outcome announcement will contain more information about relative recontracting costs when more of the firm's debt is restructured under the plan. If the unanimous consent of all creditors is required, abnormal returns at the announcement of a successful restructuring must reflect total savings in recontracting costs from avoiding bankruptcy. Given that all creditors (and stockholders) consent to the plan, the wealth of each claimholder, and thus the value of the firm, will be higher under private renegotiation than bankruptcy.

If only a subset of the firm's debt is restructured, adoption of a restructuring plan could in principle reduce the wealth of nonparticipating creditors (by granting participating creditors increased seniority interests, for example). The size of these wealth transfers will be limited, however, by the right of nonparticipating creditors to sue the firm (and other creditors), covenants that restrict the issuance of more senior debt, and cross-default provisions that restrict the firm's ability to exclude certain creditors from participation in the plan.

Abnormal common stock returns around the initial announcement of a restructuring attempt are reported in Table 3–8. We exclude the 27 bankrupt firms in the sample [see Table 3–2] for which the Chapter 11 filing was the first public announcement of financial distress, since it is not known for these firms when (or whether) private renegotiation was attempted before the bankruptcy filing. Reported returns are two-day mean market-model residuals, estimated using Center for Research in Security Prices (CRSP) daily returns for the period 250 days to 50 days prior to the announcement date, and the equally weighted market return. Since infrequent trading is an especially common problem for measuring stock returns of financially distressed firms, abnormal returns are based on Scholes-Williams estimates of the market-model parameters [Scholes and Williams (1977)].

Separate results are presented for the total sample, and for a subsample of 90 restructuring attempts (including 38 successful and 52 failed restructurings) where the initial public announcement contains a reference to either a default or what appears to be the actual commencement of negotiations with lenders. Announcements in the latter sample may contain relatively more surprise, and therefore provide a more powerful test of the market's ability to discriminate between firms that ultimately either succeed or fail to restructure their debt privately.

For the total sample, two-day average returns associated with the initial announcement of a debt restructuring equal –1.6% for firms that successfully restructure their debt, and –6.3% for firms whose restructuring attempt ultimately fails. These returns are significantly different at the 5% level (*t*-statistic of 2.50). Corresponding returns estimated for the sample of "sur-

TABLE 3–8
Two-Day Average Returns Associated with the Initial Announcement of a Private Debt Restructuring, and of the First Announcement of the Restructuring's Resolution[a]

Announcement Type	(1) Successful Debt Restructuring	(2) Unsuccessful Debt Restructuring	t-Statistic of (2) minus (1)
Panel A: Total sample			
(A) Initiation of debt restructuring [b]	−0 .016 (1.53)	−0.063 (4.03)[b]	(2.50)[c]
Sample size	68	57	
(B) Resolution of debt restructuring [b]	0.007 (0.63)	−0.167 (6.68)[b]	(6.37)[b]
Sample size	66	38	
t-statistic of (A) minus (B)	(1.51)	(3.53)[b]	
Panel B: Restructurings that begin with a default or for which actual commencement date is known			
(A) Initiation of debt restructuring [b]	−0.030 (1.94)[d]	−0.087 (3.39)[b]	(1.90)[d]
Sample size	37	31	
(B) Resolution of debt restructuring [b]	−0.009 (0.70)	−0.166 (5.98)[b]	(5.16)[b]
Sample size	34	19	
t-statistic of (A) minus (B)	(1.07)	(2.09)[c]	

[a] Figures are based on a sample of 80 firms that successfully restructured their debt to avoid bankruptcy, and 89 firms that were ultimately unsuccessful in restructuring their debt and filed under Chapter 11 of the U.S. Bankruptcy Code. Announcement dates are determined from *The Wall Street Journal*. All announcements take place between 1978 and 1988. In panel B, results are based on a subsample of 90 debt restructurings (47 successful and 43 unsuccessful) that begin with the announcement of a default or for which the actual commencement date of the restructuring is known. t-statistics are in parentheses.

See Table 3–1 for a definition of debt restructuring and bankruptcy. The two-day average return is an average of daily returns realized on *The Wall Street Journal* announcement day and the preceding day. Stock returns are obtained from the 1988 CRSP daily returns file.

[b] p-value ≤ 0.01.
[c] p-value ≤ 0.05.
[d] p-value ≤ 0.10.

prise" announcements are –3.0% and –8.7%, and are significantly different at the 10% level (*t*-statistic of 1.90). Although less significant results are obtained for the "surprise" sample (which may be attributable to the smaller sample size), both sets of results are consistent with the market being able to distinguish in advance which firms are more likely to be successful at re-structuring their debt privately. As pointed out above, these results do not allow us to identify what specific information the market uses in forming its prediction.

Table 3–8 also reports two-day abnormal returns for the announcement of the outcome of a debt restructuring. For unsuccessful attempts to restruc-ture, this is the announcement of a firm's Chapter 11 filing. For successful restructurings, abnormal returns around the outcome announcement are in-significantly different from zero, for both samples. For unsuccessful restructurings, abnormal returns are significantly negative around the an-nouncement of the Chapter 11 filing, again for both samples (respective abnormal returns are –16.7% and –16.6%, with corresponding *t*-statistics of 6.68 and 5.98).

When these results are combined with the initial-announcement re-turns, it appears that stockholders do better over the entire restructuring interval when their firms ultimately settle with creditors out of court. This impression is confirmed in Table 3–9, which reports average cumulative abnormal returns for the entire restructuring interval. For the total sample, stockholders of firms that successfully restructured realized average abnor-mal returns of 41.4% over the restructuring interval, whereas stockholders of ultimately bankrupt firms realized abnormal returns of –39.9%. Corre-sponding returns for the "surprise" subsample are 71.3% and –36.1%. For both panels, differences in returns are significant at the 5% level. These results are not driven by outliers. Seventy-two percent of cumulative returns are negative for firms that ultimately file for Chapter 11, and 58% are positive for firms that successfully restructure. The percentage of negative returns is significantly different between the two subsamples at the 5% level.

These results suggest that, for whatever reason, stockholders on aver-age fare less well in bankruptcy than in private renegotiation, and thus have incentives to settle with creditors privately. Consistent with this possibility, stockholders seldom exercise their option to file for Chapter 11 without first attempting to restructure the firm's debt privately [see Table 3–2]. An alter-native interpretation, however, is that firms that file for bankruptcy experi-ence unexpectedly worse operating performance than firms that ultimately restructure their debt privately. Thus larger stock-price declines for bankrupt

TABLE 3–9
Average Cumulative Returns for Successful and Unsuccessful Debt Restructurings[a]

Outcome of Debt Restructuring	Average Cumulative Return
Panel A: Total sample	
(A) Successful	0.414
	(2.71)[c]
Sample size	69
(B) Unsuccessful	⁻0.399
	(3.28)[b]
Sample size	55
t-statistic of (A) minus (B)	(4.17)[b]
Panel B: Restructurings that begin with a default or for which actual commencement date is known	
(A) Successful	0.713
	(3.21)[b]
Sample size	38
(B) Unsuccessful	⁻0.361
	(2.19)[c]
Sample size	30
t-statistic of (A) minus (B)	(3.88)[b]

[a] Returns are measured from one day before the commencement of restructuring to the day on which success of restructuring attempt is determined. Figures are based on a sample of 80 firms that successfully restructured their debt to avoid bankruptcy, and 89 firms that were ultimately unsuccessful in restructuring their debt and filed under Chapter 11 of the U.S. Bankruptcy Code. Announcement dates are determined from *The Wall Street Journal*. All announcements take place between 1978 and 1988. In panel B, results are based on a subsample of 90 debt restructurings (47 successful and 43 unsuccessful) that begin with the announcement of a default or for which the actual commencement date of the restructuring is known. *t*-statistics in parentheses.

See Table 3–1 for a definition of debt restructuring and bankruptcy. Stock return data are obtained from the 1988 CRSP daily returns file.

[b] *p*-value ≤ 0.01.
[c] *p*-value ≤ 0.05.

firms may not be due to the recontracting process itself, but instead reflect a selection bias resulting from the fact that bankrupt firms are inherently less profitable (subsequent to the bankruptcy filing).

Finally, attempts to relate abnormal stock returns to the explanatory variables used in the logit regressions yielded insignificant results. Cross-sectional regressions of abnormal returns against various combinations of these variables generally produced adjusted R-squares of less than 5%, and individual coefficient estimates were almost always insignificant. The insignificant results cannot be attributed to multicollinearity or heteroskedasticity of the error terms. The low explanatory power of these regressions is consistent with the market's using more information to forecast the outcome of private renegotiation than is captured by the explanatory variables.

CONCLUSION

In this study we investigate how financially distressed firms restructure their debt. For a sample of 169 distressed companies, we investigate firms' economic incentives to choose between private renegotiation and formal bankruptcy as alternative mechanisms for dealing with default. In about half of all cases, financially distressed firms successfully restructure their debt outside of Chapter 11. Financial distress is more likely to be resolved through private renegotiation when more of the firm's assets are intangible, and relatively more debt is owed to banks; private renegotiation is less likely to succeed when there are more distinct classes of debt outstanding. Analysis of stock returns suggests that the market is also able to identify in advance which firms are more likely to succeed in restructuring their debt privately. Cumulative stock returns are significantly higher when debt is restructured privately; thus on average stockholders have incentives to avoid bankruptcy and settle out of court.

One implication of our results is that troubled companies are likely to find informal alternatives to bankruptcy increasingly attractive in dealing with financial distress. As recently argued by Jensen (1989a, b), companies that have relatively more debt outstanding will default sooner if they are being mismanaged. This has the virtue of forcing management to undertake corrective changes in corporate policy sooner, thus preserving more of the firm's going-concern value. Consistent with this, the present study finds that insolvent firms with relatively high going concern value are more likely to restructure their debt privately, because more of this value tends to be lost for a variety of reasons (including through asset sales) when debt and the firm's operations are reorganized in Chapter 11. Thus, future defaults by the current generation of highly levered companies may be increasingly resolved through private renegotiation.

Our results also have important implications for interpreting recent evidence that shows an increase in the default rate of high-yield publicly traded bonds [Altman (1989), Asquith et al. (1989)]. We present evidence that restructuring of publicly traded debt almost always takes the form of an exchange offer, and is generally completed within two months. The out-of-pocket costs incurred in connection with these offers are economically insignificant (amounting on average to less than 1% of the firm's book value of assets). It remains an unanswered empirical question whether other default-related costs are sufficiently high to warrant continued concern over the recent rise in defaults.

NOTES

1. Alternatively, firms can elect to liquidate by filing under Chapter 7 of the Code. Before the Code was enacted on October 1, 1979, bankruptcy practices were governed by the Bankruptcy Act, under which corporations could choose to either liquidate under Chapter 7, or reorganize under Chapters 10 or 11. Filing for Chapter 11 is not always the exclusive right of stockholders. Creditors may file an "involuntary" Chapter 11 petition, if they can demonstrate that the firm has been delinquent in making payments on its debt. Following a default, creditors can generally accelerate full payment on their debt after 30 days have elapsed, thus giving the firm little option but to file for bankruptcy.

2. Previous empirical studies of out-of-court restructurings include Gilson (1989, 1990), who analyzes changes in corporate ownership and governance structure during financial distress; Gilson and Vetsuypens (1991), who study CEO compensation policy in distressed firms; and Hoshi et al. (1990), who investigate the resolution of financial distress in Japan. Previous theoretical research into the choice between bankruptcy and private renegotiation includes Haugen and Senbet (1978), Bulow and Shoven (1978), White (1983), Aivazian and Callen (1983), Green and Laffont (1987), Roe (1987), Kahn and Huberman (1988), Brown (1989), Giammarino (1989), Hart and Moore (1989), and Mooradian (1989). Much of this research views the firm's bankruptcy decision as the outcome of a strategic game played between stockholders and creditors. An analogous problem is addressed in the "theory of litigation," which analyzes the choice faced by plaintiffs and defendants between settling out of court or going to trial [Gould (1973)].

3. For example, if a debtor wishes to retain the services of an investment bank, it must first file an application with the bankruptcy court. Applications can be made only after appropriate "notice and hearing" has been given, which requires the firm to inform all

creditors of the application in writing, and allow sufficient time for any objections to be filed. The court rules on the application at a special hearing. The time required for approval can be shortened if the debtor requires creditors to show cause, allowing the application to be approved within a few days if no objections are raised.

4. Under section 1126(b) of the Code, any claimholder who accepts or rejects a reorganization plan that is proposed prior to filing for Chapter 11 is deemed also to have accepted or rejected the plan for purposes of plan confirmation, provided that the debtor has disclosed all relevant information for making an informed decision as provided under nonbankruptcy law.

5. Defaults on technical convenants (for example, those requiring firms to maintain a minimum level of net worth) are not explicitly considered in this definition because such covenants are frequently renegotiated by financially healthy firms when debt is privately placed. As Zinbarg (1975, p. 35) notes: "My own institution's experience [Prudential Insurance Company of America] may serve as an illustration. In any given year, we will, on average, receive one modification request per loan on the books. In no more than five percent of these cases will we refuse the request or even require any quid pro quo, because the vast majority of corporate requests are perfectly reasonable and do not increase our risk materially." For a detailed discussion of the economic function of covenants, see Smith and Warner (1979).

6. Thus, for example, if the last reference to an ongoing restructuring of a firm's bank debt was on June 15, 1982, and the next such reference occurs on September 12, 1983, these would be treated as references to two separate restructurings. Similarly, if a firm's bank debt is successfully restructured on March 22, 1980, and it begins to restructure its publicly traded debt on November 2, 1980, these would be treated as two references to the same ongoing restructuring. Five firms in the sample appear twice as two separate restructurings, and four firms appear as both a debt restructuring and a bankruptcy.

APPENDIX TO CHAPTER 3

CASE STUDIES OF ATTEMPTS BY TEN FIRMS TO RESTRUCTURE THEIR DEBT PRIVATELY TO AVOID BANKRUPTCY

This appendix presents brief case studies describing the experience of ten firms that attempted to restructure their debt privately to avoid bankruptcy. Each case study describes major events relating to the restructuring, general terms (either proposed or adopted) for restructuring the firm's debt, and other relevant information. The cases are based on information contained in published reports in *The Wall Street Journal* and disclosed in firms' 10k reports, shareholder proxy statements, and exchange offer prospectuses. The ten firms examined here represent a cross-section of various possible restructuring plan types and outcomes. At the beginning of each case each debt restructuring is classified according to the principal types of debt involved, and whether the restructuring attempt was successful (i.e., whether the firm avoided having to file for Chapter 11). In addition, for each case we report (i) the period over which the restructuring took place (as defined in section 3 of the text), (ii) the Scholes-Williams cumulative abnormal common stock return over the restructuring interval (labeled *car*), and (iii) the firm's common stock price at the beginning and end of the restructuring, or the most recent prices reported inside the restructuring interval (labelled *p0* and *p1*, respectively). Stock prices are obtained from Standard and Poor's *Daily Stock Price Record*. Reported time intervals are all rounded to the nearest month. "n.a." means that cumulative abnormal returns could not be calculated because there were insufficient stock returns available as a result of nontrading.

Brock Hotel Corporation *Classification:* Successful restructuring of bank and publicly traded debt, accompanied by stock placement with financial advisor to restructuring and common stock rights offering (6/28/85–6/26/86; *car*= n.a.; *p0*= 2⅛, *p1* = ⅞).

The company made an exchange offer to holders of its eight publicly traded debenture issues, offering a package of common stock and new debentures (having a lower coupon rate, payable in cash or common stock). Although 86% of the debentures were tendered under the offer, it was decided that the offer would not be sufficient to resolve the company's financial problems. As a result, the company implemented a comprehensive plan to restructure all of its long-term debt. Under the plan, all of the new debentures issued under the previous exchange offer were converted into various amounts of common and preferred stock, common stock options, and cash. In addition, the company acquired the bank debt and capitalized lease obligations of its operating subsidiaries (using a combination of cash, warrants, and common stock options), and exchanged new debentures for all of the preferred stock of a partly owned subsidiary. Various other debt was also restructured, including liabilities arising from canceled operating leases and company guarantees, and the lease agreement on the company's headquarters building. A critical feature of the plan was a rights offering of 266 million common shares to current stockholders (only about 13 million shares were outstanding before the offering). Following a vote of the common stockholders, the plan was adopted one year from the announcement of the initial exchange offer. A major role in the restructuring was played by The Hallwood Group Inc., which the company engaged as a financial advisor to the restructuring. In addition to managing the rights offering, Hallwood obtained secured lenders' consent to the plan by agreeing to guarantee the minimum proceeds that would be realized from selling various assets under the plan. In return for providing these and other services, Hallwood received the right to elect a majority of the company's board of directors (including its chairman), and was issued 14% of the company's common stock.

Crawford Energy Inc. *Classification:* Unsuccessful restructuring of bank and trade debt (10/20/83–9/30/85; *car*= -63.3%; *p0*= 3 ⅛, *p1*= ⅔).

Following eight months of negotiations, the company eliminated most of its $10 million in trade debt by offering new common stock to its 44 trade creditors in a negotiated exchange offer. In return for canceling almost half of the debt, trade creditors received 21% of the company's common stock. Also participating in the plan was A. Gail Crawford, the company's founder, chairman, and CEO. Mr. Crawford, who before the offer held 79% of the company's stock, was issued new stock representing 33% of the total shares outstanding after the offer, in return for his personally assuming the remainder of the debt. Four months later, the company announced an agreement in principle with its two banks to restructure its bank loans. Although payment on these loans was four months overdue, neither bank had yet formally declared the company in default. This agreement, which provided for an extension of the loans' due date, was in default eight months later. The banks then agreed to fund the company on a monthly basis while it sought to sell off assets or obtain an infusion of outside equity. Four months after that, the company filed for Chapter 11.

Crystal Oil Company *Classification:* Unsuccessful restructuring of bank, trade, and publicly traded debt (6/11/85–10/1/86; *car*= n.a.; *p0*= 2, *p1*= ⅜).

The company entered into an agreement with a major supplier to extend payment on its trade debt, in return for issuing the supplier a

secured note. As disclosed in the company's 10k report, it was also in
technical default on a secured mortgage note held by a bank, although
details concerning how (or whether) the default was resolved were not
reported. At the same time, the company undertook an exchange offer
for its six publicly traded debenture issues, offering a package of
common stock and new secured notes (having a higher coupon rate,
payable in either cash or common stock). The old debentures represented approximately 80% of the company's long-term debt. Four
months later, after extending and sweetening the offer seven times, the
company accepted all 70% of the debentures that were tendered, resulting in the issuance to noteholders of approximately 26% of the
company's common stock (following payment of interest on the new
notes with common stock, noteholders' ownership increased to 59%
within three months). Despite the success of the exchange offer, the
company subsequently found it necessary to again restructure its debt.
Within approximately a year of the conclusion of its exchange offer,
the company made a "prepackaged" Chapter 11 filing, after having
first obtained creditors' consent to a reorganization plan. The company
emerged from Chapter 11 after only three months.

Dunes Hotels and Casinos Inc. *Classification:* Successful restructuring of
bank and other privately placed debt, accompanied by outside stock placement (8/31/83–2/6/84; *car*= 102.9%; *p0*= 4⅛, *p1*= 6⅛).

For six months, the company attempted to restructure a $30 million
debt held by two private investors, Ronald and Stuart Perlman. Initially, the Perlmans agreed to acquire the company for $80 million in
notes and the assumption of $105 million in debt. This agreement was
replaced by another under which the Perlmans were to convert their
debt into approximately 45% of the company's common stock. The
restructuring of this and other debt was deemed essential to avert a
bankruptcy filing. Finally, the company reached an agreement to place
41% of its common stock with John Jack Anderson, a private investor
with prior management experience in the industry. At about the same
time, the company restructured approximately $80 million of debt
owed to its three institutional lenders (a bank, a leasing company, and
American Financial Corporation), resulting in various payment defer-
rals. Terms of the agreement gave Mr. Anderson effective voting control over additional shares held by management, increasing the
percentage of common shares he either owned or controlled to 51%.

Mr. Anderson was named chairman of the company, succeeding Morris Shenker, who prior to the restructuring held 41% of the company's stock. Mr. Shenker, who remained CEO, had filed for personal bankruptcy four months previously.

Lamson & Sessions Co. *Classification:* Successful restructuring of bank debt, accompanied by new private debt placement (12/31/82–4/29/85; *car*= 51.3%; $p0$= 3 ⅛, $p1$= 3 ⅝).

The company disclosed in its annual report that it was not in compliance with "certain" covenants in its loan agreements, and had been attempting to restructure its debt to 24 bank and insurance company lenders. The company had no publicly traded debt. Ten months into the negotiations, the company announced that the restructuring effort had stalled because of disagreements among lenders over terms. The company refused to explain what the differences were, or disclose the identity of the lenders. A debt restructuring plan was announced five months later. Under the plan, the company's institutional debt was to be converted into cash, new secured notes, and convertible preferred stock (with dividends payable in either cash or common stock). Assuming full conversion of the preferred stock, the lenders would hold 34% of the firm's common stock. The cash payment, representing 24% of the balance owed, was raised through a new short-term secured credit facility with Congress Financial Corp. As part of the plan, borrowings under this facility were to be reduced by applying part of the proceeds raised from the subsequent divestiture of an operating subsidiary. The plan was adopted three months later at the company's annual meeting, where stockholders approved a requisite increase in the number of authorized common shares. At the same meeting, the company's chairman relinquished the post of CEO to the company president, and announced that he would soon also step down as chairman. Ten months later, the company repurchased (with cash) all of the new notes for 60% of their face value, and exchanged new common stock warrants for approximately a third of the preferred stock held by lenders.

Oak Industries Inc. *Classification:* Successful restructuring of publicly traded debt accompanied by outside stock placement (2/11/85–5/6/86; *car*= –33.3%; $p0$= 2 ⅛, $p1$= 1 ⅝).

The company, which had no bank debt, offered to exchange a

package of notes, warrants, and common stock for its three outstanding publicly traded debenture issues. The new notes had a lower promised coupon rate and identical face value, and were to mature approximately ten years before the old debentures. The notes also allowed payment of interest in either cash or common stock (the company indicated that interest would be paid in common stock for the "foreseeable future"). After extending the offer three times, the company accepted all 79% of the old debentures tendered, two months following the initial announcement of the offer. Approximately one week before the offer's expiration, the company's president resigned to "pursue other business interests," amid an SEC investigation into alleged disclosure violations by the company. Seven months after the first exchange offer concluded, the company announced a new exchange offer for all of its publicly traded debt, in which holders were offered a package of cash and common stock. The cash part of the offer was financed by the sale of a major operating division and block of new equity securities to Allied-Signal Inc. (not previously a stockholder). The equity placement, which was made conditional on the success of the debt restructuring, consisted of common stock and warrants, representing about 20% of the company's common stock outstanding at the conclusion of the offer (assuming full exercise of the warrants). As part of the agreement, Allied-Signal also received three seats on the company's seven-member board of directors. The second exchange offer and the transaction with Allied-Signal were completed five months later, resulting in a doubling of the total number of common shares outstanding.

Petro Lewis Corp. *Classification:* Successful restructuring of publicly traded debt, effected through acquisition of the company (3/28/85–12/31/86; *car*= -50.2%; *p0*= 4 ⅛, *p1*= 2 ⅛).

The company attempted to restructure its publicly traded debt through a series of three exchange offers. Approximately 75% of the company's long-term debt was publicly traded. In the first offer, which took two months to complete, the company sought to exchange new (secured and unsecured) notes and common stock for one of its note issues and three issues of preferred stock. Approximately 80% of the notes, and on average 58% of the preferred stock issues, were tendered and accepted. Five months later, the company undertook a new exchange offer for four of its outstanding issues of subordinated notes and debentures. Holders were offered a package of new secured notes (carrying a higher coupon rate but lower face value), common stock, and cash. After several extensions of the expiration date, the offer concluded two months later, with about 50% of holders tendering. The third and final offer was announced five months later, and consisted of an offer to exchange a package of new secured and convertible notes and common stock for all nine of the company's publicly traded debt issues outstanding (including those that were issued under the earlier exchange offers). The company terminated this offer four months later, after deciding that it did not "represent a viable alternative for the company." Two months previously, an agreement had been announced in which Freeport-McMoRan Inc. would acquire the company to enable it to avert a bankruptcy filing, for a total price of about $770 million. Ultimately Freeport purchased the company by making a public tender offer for all of its outstanding publicly traded securities (debt as well as equity). The time that elapsed between the initial exchange offer and the consummation of the merger was approximately 20 months.

Seiscom Delta Inc. *Classification:* Successful restructuring of bank debt, followed by bankruptcy more than one year later (5/12/83–4/26/85; $car=$ –65.3%; $p0= 5\,\%$, $p1= 1\,\%$).

The company announced that it restructured its bank debt by obtaining a one-year extension of the date on which its revolving bank loans would convert to term loans. In the *WSJ* story that reported the restructuring, the company refused to identify which banks were involved, and no mention of the transaction was made in the firm's 10k report for that year. The company had no publicly traded debt outstanding. Fourteen months later, the company was granted a "second" waiver on a bank loan covenant (the first was not reported) that was in default because the company had exceeded the borrowing limit specified in its revolving credit agreement. Two weeks later, D. Gale Reese, chairman and CEO of the company, resigned under pressure from its banks. The *WSJ* quoted a company spokesman as saying, "It's just a matter of the bank being willing to do certain things provided Gale Reese was not on the team." In the same story that reported Mr. Reese's resignation, it was revealed that one of the company's banks granted a third waiver of the same loan covenant. Nine months later, a definitive agreement was reached to restructure the company's bank debt. The agreement provided for the banks to forgive 52% of the outstanding bank loan balance, and grant a seven-month waiver of interest and nineteen-month waiver of principal owed on the remaining balance. In return, the banks were given a package of common stock, convertible preferred stock, and warrants, which together represented 77% of the company's outstanding common stock (assuming full conversion of preferred stock and warrants). In addition, the banks were granted an increased security interest in all of the company's assets. The agreement also provided for forgiveness of certain lease payments owed on the company's headquarters building. Seventeen months later, the company and four of its wholly owned subsidiaries filed for Chapter 11.

Tiger International Inc. *Classification:* Successful restructuring of bank and publicly traded debt by parent company, accompanied by bankruptcy of subsidiary (2/14/83–3/25/85; *car*= 18.3%; *p0*= 7⅛, *p1*= 8⅝).

The company and its bank lenders agreed on a tentative restructuring plan four months following the company's decision to unilaterally suspend interest and principal payments on about half of its total $1.8 billion in debt. Regarding the company's decision to suspend payments on its debt, a company spokesman was paraphrased by the *WSJ* as saying that "the company chose to announce suspension of interest and principal on debt, rather than issue a joint release with lenders, because of the large number of banks involved [60, including certain other unspecified 'lending institutions'] and the complexity of the loan agreements." Under the proposed plan, the company was to be granted an extension on scheduled payments owed by three operating subsidiaries, receive a new revolving credit line from an existing lender, and implement an exchange offer for its two publicly traded issues of debentures. Regarding lenders' reaction to the plan, the firm's chairman noted: "It's in the lenders' interest to do this. All of them agree that the going concern is the important thing." On the day before the announcement of the plan, it was announced that the company's president and financial vice president had both resigned; the company denied allegations that this action had been prompted by its lenders. Interest on the new credit line was tied to the company's future earnings performance. The exchange offer took three months to complete, with approximately 81% of all bonds being tendered. Tendering debenture-holders received a package of new debentures (having a lower face value, shorter average maturity, and identical coupon rate), common stock, and warrants; interest on the new debentures was payable in either cash or common stock. Final agreement on the restructuring of subsidiary debt was reached by two of the subsidiaries seven months after the initial plan was proposed, and by the third, a year after the plan proposal date. Shortly thereafter the company undertook an additional exchange offer for two issues of publicly traded debt owed by one of its subsidiaries, offering a package of common stock and warrants. Fourteen months following the initial suspension of debt payments, the company revealed in its annual report that it was still attempting to restructure the debt of a subsidiary. Eight months later, the subsidiary independently filed for Chapter 11, after it failed to reach a standstill agreement with its banks on a $132 million secured note that was in default.

Verna Corp. *Classification:* Successful restructuring of bank and privately placed debt (12/31/82–4/29/85; *car*= –136.7%; *p0*= 4⅞, *p1*= ¹³⁄₁₆).

After reporting a quarterly loss, the company granted its two banks a security interest in 39 drilling rigs (although no default was reported). Six months later the company announced that it had restructured its bank debt. The banks, which were owed approximately $28 million, were given warrants convertible into 13% of the company's common stock, a security interest in accounts receivable, and a "fee" of $850,000. In return, the company was granted a 13-month deferral of interest and principal payments, and an increase in its borrowing limit under an existing revolving loan. Concurrently with the bank debt restructuring, the company privately placed $1 million of new secured subordinated notes with a group of three venture capital companies. In return for purchasing the notes, said companies were given common stock warrants for 8% of the common stock, and three permanent seats on the board of directors. Ten months later, both the bank debt and new notes had to be restructured, resulting in various payment deferrals and increased grants of security. Among other things, the banks were given the right to force certain asset sales to effect repayment of the debt. Eighteen months later, the company restructured its debt for a third and final time, following stockholder approval of the transaction. Debt owed to the two banks was converted into an issue of new secured notes, convertible preferred stock, and preferred stock warrants, representing 56% of the company's common stock (assuming full conversion of the banks' claims). The notes held by the three venture capital lenders were exchanged for new common stock, representing 24% of the common stock then outstanding. Three months later, four of the firm's five outside directors resigned after the company's insurer withdrew its liability coverage.

REFERENCES

Aivazian, Varouj, and Jeffrey Callen, 1983, "Reorganization in bankruptcy and the issue of strategic risk," *Journal of Banking and Finance 7*, 119–33.

Altman, Edward, 1984, "A further investigation of the bankruptcy cost question," *Journal of Finance 39*, 1067–89.

Altman, Edward, 1989, "Measuring corporate bond mortality and performance," *Journal of Finance 44*, 909–22.

Ang, James; Jess Chua; and John McConnell, 1982, "The administrative costs of corporate bankruptcy: A note," *Journal of Finance 37*, 219–26.

Asquith, Paul; David Mullins, Jr.; and Eric Wolff, 1989, "Original issue high yield bonds: Aging analyses of defaults, exchanges and calls," *Journal of Finance 44*, 923–52.

Baldwin, Carliss, and Scott Mason, 1983, "The resolution of claims in financial distress: The case of Massey Ferguson," *Journal of Finance 38*, 505–16.

Bradley, Michael; Anand Desai; and E. Han Kim, 1983, "The rationale behind interfirm tender offers," *Journal of Financial Economics 11*, 183–206.

Brown, David, 1989, "Claimholder incentive conflicts in reorganization: The role of bankruptcy law," *Review of Financial Studies 2*, 109–23.

Bulow, Jeremy, and John Shoven, 1978, "The bankruptcy decision," *Bell Journal of Economics 9*, 436–45.

DeAngelo, Harry; Linda DeAngelo; and Douglas Skinner, 1990, "An empirical investigation of the relation between accounting choice and dividend policy in troubled companies," Unpublished paper (University of Michigan, Ann Arbor, MI).

DeAngelo, Linda, 1988, "Managerial competition, information costs, and corporate governance: The use of accounting performance measures in proxy contests," *Journal of Accounting and Economics 10*, 3–36.

DeNatale, Andrew, 1981, "The creditors' committee under the Bankruptcy Code: A primer," *American Bankruptcy Law Journal 55*, 43–62.

Douglas-Hamilton, Margaret, 1975, "Creditor liabilities resulting from improper interference with the management of a financially troubled debtor," *Business Lawyer 31*, 343–65.

Eberhart, Allan; William Moore; and Rodney Roenfeldt, 1990, "Security pricing and deviations from the absolute priority rule in bankruptcy proceedings," *Journal of Finance 45,* 1457–70.

Franks, Julian, and Walter Torous, 1989, "An empirical investigation of U.S. firms in reorganization," *Journal of Finance 44,* 747–69.

Giammarino, Ronald, 1989, "The resolution of financial distress," *Review of Financial Studies 2,* 25–47.

Gilson, Stuart, 1989, "Management turnover and financial distress," *Journal of Financial Economics 25,* 241–62.

Gilson, Stuart, 1990, "Bankruptcy, boards, banks, and blockholders," *Journal of Financial Economics 26.*

Gilson, Stuart, and Michael Vetsuypens, 1991, "CEO compensation in financially distressed firms: An empriical analysis," Unpublished paper (Harvard Business School, Boston, and Southern Methodist University, Dallas).

Gould, John, 1973, "The economics of legal conflicts," *Journal of Legal Studies 2,* 279–300.

Green, Jerry, and Jean-Jacques Laffont, 1987, "Renegotiation and the form of efficient contracts," Unpublished paper (Harvard University, Cambridge, MA).

Hart, Oliver, and John Moore, 1989, "Default and renegotiation: A dynamic model of debt," Unpublished paper (Massachusetts Institute of Technology, Cambridge, MA).

Haugen, Robert, and Lemma Senbet, 1978, "The insignificance of bankruptcy costs to the theory of optimal capital structure," *Journal of Finance 33,* 383–93.

Hoshi, Takeo; Anil Kashyap; and David Scharfstein, 1990, "The role of banks in reducing the costs of financial distress in Japan," *Journal of Financial Economics 26.*

Huberman, Gur, and Charles Kahn, 1988, "Default, foreclosure, and strategic renegotiation," Unpublished paper (Columbia University, New York, NY).

Jackson, Thomas, 1986, *The logic and limits of bankruptcy law* (Harvard University Press, Cambridge, MA).

James, Christopher, 1987, "Some evidence on the uniqueness of bank loans," *Journal of Financial Economics 19,* 217–35.

Jensen, Michael, 1989a, "Active investors, LBOs, and the privatization of bankruptcy," *Journal of Applied Corporate Finance 2,* 35–44.

Jensen, Michael, 1989b, "Eclipse of the public corporation," *Harvard Business Review,* September-October, 61–74.

King, Lawrence, 1979, "Chapter 11 of the 1978 Bankruptcy Code," *American Bankruptcy Law Journal 53,* 107–31.

Klee, Kenneth, 1979, "All you ever wanted to know about cram down under the new bankruptcy code," *American Bankruptcy Law Journal 53,* 133–71.

Lang, Larry; Rene Stulz; and Ralph Walkling, 1988, "Managerial performance,

Tobin's q and the gains from successful tender offers," *Journal of Financial Economics 24,* 137–54.

Maddala, G., 1983, *Limited-dependent and qualitative variables in econometrics* (Cambridge University Press, Cambridge, England).

Manski, Charles, and Daniel McFadden, 1983, "Alternative estimators and sample designs for discrete choice analysis," in: Charles Manski and Daniel McFadden (eds.), *Structural analysis of discrete data with econometric applications* (MIT Press, Boston, MA).

Mooradian, Robert, 1989, "Recapitalizations and the free-rider problem," Unpublished paper (University of Florida, Gainesville, FL).

Myers, Stewart, 1977, "Determinants of corporate borrowing," *Journal of Financial Economics 5,* 147–76.

Roe, Mark, 1987, "The voting prohibition in bond workouts," *The Yale Law Journal 97,* 232–79.

Scholes, Myron, and Joseph Williams, 1977, "Estimating betas from non-synchronous data," *Journal of Financial Economics 5,* 309–27.

Smith, C., and Jerold Warner, 1979, "On financial contracting: An analysis of bond covenants," *Journal of Financial Economics 7,* 117–61.

Stein, Sol, 1989, *A feast for lawyers* (M. Evans and Company, Inc., New York, NY).

Titman, Sheridan, 1984, "The effect of capital structure on a firm's liquidation decision," *Journal of Financial Economics 13,* 137–51.

Trost, Ronald, 1979, "Business reorganizations under Chapter 11 of the new bankruptcy code," *Business Lawyer,* April, 1309–46.

The Wall Street Journal, 1988, "Corporate finance, 'leveraged to the hilt,'" October 25, p. A11.

Warner, Jerold, 1977a, "Bankruptcy, absolute priority and the pricing of risky debt claims," *Journal of Financial Economics 4,* 239–76.

Warner, Jerold, 1977b, "Bankruptcy costs: Some evidence," *Journal of Finance 32,* 337–47.

Weiss, Lawrence, 1990, "Bankruptcy resolution; direct costs and violation of priority of claims," *Journal of Financial Economics 26.*

White, Michelle, 1989, "The corporate bankruptcy decision," *The Journal of Economic Perspectives 3,* 129–51.

Zinbarg, Edward, 1975, "The private placement loan agreement," *Financial Analysts Journal 31,* 33–52.

CHAPTER 4

PRIVATE VERSUS PUBLIC CREDITOR EXPERIENCE IN DISTRESSED FIRM DEBT RESTRUCTURINGS

David T. Brown
Christopher M. James
Robert M. Mooradian

INTRODUCTION

Firms recontract in financial distress to resolve conflicting claims on the firm in order to permit the continued operation of the firm and to realign incentives with firm value maximization. Collectively it is in the interest of the claim holders to accomplish this reorganization. Moreover, it is in their collective interest to recontract privately and avoid costly formal bankruptcy proceedings.

While bankruptcy avoidance is in the collective interest of all of the firm's claim holders, there are a number of reasons why firms file for bankruptcy. In particular, the literature focuses on two reasons private renegotiation may fail, asymmetric information and a holdout problem.

David T. Brown, Christopher M. James, and Robert M. Mooradian are Professors of Finance at the Graduate School of Business, University of Florida.

The authors wish to thank Mitch Berlin, Jim Brickley, Stuart Gilson, Dave Hirshleifer, Greg Niehaus, Steve Sharpe, Mike Ryngaert, and René Stulz for helpful comments, and to Jon Garfinkel and Steve Cox for research assistance.

The holdout problem is particularly acute when recontracting with public bondholders because of the voting procedures imposed on the recontracting process by the Trust Indenture Act of 1939 and the fact that publicly traded debt tends to be diffusely held. The Trust Indenture Act requires that all bondholders approve any alteration of their contract. Thus, while it is in the collective interest of bondholders to restructure, individually they have the incentive to hold out. Bankruptcy law, on the other hand, mitigates the holdout problem by, for example, allowing a reorganization of public debt with only the approval of a two-thirds majority of the bondholders.[1]

The second (related) reason why firms may fail to restructure their debt privately is that bondholders are poorly informed about the firm's future prospects. In particular, if an information asymmetry exists between bondholders and insiders then a so-called lemons problem can develop in which bondholders expect management to misrepresent the firm's prospects so that management can "cut" a good deal in the private restructuring. In short it is in shareholders' or management's interest to always say that the firm's value is low to reduce the amount that bondholders receive in the restructuring. Since information asymmetries are likely to be much less important in a court supervised bankruptcy, bondholders prefer bankruptcy to private renegotiations. In contrast, if private lenders (such as banks and insurance companies) are better informed than public debt holders, they will be less likely to use the courts to determine firm value.[2] Gilson, John, and Lang (1990) provide convincing evidence that achieving a consensus outside of bankruptcy is easier with privately held claims.

This paper shows how the information problems that can arise in a debt restructuring influence the composition of an exchange offer to public debt. The nature of the securities offered bondholders can credibly convey management's private information about the firm's prospects allowing the claims to be successfully reorganized outside of Chapter 11. We then discuss how the nature of the claims offered to private debt, which is assumed to be well informed, differs from the claims offered in a reorganization of public debt.

Our analysis leads to predictions about how stock prices will respond to the announcement of a debt restructuring. Consistent with these predictions, we find that the stock price reaction to a debt restructuring depends on (1) whether the restructuring involves public or private debt, and (2) whether stock or senior securities are offered to debt holders, i.e. the composition of the offer. In particular, we find a significant positive share price reaction to exchange offers in which public bondholders are offered senior claims and a significant negative share price reaction associated with exchange offers in which bondholders are offered stock. In contrast, we find a positive stock price reaction associated with a restructuring in which private lenders are offered stock and a negative stock price reaction when private lenders are offered senior claims.

This research provides three basic insights into the process of reorganizing debt. First, we show why and how managers "signal" their private information to bondholders through the construction of public debt exchange offers. Second, the capital market's interpretation of the terms of a debt restructuring announcement depends on both the type of security exchanged for the original debt claims and the identity of the lender involved in the transaction. Third, the evidence suggests that private lenders are better informed about the issuer's prospects than public lenders.

Next, the paper analyzes the role of information asymmetries in the design of reorganizations by analyzing first the case where the lender has inferior information (the public debt case) and then the case where the lender is relatively well informed (the private debt case). Finally, we test the predictions of this analysis regarding the stock price response to different types of debt restructuring.

EXCHANGE OFFERS FOR PUBLIC DEBT

First, we analyze the firm's exchange offer design problem under the assumption that bondholders are not well informed about the "true value" of the firm but management is well informed. Suppose that the firm must restructure its public debt to avoid bankruptcy. The amount that bondholders will accept in a restructuring (or exchange offer) depends largely on what they expect to receive if the restructuring fails and the firm files for bankruptcy. Thus, since the true value of the firm is not revealed to bondholders until after a successful exchange offer or a bankruptcy, the bondholders' reservation value in a restructuring depends on their perception of the value of the firm and the costs they would bear in a formal bankruptcy.

Since the bondholders' reservation value depends on their beliefs about the value of the firm, management has an incentive to reveal negative information about firm value in order to reduce the bondholders' reservation value. One way to credibly convey negative information to bondholders is to offer to exchange equity for debt.

To see this consider the following simple numerical example. Suppose a firm has $10 in face value of public debt claims outstanding and the bondholders believe the firm is worth $8. Given their beliefs and an assumed bankruptcy cost of $0.50 borne by bondholders, bondholders are willing to accept $7.50 in new fixed claims in order to avoid a costly bankruptcy. Now suppose managers know the firm is actually worth $6. They could approach the bondholders with this assertion and offer them $5.75 in fixed claims and exact what little equity remains for the original equity holders. However, bondholders should be skeptical of this offer in that if the firm is in fact worth $8 the new equity is worth $2.25. To mitigate bondholder skepticism, managers could offer debt holders equity representing 93.75% of the reorganized firm, i.e., an offer of $5.625 if the firm is worth $6. In this case, if the firm is in fact worth $8 or more, the original bondholders' new claims will be worth at least $7.50.

In contrast, consider the case in which management has favorable private information so that the firm is "undervalued" in the market. In this case it is in stockholders' interest to offer bondholders the least contingent claim possible in the exchange offer to credibly convey favorable information. To see this return to the above example, but suppose that management knows the firm is actually worth $12 if the public debt is restructured to avoid bankruptcy. Since bondholders believe the firm is worth only $8, they will only accept equity if they get at least 93.75% of the firm. However, since the firm is worth $12, 93.75% of the firm is worth $11.25. Alternatively, managers could offer the original bondholders a new debt claim with a $10 face value, which bondholders would obviously accept since it represents no reduction in face value. Clearly equity is better off with a debt offer than an equity offer.

One implication of this logic is that exchange offers involving the issuance of stock will be associated with a negative stock price reaction, since these offers are a way of conveying unfavorable private information. In contrast, exchange offers involving the issuance of debt securities will be associated with a positive share price reaction.

Clearly, in addition to the problem of private information concerning firm value, there are other considerations in the design of exchange offers. First, if the firm is to swap new debt claims for old debt claims, it must be concerned with its ability to service the new debt. As a practical matter, most of the debt for debt exchange offers of distressed firms in the 1980s swap payment-in-kind (PIK) debt to public debt holders. Thus, the distressed firm's ability to generate cash flow sufficient to service its debt is not a concern, at least for several years. Moreover, given the use of PIK debt in exchange offers, an exchange offer conveys information about firm value through the priority of the claims offered rather than through the firm's ability to generate cash flow to meet its debt service.

Regardless of the type of debt security offered, one might argue that the capital market would respond favorably to a debt for debt offer because it indicated that management believes the firm can support this level of debt. This would imply that the capital market would also respond favorably to a reorganization of private debt where the bank accepts new debt rather than stock. However, we find exactly the opposite occurs.

A second motivation for a debt for debt offer hinges on the fact that in many debt for debt offers, the new claims are senior to the existing claims. Roe (1987), Gertner and Scharfstein (1991), and Coffee (1990) have argued that offering senior claims is a way of expropriating bondholders. When senior claims are offered, bondholders face a kind of prisoners' dilemma. If they don't tender, their bonds decline in value as the tendering bondholders jump priority. If they tender they must accept a senior bond with a lower face value than that of their original bond. In contrast, when equity is offered for debt, a holdout problem is created because as bondholders tender their bonds for stock the untendered bonds increase in value. Thus, it may be argued that bondholder wealth expropriations in debt for debt offers lead to the observed stockholder gains.

Whether offering senior claims is expropriative or not is an empirical issue. The expropriation argument implies that the bondholders are worse off with a senior debt for junior debt exchange and one would expect to see a decline in bond prices on the announcement of the offer. However, we find a positive return to bondholders on the announcement of offers that involve an increase in priority. While these tests are not exhaustive, they indicate that senior debt for junior debt offers may not be as coercive as many legal scholars have indicated.

RECONTRACTING WITH PRIVATE DEBT HOLDERS

It is generally assumed that private lenders are well informed about the true value of the firm. This may be due to more intense monitoring on the part of private lenders or perhaps access to information about deposit flows. If private lenders are well informed they should be indifferent to the composition of the offer so long as it is fairly priced.[3] However, it is important to note that the acceptance of equity on the part of private lenders indicates that at least an equity offering is feasible in the following sense. Suppose the firm has $10 in face value of debt, where $5 in face value is held by a well informed bank and the other $5 is held by public bondholders. For simplicity assume that the two debt claims are of equal priority. If the bank takes equity in exchange for its debt, the public debt becomes the most senior claim on the firm. If the value of the firm is $8 and the bank takes all the firm's equity in exchange for its debt, it has accepted new paper worth $3 in exchange for an equal priority claim on a firm worth $8. The public debt claim would benefit from the reorganization. Clearly the bank would only consider accepting equity for its claim if it believed the firm was worth at least $10. Therefore, there should be some positive information in an equity offer.

Because of the subsidy to public debt associated with the equity for private debt offer outlined above, shareholders would prefer to offer private lenders senior or secured debt in a restructuring. Suppose that the firm is equally likely to be worth $6 or $12 after the restructuring depending on the success of a new product. The debt claims would be worth either $3 or $5 with an expected value of $4. Equity could offer the bank new debt with a face value of $4 that is senior to the public debt. With this type of offer the bank is as well off and equity has lowered the face value of the firm's debt outstanding from $10 to $9. Equity and the bank form a coalition to dilute the public debt claims. This suggests that senior debt offers should be more predominate in private debt renegotiations.

While public debt expropriation may be a strong motive for offering senior debt to private lenders, both public and private debt contracts frequently contain covenants that restrict the issuance of senior claims unless approved by debt holders. In this case, the firm will be forced to issue equity unless the other classes of debt are willing to subordinate their claims. The other classes of debt will only accept subordination if the firm's prospects are sufficiently bad. The intuition is that the poorer the firm's prospects, the more private lenders will be willing to scale down their existing claims in exchange for a senior claim, since their reservation value is what they receive if the firm files. The more their claims are scaled down the less adverse the impact of subordination on the other classes of debt. Thus, the worse the firm's prospects the more likely other debt holders will accept subordination.

This argument suggests that management will only offer equity to private lenders and private lenders will only accept equity when management and private lenders have favorable information about the firm's prospects. Thus, in contrast to exchange offers involving public debt, private lenders' acceptance of equity is predicted to convey favorable information.

DATA AND SAMPLE SELECTION

To examine empirically the valuation effects of restructurings we assembled a sample of financially distressed firms that announced exchange offers involving publicly traded debt and/or restructurings of private debt claims during the period from 1980 through 1987. The sample was constructed a little differently than the sample of Gilson, John, and Lang (1990). Our firms were identified through a key word search using the Dow Jones News Retrieval Service and the Standard and Poor's Corporate News Service. The key words used in the search are *debt restructuring, financial restructuring,* and *exchange offer*. Firms identified in this search were included in our sample if the firm's common stock traded on the NYSE or AMEX 200 days prior to the announced transaction, the proposed transaction altered the priority of the original claim, and the firm is in financial distress. A firm was determined to be in financial distress if *The Wall Street Journal* article describing the transaction indicates that the purpose of the transaction was to remedy a preexisting default or an anticipated default on a debt contract. Information on the nature of the restructuring comes from the Moody's Manual and *The Wall Street Journal*.

We define a transaction as priority reducing if the existing loan or debt contract is replaced by one that provides creditors stock or warrants in exchange for some reduction in principal and there is no increase in the priority of the remaining debt claims. The 1983 exchange offer by Allis Chalmers in which the holders of the firm's 5.1% debentures were offered stock is an example of a priority reducing transaction. In contrast, a transaction is classified as priority increasing if claim holders are offered a more senior claim. The 1983 exchange offer made by Tiger International in which it offered holders of its 8 ⅝% subordinated debt a new senior debt claim is an example of a priority increasing transaction.

Based on these selection criteria we identified 54 public exchange offers and private debt negotiations. Summary statistics for the sample are provided in Table 4–1. The sample is about evenly split between public and private debt restructurings and between priority increasing and priority decreasing transactions. Note that while the number of firms filing for bankruptcy is higher for the public exchange offers the likelihood of bankruptcy does not appear to be related to the composition of the offer.

Table 4–1 contains only the transactions in which there was a change in priority. A natural question is what proportion of all restructurings include a change in priority. Only one exchange offer involving public debt was excluded. A total of 42 private debt restructurings were excluded. These involved changes in the terms of the loan agreement and in some cases the bank taking equity but no reduction in the principal value.

Most of the priority increasing exchange offers appear to have been made under the 3(a)9 exemption from registration. In addition most involved the issuance of a senior claim that pays interest in common stock or cash at the company's option. The pay-in-kind feature implies that a senior debt offering has a similar impact on the firms' cash flow obligations as swapping stock. However, the priority of the claims in bankruptcy are very different.

Several of the priority increasing transactions involve issuing a more

TABLE 4–1
Summary of Restructuring Terms for a Sample of 54 Public Debt and Bank Restructuring by Financially Distressed Firms Involving the Issuance of Equity or an Alteration in the Priority of Debt Claims

	Number	Percent of Total	Number Bankrupt[a]
A. Public Debt Exchange Offers			
1. Bondholders Offered Senior Claim[b]	13	52%	5
2. Bondholders Offered Junior Securities[c]	12	48%	4
B. Bank Loan Restructurings			
1. Bank Offered Senior Claim	13	44%	3
2. Bank Offered Junior Claims (Stock or Warrants)	16	55%	1

[a] Number bankrupt refers to the number of firms filing for bankruptcy protection within two years of the exchange offer or bank loan restructuring.
[b] A senior claim is defined as a claim with a higher priority than the debt sought in the exchange.
[c] Junior securities refer to common stock, preferred stock, or warrants. These transactions involve common or preferred stock for debt exchanges or combinations of debt and stock for debt exchanges in which the debt offered does not have a higher priority than the debt sought.

senior but lower face value claim. In these transactions it is unclear whether the priority of the debt actually increased in the sense that the tendering bondholders would receive higher payoffs in bankruptcy. However, the face value of the senior claims offered average 82% of the face value of the claims sought. Moreover, in all cases the face value of the senior claims exceeds the market value of the claims sought. The market value of claims sought equals 52% of face value.

One might conjecture that the success of the public exchange offer may depend on the composition of the offer. In particular, if the purpose of offering senior claims is to resolve a holdout problem one would expect to see higher tendering rates for offers that involve the issuance of senior claims. We obtained information on the outcome of these offers from *The Wall Street Journal* and the Moody's Manual. Surprisingly, the percent of outstanding bonds tendered for the new compensation is about the same for priority increasing and priority decreasing exchange offers: 69.5% for the priority increasing transaction versus 67.5% for the other transactions. It is tempting to say that these numbers suggest that hold out problems are not an important impediment to restructuring. However, it may be the case that firms with diffuse bondholders issue senior claims and firms with concentrated bond ownership and hence a smaller holdout problem choose to offer equity.

EMPIRICAL TESTS

The primary empirical implication of the discussion so far is that the valuation effects of a restructuring will depend on the composition of securities offered and the identity of the lender. We analyze this issue by examining common stock returns around the announcement of each type of transaction. In particular, we use the standard event study methodology to calculate average abnormal or market adjusted returns for the two days around the announcement.[4]

These results are reported in Table 4–2. Panel A contains the results for public exchange offers. Notice that consistent with the information story we find a positive and significant stock price reaction associated with exchange offers in which bondholders are offered senior claims. In contrast, when bondholders are offered stock we find a negative and statistically significant stock price reaction. Moreover the difference in returns is significant both economically and statistically (13.1% over 2 days).

TABLE 4-2

Average Two-Day Prediction Errors on Announcement of 54 Public Debt and Bank Loan Restructurings Involving the Issuance of Equity or an Alteration in the Priority of Debt Claims

	APE (z-Statistic)	Sample Size	Percent Positive
A. Public Debt Exchanges			
1. Bondholders Offered Senior Claims[a]	7.305% (3.372)	13	84%
2. Bondholders Offered Junior Claims[b]	-5.783% (-4.138)	12	8%
Difference (z-Statistic)	13.088% (5.011)		

	APE (z-Statistic)	Sample Size	Percent Positive	Difference (z-Statistic)
B. Bank Loan Restructures				
1. Bank Offered Senior or Secured Position[a]	-1.809% (-.267)	16	46%	9.11% (4.039)
2. Bank Offered Junior Claims[b]	5.66% (3.350)	13	81%	-11.84% (5.78)
Difference (z-Statistic)	-7.069% (2.41)			

[a] A restructuring is classified as one offering a senior claim if bondholders (bank) are offered debt with a higher priority than the debt sought in the exchange.

[b] An exchange is classified as one offering junior claims if bondholders (bank) are offered common stock, preferred stock, or warrants, or a combination of stock or warrants and debt in which the debt offered does not have a higher priority than the debt sought.

Recall that management will only offer equity to informed private lenders and private lenders will only accept equity if the firm's prospects are favorable. Note that in contrast to public exchange offers in private restructurings we find a positive share price reaction associated with the issuance of junior claims. In addition we find a slight negative price reaction associated with the issuance of senior claims. Finally, for the purpose of comparison, for the 42 private debt restructurings in which there was no priority change we find an average abnormal return of 1.38%, which is significantly different from the average return for transactions in which the bank takes a senior position.

Comparing the price reaction of public to private debt restructurings we find significant differences in the average stock price reaction based on the identity of the lender. Notice that for priority increasing transactions the price reaction is significantly smaller for the private restructurings. In contrast for the transactions involving the issuance of junior claims the price reaction is significantly larger for transactions involving private lenders.

ALTERNATIVE EXPLANATIONS

While the results reported in Table 4–2 are consistent with the idea that the composition of the offer provides outsiders with information about the value of the firm, there are several alternative explanations for these results. One explanation for the positive share price reaction associated with offering bondholders senior claims is that these offers are expropriative, leading to a wealth transfer from bondholders to stockholders. The idea is that by offering bondholders a senior claim that is worth less than the value of their present claim the firm can force bondholders to tender even though it is in their collective interest to reject the offer. If a single bondholder doesn't tender he/she is left with a junior claim that is worth less. Thus tendering is the better of two bad choices. Moreover, Roe (1987) and Coffee (1990) have argued that covenants prohibiting subordination provide little protection since exit consent requirements can be used to tie tendering with voting for removal of the covenant.

If bondholder expropriation explains the positive stock price reaction to public offers involving senior or secured debt then one would expect these offers to adversely affect the value of outstanding subordinated debt. In contrast the information-based story predicts that the bond values will not be adversely affected by the offer. To examine this issue we collected bond prices for 17 of the 25 firms involved in exchange offers where data were available. Ten of these firms were involved in priority increasing transactions. The average abnormal bond return on announcement for the entire sample of exchange offers is 1.59 percent (not different from zero). More important, the average abnormal bond return for the priority increasing transactions is positive (=1.58%). This result does not suggest that the positive stock price performance results from bondholder expropriation.

A second explanation for the positive share price reaction associated with offering bondholders senior claims is one based on enhanced monitoring. The share price reactions associated with the bank taking a junior position are uniformly positive. This may be explained as a reaction to the possibility that the bank will more intensely monitor the firm, and that the bank and shareholders' interests are more closely aligned. This explanation is observationally equivalent to the one that we present in the paper. Indeed, this argument is not inconsistent with the one that we present. In other words, the bank will permit its position to be subordinated and take a more active role in monitoring if, as we argue, it views the firm's prospects favorably.

SUMMARY AND CONCLUSION

We present a model that illustrates how the composition of exchange offers made by financially distressed firms conveys information about the value of the firm. The model also demonstrates why the valuation effects of restructurings depend on the identity of the lender involved. Specifically, we show that in exchange offers involving public debt, offering junior claims results in a downward revaluation of the firm. In contrast, offering equity to informed private lenders results in an upward revaluation.

Our empirical analysis of 54 restructurings by financially distressed firms provides results consistent with the predictions of our model. For example, when private lenders are offered equity, we find a positive average share price reaction of 5.66%. In contrast, when public debt is offered equity, we find a –5.78% average abnormal return to equity. Our results provide further evidence consistent with the hypothesis that private lenders have information about firm value that is not available to public securities holders.

NOTES

1. Brown (1989) discusses the role of bankruptcy law in overcoming such holdout problems.
2. This argument is developed in more detail in Giammarino (1989).
3. It has been argued that regulated lenders prefer debt for debt swaps because as long as the principal is maintained, the value of the lender's claim remains the same from the standpoint of the regulator.
4. The two-day standardized prediction error is calculated the same way as in Mikkelson and Partch (1986).

REFERENCES

D. Brown, 1989, "Claimholder Incentive Conflicts in Reorganization: The Role of Bankruptcy Law," *Review of Financial Studies, 2:* 109–23.

J. Coffee, 1990, "Coercive Debt Tender Offers: The Problem of Distorted Choice Revisited," unpublished manuscript, Columbia University School of Law.

R. Gertner and D. Scharfstein, 1991, "A Theory of Workouts and The Effects of Reorganization Law," *Journal of Finance, 46:* 1189–1222.

R. Giammarino, 1989, "The Resolution of Financial Distress," *Review of Financial Studies, 2:* 25–47.

S. Gilson, K. John, and L. Lang, 1990, "Troubled Debt Restructurings: An Empirical Study of Private Reorganization of Firms in Default," forthcoming *Journal of Financial Economics.*

W. Mikkelson and M. Partch, 1986, "Valuation Effects of Security Offerings and the Issuance Process," *Journal of Financial Economics, 15:* 31–56.

M. Roe, 1987, "The Voting Prohibition in Bond Workouts," *Yale Law Review, 97:* 232–79.

CHAPTER 5

MANAGING A DISTRESSED FIRM

Gerald P. Buccino

THE KEY LBO ASSUMPTIONS

Buccino & Associates has worked on over a dozen middle market LBOs in the past twelve months. Some engagements have been classic turnaround assignments; others have, in essence, been the last stage of due diligence prior to the commencement of restructuring negotiations. Normally, in a due diligence assignment, we attempt to answer two questions: "Does the business plan make sense?" and "Can the management team realize the plan's bottom line?" In these abnormal times, the restructuring due diligence answers two other questions: "Can the cash flow of the business be improved in a meaningful way?" and "Is the business viable?"

We often begin such due diligence engagement by reviewing the "blue book" which documented the transaction and its assumptions at funding. Translating investment banking and legal language into plain English, the key LBO assumptions regarding the fundamentals of the business can be summarized as follows:

A.   The company is "undermanaged."

   1. The corporation's overhead can be substantially reduced.

   2. G&A efficiencies, together with other efficiencies, will not affect

---

Gerald P. Buccino is President of Buccino & Associates, Inc.

the operations of the business.

3. Net sales and gross margins can be increased simultaneously.
   a. Sales increases will be double digit.
   b. New terms for vendors will contribute to increased margins.
   c. Inventories can be managed downward. JIT is the watchword.
   d. Management will be energized with an equity stake to effect change.

B.   Assets will be sold to reduce LBO-incurred debt.

1. Quick dispositions will take place at high prices.

2. The core business will not be disturbed.

C.   Nothing substantially bad will happen to:

1. The economy;

2. The company's customers;

3. The company's key employees;

4. The company's banker/lender.

D.   The exit strategy is sound.

1. In 3–5 years, a willing buyer can be found.

2. This buyer will be able to raise even more debt to acquire the business.

3. The pricing mechanism will be no less than the EBIT multiples used to value the company when initially acquired.

BUSINESS FAILURES IN HISTORICAL CONTEXT

Since 1980, business failures nationwide have increased almost fivefold, from almost 12,000 to over 60,000 in 1990, as reported by Dun & Bradstreet. Not only have the number of failures increased dramatically, the average liability of each failure has jumped from almost $400,000 to over $1,000,000 in 1990, an increase of over 150 percent. Though these statistics are startling enough, the real significance is that the failure rate per 10,000 is greater now than it was during the Great Depression. And none of these statistics include the first two stages of LBO restructurings described above.

Dun & Bradstreet lists a large number of causes of business failure; economic factors, management experience and declining sales are included. While it is possible for a business to suffer losses at the hands of natural catastrophes, government regulation, or similar occurrences, common to every turnaround is our belief that companies involved in such a situation are there as a result of (mis)management. In turnarounds, management is the single-most important ingredient in an organization, even though it does not show up on the balance sheet.

A. Historical Data

1. Business Failures Defined:

    Businesses which have ceased operations following assignment or bankruptcy; ceased operations with losses to creditors; voluntarily withdrew *leaving unpaid debts; involved in court actions,* i.e., reorganization or receivership, or voluntarily *compromised with creditors.*

2. Business Discontinuances Defined:

    Businesses that cease operations for reasons of loss of capital, inadequate profits, ill health of owner(s), retirement of owner(s), *without loss to creditors.*

3. Business Failures by Decade
1930s	177,357
1940s	59,223
1950s	111,190
1960s	133,906
1970s	93,062
1980s	424,294

4. Business Failures—1980s
1980	11,742
1981	16,794
1982	24,908
1983	31,334
1984	52,078
1985	57,253
1986	61,616

1987 61,111
1988 57,097
1989 50,361
Preliminary 1990 60,432

5. Business Failure Rate per 10,000 by Decade
   1930–39 ....86 per 10,000
   1940–49 ....26 per 10,000
   1950–59 ....42 per 10,000
   1960–69 ....52 per 10,000
   1970–79 ....36 per 10,000
   1980–89 ....91 per 10,000
   1990 ....75 per 10,000

6. Liabilities Defined:
   Liabilities at the time of failure including all accounts and notes payable, all obligations (secured or unsecured) held by banks, suppliers, or the government.

7. Average Liabilities per Failure by Decade
   1930–39 ....$ 22,900
   1940–49   31,000
   1950–59   41,100
   1960–69   92,300
   1970–79   296,000
   1980–89   599,000
   1990 1,059,771

8. Business Failures, by Industry—1989 versus 1990

	_1989_	_1990_
Services	13,679	17,673
Retail Trade	11,120	12,826
Construction	7,120	8,072
Wholesale Trades	3,687	4,376
Manufacturing	3,933	4,709
Finance/Insurance	2,932	3,881
Transportation/Utilities	2,115	2,610
Agriculture, Forestry, and Fishing	1,540	1,727
Unclassified	3,884	4,177
Mining	351	381
Totals	50,361	60,432

9. Business Failures, by City—1988–1990

	1988	*1989*	*1990*
Houston	1,287	885	1,034
Dallas	911	663	716
New York	719	124	704
Denver	612	439	522
Austin	672	367	515
San Diego	543	224	478
San Antonio	598	368	474
Los Angeles	582	484	463
Miami	545	400	452
Oklahoma City	130	349	425

10. Business Failures by Age of Business

	1989	*1990*
Three Years or less	31.4%	28.6%
Five Years or less	49.8	46.5
Six to Ten Years	24.3	25.4
Over Ten Years	25.9	28.1

11. Causes of Business Failures—1990

Economic Factors	47.4%
Finance	38.4
Management Experience	7.1
Neglect	3.4
Disaster	1.6
Strategy	1.1
Fraud	1.0

12. Causes of Business Failures

1990—Economic Factors

Industry weakness	22.2%
Insufficient profits	21.6
Inadequate sales	2.3
Not competitive	0.7
Poor growth prospects	0.3
Poor location	0.2
Inventory difficulties	0.1
High interest rates	0.0

13. Causes of Business Failures

1990—Finance
    Insufficient capital 14.5%
    Heavy operating expenses 13.5
    Burdensome institutional debt 10.4

14. Causes of Business Failures

1990—Management
    Lack of business knowledge 5.1%
    Lack of line experience 1.3
    Lack of management experience 0.7

B. Current LBO Problems

From 1980 through 1989, more than $235 billion in LBO transactions were completed, with EBIT multiples rising from barely 6× to more than 15×. While many of the middle market LBOs involved companies which had been established for many decades, the financial structure created by the LBO confronted the underlying business with a crisis from the outset: in a large number of instances, the company could not meet its debt service without immediately taking dramatic steps. In our view, such middle market LBOs should have failure rates similar to new businesses in the first five years of their existence—historically, the years of greatest risk.

Would anyone be surprised to note that retailing topped the category of most transactions completed (number of deals) in each year during the period 1986–1989? And it follows that the most spectacular failures have occurred in this market segment. Is retailing an old maid at the restructuring dance? Our suspicion is that the dance floor will soon become very crowded.

An Associated Press release of August 26, 1990, quoted the chief economist of Moody's Investors Services Inc. in reporting that in the first seven months of the year, 32 high-yield issuers defaulted, for an annualized rate of 5.8 percent. If maintained, the article noted, it would be the highest rate since the collapse of the Penn Central Railroad accounted for a 10.9 percent default rate in 1970. Moody's John Lonski concluded, "I don't think we've passed the bottom yet in all likelihood, especially for highly leveraged firms that depend on discretionary income."

Where did all the troubled deals come from?

C. LBO History

In a leveraged buyout, a company is purchased by a group, which, through the use of mostly borrowed funds, acquires all of the outstanding stock or the assets of the target company. The investment group consists of either an individual or a group which sometimes includes management, institutions, and investment bankers.

Typically, the borrowed funds are collateralized by the firm's assets, with mezzanine debt, junk bonds, or equity securities being issued to bridge the gap between the value of the company's assets and the purchase price. In asset-based lending jargon, this was often called "financing the airball" for good reason. In larger LBOs, the senior bank debt often accounted for 50–55 percent of the financing. The mezzanine debt and/or junk bonds provided 40–45 percent, and equity comprises the remaining 5–10 percent.

Initially, the dramatic increase in debt is scheduled to be reduced through the selling-off of divisions or assets, and the debt service is to be met through increased revenues and decreased expenses through cost containment measures.

LBOs known as "bootstraps" have been an accepted financing acquisition technique for over 30 years. In the early years, asset-based lenders were the only ones interested in bootstraps. They typically occurred in manufacturing and distribution companies—those able to benefit from inflationary pressures on prices. In these industries, as inflation rose, the value of the company's underlying assets rose. These bootstraps were typically financed by management teams at book value or less.

LBOs gathered momentum in the late 1970s, when commercial banks began buying commercial finance companies. Larger deals were completed due to the increased capital available to the finance companies and the availability of mezzanine financing through the commercial banks. The entrance of venture capitalists and wealthy investors further sparked interest in LBOs.

The surge of LBOs in the 1980s was created by several factors. First, there was a gradual change in the way acquiring businesses determined the value of a company. Proponents of leveraged financing advanced the notion that the incurring of debt was beneficial.

They claimed that a company's earning power, not capital structure, determined both its market value and cost of funds. This emphasis on the evaluation of earnings potential and other financial aspects of the company further widened the gap between asset value and purchase price. With cash flow stability now being the key to financing and debt service for these new LBOs, it is no surprise the name "cash flow LBOs" evolved in the early '80s.

A second important factor in the LBO boom was the emergence of investment banks into the LBO arena. This was a direct result of the change in determining the market value of a company. The cash flow LBO naturally became a product for the corporate finance departments of investment banks whose expertise lay in business evaluations and fairness opinions. Because of the lucrative fees attached to the deals, fierce competition developed among the investment banks, further driving up the purchase price for the LBO deals. And when prices became such that "bridge" loans were necessary to complete an LBO, it was but a small step for the investment banks to move from intermediary to principal, providing the "bridge" on a temporary basis.

Another important factor in the LBO surge was the general strength of the economy. The bull market of the 1980s raised stock prices dramatically (recall the Dow was at 750 in August of 1982). These stock price rises did not exclude LBO companies, so the market prices for these companies rose dramatically as well. Interest rates during this boom were also low, further keeping debt financing cheap.

The use of junk bonds kept the LBO craze flourishing. Drexel discovered a market for these higher risk, higher yielding bonds by taking the private placement concept and creating a liquid after-market for the bonds. In the late 1970s, it was very difficult to finance a less than A-rated credit in most markets. In the '80s, triple C credits were financed through junk bonds fairly easily. These bonds were often positioned below the senior debt, but above the public bondholders and stockholders. Both the deductibility of interest under the Code and the perceived "discipline" of debt schedules added to the attractiveness of junk bonds for investors.

The ability and willingness of commercial banks to lend money into LBOs was also very important in the development of the LBO market. Fueled by the recovery and strength of the economy, and facing little regulatory demand for restraint, the banks showed a willingness to lend into this risky arena.

D. Some Early Concerns

A relatively early study by Steven Kaplan, a professor at the University of Chicago's School of Business, showed that of 76 management-led buyouts between 1980 and 1986, even the successful, capable management teams over-estimated the projected increase in sales and operating earnings by 10–20%. There might be further problems, Kaplan found, in the projected earnings multiples of companies and assets that the LBO management team planned to achieve when they were to be spun off.

There was further concern that the vast amount of new debt taken on by target companies would force them to emphasize short-term goals to the detriment of long-term growth. Spending on research and development and often-needed capital improvements to remain globally competitive could be affected.

We also witnessed more and more LBOs by companies in cyclical industries. More often than not, their buyout was completed when the company was at the high point in its cycle and the numbers looked their best. As the cycle shifted back down, bankers and investors were in for a rude awakening.

A similar scenario has developed in industries which require frequent innovation and development (e.g., the toy industry). When an LBO occurs in these companies, the company is often unable to implement the required changes due to its highly leveraged position.

E. The Interest Coverage Time Bomb

Concern for interest burden on the macro level has been voiced for some time. In a *New York Times* article, dated May 9, 1989, it was reported that corporate cash flow (defined as profits plus depreciation) for the first quarter of 1989 was at its lowest since 1980. Merrill Lynch estimated that interest payments consumed 22.4% of available cash flow in the third quarter of 1990. This percentage has only been higher, since World War II, in 1974 and December of 1985, when only 17% of bank loans were below investment-grade credit; in June of 1988, it had risen to 55%.

Forbes in an article entitled "Tick, Tick, Tick" in its August 6, 1990, issue asked the disturbing question, "How did so many Wall Street firms justify their clients' issuing junk bonds in amounts and at interest rates that the clients' earnings could not cover?" Detailing fifty companies which issued in the aggregate more than $18 billion in junk which initially paid no current interest, most projected current cash flow levels insufficient to cover debt service after the trigger date. The article quoted Drexel's former head of high yield research, now at Salomon Brothers: "The aim of issuing bonds beyond company's ability to service them was 'to finance companies so they could grow into their capital structure.'" Whether they were PIKs, split coupons, or resets, they represent a time bomb about to explode in the economic marketplace. Needless to say, Wall Street sees it differently, as an opportunity to profit from failure.

CRISIS MANAGEMENT IN THE LBO CONTEXT

A.   General Description

An LBO is a turnaround by definition. Crisis managers are experienced in turnarounds and workouts, and are accustomed to dealing with the problems confronting lender and debtor. Their independence and objectivity permit them to reach the core of the situation quickly and to make and recommend the hard decisions necessary to bring stability and recovery.

In a crisis situation, the time to move from analysis to action is sometimes hours. There is no time for task forces, committees, or lengthy written reports. Crisis managers have relatively little time with which to work and are often further handicapped by having only about 70 percent of the data needed. But, because of situational experience, they are able to ensure dramatic results quickly and economically.

1. Business Failures Traceable to Management
   a. Cannot cope with crisis
   b. Emotional
   c. Cannot make "hard" decisions
   d. Often authorized business decisions which now must be done
   e. Exhausted
   f. Analysis paralysis

2. The "Crisis Manager"
   a. Independent

      b. Objective

      c. Experienced

      d. Can make hard decisions

      e. No ties to the company

         i. financial

         ii. emotional

      f. No ownership

      g. Analysis to decision quickly

  3. History of the "Crisis Manager"

      a. Profit improvement consultants

         i. 1960s

         ii. 1970s

      b. Turnaround consultants of the 1980s

         i. national firms

         ii. broad backgrounds

B.   Three Stages of a Turnaround

When it becomes apparent that a company is in serious financial trouble, one or more of the company's lenders/investors often recommend that the company retain crisis managers to put the firm back on the path to profitability and positive cash flow. Although there are no set milestones which accompany a business's slide toward insolvency, turnarounds can be tracked through three very different, but definite, stages: crisis, stability, and recovery.

  1. Crisis Stage

Crisis managers are usually called in at the crisis stage. The company has sustained heavy losses, is running out of cash, is running out of time, and cannot cope with the situation any longer. In extreme cases these losses have occurred for years. The crisis stage is characterized by several elements:

- Cash-out is greater than cash-in, and the company, running out of cash, has exhausted additional outside sources of capital.
- The lender or principal bank has indicated concern over the company's inability to move forward and is beginning to place greater restrictions on the flow of cash against the already leveraged asset base established under the loan agreement.
- Unsecured creditors have lowered lines of credit or have put the

company on credit hold. Suppliers will not ship product or raw materials. If a company has no materials to manufacture its product, it has nothing to sell and thus cannot generate cash flow, further complicating the problem.

- Key employees are leaving. Customers are not the only individuals who are worried about their future. As managers leave, the company is further weakened. This further compounds the crisis because sound management is an important contribution to a successful turnaround.

The crisis manager immediately assesses the situation on a cash-flow basis. In a turnaround, the traditional profit-and-loss statement is ignored. That has less meaning than the daily cash-in/cash-out of the company, because the firm is living day to day.

On the first day of engagement, within the first hour if possible, the "crisis break-even point" is determined because it is necessary to cost-contain the client immediately. Although there are acceptable, traditional methods for determining break-even, we do not have time for complex formulas. We must determine what expenses we can cut, how quickly we can cut them, and to what extent. In a turnaround, the expense is narrowly defined as any cash outlay, regardless of the time period it covers. For example, if a yearly insurance premium is due next week, the expense is not spread over 12 months, but is considered a cash outlay during the crisis period. Spreading expenses is bookkeeping, not crisis cash-flow management.

Cash must be conserved. Each expense must be questioned with, "Can you live without this?" If the answer is yes, it must be removed.

After the cash-out side of the business has been examined and dealt with, a quick look is taken at cash-in. An effort is made to collect accounts receivable far faster than the company has been, and this includes offering discounts.

Any slow-moving inventory is sold, even at a loss, to get cash. Excess equipment is sold and excess capacity is leased or sold. The ordering of the "to do" list is an imperative turnaround step after the analysis of the cash-in/cash-out picture. This ordering is based on a two-tiered time element.

Certain steps can be implemented quickly, such as reducing salaries, shutting down product lines and divisions, and selling equipment. Other actions take more time. Selling a division, for example, can take months and requires third-party cooperation. In mature industries, such as heavy equipment, steel, or the farm implement industry, extraordinary measures are sometimes necessary regarding long-standing labor agreements to achieve cash flow break-even or positive cash flow.

After a crisis management team has successfully completed its initial undertakings, a company will show signs of reaching a break-even point. When a company reaches this point, the move to stability is near.

a. Definition: Cash-out exceeds cash-in
b. Profile of Troubled Company
   i. Heavy losses
   ii. Reduced working capital
   iii. Credit problems
   iv. Quality problems
   v. Losing market share
   vi. Losing key employees
   vii. Management cannot cope with climate
   viii. Cash depletion
c. Symptoms
   i. Lender(s) concerns
   ii. Advance rates against collateral are reduced
   iii. Suppliers will not ship
   iv. Customers reduce dependence and seek other sources
   v. Capital improvements delayed
   vi. Maintenance is deferred
   vii. Low morale
d. Solutions and Approach to Deal with Crisis
   i. Immediate *action* required
     Interview management
     Change span of control
     Identify problems
     Establish cash flow controls
     Contain cost
     Downsize
     Redeploy assets
   ii. Contain crisis stage to 30–60 days

    e. Actions
       i. Cash break-even is determined for 90-day period
      ii. Equalize cash-in with cash-out
     iii. Develop turnaround plan

2. Stability Stage

The move from crisis to stability usually takes about 90 days, depending on how advanced the company's position was when the crisis managers arrived. Stability comes when cash-in equals cash-out. There is still no long-range planning—no acquisitions, no product development, no raises. There is no recovery, and certainly no turnaround, but the company is no longer slipping, and can now start to pay past-due creditors and meet other obligations.

With the debtor at the stability stage of a turnaround, it is possible to project the recovery stage with monthly profit and loss, balance sheet, and cash flow projections for the next year or two. Each turnaround step should be identified, together with monthly and annual contributions to improved cash flow. If these monitoring steps in this stage prove successful, the company will begin to recover.

a. Definition: Cash-in equals cash-out
b. Actions and Solutions
       i. Asset redeployment
      ii. Restructuring
     iii. Divestitures
     iv. Capital—debt and/or equity
      v. 90-day duration

3. Recovery Stage

In the recovery stage, cash-in is greater than cash-out. There is no expansion yet, and a wise debtor will operate for at least one or two years as though the company were still in a crisis environment. The firm can now concentrate on improving its product, its management team, and its plants.

a. Definition: Cash-in exceeds cash-out.
b. Actions and Solutions
       i. Fine-tune turnaround
      ii. Monitor business trends
     iii. Monitor management

        iv. Long-term capital improvement
        v. Prevent return to "business as usual"
        vi. Monthly monitoring

C. Crisis Break-Even

    1. Data Collection
      a. Obtain 90-day backlog
      b. Estimate monthly sales
      c. Calculate material costs
      d. Calculate all expenses on monthly basis
         Exclude depreciation
         Add balance sheet payments
         • Term note amortization
         • Mortgage payments
         • Equipment notes

    2. Calculation

      Divide "all cash expenses" by reciprocal of material costs to sales percentage (100% minus the percentage of material cost to sales)

D. Cost Containment

    1. List *all* expenses in detail
      a. Reduce people costs
        • Management—span of control changes
        • Labor
          √ Rates
          √ Productivity
      b. Reduce non-people costs
        • Eliminate all costs and expenses not required to produce the product or deliver the service
        • Automobiles
        • Perks, i.e., clubs, etc.

E. Downsizing

    1. Current Assets
      a. Redeployment of inventories
        • Excess stocks
        • Terminate unprofitable product lines

  b. Calculate turnovers

2. Fixed Assets
   a. Redeploy excess equipment
   b. Redeploy excess real estate

3. Divestitures
   a. Negotiate sale of division(s)
   b. Negotiate sale of company, if applicable

PART TWO

BANKRUPTCY COSTS AND DISTRESSED FIRM VALUES

CHAPTER 6

BANKRUPTCY COSTS AND
VIOLATION OF CLAIMS PRIORITY

Lawrence A. Weiss

INTRODUCTION

This chapter examines the resolution of bankruptcy for 37 New York Stock
Exchange (NYSE) and American Stock Exchange (Amex) firms that filed
petitions under the 1979 Bankruptcy Code (hereafter "the Code") between
November 1979 and December 1986. New evidence is provided on the
direct costs of bankruptcy and the violation of priority of claims.

The costs of bankruptcy have long been viewed as a potential determinant of the pricing of a firm's debt and of its capital structure. Bankruptcy
costs are direct and indirect. Direct costs encompass the legal and administrative fees, including the costs of lawyers, accountants, and other professionals involved in the bankruptcy filing. Indirect costs include a wide range
of unobservable opportunity costs.

Prior studies report direct costs of bankruptcy ranging from 4 to 25

Lawrence A. Weiss is an assistant professor of accounting at A. B. Freeman School of Business, Tulane
University.

He has received many comments and suggestions from his colleagues at Tulane University, in seminars
at Harvard and Southern Methodist University, and at the Conference on "The Structure and Governance
of Enterprise" held at Harvard Business School. He is especially grateful to Carliss Baldwin, Michael
Jensen, Robert Kaplan, Howard Stevenson, Richard Ruback, and Karen Wruck. He would also like to
thank David Harvey, Elizabeth Tashjian, Ronald Lease, Jevons Lee, Jean-François Manzoni, John
McConnell, John Page, Ralph Sanders, Eugene Salorio, Barry Schachter, and Sundararaman Thiagarajan.

percent. This study is the first to examine direct costs under the new Code and to cover a broad range of industrial firms. For the firms examined, direct costs average 3.1 percent of the book value of debt plus the market value of equity at the end of the fiscal year preceding bankruptcy. As Warner (1977a) demonstrates, such small direct costs have virtually no impact on the pricing of claims and capital structure prior to bankruptcy.

The firm's cost of capital and its capital structure may also be affected if priority of claims is not maintained in bankruptcy. Priority of claims is violated when senior claimants are not fully satisfied before junior claimants receive any payment. Economists have long argued that bankruptcy courts mistakenly fail to uphold priority of claims. Meckling (1977) asserts, "The courts, the Congress, and the Securities and Exchange Commission refuse to relegate stockholders to the status of purely residual claimants." Miller (1977) states, "Permitting stockholders to claim court protection and thereby retain control of a corporation in default would amount to giving them a call option at the expense of the creditors."

Priority of claims is violated for 29 of the 37 firms studied, consistent with prior research.[1] The breakdown of priority occurs primarily between the unsecured creditors and equity holders and among the unsecured creditors. Priority of claims holds for only one of the 18 cases filed in New York, but for 7 of the 19 cases filed outside New York. Secured creditors' contracts are upheld in 34 of the 37 cases.

The following section reviews the sample of bankrupt firms. This is followed by sections on the costs of bankruptcy and violations of priority, and a brief conclusion. Explanations of the Code and its impact on recontracting within bankruptcy appear throughout the paper.

SAMPLE SELECTION

On October 1, 1979, passage of a new bankruptcy code substantially revised bankruptcy administration. The number of businesses filing for bankruptcy skyrocketed from 44,000 in 1980 to 81,000 in 1986. I compile a list of NYSE and Amex firms declaring bankruptcy from November 1979 to December 1986 by examining (1) the Securities and Exchange Commission's (SEC's) annual report to Congress, which contains a listing of all presentations by the SEC to bankruptcy courts; (2) *The Wall Street Journal Index* (*WSJI*) listing of all firms that declare bankruptcy; (3) *Compustat*'s Research File listing of all firms that are dropped because of bankruptcy filings; and (4) firms listed as suspended or deleted from the Center for Research in Security Prices (CRSP) tapes. Financial institutions are excluded because they are not subject to the standard provisions of the bankruptcy code. The initial sample consists of 99 firms that filed for bankruptcy in 32 jurisdictions—an average of 14 firms per year, or 0.7% of the roughly 2,000 firms listed on the two exchanges. Table 6–1 classifies the sample by stock exchange, the year bankruptcy was filed, and the location of filing.

Court documents are available only at the federal court where the bankruptcy petition is filed, and there may be several jurisdictions or districts within an individual state. Because of budget and time constraints, data

TABLE 6–1
NYSE and Amex Industrial Firm Bankruptcies, by Year and Jurisdiction—November 1979–December 1986

Exchange	Year							Total
	1980	1981	1982	1983	1984	1985	1986	
NYSE	2	2	9	1	3	6	3	26
Amex	9[a]	9	10	9	13	10	13	73
Total	11	11	19	10	16	16	16	99

Jurisdiction	Number	Jurisdiction	Number
Alabama	1	Minnesota	2
Arizona	1	Missouri	1
California	8	New Jersey	3
Colorado	4	New York	30
Delaware	1	Ohio	6
Florida	5	Oklahoma	2
Georgia	1	Pennsylvania	3
Illinois	5	Texas	12
Indiana	2	Utah	1
Iowa	1	Virginia	2
Massachusetts	4	Washington, D.C.	1
Maryland	1	West Virginia	1
Michigan	1		
		Total	99

[a] Only one firm in the sample filed between the time the new bankruptcy code went into effect, on November 15, 1979, and the end of 1979. The firm, Tenna Corporation, filed on December 5, 1979, and is included in the total for 1980.

collection was confined to the following seven jurisdictions:

    Central District of California
    Southern District of Florida
    Northern District of Illinois
    District of Massachusetts
    Northern District of Michigan
    Southern District of New York
    Northern District of Ohio

These locations have a total of 51 filings, or just over half of the initial sample. An additional 14 firms were excluded because their bankruptcies were not resolved by May 31, 1989; their data were being used by a bankruptcy judge and hence were not available for study; or their data had been removed from the court to an archive.

The final sample contains 37 firms. Information on each is provided in Appendix A to Chapter 6. The average time from filing of the bankruptcy petition to resolution is 2.5 years, with a standard deviation of 1.4 years. The shortest bankruptcy took just under 8 months; the longest, more than 8.3 years. This is much less than the time required by Warner's (1977a) sample of railroad firms, which has a mean of 12.5 years. The shortest bankruptcy in Warner's sample took four years to complete. Franks and Torous (1989) report an average of 4.5 years for 16 firms filing before the Code took effect, and 2.7 years for 14 firms filing afterward (of these 14 firms, 10 are part of the current study).

The sample firms' ratio of debt to total assets is 77%, which is 50% higher than the 51% average for all nonbankrupt firms listed on *Compustat* between 1979 and 1986. For a complete discussion of the difference in financial ratios between bankrupt and nonbankrupt firms, see Weiss (1990).

THE DIRECT COSTS OF BANKRUPTCY

The direct costs of bankruptcy are the legal and other professional and administrative fees associated with the bankruptcy filing; they represent the measurable part of all bankruptcy costs. The indirect bankruptcy costs are the unmeasurable opportunity costs, including

1. Lost sales and a decline in the value of inventory. Customers may become concerned about assured supply or warranties. In certain industries (e.g., financial services) these costs can completely destroy the value of the firm (e.g., Drexel Burnham Lambert).

2. Increased operating costs. Firms may lose key employees or have to pay more to keep them from abandoning a troubled firm. Suppliers may refuse to ship on favorable credit terms, and the firm's cost of capital may increase.
3. A reduction in the firm's competitiveness. Management attention is focused on the bankruptcy, increasing the firm's vulnerability to competitors.

The Code requires the court to list all fees paid, making possible an examination of the direct costs of bankruptcy. Judges often include a summary of the fees paid in their final order on fees. Unfortunately, access to these data is not guaranteed: the court record may be incomplete or unavailable; many courts interpret the rules concerning preparation of the list as mandatory only when a trustee has been appointed; and other courts simply do not prepare the list because of staffing constraints. Despite these limitations, data for this part of the study are available for 31 of the 37 firms examined.

Three measures are used to assess the magnitude of the direct costs of bankruptcy: (1) market value of equity, (2) book value of debt plus the market value of equity, and (3) book value of total assets, all measured at the fiscal year-end prior to the bankruptcy filing. The market value of debt is not used because only a few firms in the sample (mainly the larger ones) had any publicly traded debt, and publicly traded debt represents only a fraction of total debt. Book value of debt is readily available and is used as a proxy for the market value of equity. The book value of total assets is used to ensure the results are not overstated by the large drop in market value of equity that occurs before the bankruptcy filing, as demonstrated by Weiss (1989).

On average, the direct costs of bankruptcy are 20.6% of the market value of equity (ranging from 2.0% to 63.6%), 3.1% of the book value of debt plus the market value of equity (ranging from 1.0% to 6.6%), and 2.8% of the book value of total assets (ranging from 0.9% to 7.0%). Table 6–2 displays data on the costs of bankruptcy as a percentage of different measures of firm size, a comparison with prior research, and the relationship between firm size and costs.

Both Stanley and Girth (1971) and Ang, Chua, and McConnell (1982) use much smaller firms on average and find much higher fees as a percentage of firm size (25% and 7.5% respectively) than those of Warner (1977a) and this study. Ang et al. (1982) also find the scale effect hypothesized by Warner (1977a). This study does not find a similar effect. From the results of the ordinary-least-squares regressions presented in Table 6–2, the direct costs of bankruptcy appear highly correlated with total assets but do not fit a concave function (i.e., costs as a percentage of total assets do not decline as the size of the firm increases). The difference between Warner's finding and the findings of this study may be explained by noting that Warner's cases are heavily regulated railroads with many more classes of debt than the cases in this study; the changes in the bankruptcy rules and new financing techniques may also play a part.

TABLE 6–2
Direct Costs of Bankruptcy and Their Relationship to Firm Size

Summary Statistics:

	Mean	*Median*	*High*	*Low*	*Number Firms*	*Time Period*
Current Study:						
Costs[a] / MVE[b]	20.6%	16.7%	63.6%	2.0%	31	1980–1986
Costs / D&E[c]	3.1%	2.6%	6.6%	1.0%	31	1980–1986
Costs / TA[d]	2.8%	2.5%	7.0%	0.9%	31	1980–1986
Prior Studies:						
Stanley&Girth[e]	24.9%	n/a	n/a	n/a	90	1964
Warner[f]	4.0%	n/a	9.8%	1.1%	11	1933–1955
Ang et al.[g]	7.5%	1.7%	100%	0.01%	55	1963–1978

Regression Results:

$$\text{Costs} = \underset{(0.1)}{-0.9} + \underset{(11.9)}{0.028 \times \text{TA}} \qquad R^2 = 0.83$$
$$\text{Number firms} = 31$$

$$\text{Costs} = \underset{(0.5)}{2.6} + \underset{(1.0)}{0.005 \times \text{TA}} + \underset{(5.5)}{0.00001 \times \text{TA}^2} \qquad R^2 = 0.90$$
$$\text{Number firms} = 31$$

(*t*-statistics in parentheses.)

[a] Costs = legal and other professional fees associated with the bankruptcy filing.
[b] MVE = market value of equity at the fiscal year-end prior to the bankruptcy filing.
[c] D&E = book value of debt plus the market value of equity at the fiscal year-end prior to bankruptcy.
[d] TA = book value of total assets at the fiscal year-end prior to bankruptcy.
[e] Stanley and Girth (1971) use total assets (book value) from the last financial statement filed prior to bankruptcy.
[f] Warner (1977a) uses market value of debt + market value of equity immediately prior to bankruptcy.
[g] Ang et al. (1982) use the liquidated value of the firms at the end of the bankruptcy process.

PRIORITY OF CLAIMS UNDER THE NEW BANKRUPTCY CODE

This section is divided into four subsections. The first describes how the Code allows priority of claims to be violated. The second presents the method used to investigate violation of priority of claims. The third analyzes the frequency of overall deviations from strict priority of claims, and the fourth examines patterns of deviations.

The New Bankruptcy Code and Priority of Claims

Two types of bankruptcy filings are available to corporations: Chapter 7 and Chapter 11 (these titles refer to chapters of the bankruptcy code). Chapter 7 provides for the orderly liquidation of a firm's assets by a court-appointed trustee, and payment to claimants in order of priority is always maintained. Only 2 of the 37 firms examined filed under Chapter 7. Chapter 11 provides for reorganization of a firm. Participants in a Chapter 11 filing must approve a plan of reorganization, leaving room for negotiations among the various parties and for violation of priority of claims. In a Chapter 11 bankruptcy the debtor's management operates the firm and works out the reorganization or liquidation unless an interested party can prove management is either incompetent or has committed a fraud, and then the court appoints a trustee. Bankruptcy terminology for management's remaining in control is "debtor-in-possession." The law also provides for conversion from one type of filing to the other. Thirty of the 35 firms examined that filed under Chapter 11 were reorganized, and 5 were liquidated. One firm, Cook United, initially filed under Chapter 11 and within a year of its reorganization filed under Chapter 7.[2]

Bankruptcy law alters the creditors' contracts by giving junior creditors and residual claimants the ability to delay the final resolution and to force the firm to incur additional costs—powers junior claimants do not have outside bankruptcy. The first restriction on creditors is the difficulty they face in presenting their own plan for reorganization. The debtor-in-possession or trustee is automatically given a 120-day period to formulate a plan, and during that period no one else can propose a plan. The bankruptcy judge can extend the initial exclusive period, and often does. A creditor can propose a reorganization plan if the exclusive period is over and a debtor's plan has not been accepted within 180 days of the bankruptcy filing. Creditors, unlike debtors, must support their evaluation of the firm's asset values by means of appraisals, a costly process. All this makes creditor plans for reorganization rare (there was only one case among the 37 firms examined by this study).

The voting procedure further restricts creditors. Unimpaired creditors—those who receive payment in full with interest or who have had their claims reinstated in full with any defaults cured—do not vote on the reorganization plan. All other creditors are deemed impaired. A majority in number and at least two-thirds by amount owed to the creditors who vote in each class of impaired creditors must approve the reorganization plan before it can be confirmed by the bankruptcy court. Equity holders must also approve the plan by a two-thirds majority, giving them leverage over creditors.

If the bankruptcy judge does not believe agreement will be reached, he or she can force acceptance of a plan by using a procedure termed a cram-down. Before applying a cram-down the judge must order costly valuation hearings to ensure that any dissenting class of impaired creditors receives at least as much under the plan as it would in a liquidation. The prospect of such hearings is often enough to make creditors approve a plan in which their priority is violated.

Creditors may also be willing to allow a violation of priority to obtain their proceeds in a timely manner. Initially, the trustee, management, or an outside consultant ascertains whether a class of claimants is impaired or unimpaired, and whether each class will receive more from the plan than it would if the firm were liquidated. Any claimant who disagrees with any part of the plan is allowed to argue that position in court, further delaying the resolution. If the bankruptcy judge, after hearing arguments from dissenting claimants, determines that the estimated values and status of claimants contained in the plan are unfair (the judge decides what constitutes fairness), a vote cannot be taken, and a new plan must be prepared.

Secured creditors, whose collateral is worth less than the principal plus accrued interest, may give up part of their claims to avoid losing additional interest. Bankruptcy law has traditionally been vague about whether secured creditors receive interest on their claims over the bankruptcy period. The Supreme Court has recently clarified this issue in *United Savings Association of Texas* v. *Timbers of Inwood Forest Associates, Ltd.* According to an opinion written by Justice Scalia, secured creditors receive interest on their loans at the rate specified up to the value of their secured interest. Once that maximum is reached, no further interest is allowed.

Secured creditors may also be willing to violate priority to reduce the risk of decay in the value of their collateral. Bankruptcy law instructs the trustee or debtor-in-possession to protect the interests of the secured credi-tors so they will receive, at a minimum, what they would have received if the bankruptcy petition had not been filed. Unfortunately, providing such protection is not an exact science. Numerous cases have tried to determine what constitutes adequate protection for secured creditors but the answer is still vague.

Finally, tax laws influence bankruptcy resolutions. Under current tax law, cooperation of the equity holders is essential to maintain the corporate shell and preserve tax loss carryforwards. Equity holders may receive a distribution of funds from an insolvent firm in return for their cooperation.

Method

To determine the extent to which priority of claims is violated, this study uses the figures reported in the reorganization plan confirmed by the bank-ruptcy court. The plan must designate and describe each class of creditors, say how each class will be treated, and provide adequate means of imple-mentation. It specifies the cash and securities each class will receive, when it will receive them, and whether a particular class is unimpaired or impaired. The plan also says whether a given class will receive at least as much as it would receive in a liquidation. Most plans do not formally set out the estimated amount each class would receive in a liquidation but merely state that the plan provides more.

Most plans report the percentage of claims to be repaid to each class, and where this number is not provided it usually can be calculated from other court documents. When the reorganization plan contains estimated market values for securities given to creditors in compensation for their claims, I use those market values; otherwise, I use the face value of the securities. If the final distribution is contingent on future events and the plan presents a range of possible values for what each group of claimants will receive, this study uses the median value. Whenever possible, I spoke with the lawyers involved about the negotiation process.[3]

The reorganization plan indicates whether priority of claims is violated when agreement among the parties is reached. Gains or losses because of unpredictable changes in the company and the economy between the time of the agreement and final payment to the creditors are separate from whether the claimants agree to uphold or violate priority. Further, most of the reorga-nized firms' securities do not trade in a public market and the only evidence of their value is the value provided in the reorganization plan.

The values in the plan are confirmed by an impartial judge, who is central to the decision-making process and has the benefit of all the evidence and testimony. Use of these values has several limitations, however. First, the amount of a creditor's claim is the amount allowed by the court, and the court accepts management valuations unless a creditor establishes a different value through costly hearings. Second, the court may understate the amount of the claim by failing to provide appropriate interest. Finally, the court will accept management's view of whether creditors are impaired, and creditors may decide it is not worth the effort and expense to prove otherwise. According to the lawyers interviewed, it is rare for a reorganization plan to incorrectly classify a group as unimpaired. Despite these limitations, the plan of reorganization remains the most timely and objective source of information about what each claimant expects to receive from the bankruptcy process.

For the purposes of this study, priority of claims is upheld when, according to the reorganization plan, secured creditors are satisfied first, then various grades of subordinated debt, and equity holders last. I also determine whether priority of claims is violated for both secured and unsecured creditors or for unsecured creditors alone.

Deviations from Strict Priority of Claims

Strict priority of claims is violated in 78% ($^{29}\!/_{37}$) of the cases. Table 6–3 summarizes violation of priority for the firms examined, and Appendix A to Chapter 6 provides additional information on each firm, with a brief summary of its bankruptcy filing.

Shareholders received nothing in only seven (19%) cases—five cases in which priority of claims is maintained and two cases in which it is violated. In three (8%) cases, shareholders received a cash settlement ranging from $233,000 to $1,500,000, or $0.03 to $0.10 per share. In 15 (41%) cases, shareholders received a small portion (25% or less), and in 12 (32%) cases, shareholders received a substantial portion (more than 25%) of the equity of the reorganized company.

In six cases, shareholders retain virtually all (99% or 100%) of the reorganized firm's equity. In two of these cases (Bobbie Brooks and Branch Industries) the firms' fortunes recovered sufficiently to repay the creditors fully. In two other cases (Lionel Corporation and Salant Corporation) the secured creditors are paid fully and the unsecured creditors receive over 90% of their claims. In the remaining two cases (Imperial Industries and

TABLE 6–3
Summary of Claims[a] Resolution for 37 Exchange-Listed Firms Filing for Bankruptcy Between 1980–1986

	Percentage or Description of Claims Paid to		
Firm Name	Secured Creditors	Unsecured Creditors	Equity Holders
Priority held			
Bobbie Brooks	100%	100%	100%
Branch Inds	100%	100%	100%
Brody (B) St	100%	51%	0
Flanigan's	100%	100%	0
Garland Corp	100%	100%	> 0
Ronco Telepd	100%	Balance	0
Tenna Corp	74%	0	0
U.N.A. Corp	100%	1 CS[b] per $1 claim	0
Priority violated for unsecured creditors only			
AM Intl	100%	94%	47%
Anglo Energy	100%	58%	25%
Beker Inds	100%	< 20%	38%
Berry Inds	100%	Cash & PS[c]	60%
Combustion	100%	From 49% to 82%	$316,000
Cook United	100%	93% of CS	7%
Goldblatt	100%	24%	53%
HRT Inds	100%	75%	25%
Imperial Inds	100%	37%	100%
KDT Inds	100%	36%	$1,500,000
Lionel Corp	100%	Up to 100%	100%
Manville	100%	Up to 100%	5%
McLouth Stl	100%	90% of CS	10%
Morton Cos	100%	33%	$233,000
Penn-Dixie	100%	45% of claim+50% CS	50%
Revere Copper	100%	65%	77%
Richton Intl	100%	60%	100%
Salant Corp	100%	97%	99%
Saxon Inds	100%	From 33% to 49%	PS
Seatrain Ln	100%	CS	Warrants
Shelter Res	100%	5% of CS	5%
Spencer Cos	100%	30% of claim+60% CS	17%
Tacoma Boat	100%	96% of CS	4%
Towle Mfg	100%	60%	7%
White Motor	100%	51%	10%
Wickes Cos	100%	From 59% to 92%	19%
Priority violated for secured creditors			
Crompton Co	85%	20%	0
Evans Pds	76%	87%	0
Stevcoknit	From 37–77%	33%	12%

[a] Priority of claims holds when secured creditors are satisfied first; then various grades of subordinated debt; and equity holders last.
[b] CS = Common stock
[c] PS = Preferred stock

Richton International) the secured creditors are paid in full, but the unsecured creditors receive only 37% and 60% of their claims respectively. One lawyer argued, "Shareholders were tossed a bone, crumbs off the table, to get the deal done and save any tax-loss carryforwards." It still remains a clear breach of the debt contracts for shareholders to retain anything when creditors are not fully paid.

Within the various classes of unsecured creditors (e.g., senior and subordinated debentures), strict priority of claims rarely holds. For example, in the White Motor reorganization plan, the senior unsecured bondholders received 61% of their claims; the senior unsecured creditors, 55%; the general unsecured creditors, 51%; and the subordinated unsecured bondholders, 14%. The lawyers interviewed either did not know or were unwilling to provide any insight into why the senior unsecured creditors were not fully repaid before the junior unsecured creditors received anything. The lawyers agreed that priority was largely ignored within the group of unsecured creditors but insisted the consensual settlements made everyone better off.

Priority of claims for the secured creditors is maintained in 92% ($^{34}/_{37}$) of the cases in my sample. The three cases of violation are Crompton, Evans Products, and Stevcoknit. Crompton, a textile mill that produced corduroy and velveteen products, filed for bankruptcy in New York on October 23, 1984; its reorganization plan was confirmed 1,423 days later, on September 15, 1988. Priority broke down because of litigation by the unsecured creditors against the secured creditors. The unsecured creditors argued that the secured creditors were not entitled to payment from the surplus in Crompton's pension plan and Crompton's holdings of export-related commercial paper. After prolonged negotiations, a settlement was reached whereby the secured creditors received 85% of their claims, the unsecured creditors received 20% of their claims, and the equity holders received nothing.

Evans Products, a supplier of building materials and home mortgages, was the first major case in which a creditor-initiated reorganization plan was confirmed by the court. Evans Products filed for bankruptcy in Florida on March 11, 1985, and its reorganization plan was confirmed 478 days later, on July 2, 1986. Lawyers involved with the case assert that secured creditors decided to go forward with the effort and expense of a creditor plan when they were unable to reach a settlement with Victor Posner, a Miami-based reclusive acquirer and buyout specialist, who held a controlling interest in the company's stock. The plan froze out the equity holders, but to ensure its success, the secured creditors offered the unsecured creditors a sweetened deal. Unsecured creditors actually received a higher percentage of their claims (87%) than secured creditors (76%); their total claims, however, amounted to less than one fourth of the secured creditors' claims. Many of the lawyers involved now believe that the secured creditors gave the unsecured creditors substantially more than was necessary to get the deal done.

Stevcoknit, a producer of knitted fabrics for sportswear, filed for bankruptcy in New York on November 16, 1981, and had its reorganization plan confirmed 424 days later, on January 18, 1983. According to lawyers involved in the case, the secured creditors accepted 57% of their claims because the market value of their collateral had fallen far below the value of their claims. Unsecured creditors received 33% of their claims, and equity holders were given an 11% share of the reorganized firm.

How Priority of Claims Is Violated

Discussions with lawyers indicate that two factors, firm size and location of bankruptcy, are important in predicting whether priority of claims will be violated. According to the lawyers, the larger, more complicated bankruptcies present more opportunities for equity holders and small groups of unsecured creditors to extract concessions from other creditors. Anecdotal evidence supports the lawyers' claim that different jurisdictions treat debtors differently, and debtors respond by filing in the district they think will be most favorable to them. A February 6, 1989, *Miami Review* article describes how the Southern District of Florida's chief bankruptcy judge is much tougher on debtors than judges in some other districts.

Bankruptcy falls under federal law and, except for certain state-law issues, should be uniform across the United States. To receive bankruptcy protection, a firm must file with the bankruptcy clerk in the United States court district where the firm had its principal place of business for the preceding 180 days, or where most of the firm's assets are located, or in a district that facilitates negotiations with creditors. Corporations with assets and operations in several jurisdictions have some latitude in deciding where to file.

Figures 6–1 and 6–2 illustrate, by firm size and location of bankruptcy filing, violation of priority of claims in the sample of bankruptcy resolutions. The larger firms and firms filing in New York are more likely to violate strict priority of claims. Strict priority is violated for all 20 firms having total assets over $100 million, 14 of which filed in New York. For firms with less than $100 million in assets, strict priority holds in eight of 17 cases, only

FIGURE 6–1
Priority of Claims and Bankruptcy Resolutions, by Firm Size

Number of Firms (N = 37)

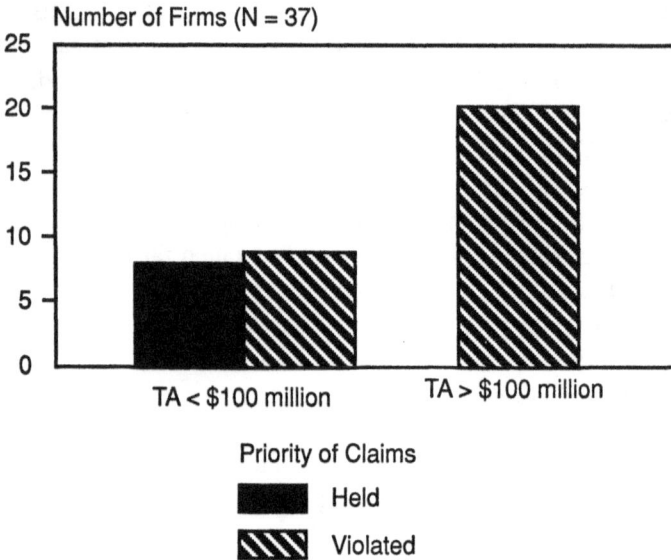

TA = book value of total assets at the fiscal year end prior to bankruptcy

one of which filed in New York. There appears to be a strong link between firm size and priority of claims.

The results on the treatment of creditors in different locations are less clear. Lawyers in both Florida and Illinois assert that judges and lawyers in their jurisdictions are more willing to freeze out equity holders than are judges and lawyers in New York. One lawyer interviewed about the Evans Products case stressed how New York lawyers involved in the case were willing to give the equity holders a sizeable piece of the reorganized company. Only after the New York lawyers became frustrated by Victor Posner's demands were the Florida lawyers able to persuade their New York colleagues to propose a creditor plan and freeze out the shareholders. Priority of claims held for only one of the 18 cases filed in New York, and in that case the firm's fortunes turned around during the bankruptcy so there were sufficient funds to repay all creditors in full. Priority of claims held for seven of the 19 cases filed outside of New York.

Lawyers in New York acknowledge the high number of filings there and the favorable treatment of debtors. They say there is less fighting among

FIGURE 6–2
Priority of Claims and Bankruptcy Resolutions, by Location of Filing

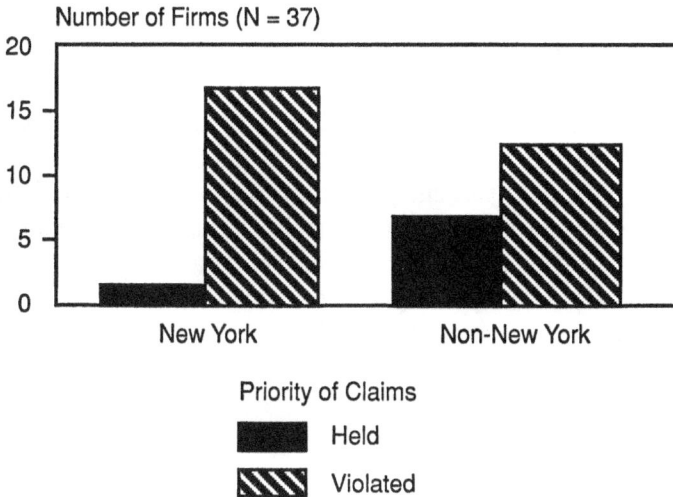

Number of Firms (N = 37)

Priority of Claims
Held
Violated

parties in New York because of the greater sophistication of the creditors, the professional actions of the bankruptcy lawyers, and a willingness by creditors to compromise priority to settle the case quickly. No evidence, however, supports the lawyers' assertion that New York cases are resolved faster than cases filed in other parts of the country. The average time needed to resolve the New York cases is 974 days, compared with 850 days for the cases outside New York. The New York cases take longer than non-New York cases whether the cases examined are large or small (total assets of more or less than $100 million before the bankruptcy filing).[4]

The process of assigning judges to New York cases does not appear to be random as claimed by the court. As of August 1990, five bankruptcy judges (Abram, Buschman, Blackshear, Brozman, and Lifland) preside over all bankruptcy cases in the Southern District of New York. Of the 18 New York cases examined, six (33%) were handled by the Honorable Burtan R. Lifland; the Honorable Prudence Abram and the Honorable Edward J. Ryan each handled three cases (17% each); the Honorable Howard C. Buschman III and the Honorable John J. Galgay each handled two cases (11% each); and the Honorable Cornelius Blackshear and the Honorable Joel Lewittes each handled one case. Too few cases were examined in each of the other districts for me to determine whether any particular judge dominated the larger cases filed there.

All the non-New York cases were filed in the jurisdiction where the firm's headquarters or principal place of business was located. Six of the 18 firms filing in New York (Beker, HRT, KDT, Manville, Tacoma Boat-building, and Towle) did not have their headquarters or principal place of business in New York. The available evidence is insufficient to show why New York attracts a disproportionate share of the bankruptcy filings. New York may have more lawyers and judges with the expertise to work on large cases; it may be a convenient location for the firm and its creditors; it may happen to be the location of the firm's headquarters and/or principal place of business; or New York judges may have different biases than judges in other districts. Whatever the reason, equity holders appear to receive better treatment in New York.

CONCLUSION

Bankruptcy represents a legal framework for recontracting when various interested parties cannot reach an accord following a firm's default on a debt contract. If either the direct costs of resolving a bankruptcy are high or creditors cannot be confident that priority of claims will be honored, creditors will require somewhat higher interest rates, raising the cost of corporate borrowing and altering the firm's capital structure. This paper presents new evidence on the direct costs of bankruptcy and the degree to which priority of claims is violated in bankruptcy proceedings of NYSE and Amex firms.

I find lower direct costs of bankruptcy than previous researchers, a finding that may be explained by differences in the size and type of firms studied, the methods used to calculate firm size, the time periods considered, or changes in the bankruptcy law. On average, direct costs of bankruptcy are 3.1% of the book value of debt plus the market value of equity at the fiscal year-end prior to the bankruptcy filing, with a range from 1% to 6.6%. These low direct costs, as demonstrated by Warner (1977a), will have little or no impact on the pricing of claims prior to bankruptcy.

Priority of claims is violated in 29 of the 37 cases examined. Unsecured creditors are frequently denied priority over both equity holders and lower-ranked unsecured creditors. Secured creditors receive their full claim in all but three of the 37 cases. Creditors are likely to demand higher interest rates to compensate them for the violation of priority of claims that occurs in bankruptcy.

Equity holders of larger firms appear to fare better than their smaller-firm counterparts, probably because junior claimants are better able to delay the resolution in the larger, more complex cases, and to threaten the loss of tax loss carryforwards. The disproportionate number of cases in which equity holders in New York receive some compensation in violation of priority of claims, combined with the disproportionate number of cases filed there, seems to indicate that debtors may shop around for the best place to file—and correctly choose New York. Of all the cases where priority of claims held, only one was in New York. Because New York is the headquarters for a majority of the larger firms studied, however, it may simply be a proxy for firm size and complexity of capital structure.

Olson (1965) declares that "unless the number of individuals in a group is quite small, or unless there is coercion or some other special device to make individuals act in their common interest, rational, self-interested individuals will not act to achieve their common or group interest." Bankruptcy is a social institution designed to deal with just such a collective-action problem by: (1) preserving the value of the firm and preventing premature liquidation after the firm has defaulted on its debt, and (2) enforcing creditors' rights. Bankruptcy has always sought to prevent creditors from racing to grab assets; however, there is no reason it could not deliver the reorganized firm into the hands of the creditors and keep the stockholders in their place as residual claimants. A lack of belief in markets may be the underlying reason the law perceives it necessary to allow violation of priority of claims.

NOTES

1. See Franks and Torous (1989) and Eberhart, Moore, and Roenfeldt (1990).
2. The second bankruptcy filing was outside the period under study, so only the resolution of the Chapter 11 filing is included here.
3. Fourteen lawyers were contacted, half by phone and half in person. Most of the lawyers had worked on several of the cases under study.
4. The larger New York cases (average total assets of $457 million) spend an average of 988 days from the filing of the bankruptcy petition to the court's confirmation of a reorganization plan, compared with 873 days for non-New York cases (average total assets of $691 million). The smaller New York cases (average total assets of $61 million) average 925 days in bankruptcy, compared with 818 days for non-New York cases (average total assets of $34 million).

REFERENCES

Altman, Edward I., 1984, "A further empirical investigation of the bankruptcy cost question," *Journal of Finance 39*, 1067–89.

Ang, James S., and Jess H. Chua, 1980, "Coalitions, the me-first rule, and the liquidation decision," *Bell Journal of Economics 11*, 355–59.

Ang, James S.; Jess H. Chua; and John J. McConnell, 1982, "The administrative costs of corporate bankruptcy: A note," *Journal of Finance 37*, 219–26.

Baird, Douglas G., and Thomas H. Jackson, 1984, "Corporate reorganizations and the treatment of diverse ownership interests: A comment on adequate protection of secured creditors in bankruptcy," *University of Chicago Law Review 51*, 97–130.

Baldwin, Carliss Y., and Scott P. Mason, 1983, "The resolution of claims in financial distress: The case of Massey Ferguson," *Journal of Finance 38*, 505–23.

Barrickman, Ray E., 1979, *Business Failure: Causes, Remedies, and Cures* (University Press of America, Washington, D.C.).

Cohn, Daniel C., 1982, "Subordinated claims: Their classification and voting under chapter 11 of the bankruptcy code," *American Bankruptcy Law Journal 56*, 293–324.

Demsetz, Harold, 1972, "When does the rule of liability matter?" *Journal of Legal Studies 1*, 13–28.

Dodd, Peter, and Richard Leftwich, 1980, "The market for corporate charters: 'Unhealthy competition' versus federal regulation," *Journal of Business 53*, 259–83.

Easterbrook, Frank H., and Daniel R. Fischel, 1982, "Corporate control transactions," *Yale Law Journal 91*, 698–737.

Eberhart, Allan C.; William T. Moore; and Rodney L. Roenfeldt, 1990, "Security pricing and deviations from the absolute priority rule in bankruptcy proceedings," *Journal of Finance 45*, 1457–70.

Franks, Julian R., and Walter N. Torous, 1989, "An empirical investigation of U.S. firms in reorganization," *Journal of Finance 44*, 747–79.

Jackson, Thomas H., 1986, "Of liquidation, continuation, and delay: An analysis of bankruptcy policy and nonbankruptcy rules," *American Bankruptcy Law Journal 60*, 399–428.

Jackson, Thomas H., 1987, *The Logic and Limits of Bankruptcy Law* (Harvard University Press, Cambridge, MA).

Jensen, Michael C., and William H. Meckling, 1976, "Theory of the firm: Managerial behavior, agency costs and ownership structure," *Journal of Financial Economics 3*, 305–60.

Lopucki, Lynn M., 1983, "The debtor in full control—Systems failure under Chapter 11 of the bankruptcy code?" *American Bankruptcy Law Journal 57*,

99–126, 247–73.

Meckling, William H., 1977, "Financial markets, default, and bankruptcy: The role of the state," *Law and Contemporary Problems 41*, 13–38.

Meckling, William H., et al., 1977, "Discussion—The economics of bankruptcy reform," *Law and Contemporary Problems 41*, 124–77.

Miller, Milton H., 1977, "The wealth transfers of bankruptcy: Some illustrative examples," *Law and Contemporary Problems 41*, 39–46.

Nelson, Philip B., 1981, *Corporation in Crisis: Behavioral Observations for Bankruptcy Policy* (Praeger, New York).

Nimmer, Raymond T., 1983, "Executory contracts in bankruptcy: Protecting the fundamental terms of the bargain," *University of Colorado Law Review 54*, 507–54.

Olson, Mancur, 1965, *The Logic of Collective Action* (Harvard University Press, Cambridge, MA).

Raiffa, Howard, 1982, *The Art and Science of Negotiation* (Harvard University Press, Cambridge, MA).

Rodriguez, Eva M., 1989, "Fleeing southern justice," *Miami Review 63* (February 6), 164.

Roe, Mark J., 1983, "Bankruptcy and debt: A new model for corporate reorganization," *Columbia Law Review 83*, 527–602.

Smith, Clifford W., Jr., and Jerold B. Warner, 1979, "On financial contracting—An analysis of bond covenants," *Journal of Financial Economics 7*, 117–61.

Stanley, David T., and Marjorie Girth, 1971, *Bankruptcy: Problems, Process, Reform* (Brookings Institution, Washington, D.C.).

Warner, Jerold B., 1977a, "Bankruptcy costs: Some evidence," *Journal of Finance 32*, 337–47.

Warner, Jerold B., 1977b, "Bankruptcy and the pricing of risky debt," *Journal of Financial Economics 4*, 239–76.

Weiss, Lawrence A., 1989, "Bankruptcy: The experience of NYSE and ASE firms from 1980 to 1986," Doctoral thesis (Harvard University, Cambridge, MA).

Weiss, Lawrence A., 1990, "Bankruptcy prediction: A methodological and empirical update," Working paper (Tulane University, New Orleans, LA).

Weistart, John, C., 1977, "The costs of bankruptcy," *Law and Contemporary Problems 41*, 107–22.

White, Michelle J., 1980, "Public policy toward bankruptcy: Me-first and other priority rules," *Bell Journal of Economics 11*, 550–64.

White, Michelle J., 1983, "Bankruptcy costs and the new bankruptcy code," *Journal of Finance 38*, 477–504.

APPENDIX A TO CHAPTER 6

SUMMARY OF FIRMS EXAMINED

AM International—Business graphics equipment and systems
04/14/82, bankruptcy petition filed in Illinois; 09/11/84, plan confirmed
881 days in bankruptcy
Listed on NYSE
Direct costs of bankruptcy = $14,765,000
Total assets prior to bankruptcy = $546,213,000
Direct costs/total assets = 2.70%
Debt/total assets prior to bankruptcy = 97.5%
Priority violated for unsecured creditors—Firm reorganized.

Secured creditors received 100% of their claims. Unsecured creditors received an average of 94% of their claims. Equity holders retained 47% of the common stock of the reorganized company.

The firm had a $203 million write-down of assets, and the SEC charged Price Waterhouse and three of its partners with violating security laws. The firm blamed its bankruptcy on poor planning, sloppy management, and inadequate financing.

Anglo Energy—Oil and gas extraction
11/04/83, bankruptcy petition filed in New York; 07/14/86, plan confirmed
983 days in bankruptcy
Listed on Amex
Direct costs of bankruptcy = $9,066,000
Total assets prior to bankruptcy = $229,596,000
Direct costs/total assets = 3.94%
Debt/total assets prior to bankruptcy = 85.1%
Priority violated for unsecured creditors—Firm reorganized.

Secured creditors received 100% of their claims. Unsecured creditors received 50% of their claims in cash and notes, and 8% in common shares and warrants. Equity holders retained 25% of the common stock of the reorganized company.

The firm blamed its bankruptcy on the decline in the oil and gas business in 1982.

Beker Industries—Chemicals (concentrated phosphate)
10/21/85, bankruptcy petition filed in New York; 10/06/88, plan confirmed
1,081 days in bankruptcy

Listed on NYSE
Direct costs of bankruptcy = $5,042,000
Total assets prior to bankruptcy = $341,087,000
Direct costs/total assets = 1.57%
Debt/total assets prior to bankruptcy = 61.1%
Priority violated for unsecured creditors—Firm reorganized.
Secured creditors received 100% of their claims. Unsecured creditors re-
ceived a variety of assets (from land to different forms of equities) representing less
than 20% of their claims. Equity holders retained 38% of the reorganized firm.

The firm blamed its bankruptcy on the decline in the market price of its
principal product.

Berry Industries—Oil and gas extraction equipment and service
10/05/84, bankruptcy petition filed in California; 11/16/87, plan confirmed
1,137 days in bankruptcy
Listed on Amex
Direct costs of bankruptcy = $620,000
Total assets prior to bankruptcy = $39,608,000
Direct costs/total assets = 1.57%
Debt/total assets prior to bankruptcy = 59.2%
Priority violated for unsecured creditors—Firm reorganized.
Secured creditors received 100% of their claims. Unsecured creditors re-
ceived the balance of cash from one of the subsidiaries and a new class of preferred
stock, and could vote for two of the five members on the board of directors. Equity
holders retained their shares.

The firm blamed its bankruptcy on the decline in the oil market.

Bobbie Brooks—Manufacture sportswear and swimwear
01/15/82, bankruptcy petition filed in Ohio; 02/15/83, plan confirmed
397 days in bankruptcy
Listed on NYSE
Direct costs of bankruptcy = $1,537,000
Total assets prior to bankruptcy = $87,005,000
Direct costs/total assets = 1.76%
Debt/total assets prior to bankruptcy = 65.9%
Priority of claims held—Firm reorganized.
Secured and unsecured creditors were paid in full and equity holders retained
their interest in the company.

The firm blamed its bankruptcy on unprofitable operations.

Branch Industries—Trucking and warehousing
08/16/84, bankruptcy petition filed in New York; 03/31/88, case dismissed

1,323 days in bankruptcy
Listed on Amex
Direct costs of bankruptcy =$1,229,000
Total assets prior to bankruptcy = $52,458,000
Direct costs/total assets = 2.34%
Debt/total assets prior to bankruptcy = 86.3%
Priority of claims held—Firm reorganized.
Secured and unsecured creditors were fully paid and the company's bankruptcy petition was dismissed.

The firm blamed its bankruptcy on the increased competition and rate cutting that followed deregulation of the trucking industry.

Brody (B) Seating—Manufacture furniture
02/04/80, bankruptcy petition filed in Illinois; 01/09/81, plan confirmed
340 days in bankruptcy
Listed on Amex
Direct costs of bankruptcy = $224,000
Total assets prior to bankruptcy = $3,823,000
Direct costs/total assets = 5.85%
Debt/total assets prior to bankruptcy = 65.7%
Priority of claims held—Firm liquidated under Chapter 11.
Secured creditors received 100% of their claims. Unsecured creditors received 51% of their claims. Equity holders received nothing.

The firm blamed its bankruptcy on a general softening of the furniture market combined with increasing interest rates.

Combustion Equipment—Air pollution and agricultural equipment
10/20/80, bankruptcy petition filed in New York; 12/21/83, plan confirmed
1,157 days in bankruptcy
Listed on Amex
Direct costs of bankruptcy = $2,123,000
Total assets prior to bankruptcy = $177,991,000
Direct costs/total assets = 1.19%
Debt/total assets prior to bankruptcy = 74.4%
Priority violated for unsecured creditors—Firm reorganized.
Secured creditors received 100% of their claims. Senior unsecured creditors received cash for 82% of their claims plus stock, and subordinated creditors received 49% of their claims plus stock. Equity holders were paid $316,000.

The firm blamed its bankruptcy on cost overruns, strikes, and a failure to obtain necessary operating permits.

Cook United—General merchandise discount department stores
10/01/84, bankruptcy petition filed in Ohio; 09/30/86, plan confirmed

729 days in bankruptcy
Listed on NYSE
Direct costs of bankruptcy = $4,926,000
Total assets prior to bankruptcy = $166,161,000
Direct costs/total assets = 2.96%
Debt/total assets prior to bankruptcy = 95.5%
Priority violated for unsecured creditors—Firm reorganized.
Secured creditors received 100% of their claims. Unsecured creditors received 92% of the common stock of the new company, the union received 1%, and equity holders received 7%.

Within a year after the plan of reorganization was confirmed, the company refiled a Chapter 7 bankruptcy petition, the company was liquidated, and strict priority of claims held. The results of the first bankruptcy, where priority held for the secured creditors only, are used for this study.

The firm blamed its bankruptcy on insufficient sales and excess inventory.

Crompton Co—Textile mill (corduroy and velveteen) products
10/23/84, bankruptcy petition filed in New York; 09/15/88, plan confirmed
1,423 days in bankruptcy
Listed on Amex
Direct costs of bankruptcy = $922,000
Total assets prior to bankruptcy = $97,064,000
Direct costs/total assets = 0.94%
Debt/total assets prior to bankruptcy = 60.0%
Priority violated for secured creditors—Firm liquidated under Chapter 11.
Secured creditors received approximately 85% of their claims. Unsecured creditors received approximately 20% of their claims. Equity holders received nothing.

The firm blamed its bankruptcy on competition from Far Eastern textile producers and a weak domestic market.

Evans Products—Building materials, and home mortgages
03/11/85, bankruptcy petition filed in Florida; 07/02/86, plan confirmed
478 days in bankruptcy
Listed on NYSE
Direct costs of bankruptcy = $12,347,000
Total assets prior to bankruptcy = $803,228,000
Direct costs/total assets = 1.53%
Debt/total assets prior to bankruptcy = 86.0%
Priority violated for secured creditors—Firm reorganized.
Secured creditors received 76% of their claims. Unsecured creditors received 87% of their claims. Equity holders received nothing.

Evans was the first major case in which the creditor plan of reorganization was confirmed by the court. When the creditors and Victor Posner—who held a controlling interest in Evans—could not agree, the secured creditors decided to go forward with the expense of a creditor plan and freeze out the equity holders. To ensure success of the plan, the secured creditors offered the unsecured creditors a sweetened deal that many lawyers today believe was unnecessary.

The firm blamed its bankruptcy on the increase in interest rates that occurred after it extended fixed-rate mortgages while borrowing at rates tied to prime.

Flanigan's Enterprises—Retail liquor stores
  11/04/85, bankruptcy petition filed in Florida; 05/07/87, plan confirmed
  549 days in bankruptcy
  Listed on Amex
  Direct costs of bankruptcy = not available
  Total assets prior to bankruptcy = $26,779,000
  Direct costs/total assets = not available
  Debt/total assets prior to bankruptcy = 83.5%
  Priority of claims held—Firm liquidated.

Secured creditors received 100% of their claims. Unsecured creditors received the balance, which was estimated to be 100% of the face value of the claims but was paid over one and a half years. Equity holders received nothing.

The firm blamed its bankruptcy on significant rental increases on leases (tied to the consumer price index) and declining sales.

Garland Corp—Knitted textile products
  04/29/80, bankruptcy petition filed in Massachusetts; 12/22/80, plan confirmed
  237 days in bankruptcy
  Listed on Amex
  Direct costs of bankruptcy = $805,000
  Total assets prior to bankruptcy = $25,423,000
  Direct costs/total assets = 3.16%
  Debt/total assets prior to bankruptcy = 55.2%
  Priority of claims held—Firm liquidated.

Secured and unsecured creditors were paid in full, with funds left over for shareholders.

After management walked out, a trustee turned the company around by completing work in progress and manufacturing more goods.

The firm blamed its bankruptcy on five years of substantial losses.

Goldblatt Brothers—General merchandise department stores
  06/16/81, bankruptcy petition filed in Illinois; 10/14/83, plan confirmed
  850 days in bankruptcy

Listed on Amex
Direct costs of bankruptcy = $2,736,000
Total assets prior to bankruptcy = $67,601,000
Direct costs/total assets = 4.04%
Debt/total assets prior to bankruptcy = 85.3%
Priority violated for unsecured creditors—Firm reorganized.
Secured creditors received 100% of their claims. Unsecured creditors received 24% of their claims. Equity holders received 52.5% of the common stock of the reorganized company. The value of the equity was very low, considering that another firm received the remaining 47.5% of the common stock for providing a loan of $3 million.

The firm blamed its bankruptcy on competitive pressures, changing trends, higher operating costs, and increased interest rates.

HRT Industries—General merchandise discount department stores
11/23/83, bankruptcy filed in New York; 02/10/84, plan confirmed
444 days in bankruptcy
Listed on Amex
Direct costs of bankruptcy = $6,158,000
Total assets prior to bankruptcy = $211,146,000
Direct costs/total assets = 2.91%
Debt/total assets prior to bankruptcy = 73.5%
Priority violated for unsecured creditors—Firm reorganized.
Secured creditors received 100% of their claims. Unsecured creditors received an average of 75% of their claims (in various combinations of cash and stock). Equity holders received one new share for every four old shares.

The firm blamed its bankruptcy on declining sales caused by general economic conditions.

Imperial Industries—Stone, clay, and glass products
09/29/86, bankruptcy petition filed in Florida; 06/02/87, plan confirmed
246 days in bankruptcy
Listed on Amex
Direct costs of bankruptcy = not available
Total assets prior to bankruptcy = $19,315,000
Direct costs/total assets = not available
Debt/total assets prior to bankruptcy = 120.0%
Priority violated for unsecured creditors—Firm reorganized.
Secured creditors received 100% of their claims. Unsecured creditors received 37% of their claims. Equity holders retained their equity interest.

The firm blamed its bankruptcy on declining sales caused by general economic conditions.

KDT Industries—General merchandise discount department stores
> 08/05/82, bankruptcy petition filed in New York 03/24/84, plan confirmed
> 597 days in bankruptcy
> Listed on Amex
> Direct costs of bankruptcy = $3,460,000
> Total assets prior to bankruptcy = $239,555,000
> Direct costs/total assets = 1.44%
> Debt/total assets prior to bankruptcy = 82.9%
> *Priority violated for unsecured creditors—Firm reorganized.*

Secured creditors received 100% of their claims. Senior unsecured creditors received an initial distribution of stock plus cash for 36% of their claims and the potential for a future cash distribution of up to 17% of their claims. Subordinated unsecured creditors received similar treatment with a smaller percentage of their claims. Equity holders received Ames common stock (Ames took over KDT) worth $1.5 million and the potential for an additional distribution of up to $0.10 per share (or an additional $500,000).

The firm blamed its bankruptcy on changing consumer spending habits, competition from other chains, high interest rates, and a prolonged recession.

Lionel Corp—Retail toy and leisure products
> 02/19/82, bankruptcy petition filed in New York; 09/12/85, plan confirmed
> 1,301 days in bankruptcy
> Listed on NYSE
> Direct costs of bankruptcy = $5,466,000
> Total assets prior to bankruptcy = $221,619,000
> Direct costs/total assets = 2.40%
> Debt/total assets prior to bankruptcy = 85.1%
> *Priority violated for junior unsecured creditors—Firm reorganized.*

Secured creditors and senior unsecured creditors received 100% of their claims. General unsecured creditors received some cash and common stock. Equity holders retained their old shares and received warrants to purchase new shares.

The firm blamed its bankruptcy on high interest rates and energy costs, combined with a poor 1981 Christmas season.

Manville Corp—Asbestos products
> 08/26/82, bankruptcy petition filed in New York 12/15/85, plan confirmed
> 1,207 days in bankruptcy
> Listed on NYSE
> Direct costs of bankruptcy = $82,475,000
> Total assets prior to bankruptcy = $297,814,000
> Direct costs/total assets = 3.58%
> Debt/total assets prior to bankruptcy = 35.9%

Priority violated for unsecured creditors—Firm reorganized.

Secured creditors received 100% of their claims. Unsecured creditors received 76% of their claims in cash and debentures, and equity for the balance (essentially losing some accrued interest). Tort asbestos claimants received cash and shares valued at $2.3 to $2.6 billion. Shareholders received approximately 5% of shares of the reorganized firm.

The firm blamed its bankruptcy on thousands of product-liability lawsuits.

McLouth Steel—Steel manufacture and motor carrier

12/08/81, bankruptcy petition filed in Michigan; 12/11/84, plan confirmed

1,099 days in bankruptcy

Listed on NYSE

Direct costs of bankruptcy = not available

Total assets prior to bankruptcy = $446,085,000

Direct costs/total assets = not available

Debt/total assets prior to bankruptcy = 72.7%

Priority violated for unsecured creditors—Firm reorganized.

Secured creditors received 100% of their claims. Unsecured creditors received slightly over 90% of the common stock of the reorganized firm, with equity holders receiving the balance.

The firm blamed its bankruptcy on a dramatic rise in labor and energy costs, combined with increased foreign competition.

Morton Shoe—Manufacture and retail footwear

01/05/82, bankruptcy petition filed in Massachusetts; 08/15/83, plan confirmed

587 days in bankruptcy

Listed on Amex

Direct costs of bankruptcy = $708,000

Total assets prior to bankruptcy = $30,818,000

Direct costs/total assets = 2.32%

Debt/total assets prior to bankruptcy = 93.6%

Priority violated for unsecured creditors—Firm liquidated under Chapter 11.

Secured creditors received 100% of their claims. Unsecured creditors received an average of 33% of their claims. Equity holders received $233,000, or just under 10% of the amount paid to the unsecured creditors.

The firm blamed its bankruptcy on continuing losses.

Penn Dixie—Manufacture steel and cement

04/07/80, bankruptcy petition filed in New York; 03/04/82, plan confirmed

696 days in bankruptcy

Listed on NYSE

Direct costs of bankruptcy = $3,760,000

Total assets prior to bankruptcy = $176,728,000
Direct costs/total assets = 2.12%
Debt/total assets prior to bankruptcy = 68.7%
Priority violated for unsecured creditors—Firm reorganized.
Secured creditors received 100% of their claims. Unsecured creditors received cash for 45% of their claims and slightly less than 50% of the common stock of the reorganized firm. Equity holders received slightly over 50% of the common stock of the reorganized firm. The judge awarded the lawyers involved a 10% premium on their fees for their expeditious handling of the case.

The firm blamed its bankruptcy on the wasteful and fraudulent investments made by the firm's CEO, Jerome Castle.

Revere Copper and Brass—Manufacture metals and metal products
10/27/82, bankruptcy petition filed in New York; 07/29/85, plan confirmed
1,066 days in bankruptcy
Listed on NYSE
Direct costs of bankruptcy = $7,560,000
Total assets prior to bankruptcy = $473,756,000
Direct costs/total assets = 1.59%
Debt/total assets prior to bankruptcy = 60.2%
Priority violated for unsecured creditors—Firm reorganized.
Secured creditors received 100% of their claims. Unsecured creditors received an average of 65% of their claims (cash value). Equity holders retained their shares (diluted to 77% of total outstanding).

The firm blamed its bankruptcy on its inability to expand production and reduce the unit cost at its rolling mill and reduction plant.

Richton International—Manufacture jewelry and sportswear
03/18/80, bankruptcy petition filed in New York; 08/26/81, plan confirmed
526 days in bankruptcy
Listed on Amex
Direct costs of bankruptcy = $1,076,000
Total assets prior to bankruptcy = $53,477,000
Direct costs/total assets = 2.01%
Debt/total assets prior to bankruptcy = 50.2%
Priority violated for unsecured creditors—Firm reorganized.
Secured creditors received 100% of their claims. Unsecured creditors received 60% of their claims. Equity holders were unimpaired and retained their equity position.

The firm blamed its bankruptcy on losses in both its jewelry and sportswear businesses.

Ronco Teleproducts—Wholesale miscellaneous durable goods
02/02/84, bankruptcy petition filed in Illinois; 04/28/87, converted to Chapter 7
1,181 days in bankruptcy
Listed on Amex
Direct costs of bankruptcy = not available
Total assets prior to bankruptcy = $20,543,000
Direct costs/total assets = not available
Debt/total assets prior to bankruptcy = 70.0%
Priority of claims held—Firm liquidated under Chapter 7.
Secured creditors were fully paid, and the unsecured creditors received the balance.
The firm blamed its bankruptcy on an optimistic expansion combined with a decline in sales.

Salant Corp—Apparel and other textile products
02/22/85, bankruptcy petition filed in New York; 05/19/87, plan confirmed
816 days in bankruptcy
Listed on NYSE
Direct costs of bankruptcy = $7,003,000
Total assets prior to bankruptcy = $110,439,000
Direct costs/total assets = 6.34%
Debt/total assets prior to bankruptcy = 77.4%
Priority violated for unsecured creditors—Firm reorganized.
Secured creditors received 100% of their claims. Unsecured creditors received approximately 97% of their claims (45% in cash, 50% in debentures, and 2% in common shares). Equity holders were unimpaired except for a slight dilution of their holdings.
The firm blamed its bankruptcy on the combination of a costly failed engineering attempt to reduce manufacturing costs and a reduction in the general demand for jeans and slacks.

Saxon Industries—Paper and allied products
04/15/82, bankruptcy petition filed in New York; 03/22/85, plan confirmed
1,072 days in bankruptcy
Listed on Amex
Direct costs of bankruptcy = $14,216,000
Total assets prior to bankruptcy = $486,617,000
Direct costs/total assets = 2.90%
Debt/total assets prior to bankruptcy = 74.0%
Priority violated for unsecured creditors—Firm reorganized.

Secured creditors received 100% of their claims. Senior unsecured creditors received between 45% and 49% of their claims. General creditors received 37% of their claims. Debenture holders received 33% of their claims. Equity holders exchanged their shares for preferred shares.

The firm blamed its bankruptcy on a dramatic downturn in the oil business combined with increased costs.

Seatrain Lines—Water transportation (vessel chartering)
02/11/81, bankruptcy petition filed in New York; 03/27/87, plan confirmed
2,235 days in bankruptcy
Listed on NYSE
Direct costs of bankruptcy = $15,422,000
Total assets prior to bankruptcy = $913,414,000
Direct costs/total assets = 1.68%
Debt/total assets prior to bankruptcy = 101.4%
Priority violated for unsecured creditors—Firm reorganized.

Secured creditors received 100% of their claims. Unsecured creditors received new common shares. Equity holders received new Seatrain warrants.

The firm blamed its bankruptcy on the increase in oil prices through the 1970s, which halted construction of new vessels.

Shelter Resources—Wood buildings and consumer products
09/09/82, bankruptcy petition filed in Ohio; 07/26/85, plan confirmed
1,051 days in bankruptcy
Listed on Amex
Direct costs of bankruptcy = $2,638,000
Total assets prior to bankruptcy = $37˙728,000
Direct costs/total assets = 6.99%
Debt/total assets prior to bankruptcy = 103.3%
Priority violated for unsecured creditors—Firm reorganized.

Secured creditors received 100% of their claims. Unsecured creditors received a small amount of cash and 5% of the common stock of the reorganized firm. Equity holders received 5% of the common stock of the reorganized firm. The balance of the common stock was sold to an outsider.

The firm blamed its bankruptcy on increasing interest rates and reduced housing starts.

Spencer Companies—Manufacture and retail apparel
11/19/86, bankruptcy petition filed in Massachusetts; 11/30/88, plan confirmed
742 days in bankruptcy
Listed on Amex
Direct costs of bankruptcy = $1,789,000

Total assets prior to bankruptcy = $34,554,000
Direct costs/total assets = 5.17%
Debt/total assets prior to bankruptcy = 60.7%
Priority violated for unsecured creditors—Firm reorganized.
Secured creditors received 100% of their claims. Unsecured creditors received a cash payment for 10% of their claims and 60% of new Spencer common stock. They also received notes for 20% of their claims and warrants for the purchase of 2 million additional shares. Equity interests retained their common shares, which accounted for 17% of the total outstanding.

The firm blamed its bankruptcy on losses in businesses other than the retail sales of footwear.

Stevcoknit—Textile mill products
11/16/81, bankruptcy petition filed in New York 01/14/83, plan confirmed
424 days in bankruptcy
Listed on Amex
Direct costs of bankruptcy = $1,279,000
Total assets prior to bankruptcy = $39,297,000
Direct costs/total assets = 3.25%
Debt/total assets prior to bankruptcy = 67.0%
Priority of claims violated—Firm reorganized.
Secured creditors received between 37% and 77% of their claims. Unsecured creditors received 33% of their claims. Equity holders received 11.5% of the reorganized firm's stock. Lawyers interviewed declared that the secured creditors accepted less than 100% because the value of their collateral had fallen far below the value of their claims.

The firm blamed its bankruptcy on poor economic conditions in the textile industry.

Tacoma Boatbuilding—Ship building and repair
09/23/85, bankruptcy petition filed in New York; 08/17/87, plan confirmed
693 days in bankruptcy
Listed on Amex
Direct costs of bankruptcy = not available
Total assets prior to bankruptcy = $277,954,000
Direct costs/total assets = not available
Debt/total assets prior to bankruptcy = 103.3%
Priority violated for unsecured creditors—Firm reorganized.
Secured creditors received 100% of their claims. Unsecured creditors received 96% of new common stock. Equity holders received 4% of new common stock.

The firm blamed its bankruptcy on a ten-week strike in 1983 that caused a loss of skilled workers, disrupted schedules, and hurt efficiency, and on no new contracts in 1985.

Tenna Corp—Electronic and other electrical equipment
 12/05/79, bankruptcy petition filed in Ohio 04/06/88, case closed
 3,045 days in bankruptcy
 Listed on Amex
 Direct costs of bankruptcy = $472,000
 Total assets prior to bankruptcy = $29,130,000
 Direct costs/total assets = 1.62%
 Debt/total assets prior to bankruptcy = 62.0%
 Priority of claims held—Firm liquidated under Chapter 7.
 Secured creditors received 74% of their claims. Unsecured creditors and equity holders received nothing. This was a Chapter 7 bankruptcy filing.
 The firm blamed its bankruptcy on declining sales due to a sharp reduction in shipments to automakers.

Towle Manufacturing—Manufacture silverware and giftware
 03/24/86, bankruptcy petition filed in New York; 09/30/87, plan confirmed
 555 days in bankruptcy
 Listed on NYSE
 Direct costs of bankruptcy = $7,519,000
 Total assets prior to bankruptcy = $239,627,000
 Direct costs/total assets = 3.13%
 Debt/total assets prior to bankruptcy = 73.0%
 Priority violated for unsecured creditors—Firm reorganized.
 Secured creditors received 100% of their claims. Unsecured creditors received 60% of their claims (12% in cash, 31% in debentures, and 17% in new common stock). Old preferred shareholders received 6.6% of new common stock, and old common shareholders received 3.3% of new common stock.
 The firm blamed its bankruptcy on reorganization of its distribution facilities, which caused late deliveries and canceled orders.

U.N.A. Corp—Wholesale durable goods
 12/01/86, bankruptcy petition filed in Massachusetts; 06/17/88, plan confirmed
 564 days in bankruptcy
 Listed on Amex
 Direct costs of bankruptcy = not available
 Total assets prior to bankruptcy = $18,217,000
 Direct costs/total assets = not available
 Debt/total assets prior to bankruptcy = 98.5%
 Priority of claims held—Firm reorganized.

Secured creditors were fully paid. Unsecured creditors received one common share for each dollar of claim. Equity holders received nothing.

The firm blamed its bankruptcy on continued losses.

White Motor—Motor vehicles and equipment
09/04/80, bankruptcy petition filed in Ohio; 11/18/83, plan confirmed
1,170 days in bankruptcy
Listed on NYSE
Direct costs of bankruptcy = $21,168,000
Total assets prior to bankruptcy = $630,150,000
Direct costs/total assets = 3.35%
Debt/total assets prior to bankruptcy = 63.4%
Priority violated for unsecured creditors—Firm reorganized.

Secured creditors received 100% of their claims. Unsecured creditors received an average of 51% of their claims with over 90% in cash and the balance in shares. Equity holders retained a 10% interest in the common stock of the reorganized firm.

The firm blamed its bankruptcy on volatility of demand for heavy-duty trucks and farm equipment, combined with a substantial level of borrowing pegged to an increasing prime rate.

Wickes Companies—Building materials and supplies
04/24/82, bankruptcy petition filed in California; 09/21/84, plan confirmed
881 days in bankruptcy
Listed on NYSE
Direct costs of bankruptcy = $20,345,000
Total assets prior to bankruptcy = $551,509,000
Direct costs/total assets = 1.31%
Debt/total assets prior to bankruptcy = 98.5%
Priority violated for unsecured creditors—Firm reorganized.

Secured creditors received 100% of their claims. Senior unsecured creditors received 74.5% of their claims in cash and another 17.5% in common stock (53% of the total outstanding) of the reorganized firm. Subordinated creditors received 50.9% of their claims in cash and 6.1% in common stock (28% of the total outstanding) of the reorganized firm. Equity holders received 19% of the common stock of the reorganized firm (4% to the old preferred shareholders and 15% to the old common shareholders).

The firm blamed its bankruptcy on a decline in earnings, combined with an increase in interest rates after it incurred approximately $1.7 billion of debt to pay for acquisitions.

CHAPTER 7

A MARKET ASSESSMENT OF BANKRUPTCY COSTS AND LIQUIDATION COSTS

Dana J. Johnson
Glenn Wolfe
Larry A. Lynch

INTRODUCTION

Considerable debate and research have focused on the gains and losses in shareholder wealth of firms that file bankruptcy. According to much of the capital structure literature, the value of equity is modeled as being negatively related to the expected value of deadweight bankruptcy costs [e.g., Stiglitz (1969), Castinas (1983), Chen and Kim (1979), and Myers (1977)]. Prior studies suggest that the direct costs of bankruptcy are approximately 5.3 percent of the firm's market value three years prior to bankruptcy [Warner (1977)]. Altman (1984) estimates that the indirect costs of bankruptcy, defined as the difference between actual and expected earnings, are in the range of 11 to 17 percent three years prior to bankruptcy and 20 percent of the value of the firm immediately preceding the bankruptcy filing.

Dana J. Johnson is Professor of Finance at Virginia Polytechnic Institute and State University.
Glenn Wolfe is at the University of Toledo and Larry A. Lynch is at Roanoke College.

Haugen and Senbet (1978, 1988) contend that only a small portion of the decline in the value of a firm approaching bankruptcy is attributable to expected and/or indirect bankruptcy costs and that a large proportion of the loss in value is due to expected liquidation costs. Specifically, they argue that the observed deterioration in product demand and decreased profitability prior to filing bankruptcy are attributable to the likelihood of liquidation rather than bankruptcy. The loss in the value of the firm is attributable not only to ex ante liquidation costs but also to the expected value of the costs associated with liquidation at the time of its occurrence. They distinguish between liquidation and bankruptcy costs by defining liquidation costs as a deteriorating profitability that eventually leads to a costly piecemeal liquidation of the firm's operations and the bankruptcy costs as the direct and indirect costs associated with a transfer of ownership.[1] Furthermore, Haugen and Senbet (1988) argue that there is no conceptually sound basis for inferring or assuming liquidation and bankruptcy costs are related, a position which is in sharp contrast to that of Titman (1984), who suggests a link between financial structure and liquidation.

While prior studies examine the excess returns of firms that file bankruptcy, comparative analysis of shareholder wealth effects according to whether a firm liquidates or continues after filing have been largely ignored.[2] Still, this is the essence of the bankruptcy versus liquidation cost argument. That is, to the extent that liquidation costs are the source of value loss during the years before bankruptcy, those companies that eventually liquidate should have larger losses in value prior to filing bankruptcy than those that continue. Those firms that continue could also experience a loss in value due to expected liquidation costs; however, efficient markets imply that on the average the loss in value should not be as great as for those firms that actually liquidate. Furthermore, if bankruptcy and liquidation costs are unrelated events, the change in shareholder wealth just prior to the filing date when bankruptcy is highly probable through the filing date when it is certain should be invariant to the outcome. The purpose of the present chapter is to examine the relative magnitude of liquidation and bankruptcy costs by focusing on the behavior of shareholder excess returns according to the outcome of the bankruptcy filing. The analysis develops hypotheses and empirical tests for the period prior to the bankruptcy filing, the 21-day period surrounding the filing date, and the period following the filing. In addition, the effect of the 1978 Bankruptcy Reform Act on the hypothesized behavior of firms is addressed both conceptually and empirically.

In the next section, a simple valuation model incorporating liquidation and bankruptcy costs is presented along with corresponding testable hypotheses. The third section discusses the methodology and sample selection. The results of the empirical study are presented and discussed in the fourth section, and a summary is given in the final section.

THE HYPOTHESES DEVELOPMENT

Assume that the values of the firm's assets, debt, and equity gross of liquidation and bankruptcy costs are $V(A)$, $V(D)$, and $V(E)$, respectively. Then

$$V(A) = V(D) + V(E)$$

Now let liquidation costs be defined as the direct costs of dismantling operations at the time of liquidation as well as the indirect costs of liquidation, encompassing the lost profits due to loss of customer and supplier confidence in the firm's ability to continue.[3] Prior to liquidation, the present value of expected liquidation costs is defined as:

$$V(L) = \pi_L L$$

where π_L represents the probability of liquidation occurring at some future date and L represents the present value of the associated liquidation costs.

Assume that a firm can file bankruptcy only under one chapter so that the cost of bankruptcy cannot be attributed to a particular type of filing.[4] Moreover, for those firms that file bankruptcy and liquidate, the bankruptcy filing must occur prior to liquidation. The expected costs of bankruptcy are then defined as the costs of filing bankruptcy and the associated proceedings. Furthermore, they also encompass the indirect costs of bankruptcy attributable at any lost operating profits due to the expected bankruptcy event. While Haugen and Senbet (1978, 1988) argue that costs associated with lost profits are attributable to the uncertainty of the firm's continuance (i.e., liquidation), it is possible that even for firms which continue that the court trustee and creditors could impede the operation of the firm while it is in bankruptcy proceedings such that supplier and customer relationships are affected.[5] To the extent these costs are associated with the bankruptcy process, they should be included in expected bankruptcy costs. The expected value of the present value of the firm's bankruptcy costs is defined as follows:

$$V(B) = \pi_B B$$

where π_B represents the probability of filing bankruptcy at some future date and B represents the present value of the associated bankruptcy costs.

Then the value of the firm's assets net of expected liquidation and bankruptcy costs, $V(NA)$, is given as follows:

$$V(NA) = V(D) + V(E) - V(B) - V(L)$$

Let the proportional costs of liquidation and bankruptcy borne by the equity holders be g and that of debt holders $(1 - g)$.[6] Then $V(NA)$ can be rewritten as follows:

$$V(NA) = V(D) - (1 - g)[V(B) + V(L)] + V(E) - g[V(B) + V(L)]$$

The value of equity net of expected liquidation and bankruptcy costs can be written as follows:

$$V(NE) = V(E) - g[V(L) + V(B)]$$
$$= V(E) - g[\pi_L L + \pi_B B]$$

Period Preceding the Bankruptcy Filing

Prior to bankruptcy and therefore liquidation, the values of π_L and π_B are less than one. Thus, when the firm files bankruptcy, the probability of bankruptcy, π_B, is 1.0 which should produce a decrease in the value of equity equal to the uncapitalized portion of the bankruptcy costs plus any reassessment of the probability of liquidation.

If the market correctly assesses the probability of liquidation, the higher probability of liquidation, π_L, and liquidation costs, $V(L)$, should be observed prior to filing for firms that actually do liquidate versus those that do not. Thus, for firms that eventually liquidate, the prefiling decline in the net value of equity, $V(NE)$, should be larger that that for firms that continue. Moreover, the prefiling net value of equity for firms that continue after the filing also includes a component for $V(L)$, but due to the lower probability of liquidation, the prefiling magnitude of $V(L)$ is less than that for firms that liquidate. If the indirect costs of liquidation are the costs that often are referred to as ex ante or indirect bankruptcy costs, firms that liquidate after the filing should have larger losses in value prior to the filing than those that continue. This leads to the following null hypothesis:

$H1_0$: Shareholder excess returns prior to filing bankruptcy are invariant with respect to whether the firm eventually continues or liquidates.

After filing bankruptcy a firm can continue either through reorganization, in which case the original firm emerges from bankruptcy, or through acquisition. White (1983) includes such acquired firms in a sample of liquidated firms; however, these firms continue to operate similarly to reorganized firms. The fact that such firms neither liquidate nor reorganize implies that they possess unique characteristics that make them attractive acquisition candidates. For example, firms acquired in the bankruptcy process may have tax-based value from unused NOLs or the potential from asset base revaluations that an acquiror with positive net operating income could begin realizing immediately. In reorganization the value of these tax benefits can be realized only when the firm has positive income against which to offset these losses; in a liquidation, such benefits are lost.[7] Studies predicting mergers provide evidence that the market does in fact foresee the likelihood of acquisition [e.g., Palepu (1986)]. To the extent the market realizes the marketability of the attractive attributes of these firms and therefore places a high probability on acquisition prior to filing, the lower $V(B)$ and $V(L)$ are, the smaller should be the associated loss in value prior to filing bankruptcy. Thus, prior to filing bankruptcy the smallest loss in value attributable to $V(L)$ should occur in acquired firms, with the next largest decrease for reorganized firms followed by those that are liquidated. This lead to the second null hypothesis:

$H2_0$: There should be no statistical difference in excess return prior to the filing for firms that are acquired, reorganized, or liquidated.

The Filing Period

If liquidation costs are not associated with bankruptcy costs as Haugen and Senbet (1988) assert, both firms that eventually liquidate and those that are not liquidated should have proportionately equal $V(B)$ immediately preceding the bankruptcy filing date when the probability of bankruptcy is close to 1.0.[8] If liquidation costs and bankruptcy costs are positively related as asserted by Titman (1984), however, then $V(B)$ should be higher for firms that liquidate than those that continue.

For firms that are acquired, the market's anticipation of an acquisition prior to filing may cause delays in capitalizing liquidation costs until the filing date is close. At the announcement of the bankruptcy filing, $\pi_B = 1.0$ and the decrease in value $V_0(NE)$ for the acquired firms should reflect the *PV* of bankruptcy costs. In addition, if the market places a high probability on acquisition and a low probability on liquidation prior to the filing, there may also be an increase in π_L and an additional decrease in value attributable to uncapitalized liquidation costs at the time of filing. Thus, for firms that are acquired after the filing, the loss in value at the announcement of bankruptcy may be higher than for those firms that liquidate or reorganize. This leads to the third null hypothesis given as follows:

H3_0: The excess returns at the filing should be the same regardless of whether a firm liquidates, reorganizes, or is acquired.

The Period Following the Filing

To the extent the market capitalizes a large portion of the liquidation and bankruptcy costs during the period prior to through the bankruptcy filing date, market efficiency suggests that no excess returns should occur in the period following the filing. Warner (1977) finds significant positive excess returns for the bonds of railroads that reorganized after the filing and attributes these findings to informational inefficiencies. Specifically, the source of value change could be attributable to the release of detailed information on the firm's financial condition as a result of the filing. This information could lead to a revision of expectations about the fate of the firm's equity holders relative to expectations prior to the filing. Whether excess returns are negative or positive depends on the type of information released at the filing relative to investors' expectations prior to it. For instance, if the information reveals that the company's fate is worse than expected, negative excess returns should be observed after the filing. Similarly, if the firm's fate is better than expected, excess returns after the filing would be positive. This leads to the following null hypothesis corresponding to the presence of informational efficiency:

H4_0: Shareholder excess returns are zero for the period following the filing, regardless of the outcome.

The 1978 Reform Act

A potentially important consideration in examining the liquidation versus continuance alternatives is the effect of the 1978 Bankruptcy Reform Act.

According to White (1983), the 1978 Bankruptcy Reform Act makes reorganization more difficult, thereby forcing inefficient firms out of operation. Thus, prior to the Act, inefficient firms with going-concern values less than their liquidated values were allowed to reorganize rather than being forced into the economically efficient alternative of liquidation. In the context of the preceding model, the 1978 Act should increase the probability of liquidation of an inefficient firm for which liquidation is the economically efficient alternative. While the present value of the costs of liquidation would not be affected by the 1978 Reform Act, the probability of liquidation would be higher after the Act. Thus, the present value of expected liquidation costs, $V(L)$, should be smaller for those filing before the Act relative to those filing after it. As a result, the loss in value due to increased expected liquidation costs of firms reorganizing prior to the Act should be smaller than the loss in value for firms reorganizing after the Act.

Two empirical studies address the effect of the 1978 Reform Act. Morse and Shaw (1988) report that excess returns over the three-year period following the filing are not statistically different for those firms that filed for reorganization before the Act versus those that filed after the law change. White (1983) provides support for her hypothesis by demonstrating that proportionately more companies liquidate after the Act than before it.

Both studies, however, have methodological shortcomings. The problem with White's methodology is that it examines the proportion of firms filing liquidation versus reorganization rather than the magnitude of the losses from liquidation and reorganization. The alternative approach of Morse and Shaw, which examines the loss in value after the filing, has two problems. First, it ignores the fact that it is only the portfolio of the firms that eventually reorganize that should have higher excess returns after the Act rather than the larger sample of all firms filing (i.e., reorganized, liquidated, and acquired combined). Second, examining the excess returns after the filing assumes that no anticipation of the outcome occurred prior to the filing which is highly unlikely. If the 1978 Act increases the efficiency of the bankruptcy process, excess returns of those firms actually reorganizing (as opposed to filing for reorganization) after the Act should be less negative than those reorganizing before the Act. This leads to the following null hypothesis:

$H5_0$: The cumulative excess returns of firms reorganizing after the 1978 Bankruptcy Reform Act are not significantly different from those filing before it.

The remainder of the chapter reports the empirical evidence from tests of the firms' hypotheses. The sample description and methodology for the empirical analysis are presented in the next section.

METHODOLOGY AND SAMPLE DESCRIPTION

Sample Selection

The initial sample consists of the 154 firms that filed bankruptcy from 1970 through 1985 for which the outcome of the filing can be determined.[9] This sample was obtained by searching *The Wall Street Journal Index* and filtering the *Compustat* Annual Research File for firms that filed bankruptcy during the aforementioned time period. *The Wall Street Journal Index*, individual *Wall Street Journal* articles, and the National Quotation Bureau "Pink Sheets" were used to identify the outcome of each bankruptcy filing.

Chapter 7 filings were dropped from the sample because only three firms, an insufficient number for further analysis, fell into this category.[10] In addition, six firms not contained on the CRSP tapes were eliminated, reducing the sample to 145 firms. Return data ceased to exist more than 252 days prior to the filing date for 27 of the remaining 145 firms and, consequently, these firms were purged from the sample. Unfortunately, even the 118 firms remaining in this reduced sample are plagued with the problem of missing returns during the 504-day period of analysis (extending from $t = -252$ through $t = +252$) chosen for this study. Therefore, in order for a firm to remain in the sample a minimum of 150 returns must be available during the period $t = -252$ through $t = 0$. This requirement eliminated another 17 firms from the remaining subset of firms, resulting in a final sample of 101 firms. Returns for each of these firms were obtained from the CRSP Daily Returns File and/or the CRSP NASDAQ Master Returns File for an event period extending from day -252 through day $+252$ relative to the bankruptcy filing date denoted $t = 0$. A nonparametric chi-square test of independence is then employed to test the null hypotheses that the availability of sufficient return data is unrelated to (1) filing year, (2) filing before or after the bankruptcy law change, or (3) outcome.

The distribution of bankruptcy filings by year is presented in Table 7–1 for the reduced sample (Panel A) and the final sample (Panel B). The null hypothesis that the availability of sufficient return data is unrelated to filing year cannot be rejected at the .01 level of significance ($x^2 = 18.145$; PR ≥ 0.200). For the reduced sample, 76 (64.4%) occurred prior to the effec-

TABLE 7–1
Distribution of Bankruptcy Filing by Year

Panel A. Initial Sample of 118 Firms

Year	Frequency	Year	Frequency	Year	Frequency
1970	5	1975	10	1980	8
1971	2	1976	4	1981	9
1972	2	1977	11	1982	13
1973	14	1978	10	1983	7
1974	12	1979	7	1984	4

Panel B. Sample of 98 Firms with Minimum of 150 Returns

Year	Frequency	Year	Frequency	Year	Frequency
1970	5	1975	6	1980	8
1971	2	1976	3	1981	8
1972	2	1977	9	1982	13
1973	13	1978	9	1983	5
1974	10	1979	4	1984	4

tive date of the 1978 Bankruptcy Reform Act, while 42 (35.6%) occurred following the effective date. In comparison, for the final sample, 62 (61.4%) occurred prior to the effective date of the 1978 Bankruptcy Reform Act, while 39 (38.6%) occurred following the effective date. The null hypothesis that the availability of sufficient return data is unrelated to filing before or after the bankruptcy law change likewise cannot be rejected at the .01 level of significance ($x^2 = 2.790$; PR≥ 0.095).

The distribution of outcomes is displayed in Table 7–2 for the reduced sample (Panel A) and the final sample (Panel B). The null hypothesis that the availability of sufficient return data is unrelated to outcome cannot be rejected at the .01 level of significance ($x^2 = 1.595$; PR ≥ 0.450).

The distribution of outcome by chapter filing for those filings occurring after the bankruptcy law change in the initial sample and the final sample are displayed in Table 7–3. The null hypothesis that the availability of sufficient return data is unrelated to outcome cannot be rejected at the .01 level of significance ($x^2 = 2.669$; PR ≥ 0.263).

TABLE 7–2
Sample Distribution of Outcome

Panel A

		Outcome		
	Liquidation	Reorganization	Acquisition	Totals
n	36	66	16	118
%	30.51	55.93	13.56	100

Panel B

		Outcome		
	Liquidation	Reorganization	Acquisition	Totals
n	33	55	13	101
%	32.67	54.46	12.87	100

TABLE 7–3
Sample Distribution of Outcome for Chapter 11 Filings after Bankruptcy Reform Act

Panel A

		Outcome		
	Liquidation	Reorganization	Acquisition	Totals
n	13	23	6	42
%	30.95	54.76	14.29	100

Panel B

		Outcome		
	Liquidation	Reorganization	Acquisition	Totals
n	13	20	6	39
%	33.33	51.28	15.38	100

Methodology

To compare the behavior of cumulative excess returns over the one-year period leading up to the bankruptcy filing, the period surrounding the filing, and the one-year period after the filing, standardized prediction errors and cumulative prediction errors (CPE) are calculated for each firm over the period; then cross-sectional mean CPEs are calculated for the group of such firms. The CPE methodology is similar to the event time methodology used by Dodd and Warner (1983) and Hite, Owers, and Rogers (1987). The specific formulations are given below.

The prediction error for security j on trading day t is defined as follows:[11]

$$PE = R_{jt} - R_{Mt} \qquad (7.1)$$

where

R_{jt} = the return on security j on trading day t
R_{Mt} = the return on the market index on trading day t

Next, the prediction errors for each trading day t are averaged cross-sectionally and the resulting average prediction errors, PE_t, are tested for statistical significance using a standard T-test.

The cumulative prediction errors for each security j over the period $t = K$ through L are then calculated as follows:

$$CPE_j = \sum_{t=K}^{L} PE_{jt} \qquad (7.2)$$

Next, the cumulative prediction errors for each security j are averaged cross-sectionally and the resulting average cumulative prediction errors, CPE, are test for statistical significance.

The test statistic for CPE relies on standardized prediction errors which are defined as follows:

$$SPE_{jt} = \frac{PE_{jt}}{\sigma PE_j} \qquad (7.3)$$

where

$\sigma_{PEj} =$ standard deviation of prediction errors for security j over the period $t = -379$ through -253. The test statistic is then given as follows:[12]

$$Z = \sum_{j=1}^{N} \frac{SCPE_j}{\sqrt{\tilde{N}}} \qquad (7.4)$$

where

$$SCPE_j = \sum_{t=K}^{L} \frac{SPE_{jt}}{\sqrt{\widetilde{L-K+1}}}$$

T-tests are then used to test for statistical differences among the subgroup's CPEs and PEs. The decision to use a T-test assuming equal or unequal variances for the two subgroups is based on an F-test for the null hypothesis of no differences in the variances of the two groups. A nonparametric Kruskall Wallis test is also used to test for statistically significant differences.

EMPIRICAL RESULTS

CPEs According to the Outcome

The analysis is divided into three event periods corresponding to the hypotheses stated in the second section. The pre-event period extends from $t = -252$ through -11 and corresponds to a period when the market capitalizes liquidation costs. The event period, covering the period $t = +11$ through $+252$ is the period during which information released in the filing may lead to a revision of expectations. Note this period does not generally cover the point in time the firm emerges from bankruptcy and the various court decisions. Rather, it represents a period during which detailed information about the firm's financial condition is made public.

The Pre-Event Period (t = -252 through -11)
The CPEs according to the outcome of the bankruptcy filing for the pre-event period extending from $t = -252$ through -11 are presented in Table 7–4. A corresponding graph of the CPEs by outcome over the period $t = -252$

TABLE 7–4
CPEs for Pre-event Periods $t = -252$ through -11[a]

Pre-event Period	Acquisition	Reorganization	Liquidation
−252 through −127	0.08010 (0.125; 12/13)	−0.05717 (−0.966; 52/53)	−0.15758 [c] (−2.539; 31/31)
−252 through −61	0.07854 (−0.540; 12/13)	−0.09313 (−1.712; 52/52)	−0.44071 [c] (−5.533; 31/26)
−252 through −40	0.15222 (−0.219; 12/13)	−0.24795 [b] (−2.191; 52/50)	−0.54865 [c] (−6.266; 31/25)
−252 through −11	0.16833 (−0.349; 12/13)	−0.22822 [c] (−3.933; 52/41)	−0.66909 [c] (−7.527; 31/21)
−40 through −11	0.03935 (0.487; 13/13)	−0.05961 [c] (−2.567; 50/41)	−0.13474 [c] (−4.841; 25/21)

[a] CPEs are presented with the Z-value and beginning and ending sample sizes in parentheses beneath the CPE. For example, (0.125; 12/13) for the period −252 through −127 means that the CPE has a Z of 0.125 and there are 12 observations at the beginning of the period and 13 at the end.
[b] significant at 5% level.
[c] significant at 10% level.

through −11, presented in Figure 7–1, reveals that the CPEs behave as predicted; that is, the CPEs of the acquired companies are larger than those of the reorganized companies which are larger than those of the liquidated companies.

A closer examination of the CPEs of the *acquired* companies in Table 7–4 shows that for the period $t = -252$ through −11 a positive 16.833% is earned. However, the gain in value during the subperiod closest to the filing ($t = -40$ through −11) is only 3.935%. No general statement can be made concerning the potential for large gains because the CPE for the acquired firm is not statistically significant in any of the reported subperiods during the pre-event period.

CPEs for firms that *reorganize* are negative and statistically significant for the pre-event subperiods of $t = -252$ through −40 with CPEs of −14.795%, $t = -40$ through −11 of −5.961%, and $t = -252$ through −11 of −22.822%. Interestingly, the CPEs for $t = -252$ through −127 and −252 through −61 are not statistically significant although they are negative. In

FIGURE 7–1
CPEs for $t = -252$ through $t = -11$ by Outcome

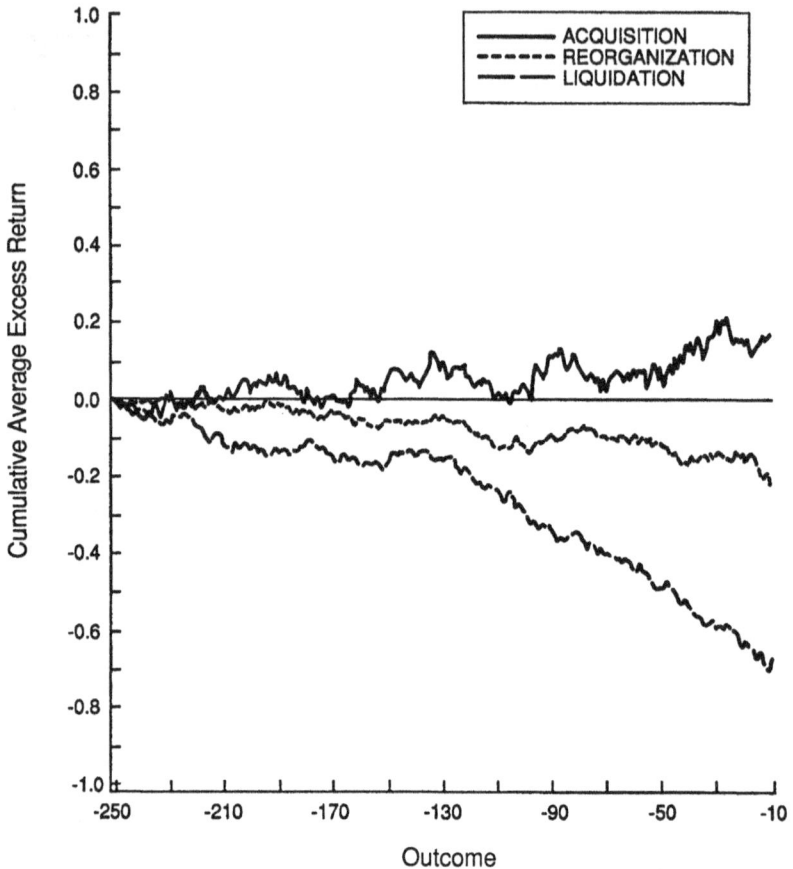

contrast to the acquired sample the CPEs for the reorganized sample are in no case statistically different from those of the acquired sample. This is largely attributable to the large dispersion of the individual firm CPEs of the acquired group which implies that while these firms may have attractive qualities in terms of acquisition, the likelihood of an acquisition being consummated prior to filing substantially varies across the sample. In short, null hypothesis $H2_0$ cannot be rejected for a comparison of pre-event CPEs for acquired and reorganized firms.

The CPEs of the *liquidated* sample during the pre-event period (Table 7-4) are negative and significant in each of the subperiods presented with a

CPE of –66.909% for the total period $t = -252$ through –11. Recall that CPEs of the reorganized sample are not significant for the earlier pre-event periods of $t = -252$ through –127 and $t = -252$ through –61 nor for any of the subperiods for the same subperiods for the acquired sample. Further observe that the magnitude of the liquidated CPEs for the same subperiods are much smaller (more negative) than for the acquired and reorganized samples. This implies that the market correctly assesses the probability of liquidation and impounds the expected liquidation costs into the price of the firm's stock as Haugen and Senbet (1988) assert. This implication is further supported by statistical tests of significance which reveal that the differences in pre-event CPEs for all reported subperiods are statistically significant for the liquidated and reorganized samples as well as the liquidated and acquired samples. Thus, null hypothesis $H1_0$ is rejected as well as $H2_0$ for comparison of the liquidated sample with the acquired and reorganized samples.

Event Period (t = –10 through +10)
The event period defined as $t = -10$ through +10 corresponds to the point of filing in the hypotheses developed in the second section. Recall that the null hypothesis $H3_0$ suggests that, if bankruptcy costs are not related to whether a firm liquidates or continues, the difference in excess returns at the filing should not be significant. The CPEs and PEs for the 21-day event period are presented in Table 7–5, and a corresponding graph is presented in Figure 7–2. Note that for the acquired firms there is a loss of 52.196% over the entire 21-day event period ($t = -10$ through +10). Of this amount, 4.323% is lost over the period $t = -10$ through –3, and an additional 40.401% is lost during the period $t = -2$ through $t = +2$. On the event date $t = 0$, a loss of 20.440% is incurred.

The reorganized sample has a CPE over $t = -10$ through +10 of –39.485%. This loss in value is attributable to a 9.794% loss for the period $t = -10$ through –3 and an additional loss of 37.421% over the five-day period $t = -2$ through +2. For the period $t = +3$ through +10, however, a statistically significant CPE of 7.550% is earned.

The liquidated firms lose 46.063% over the period $t = -10$ through +10 of which 5.642% is lost over the period $t = -10$ through –3 and an additional 41.351% over the five-day period surrounding the event ($t = -2$ through +2). Similar to the reorganized sample, the liquidated sample has a positive CPE of 0.94% over the period $t = +3$ through +10.

There are no statistically significant differences in the event period

TABLE 7–5
CPEs and PEs for the Event Period $t = -10$ through $+10$ [a]

Event Period	Acquisition	Reorganization	Liquidation
CPEs			
−10 through −3	−0.04323	−0.09794	−0.05642
	(−1.016; 13/11)	(−2.050; 41/28)	(−1.859; 21/16)
−2 through +2	−0.40401	−0.37241	−0.41361
	(−9.941; 10/5)	(−24.724; 26/20)	(−12.099; 12/6)
−1 through +1	−0.36477	−0.36119	−0.39002
	(−14.213; 7/5)	(−32.103; 17/20)	(−16.764; 6/6)
−5 through +5	−0.33450	−0.42150	−0.47792
	(−3.821; 12/5)	(−18.576; 33/19)	(−5.577; 19/6)
+3 through +10	−0.07472	−0.07550	−0.00940
	(−1.128; 5/3)	(3.573; 20/12)	(0.833; 6/5)
−10 through +10	−0.52196	−0.39485	−0.46063
	(−5.545; 13/3)	(−11.691; 41/12)	(−5.211; 21/5)
PEs			
$t = -10$	−0.00798	0.00997	−0.02878 [d]
	(−0.454; 13)	(1.284; 41)	(−3.652; 21)
$t = -9$	−0.02174	−0.00567	−0.01506 [c]
	(−1.236; 13)	(−0.730; 38)	(−1.910; 21)
$t = -8$	−0.01771	0.00476	−0.00699
	(−1.008; 13)	(0.612; 38)	(−0.887; 21)
$t = -7$	−0.01502	−0.04062 [d]	0.00390
	(−0.854; 12)	(−5.230; 36)	(0.495; 20)
$t = -6$	−0.02476	0.02182 [d]	−0.00526
	(−1.408; 12)	(2.809; 33)	(−0.668; 19)
$t = -5$	0.04170	−0.04017 [d]	0.01522 [b]
	(2.371; 12)	(−5.172; 33)	(1.931; 19)
$t = -4$	0.00474 [c]	−0.00989	0.00491 [d]
	(0.2700; 11)	(−1.273; 33)	(0.623; 18)
$t = -3$	−0.00245	−0.0813 [d]	−0.02435 [d]
	(−0.1390; 11)	(−4.909; 28)	(−3.091; 16)
$t = -2$	−0.03339 [c]	−0.03979 [b]	−0.06363 [b]
	(−1.8980; 10)	(−5.123; 26)	(−8.073; 12)
$t = -1$	−0.10925 [b]	−0.122177 [b]	−0.10598 [b]
	(−6.2110; 7)	(−15.729; 17)	(−13.446; 6)
$t = 0$	−0.20440 [b]	−0.21775 [b]	−0.13238 [b]
	(−11.6210; 7)	(−28.035; 20)	(−16.796; 5)
$t = +1$	−0.09621 [b]	−0.02126 [b]	−0.15166 [b]
	(−5.4700; 5)	(−2,737; 20)	(−19.243; 6)
$t = +2$	0.03924 [c]	0.02856 [c]	0.04004 [b]
	(2.2310; 5)	(3.677; 20)	(5.080; 6)
$t = +3$	0.01266	0.02754 [b]	−0.04739 [c]
	(0.720; 5)	(3.545; 20)	(−6.013; 6)
$t = +4$	0.03203 [d]	−0.01332 [d]	−0.05079 [b]
	0.03203 [d]	−0.01332 [d]	−0.05079 [b]
$t = +5$	−0.01917	−0.02488 [d]	0.03810
	(−1.090; 5)	(3.204; 19)	(4.835; 6)
$t = +6$	−0.01156	−0.01833 [b]	0.03727 [b]
	(−0.657; 5)	(−2.361; 19)	(4.729; 6)
$t = +7$	−0.01983	0.0319	0.04871 [b]
	(−1.127; 5)	(0.410; 18)	(6.180; 6)

TABLE 7–5, continued

Event Period	Acquisition	Reorganization	Liquidation
PEs (continued)			
$t = +8$	−0.04125 [b]	0.01547 [c]	−0.02224 [b]
	(−2.345; 5)	(1.992; 18)	(−2.822; 6)
$t = +9$	−0.01494	0.05380 [b]	0.00859
	(−0.850; 4)	(6.926; 18)	(1.090; 6)
$t = +10$	−0.01266	−0.01773 [c]	−0.00285
	(−0.720; 3)	(−2.282; 12)	(−0.362)

[a] CPEs are presented with the Z-value and beginning and ending sample sizes in parentheses beneath the CPE. For example, (0.125; 12/13) for the period −252 through −127 means that the CPE has a Z of 0.125 and there are 12 observations at the beginning of the period and 13 at the end.
[b] significant at 1% level.
[c] significant at 5% level.
[d] significant at 10% level.

FIGURE 7–2
CPEs for $t = -10$ through +10 by Outcome

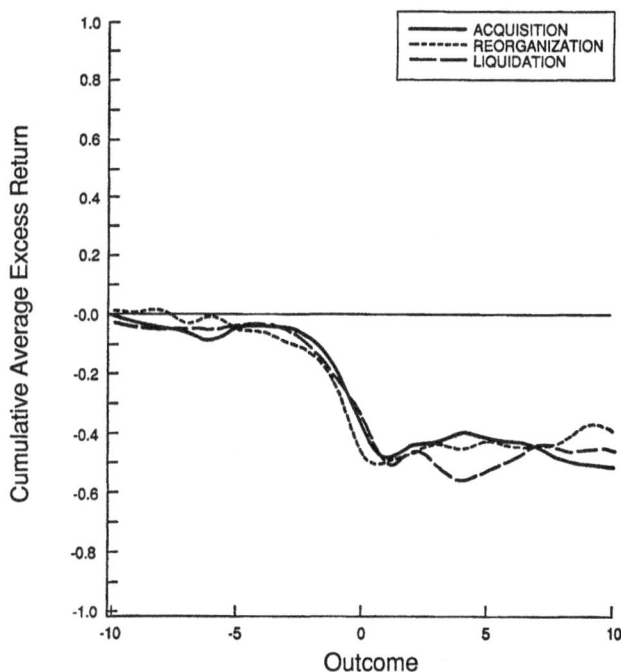

CPEs for any of the subperiods; thus, $H3_0$ cannot be rejected. To the extent the largest proportion of the bankruptcy costs are capitalized close to the filing date, there are no statistical differences in event period excess returns according to the outcome. While it could be argued that those firms included in the event period tests are statistically different from those that are deleted due to missing excess returns in the same period, tests of significance for differences in pre-event and event period CPEs for those firms with available excess returns on the event day relative to those without event-day excess returns reveal that the pre-event and event CPEs are not statistically different for the two groups, even after adjusting for the filing outcome.[13]

Post-Event Period (t = +11 through +252)

The post-event period $t = +11$ through $+252$ is used to test for informational efficiency which implies that excess returns over this period should be zero as stated in hypothesis $H4_0$. The post-event CPEs are presented in Table 7–6 and the graph over this period can be found in Figure 7–3.

The acquired sample has positive CPEs of 9.775% for the period $t = +11$ through $+43$ and 5.754% for $t = +11$ through $+252$. In the subperiod $t = +11$ through $+252$, a *CPE* of –5.596% is reported. In no case is *CPE* significant. However, statistical tests of significance are largely meaningless given a sample size ranging from 1 to 2 firms.

The reorganized sample has a statistically significant CPE of 15.007% for the period $t = +11$ through $+43$ and 19.225% for $t = +11$ through $+126$.

TABLE 7–6
CPEs and PEs for Post-Event Period t = +11 through +252 [a]

Event Period	Acquisition	Reorganization	Liquidation
+11 through +43	0.09775	0.15007 [b]	0.10257
	(0.4950; 2)	(3.059; 10/13)	(1.883; 5/6)
+11 through +126	0.05754	0.19225 [c]	0.26834 [b]
	(0.1600; 2)	(2.009; 10/11)	(2.798; 5/5)
+11 through +252	–0.05596	0.15758	0.21404 [c]
	(–0.0782; 2/1)	(1.408; 10/9)	(2.350; 5/5)

[a] CPEs are presented with the Z-value and beginning and ending sample sizes in parentheses beneath the CPE. For example, (0.125; 12/13) for the period –252 through –127 means that the CPE has a Z of 0.125 and there are 12 observations at the beginning of the period and 13 at the end.
[b] significant at 5% level.
[c] significant at 10% level.

FIGURE 7–3
CPEs for t = +11 through +252 by Outcome

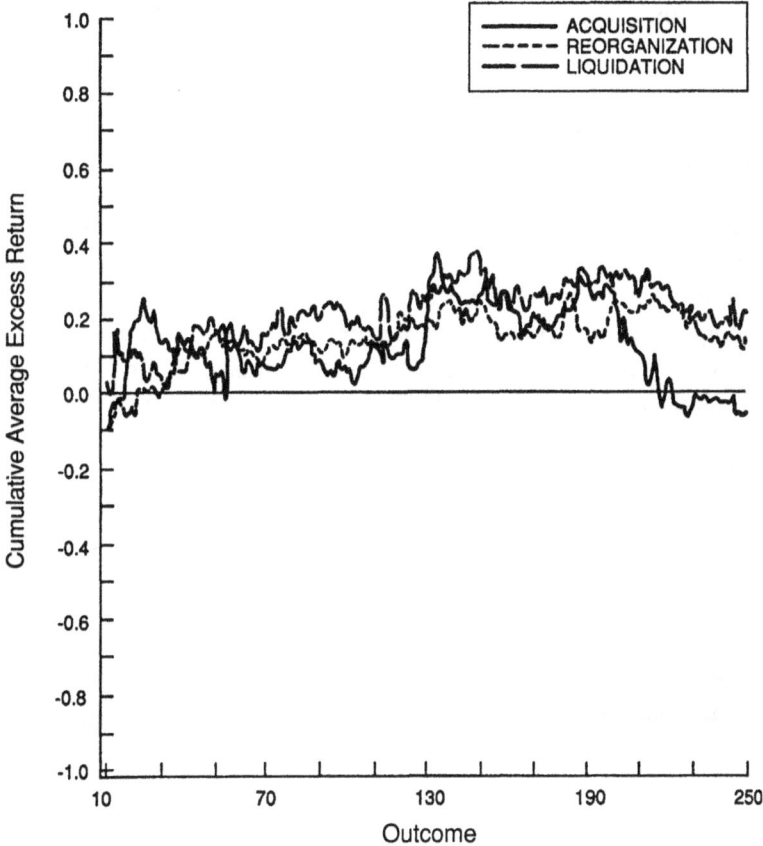

Similarly, the liquidated sample has a statistically significant positive CPE of 26.834% over the period $t = +11$ through $+126$. These gains are highlighted by the statistically significant gains reported in the event subperiod $t = +3$ through $+10$ for both samples. These results lead to a rejection of null hypothesis $H4_0$ concerning informational efficiency. That is, information released about the health of a company at the filing leads to a positive revision of expectations for firms that eventually liquidate or reorganize.

With respect to prior studies reporting opportunities for gains after the filing, the results of the analysis reveal that there is an opportunity for making short-term excess returns by investing in bankrupt firms after the filing. Due to missing observations, it is difficult to make a statement regarding longer term excess returns in the present study. However, Morse and Shaw (1988) report that they are not statistically significantly different from zero.

Effect of Change in Bankruptcy Law for Firms that Reorganize

Recall that White (1983) proposes that the 1978 Reform Act is more efficient than the preceding bankruptcy law because under the Reform Act it is more difficult for inefficient firms to reorganize. From a market perspective, firms reorganizing under the 1978 Reform Act should have larger CPEs than those reorganizing prior to it since firms reorganizing prior to the Act would include a subset that should have been liquidated. The CPEs and PEs for these two groups of reorganized firms are presented in Table 7–7.

The overwhelming observation is that firms reorganizing under the 1978 Reform Act have larger CPEs for every reported pre-event period. In no case, however, is the difference significant. Similarly, there are no statistically significant differences in the event period CPEs.[14] Thus, null hypothesis $H5_0$ cannot be rejected.

Thus, the implications of the present study are consistent with those of Morse and Shaw (1988) and do not support the position that the 1978 Reform Act induced more efficiency into the bankruptcy process by making it more difficult for inefficient firms to continue.

SUMMARY

The present study develops and tests hypotheses concerning market efficiency with respect to liquidation costs and bankruptcy costs. Specifically, efficient markets suggest that the market correctly assesses the liquidation outcome and impounds the associated costs in the price of the stock prior to the bankruptcy filing and subsequent liquidation. The results of the study support this assertion. Furthermore, Haugen and Senbet's argument that bankruptcy costs and liquidation costs are unrelated is also supported.

Tests of informational efficiency regarding information released at the filing reveal that the stocks of companies that eventually liquidate or reorganize are not informationally efficient. Specifically, statistically significant positive excess returns for such firms in the six months following bank-

TABLE 7–7
CPEs for Reorganized Firms According to Filing Before or After the 1978 Reform Act

Event Period	Before 1978 Act	After 1978 Act
Pre-Event Period		
−252 through −11	−0.25919	−0.18152
	(−2.9202; 24/34)	(−1.4227; 16/20)
−252 through −40	−0.16383	−0.12122
	(−2.0559; 31/34)	(−0.7448; 17/20)
−252 through −61	−0.12624	−0.03542
	(−1.9123; 32/34)	(0.1288; 17/20)
−252 through −127	−0.10020	0.01863
	(−1.5539; 32/34)	(0.4004; 18/20)
−40 through −11	−0.08115	−0.02912
	(−2.6432; 24/31)	(−0.7671; 16/19)
Event Period		
−10 through −3	−0.13211	−0.04829
	(−5.5005; 14/24)	(2.5880; 17/17)
−2 through +2	−0.41402	−0.33228
	(−19.1510; 7/13)	(−14.9150; 11/14)
−1 through +1	−0.36035	−0.36886
	(−21.2900; 6/7)	(−23.1870; 11/14)
+3 through +10	−0.04360	0.06140
	(−2.2818; 3/6)	(5.6109; 9/14)
−5 through +5	−0.49513	−0.38276
	(−12.104; 6/18)	(−12.723; 13/15)
−10 through +10	−0.46182	−0.40685
	(11.603; 3/24)	(−4.0224; 9/17)
Post-Event Period		
+11 through +43	0.02331	0.22359
	(0.44877; 3/3)	(3.19634; 7/9)
+11 through +126	0.57611	0.11792
	(2.1601; 3/2)	(1.6656; 7/9)
+11 through +252	0.44986	0.10728
	(0.96574; 3/2)	(1.06797; 7/8)

ruptcy indicating that the market reassesses the value of the company as information is released after the filing.

Finally, tests of the effect of the 1978 Bankruptcy Reform Act in increasing the efficiency of the bankruptcy process is studied. The results offer no support for the position that the 1978 Act increased overall economic efficiency by channeling firms into this most efficient outcome of liquidation or that continuation makes the bankruptcy process more efficient.

NOTES

1. Altman (1984) also includes the loss of key personnel due to bankruptcy. It is conceivable that the resultant transfer of ownership could very likely cause key managers to leave. However, the same managers may be the cause of bankruptcy and, thus, should not be retained. In this case, the loss of these individuals could be viewed as a cost reduction.

2. The returns to shareholders of firms filing for reorganization over a period of time preceding the filing date have been examined by Aharony, Hones, and Swary (1980), Clark and Weinstein (1983), and Baldwin and Mason (1983). The evidence indicates that shareholder excess returns are negative as much as five years before the bankruptcy event. Moreover, an additional loss is reported by Clark and Weinstein (1983) at the announcement of the bankruptcy filing. Evidence on the gains to shareholders after the filing is mixed. Barrett and Sullivan (1988) contend that investing in the stocks of firms after they file bankruptcy potentially generates large shareholder gains. Morse and Shaw (1988) report that no statistically significant excess returns are earned during the three-year period following the bankruptcy filing. According to Warner (1977a), the existence of nonzero excess returns after the filing supports informational inefficiency prior to the bankruptcy filing.

3. Liquidation in the present study is assumed to occur when the firm liquidates due to their inability to generate profits. This is distinct from the cases in which the firm voluntarily liquidates due to factors other than financial distress. For a more in-depth discussion of voluntary liquidations, see Kim and Schatzberg (1987).

4. Some argue that the initial chapter filing is an important consideration [e.g., Clark and Weinstein (1983), White (1989)]. As the subsequent sample description reveals, all of the firms included in the empirical tests filed for reorganization.

5. Such actions would not be in the best interests of the firm's claimants if they are in fact value reducing and, thus, should not occur.

6. See Warner (1977a, b) and White (1989) for a discussion of the distribution of bankruptcy costs among the firm's claimants.

7. Of course in a well-functioning capital market the acquisition of such firms should occur prior to the bankruptcy filing.

8. According to Haugen and Senbet (1988) in well-functioning capital markets, arbitrage by the security holders and complex financial contracting should avoid the costly bankruptcy process. Giammarino (1989) demonstrates that under asymmetric information and with judicial discretion permitting courts to impose a reorganization, firms may rationally select reorganization. Brown (1989) demonstrates that with perfect information the successful bid for the other claimants' securities without filing will be identical to the value received after reorganization. Thus, claimants will avoid the bankruptcy process only when the prebankruptcy settlement is the value-maximizing alternative.

9. Use of more recent filings presents problems in determining the outcome. In some cases, the period between filing and resolution is three years.

10. In addition, the model assumes that firms can file only one type of bankruptcy. In the present empirical analysis, firms file only for reorganization. Prior to the 1978 Reform Act, firms could file for two types of reorganization, Chapter 10 or Chapter 11. Tests

for differences in excess returns according to these two types of filings revealed no statistical differences; thus, the two groups are treated as homogeneous.

11. Risk adjusted measures of prediction errors are not used because there is substantial nonstationary and nonsynchronous trading, which affect estimates of the market model. See Johnson (1989) for a detailed discussion of the problems of estimating beta for firms approaching bankruptcy.

12. As will be revealed in the empirical results section of this chapter, the number of firms used in calculating the CPE over a given event period frequently changes over the event period. In the present study, the CPE for each firm is calculated using L and K covering the first and last day a security traded during the event period rather than the event period itself. The effect of this appears to be that the SCPEs are larger than they would be if the entire event period were used and the Z-test statistic is inflated. However, using the entire event period and assigning a value of zero to the PE on days after the firm stopped trading produced upward-biased PEs since prior to this time they are generally negative.

13. Both t-tests and nonparametric tests reveal no statistical differences even at $\alpha = 10\%$. The test statistics are available from the authors.

14. Similar analyses were undertaken for the acquired and liquidated groups. Since the statistical tests of significance for differences in SPEs were not significant for either of these samples, the results are not reported here but are available from the authors.

REFERENCES

Aharony, J.; C. Jones; and I. Swary, "An Analysis of Risk and Return Characteristics of Corporate Bankruptcy Using Capital Market Data," *Journal of Finance* (September 1980), pp. 1001–16.

Altman, E. I., Discussion of "The Behavior of Common Stock of Bankrupt Firms," *Journal of Finance* (May 1983), pp. 517–22.

Altman, E. I., "A Further Empirical Investigation of the Bankruptcy Cost Question," *Journal of Finance* 39 (September 1984), pp. 1067–89.

Baldwin, C., and S. Mason, "The Resolution of Claims in Financial Distress," *Journal of Finance* (May 1983), pp. 505–16.

Barret, P., and A. Sullivan, "Usually Last in Line, Holders Become Vocal in Bankruptcy Actions," *The Wall Street Journal* (January 21, 1988).

Brown, D. T., "Claimholders Incentive Conflicts in Reorganization," *The Review of Financial Studies*, Vol. 2, No. 1 (1988), pp. 109–23.

Casey, C.; V. McGee; and C. Stickney, "Discriminating Between Reorganized and Liquidated Firms in Bankruptcy," *The Accounting Review* (April 1986).

Castinias, R., "Bankruptcy Risk and Optimal Capital Structure," *Journal of Finance* 38 (December 1983), pp. 1617–84.

Chen, A., and E. Kim, "Optimal Capital Structure: A Synthesis," *Journal of Finance* 34 (May 1979), pp. 371–84.

Clark, T., and M. Weinstein, "The Behavior of Common Stock of Bankrupt Firms,"

Journal of Finance (May 1983), pp. 489–504.

Dodd, P., and J. Warner, "On Corporate Governance: A Study of Proxy Contests," *Journal of Financial Economics* 11 (1983), pp. 401–38.

Giammarino, R. M., "The Resolution of Financial Distress," *The Review of Financial Studies,* Vol. 2, No. 1 (1989), pp. 25–47.

Haugen, R., and L. Senbet, "The Insignificance of Bankruptcy Costs to the Theory of Optimal Capital Structure," *Journal of Finance* (May 1978), pp. 383–93.

Haugen, R., and L. Senbet, "Bankruptcy and Agency Costs: Their Significance to the Theory of Optimal Capital Structure," *Journal of Financial and Quantitative Analysis* 1 (March 1988), pp. 27–38.

Hite, G.; J. Owers; and R. Rogers, "The Market for Interfirm Asset Sales: Partial Selloffs and Total Liquidations," *Journal of Financial Economics* 11 (1987), pp. 229–52.

Jensen, M. C., and W. H. Meckling, "The Theory of the Firm: Managerial Behavior, Agency Costs, and Ownership Structure," *Journal of Financial Economics* 4 (October 1976), pp. 305–60.

Johnson, D. J., "The Risk Behavior of Firms Approaching Bankruptcy," *Journal of Financial Research* (Spring 1989).

Kim, E. H., and J. D. Schatzberg, "Voluntary Corporate Liquidations," *Journal of Financial Economics* 19 (1987), pp. 311–28.

Morse, D., and W. Shaw, "Investing in Bankrupt Firms," *Journal of Finance* 5 (December 1988), pp. 1193–1206.

Myers, S., "Determinants of Corporate Borrowing," *Journal of Financial Economics* 4 (1977), pp. 147–76.

Palepu, K., "Predicting Takeover Targets: A Methodological and Empirical Analysis," *Journal of Accounting and Economics* (March 1986), pp. 3–35.

Stiglitz, J. E., "A Re-Examination of the Modigliani–Miller Theorem," *American Economic Review* 5 (December 1969), pp. 784–93.

Titman, S., "The Effects of Capital Structure on a Firm's Liquidation Decision," *Journal of Financial Economics* 13 (March 1984), pp. 137–51.

Warner, J. B., "Bankruptcy, Absolute Priority, and the Pricing of Risky Debt Claims," *Journal of Financial Economics* 4 (1977a), pp. 239–76.

Warner, J. B., "Bankruptcy Costs: Some Evidence," *Journal of Finance* 32 (May 1977b), pp. 337–48.

White, M., "Public Policy Toward Bankruptcy: Me-First and Other Priority Rules," *The Bell Journal of Economics* (Autumn 1980).

White, M., "Bankruptcy Costs and the New Bankruptcy Code," *Journal of Finance* (May 1983), pp. 477–88.

White, M., "The Corporate Bankruptcy Decision," *Journal of Economic Perspectives* 3 (Spring 1989), pp. 129–51.

CHAPTER 8

INDUSTRY CONTAGION EFFECTS OF BANKRUPTCY AND FIRM SIZE

Larry H. P. Lang
Rene M. Stulz

INTRODUCTION

In Lang and Stulz (1991) we investigate the stock-price effect of bankruptcy announcements on the competitors of the firm making the announcement. We find that a bankruptcy announcement has a small but reliable negative effect on the value of the common stock of competitors. We argue in that paper that a bankruptcy announcement has two effects on competitors: it conveys information about the value of investments in the industry (contagion effect) and it changes the competitive position of firms within the industry (competitive effect).

The contagion effect should most typically be negative. If a firm announces a bankruptcy filing, it conveys information to the market that it is doing less well than previously thought, as evidenced by the literature on the information content of the bankruptcy announcement for the firms making the announcement.[1] Investors will therefore adjust their estimates of the value of comparable firms to reflect their newly acquired information that a

Larry H. P. Lang is Assistant Professor of Finance at Stern School of Business, New York University.
Rene M. Stulz holds the Rklis Chair in Business at Ohio State University.

firm in the industry is doing poorly. Since profitability is correlated across firms in an industry, part of this adjustment typically reflects information that the industry as a whole is doing more poorly than expected.

At the same time, however, a bankruptcy announcement conveys information about the relative position of firms within an industry. If a firm is doing worse in an industry relative to other firms, then the other firms must be doing relatively better. If bankruptcy provides information that a firm has or will lose some of its ability to compete, this is good news for other firms in the industry since they can prey on the weakness of the bankrupt firm. Hence, the competitive effect will typically be positive. However, whereas the dichotomy between competitive effects and contagion effects is useful, it should not be overdone. In particular, one might argue that in some cases bankruptcy enhances the competitive position of the bankrupt firm by enabling it to renegotiate contracts.

In this paper, we extend the analysis of Lang and Stulz (1991) to see whether the effect of bankruptcy announcements on competitors differs for the large and small firms in an industry. One would expect the contagion effect to be smaller for small firms because they are less likely to be affected by industry factors. For instance, small firms are less likely to serve the national market and hence are more likely to be affected by regional factors that are uncorrelated across firms operating in different regions. On the other hand, there is little reason to suspect that the small firms will experience less of a competitive effect because these firms could use the difficulties of the bankrupt firm to grow. Hence, we would expect the return of small firms in an industry associated with the bankruptcy announcement to be higher than the return of large firms—i.e., shareholders of small firms should lose less in percentage terms than shareholders of large firms.

In the second section, we describe our sample and the technique used to compute industry returns. In the third section, we report and interpret our results for small and large firms. In the final section, we provide concluding remarks.

THE SAMPLE

Our sample consists of all bankruptcies before 1990 of firms with liabilities in excess of $120 million reported in Altman (1991). We focus on large bankruptcies to restrict our attention to cases where a bankruptcy can have an industry-wide effect. We eliminate from the sample all bankrupt firms for which a four-digit SIC code is not available from *Compustat*. Our sample includes stocks traded on the NYSE, the AMEX, and NASDAQ. We define as a bankrupt firm's industry all other firms that have the same 4-digit industry SIC code. To compute the shareholder wealth effect of a bankruptcy announcement on the bankrupt firm's competitors, we form an equally-weighted portfolio of all firms in the same industry with stock returns available from CRSP data files. We construct an industry portfolio for each bankruptcy. Hence, when we have two bankruptcies in an industry, the industry portfolio is likely to differ because firms will have entered or exited the industry.[2]

In this study, we use as the event date the date of *The Wall Street Journal* announcement of the Chapter 11 filing. For a given bankruptcy, the abnormal return on a particular date is defined as the industry portfolio return minus the market return on that day.[3] We compute standard deviations of estimates using the cross-sectional standard deviations of industry portfolio returns.

The size portfolios are constructed as follows. For each bankruptcy, we divide the firms in the industry portfolio into two groups: the firms for which the total book value of assets exceeds or equals the median of the industry and the firms for which the total book value of assets is lower than the median. Without constructing size portfolios, our sample includes 59 bankruptcies for which we can compute industry portfolios. For 2 of these 59 bankruptcies, the industry portfolio has only one firm. These two bankruptcies are excluded from the sample in this study.

THE INDUSTRY RETURNS FOR SIZE PORTFOLIOS

To investigate whether the percentage market adjusted wealth losses differ depending on firm size, we provide in Table 8–1 estimates of average abnormal returns for industry portfolios of large and small firms. For the large firms, there is a significant negative abnormal on days –2, 0, and +1. Further, the abnormal return is negative on all days except two over the sample period from 5 days before *The Wall Street Journal* announcement to 5 days after. In contrast, for the small firms, the abnormal return is significantly negative on days +1 and +2 and significantly positive on day +4. The abnormal return is also nonnegative for 4 days out of 11.

Looking at individual days shows that both size portfolios experience a significant contagion effect. However, the large firm portfolios seem to

TABLE 8–1
Average Percentage Shareholder Abnormal Return Associated with Bankruptcy Announcements for Sized-Based Industry Portfolios[a]

Day Relative to Event Day	Large firms %Loss	t-stat	Small firms %Loss	t-stat
−5	−0.08	(−0.54)	0.09	(0.41)
−4	−0.21	(−1.23)	−0.22	(−1.00)
−3	−0.02	(−0.12)	0.16	(0.72)
−2	−0.31	(−2.07)	−0.33	(−1.34)
−1	−0.27	(−1.25)	0.13	(0.49)
0	−0.31	(−1.70)	−0.07	(−0.36)
+1	−0.60	(−2.55)	−0.37	(−1.94)
+2	−0.11	(−0.81)	−0.49	(−2.11)
+3	0.02	(0.12)	−0.08	(−0.37)
+4	0.27	(1.48)	0.49	(2.79)
+5	−0.09	(−0.04)	−0.07	(−0.30)
(−1, 0)	−0.58	(−1.82)	0.06	(0.17)
(−5, 0)	−0.74	(−1.58)	−0.25	(−0.42)
(−1, +1)	−1.18	(−2.61)	−0.31	(−0.68)
(−5, +5)	−1.71	(−2.33)	−0.78	(−1.08)

[a] The portfolios include the firms whose total assets exceed the median total assets in the industry (large firms) and of the other firms (small firms), respectively. The percentage abnormal return equals the portfolio return minus the market return for the relevant period. t-statistics are computed using the cross-sectional standard deviation of industry portfolio returns. The sample includes bankruptcies before 1990 of firms with more than $120 million in liabilities for which a 4-digit SIC code is available from the *Compustat* data files and for which the industry includes more than two firms (57 bankruptcies).

incorporate news about the bankruptcy announcement faster than the small firms. After day +1, there is no significant abnormal return for the large firms, but there are two significant abnormal returns of opposite signs for the small firms. To the extent that small firms trade less frequently and are followed less actively, one would expect their stock price to incorporate news less quickly than large firms. One should therefore not interpret the pattern of abnormal returns as evidence of profit opportunities that could be captured by selling the stock short on the day of *The Wall Street Journal* announcement. In any case, the gain of about 0.9% that results from cumulating the abnormal returns for days +1 and +2 and applying them to a short position are gross of transaction costs and most likely would disappear if transaction costs were taken into account.

The second part of the table reports abnormal returns for various subperiods. For three out of four subperiods, the cumulative average abnormal return of large firm portfolios is significantly negative. The cumulative average abnormal return is not negative for the period from –5 days to the day of the announcement. This is not surprising since the market's anticipation of the announcement does not seem to change much in the days immediately preceding the announcement—the highest abnormal return before the day of *The Wall Street Journal* announcement is half in absolute value the abnormal return on day +1. The fall in the value of the large firm portfolio of 1.71% over the period from 5 days before the announcement to 5 days after is slightly higher than the results we report in Lang and Stulz (1991) using value-weighted industry portfolios. In that paper, Lang and Stulz argue that the contagion effect dominates the competitive effect, and such a conclusion is warranted for the large firm portfolios.

For the small firm portfolios, none of the subperiod abnormal returns are significantly different from zero. Hence, we cannot argue for these portfolios that the contagion effect dominates the competitive effect. The smaller average wealth loss for the small firm portfolios supports the hypothesis discussed in the introduction that one would expect the absolute value of the contagion effect to be smaller for small firms because they are less likely to be affected by common industry factors. However, it should be pointed out that, whereas the average cumulative abnormal returns for the small firms are not reliably different from zero, they are not reliably different from the cumulative abnormal returns for large firms either.

CONCLUSION

In this study, we extend the study of Lang and Stulz (1991) by showing that a bankruptcy announcement on average significantly decreases the value of large firms in the industry of the bankrupt firm but not the value of small firms. We interpret this evidence as supportive of the hypothesis that the contagion effect of bankruptcy announcements is stronger for firms that are more similar to the bankrupt firm. Since we investigate large bankruptcies, large firms in the bankrupt firm's industry are more likely to have a market and costs that are similar to the bankrupt firm than smaller firms which often will be firms with a regional market.

Even for large firms the announcement effect of bankruptcy is relatively limited since it averages 1.7% for the 11 days that surround the announcement. This might be because the difficulties of the bankrupt firm are well-known and the information they convey is already incorporated in the stock price of competitors. Alternatively, this might be because bankruptcy announcements and the difficulties of the bankrupt firm are mostly due to idiosyncratic factors that have only limited implications for competitors. At the very least, however, our evidence indicates that large bankruptcies have only moderate contagion effects and hence that these effects should not be of great concern to policy makers.

NOTES

1. See, for instance, Clark and Weinstein (1983) and Lang and Stulz (1991).
2. For industries with more than 50 firms in *Compustat*, we randomly select 50 firms to form the industry portfolio and retrieve return data from the CRSP files.
3. This approach differs from Lang and Stulz (1991) where abnormal returns are risk-adjusted using beta estimates from market model regressions for industry portfolios.

REFERENCES

Altman, E., 1991, *Distressed Securities,* Chicago: Probus Publishing Co.

Clark, T. A., and M. Weinstein, 1983, "The behavior of the common stock of bankrupt firms," *Journal of Finance 38,* 489–504.

Lang, L.H.P., and R. M. Stulz, 1991, "Intra-industry competition and contagion effects of bankruptcy announcements," The Ohio State University unpublished working paper.

PART THREE

INVESTING AND TRADING
IN HLT BANK LOANS

CHAPTER 9

HLT BANK LOANS: A NEW MARKET FOR RELATIVE VALUE INVESTORS

Paul H. Ross, CFA
Dennis G. Dolan
Christopher R. Ryan
James B. Windle

OVERVIEW

Assignments and participations by money center banks of their commercial loans to smaller and regional, domestic, and foreign financial institutions were a hallmark of the growth of leveraged loan transactions in the 1980s. Such senior bank loan sales allowed agent and lead banks to accelerate their origination rates, while the selldowns gave the purchasers access to previously unavailable assets. However, such loans had limited appeal and remarketability outside the interbank market. In addition, the pricing and valuation of these loans lacked any particular scientific basis by which their prospective returns could be compared with those of other financial assets. As a result, most highly leveraged transaction (HLT) bank loans traded near par with little price differentiation for fundamental credit variables. This

Paul H. Ross, Dennis G. Dolan, Christopher R. Ryan, and James B. Windle are with the firm of Salomon Brothers, Inc. in New York.

once-restricted market now is set to change, and investors who demand a security with remarketability soon will have access to HLT bank loans.

During the 1990s, we believe that many more portfolio managers will recognize the attractive returns available from the almost $800 billion HTL bank loan market. Several nonbank investors, such as insurance companies and bank loan mutual funds, already are involved and may become more substantial players. Either directly as before or through trust vehicles, these loans will become increasingly available in a format agreeable to bond portfolio managers. And because these HLT bank loans have senior ranking, security, and strong protective covenants, high-yield investors will prefer them to many of the subordinated bonds on the balance sheets of highly leveraged issuers, as well as to the unsecured senior bonds of these same issuers.

This chapter reviews the rationale for this emerging new market for both fixed-income and equity investors. We compare the structure of HLT bank loans to that of other high-yield instruments and suggest a valuation convention to compare yields and relative value.

HIGH-YIELD BONDS REVISITED

Three recent market characteristics have caused many investors to become wary of a lot of the leveraged buyout and recapitalization issues that comprise the $210 billion universe of publicly registered high-yield bonds. First, the overwhelming majority of high-yield bonds are subordinated: this junior balance sheet priority ranking, while not significant when operating performance is strong, is doubly harmful when results decline and credit quality wanes. Second, because economic and viability risk has become such an overwhelming concern, the price volatility of many low-quality bonds is tied more to the price of their underlying equity shares than to the duration characteristics that affect their investment-grade cousins. Third, the prospective onslaught of recession is highlighting the riskiness of highly leveraged balance sheets and the limitations of support available from traditional sources and lenders of capital. Despite these drawbacks, many investors are still seeking high returns and yield spreads wider than those currently available from investment-grade bond issues or bank loans, and they are finding that HLT bank loans satisfy these goals.

HLT BANK LOANS VERSUS HIGH-YIELD BONDS

In the 1980s, demand for high-yield returns caused many loans to be securitized in the form of public and private high-yield bonds. In the 1990s, we expect this flow to reverse, since HLT bank loans can provide investors with nearly all of the favorable attributes of bonds. Banks are increasingly subject to regulatory and investor scrutiny of their asset quality and profitability. We believe that many of the estimated $800 billion of domestic HLT bank loans will become available, as more banks adopt a capital utilization and a total rate of return focus, rather than the traditional yield spread orientation, to managing their assets.

Historically, floating-rate-based HLT bank loans were unacceptable to most traditional high-yield buyers, who generally bought fixed-rate assets either to match their fixed-rate liabilities or to seek capital gains associated with duration. High-yield buyers also had a preference, in good economic times, for investments with low balance sheet priority such as straight subordinated debt or convertible bonds. HLT bank loans had other distinctive disadvantages as well—burdensome documentation, high transaction costs, potential conflicts of interest stemming from access to confidential information, and covenants that limited eligible investees and required pro rata investments in revolvers and term loans. In addition, selective investment policies restricted the purchase of HLT bank loans.

We believe the risk/reward matrix has changed: The historical constraints on the HLT bank loan market now are more than offset by these obligations' collateral and their senior priority position on high-yield issuers' balance sheets. Even in bankruptcy, the courts can quickly judge the collateral position of a secured lender and will mandate payment or accrual of interest, as appropriate in each case. HLT bank loans lack a bond's redemption protection, but purchasing an HLT bank loan at a discount to its face amount will mitigate this risk. On balance, we believe that many investors will find HLT bank loans a preferable way to participate in a given borrower's capital-raising activities. The essential differences between an HLT bank loan and a subordinated high-yield bond are summarized in Figure 9–1.

Although subordinated issues constituted the bulk of new high-yield bond issuance in the 1980s, many senior unsecured issues that once had investment-grade ratings also populate the high-yield market. Indentures of these senior unsecured issues typically include negative pledge clauses (limitations on the granting of liens), which give equal access to the collat-

FIGURE 9–1
HLT Bank Loans versus High-Yield Bonds

Bank Loans	Junk Bonds
Senior	Subordinated
Secured	Unsecured
Short Maturity	Long Maturity
Quarterly Interest in Cash	Semiannual Interest, Sometimes Not in Cash
First Claim on Cash Flows and Specific Claims on Assets	Junior Claim on Cash Flows and No Specific Claims on Assets

eral granted to newly secured creditors. However, some negative pledge clauses were not written to include all assets, and working capital often is carved out. While senior unsecured bonds with negative pledge clauses were designed to assure their holders of *pari passu* status with other senior lenders who are granted collateral interests, secured bank loans enjoy the benefits of accelerated repayment covenants, tighter financial covenants, and often access to more collateral.[1]

TRUST STRUCTURE OVERVIEW

In the past, HLT bank loans were syndicated by their agents to reduce their exposure and to serve the buyers' needs for assets. Loans can be syndicated in three ways: (1) assignments, in which the buyer replaces the selling bank and undertakes the responsibilities and rights of the seller; (2) novation, by which the credit agreement is amended to include a new lender; and (3) participation, in which limited rights and responsibilities are transferred to the buyer, while the seller retains such rights as voting privileges. Syndication methods are unique to each bank agreement, and most bank agreements have been restrictive in allowing syndication. At this time, we believe that high-yield buyers' growing preference for secured HLT bank loans and the willingness of many banks to meet this demand will cause a favorable adjustment in covenants to facilitate securitization of these loans.

Holding HLT bank loans in a trust format, as presented in Figure 9–2, offers numerous advantages. First, this creates a security as defined by the Securities Act of 1933. Because bank loans are not securities as defined by

FIGURE 9–2
HLT Bank Loans Held in a Trust Format

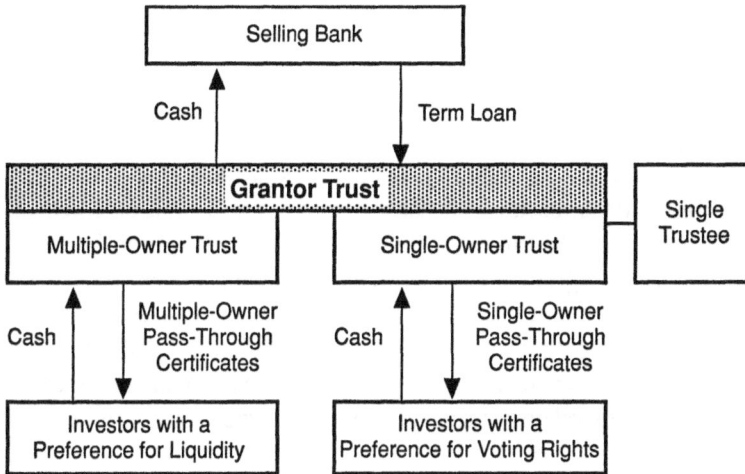

this act, many investors are restricted from purchasing them. Second, the trust format reduces transaction costs for secondary trades, because trust certificates are transferrable without the documentation and restrictions that make all direct bank loan trades cumbersome. Third, trusts may also be structured to permit certificate holders to tailor the flow of information to their own needs. Holders who wish to trade other securities of the same borrower may elect not to receive the nonpublic information that borrowers typically provide to bank lenders.

Such a trust, while a new mechanism for HLT bank loans, is the mandated format for other securitized secured bonds, such as auto receivables (CARs), collateralized mortgage obligation pass-throughs, and credit cards receivables (CARDs).

VALUATION MECHANISM

Bank term loans are floating-rate instruments with scheduled principal payments over the life of the loan. The borrower periodically selects from the available interest rate options, which typically are based on the prime rate, the London interbank offered rate (LIBOR) or the certificate of deposit rate.

Afterwards, many borrowers access the interest rate swap market to fix their borrowing costs. While buyers of floating-rate bank loans can compare these assets with other floating-rate assets on a discounted margin basis,[2] investors need an objective methodology to compare the risk/return characteristics of bank loans with those of other fixed-rate senior or subordinated high-yield bonds of the same and other issuers. An internal rate of return calculation provides such a mechanism.

Traditional yield to maturity calculations are less than ideal for floating-rate bank loans, because the base interest rate cannot be forecast over the life of the loan. Therefore, we believe that the most appropriate valuation convention is to segregate each principal payment and its related interest payments into separate floating-rate notes. By applying an interest rate swap to each separate floating-rate note, we can calculate a fixed-rate stream of coupon payments. Then, by aggregating the new stream of coupon payments with the mandatory principal payments, we can derive a stream of expected cash flows from the loan. This stream of expected cash flows may be used to calculate a semiannual yield to maturity, which is, in fact, a realized internal rate of return (see Appendix A to Chapter 9 for an example).

This valuation methodology poses a few problems. First, many term loans have an interest rate stepdown feature that is activated when the company's performance improves on a quantitative basis. When performance measures deteriorate, stepdowns reverse. Some bank loans also have this feature tied to changes in bond ratings. Unlike fixed rate bonds, this feature reduces the investor's embedded return when credit quality improves; yet the borrower's coupon saving typically is limited to 25 basis points. Second, the borrower has the option to select a different base rate each period, and he therefore can play the yield curve, if only for limited periods of time. The yield to maturity calculation at the purchase date is based on the rate mechanism that the borrower last selected. The borrower holds this option, and the investor's return is somewhat less precise.

Our yield to maturity calculation also does not account for the possibility of prepayments. Unlike the typical covenants of corporate bonds, most HLT bank loan covenants have early escape mandates that reduce each lender's loan exposure in the event that certain performance benchmarks are breached; furthermore, asset sales and capital-raising activities usually require loan principal prepayments. The HLT bank loan buyer's prepayment risk is mitigated to the extent he purchases the bank loan at a discount to the borrower's par repurchase price.

CONCLUSION

HLT bank loans in a tradeable format represent a new form of investment for portfolio managers. We believe that both performing "par" and distressed HLT bank loans will be made available by HLT bank loan holders who elect to manage their capital and assets more actively. Bank loans are short-dated assets that offer high yields, interest rate protection, quarterly interest payments, and a senior and secured position in the borrower's capital structure. Securitization of HLT bank loans will mitigate many of the negative factors that previously constrained the development of a broad audience. In the 1990s, we expect that a growing universe of institutional customers will come to appreciate the relative merits and value of HLT bank loans.

NOTES

1. See *Leveraged Buyouts and Leveraged Restructurings: Risks and Rewards for Pre-existing Bondholders,* Salomon Brothers Inc., November 2, 1988, for further discussion of the negative pledge covenant.
2. See *Understanding the Duration of Floating-Rate Notes,* Salomon Brothers Inc., September 1987.

APPENDIX A TO CHAPTER 9

VALUING HLT BANK LOANS ON A YIELD TO MATURITY BASIS

Assumptions
- Seven-year term loan.
- Eight quarterly principal repayments of 12.5% of the loan beginning at the end of the first quarter of the sixth year.
- Interest rate of reserve-adjusted LIBOR plus 250 basis points.

Step One
Segregate the loan into eight floating-rate notes with maturities corresponding to each principal payment:
1. 5 years, 3 months
2. 5 years, 6 months
3. 5 years, 9 months
4. 6 years
5. 6 years, 3 months
6. 6 years, 6 months
7. 6 years, 9 months
8. 7 years

Step Two
Determine the fixed-rate equivalent for the seven-year floating rate note:

	Seven-Year Swap versus LIBOR 9.39%
plus	250 Basis Points..2.50
plus	Reserve Adjustment 0.26
minus	Trust Administration Costs ....(0.05)
	Fixed-Rate Equivalent..12.10%

Repeat for the other seven floating-rate notes.

Step Three
Calculate quarterly interest payments for each floating-rate note based upon each note's fixed-rate equivalent. Then compile quarterly cash flows for all the notes.

Step Four
Calculate the yield to maturity based upon the assumed purchase price:

Price	Bond-Equivalent Yield
$95.00	13.08%
96.00	12.95
96.50	12.82
97.00	12.70
97.50	12.57
98.00	12.45
98.50	12.33
99.00	12.21

CHAPTER 10

REGULATORY ISSUES IN SECONDARY TRADING OF DISTRESSED BANK LOANS

Martin S. Fridson, CFA

Opinions differ concerning the evolutionary niche filled by the emerging secondary market in distressed bank loans. Some observers consider it a logical successor to the trading of public securities of leveraged buyouts as a growth business for Wall Street.[1] Others view the market for bank debt of troubled companies as a natural extension of the existing traffic in loans to less-developed countries (LDCs) and nondistressed corporations.[2]

In truth, the buying and selling of highly leveraged transaction (HLT) senior bank debt have ties of kinship with the markets in both high yield bonds and Third World obligations. As such, they are likely to inherit a number of regulatory issues from each. Certain controversies that have arisen in the realm of asset securitization will probably also be replayed in HLT debt trading.

The following survey covers six broad areas of potential regulatory activity. Emphasis throughout is on identifying issues, rather than on debating the merits or on estimating the likelihood of legislative or regulatory action.

Martin S. Fridson, CFA, is Managing Director of High Yield Research at Merrill Lynch & Co.

RECOURSE

The issue on which regulatory policy formulation is currently at the most advanced stage is recourse. On June 29, 1990, the Federal Financial Institutions Examination Council (FFIEC), representing five federal agencies charged with regulating depository institutions, requested comments on treatment of recourse arrangements for purposes of calculating regulatory capital.[3] Currently, the FFIEC is reviewing the comments it received and estimates that a cross-agency policy on the credit risk aspects of recourse will be in place by the end of 1991. The critical importance of recourse questions in the field of asset securitization—a huge market ever since the inception of federally sponsored pooling of residential mortgages in the 1970s—accounts for the comparatively well-developed state of regulatory response. Implications for the secondary HLT market of decisions concerning recourse include the following:

1. In accordance with principles embodied in an international framework established in July 1988 by the Basle Committee on Banking Supervision, U.S. regulators require all quantifiable risks to a financial institution to be supported by capital. Recourse, which may exist in a subtle form even though an institution has ostensibly shed an asset, poses a risk of loss and therefore affects the application of risk-based capital standards to the institution.

2. The determination that there is recourse back to the seller may establish that the selling bank has excessive exposure to a particular borrower, even though its outstanding loans to that borrower are within the applicable regulatory limit.

3. Performance ratios such as return on assets will decline if loans previously sold and therefore removed from a bank's balance sheet are restored on the grounds that the sales were not truly free of recourse. Lower performance ratios, in turn, adversely affect examiners' reports and securities analysts' assessments of the bank's credit quality and investment value.[4]

4. If the loan purchaser happens to be another bank and the sale is made with recourse to the selling bank, then the purchaser must treat the transaction as a loan to the selling bank rather than as a loan to the ultimate borrower. Multiplied several times over through a series of loan purchases from a particular bank, this situation may cause the purchaser to bump up against its loan limit for that bank. No such problem would arise if the purchaser bought, from a single bank and

without recourse, the loans of several different corporate borrowers.

To readers who are unfamiliar with the intricacies of loan sales, resolution of the foregoing questions may appear simple and straightforward. After all, the purchaser and seller of a loan might logically be expected to spell out clearly such an important term as which party is ultimately liable for a loss. In reality, though, many loan sales contracts are not crystal clear on the issue. The purchaser wishes to limit its risk of loss by obtaining the right to "return the loan for a refund." Such a right can be viewed as a put option, the value of which the loan's seller is eager to capture through the higher price that the asset will fetch with the option attached. At the same time, the seller wants to be able to demonstrate that it has eliminated the risk of loss associated with the loan.

The following list includes some, but not all, means by which a loan sales agreement may leave the seller with actual or potential exposure to loss. Deciding whether, in each instance, recourse should be deemed to exist defines the regulatory issue for HLT trading, as well as for other forms of loan resale and securitization.

1. Explicit recourse may exist in the loan sale contract, even though the seller retains no credit risk. Increasingly, sellers are offering assurances against losses arising from interest rate swings and prepayments, foreign exchange fluctuations, reductions in liquidity or marketability, regulatory noncompliance by borrowers, or uninsurable hazards. Similarly, recourse may be inferred if buyers of HLT loans succeed in obtaining "fair representation clauses" based on findings of fraudulent conveyance.[5] This type of clause in effect creates a put option against the seller in the event of an adverse legal decision.

2. Regulators may impute implicit recourse to a transaction if the seller has demonstrated a pattern of repurchasing loans that unexpectedly go sour, despite having no legal obligation to do so. The selling bank's motive might be to preserve the goodwill of purchasers or to maintain a reputation for providing high-quality merchandise to the resale market.

    In a similar vein, commercial bankers speak of a convention involving an informal obligation on the part of the selling bank to repurchase a loan that becomes troubled. Suppose a bank buys a portion of a loan, without recourse, from an agent bank, then in turn sells a participation to a smaller bank. The smaller bank, having no relationship with the borrower, may expect the institution with which it does have a relationship to repurchase any loan that goes sour.

   Even if the selling bank does not feel honor-bound to repurchase a problem loan it has sold to a small bank, it may end up doing so for an entirely pragmatic reason. That is, the small bank may refuse to go along with a covenant waiver or modification that is essential to the borrower's continued solvency and requires 100% approval of lenders. By "holding out" in this fashion, the small bank may effectively compel the selling bank to repurchase the loan in order to avoid an undesired bankruptcy filing that would jeopardize its own position.

3. Subtle forms of recourse may arise from structural differences between the original loan and the obligation that is sold to the purchaser. For example, the purchaser may obtain a maturity that is shorter than that of the loan originally made by the seller. A risk of loss will then exist for the seller during the period between the two maturities. Similarly, the originating bank may sell a 90-day loan made under a two-year revolving credit agreement. If the borrower were to become unable to repay the loan during the three-month period, the originating bank could remain obligated to extend credit. This would imply that it had potential liability even at the point at which no loan was on its own books.

Information and Disclosure

As the foregoing discussion of recourse makes clear, the transfer of risk is an economically critical, as well as a highly sensitive, aspect of a loan sale. As long as the risk transfer occurs with the full knowledge of both parties, it can be reflected in the price that they jointly determine through negotiation. In principle, the appropriateness of prices agreed upon under conditions of adequate disclosure should not be the subject of regulation. If, on the other hand, risk is transferred without the purchaser's complete knowledge, regulatory intervention may be in order.

   The reason for a purchasing institution's lack of sufficient information, resulting in an economically unwise decision, may simply be its own failure to perform due diligence. In such a case, a regulated entity (e.g., depository institution, insurance company) cannot offer the excuse that it relied on the seller's own credit investigation. Examiners may criticize any transaction— even if no loss has occurred—on the grounds of insufficient support for the investment decision.

Conceivably, an originating bank could initiate a policy of emphasizing loan sales and begin to make certain loans with the specific intention of selling them, rather than holding them in portfolio. In time, a more liberal credit standard could be systematically applied to loans targeted for sale without recourse. Under such circumstances, the originator's reputation for thorough credit analysis would be an even thinner reed for buyers to lean upon than ordinarily. In addition, this scenario might create a credit problem for the originating bank. If the market began to perceive a two-tiered credit standard of the sort described, the seller could suddenly be stuck with unsalable loans of lesser quality in its origination-for-sale "pipeline."

The second way in which inadequate information may accompany the transfer of risk in a loan sale is as a result of deliberately incomplete or misleading disclosure by the seller. Although under current market practice the buyer generally has a full obligation to perform due diligence, the borrower may not wish to have its nonpublic financial data and forecasts indiscriminately disseminated. Control of the information flow will then reside with the originating bank, which may have the additional advantage of a long-established relationship with the borrower. There may be a temptation on the part of a bank in this situation to downplay information concerning risks that might scare off potential buyers of the loan. Legislative, judicial, and regulatory solutions may all be required to settle questions of materiality in the conveyance of information.

One additional regulatory concern arises from the sensitivity of nonpublic information. Certain institutions involved in trading or investing in public bonds of leveraged-buyout companies also deal in HLT loans to the same companies. Bank lenders routinely receive projections and other nonpublic financial information from borrowers. Consequently, from a firmwide standpoint, such institutions may come into possession of information that, in the absence of procedures designed to preclude the misuse of such information, could compromise their ability to trade public issues. As in certain other potential conflicts, such as participation by investment banks in both financial advisory work and stock trading, "Chinese walls" may be necessary between departments that are privy to nonequivalent levels of disclosure.[6] It has also been suggested that trading loans via trust vehicles will minimize the likelihood that such information will be received and therefore insulate investors from information they might, on balance, prefer not to have. This proposed solution, however, does not address the issue of inequality of information between the original seller and the buyer.

LIQUIDITY

Like the markets for privately placed bonds, public noninvestment grade bonds, and LDC debt, the HLT loan market has certain characteristics that limit its liquidity. Final investors and market makers are comparatively few in number, documentation is not completely standardized, and credit information (partly for the reasons discussed immediately above) is at times sparse. In terms of trading mechanics, liquidity-enhancing devices such as short-selling and hedging are not readily available. Given these constraints, it is hardly surprising that most HLT loans exhibit low turnover, infrequent transactions, and wide bid/asked spreads.

Contrary to the impression held by many, this sort of illiquid trading environment characterizes the majority of financial markets, with elite sectors such as large-capitalization listed stocks and Treasury bills representing the exception rather than the rule.[7] Most financial instruments are by their nature prone to trade irregularly, resulting in unavoidable uncertainty about their values at any point other than the instant of an actual transaction. Nevertheless, legislators (and probably many prospective investors) have tended to view the high yield bond market's limited liquidity as a concern— one that, moreover, can and should be ameliorated.[8] Fueling attempts to correct what in reality may be a natural state of affairs for such instruments have been allegations of past manipulation of high yield issues by certain dealers. The premise has been advanced that such manipulation could be prevented if only centralized markets with real-time quote streams were developed. This "solution" neglects the fact that even if all transactions were recorded centrally, they would not occur frequently enough to make up-to-the-minute quotations representative of the levels at which securities could realistically be bought or sold. In the event of any hint of manipulation in the HLT sector, however, it is to be expected that calls will arise for the creation of a "normal" market in the obligations. This, though, would ignore the fact that even in the absence of manipulation, liquidity in the instruments will be limited.

PRICING AND ACCOUNTING

Aside from the threat of manipulation, the main regulatory concern arising from illiquidity involves institutions' use of prices that are frequently by definition merely estimates, since they are not always derived from actual transactions. A mutual fund, for example, charges its shareholders a management fee calculated as a percentage of its net asset value (N.A.V.). Determining the N.A.V. of a fund that holds bank loans depends on estimated prices,[9] so a fair value must be derived through the fund's directors acting diligently and in good faith. So far, the Securities and Exchange Commission has not endorsed any particular method for valuing loans, but has instead indicated that fund managers must use diligent efforts and good judgment.

In the realm of commercial banks, the reliability of prices derived from secondary trading of HLT loans affects an ongoing debate about mark-to-market accounting. By way of background, Securities and Exchange Commission Chairman Richard Breeden has strongly advocated the adoption of current-cost-basis accounting for financial assets. The Financial Accounting Standards Board intends to implement a proposal based on that principle by late 1991, despite strong opposition within the banking industry.

To many who favor the mark-to-market approach, the existence of a quoted market below par on a loan strongly implies that the portion of the loan remaining on banks' books has fallen in value and should therefore be revalued for accounting purposes. Stalwarts of the historical-cost-basis approach counter that at present, HLT secondary activity is too thin to be regarded as a generator of truly representative prices. Subpar quotations on a loan may not reflect actual transactions and therefore do not prove the willingness of holders to take losses on the obligation. Even when a quotation is generated by an actual trade, a holder who did not sell at the depressed price may argue that the sale was made under duress in a market lacking depth and was therefore not representative of intrinsic value. Notwithstanding such arguments, if a bank willingly sells part of its share of a loan at a severely depressed price, it is likely to have difficulty persuading regulators that the balance is unimpaired and should remain on its books at full face value.

Potentially even more unfavorable, from a bank's standpoint, than mandatory mark-to-market accounting is lower-of-cost-or-market (LOCOM) treatment. Under certain circumstances, auditors or examiners could extend this method from the portion of a bank's loans that it holds for sale (mandatory treatment for all banks) to its entire portfolio. LOCOM accounting generally produces a lower portfolio value than marking to market, since both methods recognize declines from original cost but only the latter recognizes gains.

The rationale for applying LOCOM to a bank's total portfolio would be an observed, recurrent pattern at the institution of selling troubled loans and retaining healthy ones. Since the bank's officers cannot ascertain ahead of time which loans will become troubled, the entire portfolio could be deemed potentially held for sale and therefore subject to LOCOM valuation.

Equally subject to criticism by examiners is the opposite pattern, i.e., selling of healthy loans that can be sold at a profit and retention of troubled ones. Examiners might deem such activity "gains trading," which they consider an unsound banking practice. (Gains trading artificially inflates performance ratios by realizing gains on loans while essentially burying offsetting losses.)

TRADING PRACTICES

"Gains trading" is but one of many trading practices that, if found to be either widespread or executed on a vast scale, could result in greater regulatory focus on the HLT market.

The investigation of possible manipulation in the LDC market in December 1990[10] underscored the potential for abuse that exists in any trading operation, but the context—a bank loan market—made the development especially pertinent to HLT traders. According to allegations published in *The Wall Street Journal,* funds were diverted from institutional accounts through trades executed at non-arm's-length prices. In language characteristic of the criticism that is periodically aimed at less-regulated markets, the *Journal* reporter characterized LDC loan trading as a "global bazaar almost wholly invisible to regulators." In the LDC market, he added, "There's no exchange, no official leadership, no written rules, no reporting system."

Such characteristics do not necessarily prove that a market is either fatally flawed or unusually susceptible to improper trading activity, but they could act as red flags. Accordingly, cries for new trading controls will likely be heard if the glare of negative publicity should for any reason fall on HLT loan trading, another sector not highly regulated at this point.

The absence of regulation specifically designed to target HLT trading does not mean that trading abuses would go undetected, however. For example, a commercial bank might conceivably sell a loan at an indifferent or unattractive price for purely cosmetic reasons, i.e., to reduce its exposure to a troubled borrower below a limit that would trigger a specific disclosure requirement. Examiners would likely judge a transaction of this nature "unsafe and unsound" and criticize it. Magnitude is a consideration in such cases, but the threshold is probably low enough and the judgmental element large enough to deter most institutions from brazenly engaging in noneconomically motivated trades.

OTHER ISSUES

Assuming the secondary market in HLT loans will continue to grow and, as a natural consequence, begin to attract increased attention from agencies and legislators, the regulatory discussion is bound to expand and incorporate various issues that have been vigorously debated in other financial markets. Two examples follow.

First, the "level playing field" concept has become a major talking point as innovation and deregulation have blurred traditional boundaries within the financial services industry. Firms have frequently complained of allegedly unfair competition from other types of institutions operating under different regulatory regimes.

In the HLT loan market, a broker-dealer could be disadvantaged vis-à-vis commercial bank requirements by heavier capital requirements to support trading operations. Engaging in HLT debt trading through an unregulated subsidiary (if legally permitted), though, could enable the broker-dealer to escape the disadvantage.

Playing fields may also be unlevel because of cross-border differences in the regulation of a given type of institution. Trading operations may even seek to exploit such differences by booking transactions in the most advantageous jurisdiction, a comparatively easy matter with today's advanced telecommunications technologies. In *The Wall Street Journal* article referred to above, the author noted that in the LDC debt market "the extent of the overseas activity, involving foreign firms or foreign units of U.S. firms, puts most of the activity beyond the reach of U.S. regulators."[11] The international scope of the HLT loan market, which has been well documented in press accounts,[12] makes cross-border regulatory differences a likely subject of future discussion.

Another issue that is likely to spill over from other markets involves the change in traditional banking practices that loan sales might induce. Already, some borrowers have demanded pricing concessions to compensate for the possibility that their loans will be sold to third parties (including institutions other than banks) with which they have no long-term relationships. The borrowers' concern is that accommodations on terms, required either to get through difficult periods or to capitalize on special opportunities, will become harder to obtain once their debt is held by parties with no incentive, in the form of potential future business, to be flexible. The regulatory imperatives produced by the weakening of relations are by no means clear, but the relevant agencies will probably not remain impassive in the face of such a major transformation of banking services.

CONCLUSION

Unless secondary bank loan market participants are very different from their counterparts in other sectors of financial services, the prospect of increased regulation is likely to raise concerns about the effect that proposed regulatory burdens could have on a dynamic, innovative market. Consequently, regulators will, we hope, take care to ensure that their actions are necessary in light of real or potential abusive behavior and no more intrusive than is needed to achieve legitimate regulatory objectives.

Realistically, though, no financial market is likely to remain large for long without attracting the attention of regulators. By responding intelligently and openly, investors and dealers may be able to head off draconian measures. Perhaps it is not even too Panglossian to hope that a number of cautious institutional investors will be more inclined to buy loans once a regulatory agency or an industry self-policing mechanism is given the mission of watching for flagrant abuses. Under these assumptions, present participants are well-advised to try to anticipate the questions that will be raised when the issue of regulation specifically designed to cover the trading of distressed bank paper is given further attention.

NOTES

1. See, for example, Steven C. Miller, "The Emerging Market for Distressed Senior Bank Loans," Loan Pricing Corporation (November 1990), p. 3. The author lists four major investment banks "which have attempted to apply their knowledge of the market for publicly traded, speculative grade 'junk bonds' and distressed debt to the bank loan market."
2. See, for example, Steven Lipin, "A Market in Bad Loans Takes Shape," *American Banker* (June 5, 1990), p. 1. The author writes, "The trading activity, participants said, would be patterned after the growing market for less-developed country loans." Lipin also characterizes HLT loan trading as "[e]ssentially an offshoot of the thriving secondary market in which healthy loans are routinely sold."

3. Federal Financial Institutions Examination Council, "Recourse Arrangements," Request for Comment in Federal Register, vol. 55, no. 126 (Washington, D.C.: United States Government Printing Office, June 29, 1990), pp. 26766–75.

4. Note that a bank's liquidity may improve—a tangible benefit to credit quality—as the result of a loan sale, even if regulators or auditors require the loan to remain on the books due to the existence of recourse.

5. "Fraudulent conveyance" refers to a potential liability that may arise for lenders and shareholders if a court finds that a highly leveraged transaction rendered the borrower insolvent. (Certain other factors also affect the determination of fraudulent conveyance.) For a fuller discussion of the issue, see Martin J. Bienenstock, *Bankruptcy Reorganization* (New York: Practising Law Institute, June 1987), pp. 399–412.

6. For a detailed discussion of this issue, see Steven Lipin, "Loan Sales Growth Heightens Legal Risks," *American Banker* (November 14, 1990), p. 1.

7. Examples of financial instruments for which investors cannot automatically expect prompt execution at levels very near the quoted markets include all but the most actively traded corporate and municipal bonds, over-the-counter stocks, and less-than-prime commercial paper. For perspective on degrees of liquidity, see Martin S. Fridson, "The Economics of Liquidity," *Extra Credit* (December 1989), pp. 4–13.

8. An October 5, 1989, letter from Senate Banking Committee Chairman Donald W. Riegle, Jr. (D., Michigan), to Treasury Secretary Nicholas F. Brady captures the spirit of attempts to fix the perceived problems of the high yield debt market. It reads in part, "In addition, thought must be given to improving the information about the market for these less than investment grade securities so that individual investors and others may be informed on a real time basis what the bid and ask prices are for these instruments and the extent to which they are liquid and marketable in the secondary market. Given the fact that secondary markets have been a central element in the growth of junk bond financing, the SEC must take steps to ensure that a modernized quotation system is put into place."

9. "Estimation" does not imply guesswork. Numerous research organizations have developed sophisticated models for valuing loans, based on borrowers' financial statements and the options embedded in loan documents.

10. Peter Truell, "Global Bazaar: U.S. Grand Jury Probes a Wild, Murky Market in Third World Debt," *The Wall Street Journal* (December 12, 1990), pp. A1, A6.

11. Ibid., p. A1.

12. See, for example, James R. Krauss, "Unit of Dutch Bank to Trade Shaky U.S. Corporate Loans," *American Banker* (October 3, 1990), p. 1.

PART FOUR

STRATEGIC ISSUES FOR DISTRESSED FIRMS AND INVESTORS

CHAPTER 11

FINANCIAL DISTRESS, REORGANIZATION, AND ORGANIZATIONAL EFFICIENCY

Karen Hopper Wruck

INTRODUCTION

Financial distress has changed dramatically over the last decade, in part because of major changes in the law and in financial markets. Since the adoption of the Bankruptcy Reform Act in October 1979, the number of Chapter 11 petitions has increased greatly. In 1980, the first full year after the new bankruptcy act, the number of bankruptcy petition filings increased 85% to 5,637 (up from 3,042 in 1979). In addition, since October 1979 there have been more than 20 Chapter 11 filings involving over $1 billion in liabilities.[1] Texaco's Chapter 11 filing in April 1987 was the largest in U.S. history, with $21.6 billion in liabilities; Campeau filed the second largest bankruptcy petition, in January 1990, with $9.9 billion in liabilities. The size of the liabilities and the circumstances surrounding many of the filings—legal judgments, product-liability claims, labor problems, leveraged acquisi-

Karen Hopper Wruck is an Assistant Professor at Harvard University Graduate School of Business Administration. The author would like to thank George Baker, Michael Gibbs, Krishna Palepu, Richard Ruback, Eric Wruck, and especially Michael Jensen and Jerold Warner, the referee, for their comments and suggestions. The author would also like to thank Amy Smith for her library work. This chapter is reprinted with permission from the *Journal of Financial Economics*, and approved in the October 1990 (Vol. 27, No. 2) issue.

tions, and leveraged buyouts—have stimulated debate and controversy among the press, investors, and researchers.

In financial markets over the last decade, firms began to substitute public original-issue high-yield debt, so called junk bonds, for commercial loans from the banking and insurance sector. The number of new high-yield debt offerings increased from 22 in 1977 to a peak of 217 in 1986, falling to 111 in 1989.[2] Through both takeovers and voluntary changes in capital structure, high-yield debt has facilitated the restructuring of many U.S. corporations. In addition, the development of a liquid market for high-yield debt focused attention on private workouts and exchange offers often used by firms to resolve financial distress. The number of investors buying and selling the securities of distressed firms and the capital available for such investments have grown spectacularly. Some of these "vulture capitalists" accumulate positions and participate directly in negotiations to reorganize the firm.

Financial distress is an emerging field steeped in confusion and complexity. Some of the confusion can be resolved by understanding the diverse nature of financial distress; it is not synonymous with corporate death. Firms in distress face a variety of situations having very different effects on their values and claimholders. This diversity, in conjunction with conflicts of interest among claimholders, leads to an information problem that makes valuing a distressed firm difficult. The valuation problems exacerbate the conflicts of interest. The second section of this chapter discusses the nature of financial distress, conflicts of interest, and the information problem facing a distressed firm's claimholders. Firms can resolve financial distress privately through a workout or liquidation, or under the supervision of the Bankruptcy Court. The third section discusses the methods available for resolving distress and evidence on the factors affecting their use.

Until recently, research on financial distress focused on distress costs and financial restructuring. The possibility that financial distress could result in beneficial outcomes was generally ignored. New empirical evidence demonstrates that financial distress has both benefits and costs, and that financial and ownership structure affect the net costs. Financial distress is often accompanied by comprehensive organizational changes in management, governance, and structure. This organizational restructuring can create value by improving the use of resources. For example, individual firms in declining industries tend to continue to operate and invest in economic activities even though efficiency dictates a capacity reduction. Financial distress frees resources to move to higher-valued uses by forcing managers and directors to reduce capacity and to rethink operating policies and strategy decisions. This kind of organizational change is unlikely to occur in an all-equity firm because without leverage, poor performance does not lead to financial distress. It is financial distress that gives creditors a legal right to demand restructuring. The fourth section discusses the benefits and costs of financial distress, and presents evidence on the performance of distressed firms in Japan. The fifth section concludes.

FINANCIAL DISTRESS, THE INFORMATION PROBLEM AND CONFLICTS OF INTEREST

A Definition of Financial Distress

This chapter defines financial distress as a situation where cash flow is insufficient to cover current obligations. These obligations can include unpaid debts to suppliers and employees, actual or potential damages from litigation, and missed principal or interest payments under borrowing agreements (default). Technical default, the violation of a debt covenant other than one specifying principal and interest payments (e.g., minimum-net-worth requirements or working-capital constraints), can be a warning that distress is imminent. Financial distress generally leads to negotiations with at least one group of the firm's creditors. Cross-default provisions are debt covenants in which default on one debt security is a condition for technical default on another. Such provisions result in much more complicated negotiations to resolve distress.

Some confusion arises because the word insolvent is often used as a synonym for financial distress. Insolvency can be interpreted as pertaining to stocks or flows, and the two are often confused. For example, Webster's *New World Dictionary (Second College Edition)* defines "insolvent" first as "not enough to pay all debts," and then as "unable to pay debts as they become due." A stock-based definition describes as insolvent a firm with a negative economic net worth: the present value of its cash flows is less than its total obligations.[3] A firm in financial distress is insolvent on a flow-basis; it is unable to meet current cash obligations.[4] Flow-based insolvency gives unpaid creditors the right to demand restructuring because their contract with the firm has been breached. If a firm is insolvent on a stock basis, but solvent on a flow basis, its creditors have little power, because their claims are paid to date. Creditors can expect little help from shareholders in such a situation because their equity claims are still valuable. In the unlikely event that firm value increases dramatically, shareholders capture the benefits.

Bankruptcy and liquidation are also used as synonyms for financial distress. In this paper, bankruptcy refers to the court supervised process for breaking and rewriting contracts. Liquidation refers to a sale of the firm's assets and distribution of proceeds to claimants.

The Information Problem and Conflicts of Interest

The information problem faced by a distressed firm's claimholders is how to obtain reliable data to determine whether the firm is insolvent on a stock, as well as a flow, basis. The extreme examples presented in Figure 11–1 help illustrate the problem. It shows actual cash flows for two firms. At time 1 the firms have identical historical cash flows, and future cash flows through time 2 are identical. It is only after time 2 that cash flows will differ. At time 1 both firms become distressed. The firm in panel A is insolvent on both a stock and a flow basis—cash flow after time 1 is permanently lower than the level of obligations. The panel B firm is insolvent on a flow basis only. Its cash flow will return to pre-distress levels after time 2.

The information problem boils down to deciding whether a distressed firm's situation is better described by panel A or panel B. This is important because the value-maximizing way to resolve distress differs between panels. The panel B firm can meet its obligations by persuading claimants to agree to a new payment schedule. Except for the costs of renegotiating, it suffers no penalty for financial distress. Resolving distress for the panel A firm requires major effort, including reducing fixed claims or reorganizing (if feasible) in a way that creates enough value to cover the claims.

At the time of financial distress (time 1) investors know the history of actual cash flows, but must make predictions about future cash flows with incomplete information. This can lead to honest disagreement about the firm's future prospects. Even if all parties could accurately predict future cash flows there would still be conflict over the best way to resolve distress, because different reorganization policies distribute wealth across managers, creditors, and shareholders differently. Therefore, reorganization policies are advocated both out of concern for value-maximization and out of self-interest. Where the two differ, there is potential for value-destroying behavior. As discussed in detail in "Enforcement of Absolute Priority Under Bankruptcy Law" (below, p. 265), the rules of the game for reorganization in the United States exacerbate these conflicts.

FIGURE 11–1
The Information Problem and Conflicts of Interest in Financial Distress

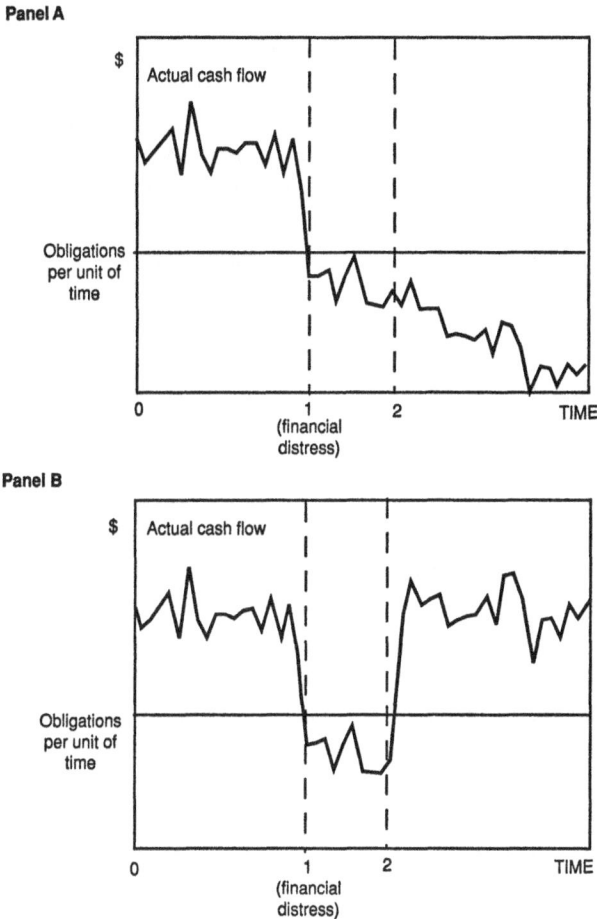

Panel A

Panel B

Panels A and B illustrate actual cash flows for two firms that become flow-based insolvent at time 1. Investors in a distressed firm face an information problem—they cannot tell whether their firm has cash flows more like those in panel A or B. The firm in panel A is insolvent due to a permanent reduction in cash flow, while the firm in panel B is insolvent due to a temporary reduction in cash flow—at time 2 its cash flow returns to a pre-distress level. Cash flows to the time of financial distress are identical for the two firms. At time 1, no one has both the relevant information about cash flows and the incentive to reveal it to the firm's claimholders. Out of self-interest shareholders will argue that panel B represents the firm's situation, while creditors will argue that panel A is more realistic. Managers will tend to side with the party less likely to fire them.

In pursuing their own interests, claimants have incentives to present biased and inaccurate data as though it were unbiased and accurate. Shareholders have incentives to claim the firm is insolvent only on a flow basis (like the panel B firm) because it increases the likelihood that they will retain their equity stake and therefore preserve the option value of their claim. Creditors have incentives to claim the firm is insolvent on a stock basis (like the panel A firm) because it increases the likelihood that they will be awarded the equity. Managers have an incentive to side with the party less likely to fire them. Resolving these conflicts consumes resources and, in the extreme, can destroy huge amounts of value. For example, a panel B firm can be turned into a panel A firm as claimants fight over the distribution of wealth, or if a value-reducing reorganization policy is chosen because it furthers the interests of a persuasive class of claimants.

The most reliable estimate of future cash flows can be obtained when accurate information is shared by managers and claimholders. Managers generally have better information about the firm's internal operations than outside investors, but they may lack the ability or incentives to make the best use of that information. A management team committed to a poor strategy or to preserving its control over the firm is using its superior information to make poor decisions. Despite their lack of detailed information about the firm's operations, both creditors and shareholders are often better able to assess the firm's situation. Large creditors have employees who are expert analysts, and in addition creditors sometimes receive special reports from the firm containing information not available to the public. Active shareholders are often better able to assess industry trends, the firm's strategy, and the effectiveness of top management. Unfortunately, no party has both the information and incentives to reveal that information to others.

Workout specialists, whose reputation suffers if they mislead claimholders, could help solve the information problem. As such a specialist, Drexel Burnham Lambert's ability to execute hundreds of exchange offers in the high-yield market suggests that its reputation played a role in attenuating information problems. The role of specialists in resolving financial distress quickly and inexpensively has been drastically curtailed with the demise of Drexel and by recent court decisions. In particular, Judge Lifland's January 1990 decision in the LTV bankruptcy case makes it more costly to resolve distress outside the courtroom. He ruled that LTV's bondholders who participated in out-of-court exchange offers before the firm's Chapter 11 filing were not entitled to a claim equal to the face value of their old bonds. Instead their claims were limited to the market value of their new bonds. Since his decision only one major private workout has been successfully completed, and it was structured to circumvent the effect of his ruling should the firm later file Chapter 11.[5]

RESOLVING FINANCIAL DISTRESS

Financial distress is resolved in an environment of imperfect information and conflicts of interest. Yet evidence on the frequency distribution of outcomes for firms in distress proves that it is not synonymous with corporate death. Financial distress is often resolved through private workouts or legal reorganization under Chapter 11 of the U.S. Bankruptcy Code. Only much more rarely are distressed firms liquidated under Chapter 7 of the code. Figure 11–2 traces firms in financial distress to their final outcomes based on data from five empirical studies. From left to right the figure presents the sample criteria for each study and follows each set of sample firms to their final outcomes. Gilson (1989, 1990) and Gilson, John, and Lang (1990) provide evidence on the fate of firms that experienced extremely poor stock price performance. Weiss (1990) and Morse and Shaw (1988) provide evidence on outcomes for firms filing Chapter 11.

Outcomes Conditional on Poor Stock Price Performance

Gilson (1989, 1990), and Gilson, John, and Lang (1990) study New York (NYSE) and American Stock Exchange (Amex) firms whose three-year cumulative stock price performance is in the bottom 5% of all firms listed on the two exchanges between 1978 and 1987. Of these firms 51% become distressed, either defaulting or restructuring their debt. The remaining 49% do not default or restructure their debt.[6] Of the distressed firms with available data, 47% (80) are able to resolve distress through a private workout.

In a workout, the firm and its creditors renegotiate their contracts privately, resolving distress without resorting to the bankruptcy courts.[7] The outcome of a workout can range from a one-time waiver of payment to a restructuring of all liabilities and equity claims. With publicly traded debt securities, the restructuring is often achieved through an exchange offer in which the distressed debt securities are exchanged for new debt securities and sometimes preferred or common stock. The remaining 53% (89) of the sample firms file for protection under Chapter 11 of the U.S. Bankruptcy Code.

FIGURE 11–2
Evidence on the Outcomes of Financial Distress Based on Data from Five Empirical Studies

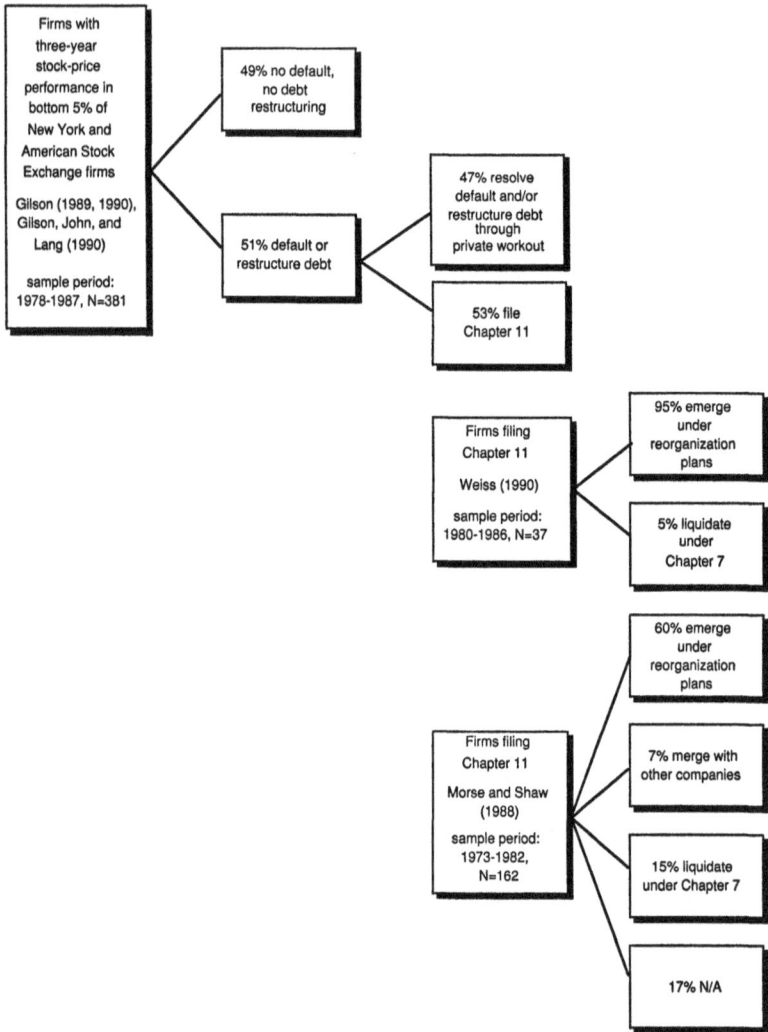

Firms with three-year stock-price performance in bottom 5% of New York and American Stock Exchange firms

Gilson (1989, 1990), Gilson, John, and Lang (1990)

sample period: 1978-1987, N=381

49% no default, no debt restructuring

51% default or restructure debt

47% resolve default and/or restructure debt through private workout

53% file Chapter 11

Firms filing Chapter 11

Weiss (1990)

sample period: 1980-1986, N=37

95% emerge under reorganization plans

5% liquidate under Chapter 7

Firms filing Chapter 11

Morse and Shaw (1988)

sample period: 1973-1982, N=162

60% emerge under reorganization plans

7% merge with other companies

15% liquidate under Chapter 7

17% N/A

The trees trace the frequency distribution of outcomes for firms in financial distress. The first box in each tree presents authors of the studies and summarizes their sample period, size, and selection criteria. Gilson (1989, 1990), and Gilson, John, and Lang (1990) study a sample of 381 NYSE and Amex firms with very poor three year cumulative stock returns during the period 1978–1987. Weiss (1990) and Morse and Shaw (1988) study samples of 37 and 162 firms filing bankruptcy petitions in the period 1980–1986 and 1973–1982, respectively.

Outcomes Conditional on Legal Bankruptcy

Figure 11–2 also follows firms that file Chapter 11 from the Weiss (1990) and Morse and Shaw (1988) samples, respectively. Their samples include firms that file Chapter 11 whether or not they had extremely poor stock price performance. A firm or its creditors can file for bankruptcy protection, which provides a court-supervised setting in which to rewrite contracts with creditors. After a firm files for bankruptcy, it continues to be run by the incumbent management team, although if management has committed fraud or is proven incompetent, the court appoints a trustee to manage the company.

Most firms entering Chapter 11 emerge after debtholders have agreed to exchange their original claims for new debt and/or equity in the company. The new debt usually has smaller payments spread over more years. Weiss (1990) studies the reorganization plans of 37 NYSE and Amex firms that enter Chapter 11. Of the 37 firms, 95% (35) emerged from Chapter 11 under accepted reorganization plans, and 5% (2) are eventually liquidated under Chapter 7. Morse and Shaw (1988) study post-Chapter 11 stock-price performance of 162 firms filing between 1973 and 1982. Of their sample firms, 60% (98) emerge from Chapter 11 under reorganization plans, 7% (11) merge with other companies, and 15% (25) liquidate under Chapter 7. Morse and Shaw could not determine with certainty the outcome for the remaining 17% (28) of their sample firms.

A firm liquidates by converting some or all of its assets to cash and distributing that cash to its claimants. When assets are less valuable to the firm than to a third party, they can be sold piecemeal or as a productive group, whichever yields the highest proceeds. Under Chapter 7 of the Bankruptcy Code, liquidation is supervised by the court. This means the bankruptcy court judge oversees the conversion of the firm's assets into cash and the distribution of the proceeds to claimholders in order of their priority.

The Role of Organizational Form and Creditors

Evidence from the United States
Many previous studies of financial distress focus on estimating the unconditional probability that a firm will file bankruptcy.[8] These studies generally analyze matched samples of bankrupt and nonbankrupt firms, using accounting information and other firm characteristics as explanatory variables. Gilson, John, and Lang (1990) estimate the probability of Chapter 11 condi-

tional on poor stock price performance. They study how asset and liability structures help predict whether financial distress is resolved through a private workout or through formal bankruptcy under Chapter 11.

Financial Structure   By design, Gilson, John, and Lang's sample contains firms for which a large percentage of the equity value has been destroyed before a default. At the median, firms in their sample that renegotiate their liabilities privately lose 50% of their equity value over the three years before the default, and firms filing for Chapter 11 lose over 60% of their equity value. They find that private renegotiation is more likely the higher the ratio of bank debt to total liabilities. The more complex the firm's capital structure (as represented by the number of classes of debt), the less likely private renegotiation is to be successful. These findings confirm some intuitive insights about bargaining and negotiation: more concentrated borrowings are easier to renegotiate, and it is easier to negotiate with fewer groups. For managers concerned about their firm's ability to reorganize privately, these results highlight the factors to consider when choosing a financing strategy.

Asset Structure   Gilson et al. also find that when Tobin's Q (the ratio of market value to replacement cost of assets) is higher, private renegotiation is more likely. They interpret their results as evidence that private reorganization is more likely in distressed firms whose economic activities generate substantial intangible assets. This is true, they argue, because the value of intangible assets is more likely to be destroyed in bankruptcy than in a private workout.[9] An alternative explanation for their results is that cross-sectional differences in Q reflect variation in pre-distress capital structure as well as in the nature of firms' assets.

A simple numerical example illustrates how this happens. Consider two firms each worth $100, with an asset replacement cost of $10 (equal to liquidation value). Firm 1 finances itself with $90 of debt and $10 of equity, whereas firm 2 finances itself with $10 of debt and $90 of equity. Suppose that for each firm half the equity value is lost and the firm defaults, entering the Gilson, John, and Lang sample. Firm 1 is worth $95 and has a Q of 9.5. Firm 2 is worth $55 and has a Q of 5.5. If firm 1 liquidates, $85 of value is destroyed and debtholders receive only 11% of their claim. If firm 2 liquidates, only $45 of value is destroyed and debtholders receive 100% of their claim. Firm 1's debt and equityholders have stronger incentives to reorganize quickly, and probably privately, once default occurs. This has nothing to do with the nature of the firm's assets, but rather with the control function of debt.[10]

International Evidence

Most of the available evidence on financial distress is based on the experience of U.S. firms. Hoshi, Kashyap, and Scharfstein (1990) provide evidence on the experience of Japanese firms. They examine the industry-adjusted investment and sales performance of 121 Japanese firms approaching financial distress between April 1978 and March 1985.[11] In selecting their sample, Hoshi, Kashyap, and Scharfstein assume a firm is approaching distress when the ratio of operating income to interest expense (interest coverage) falls below one. Sample firms have one year of healthy coverage followed by two years of poor coverage.

The evidence of Hoshi et al. indicates that cross-sectional differences in financial structure explain differences in sample firms' performance. Strong ties to financial institutions and other firms are associated with higher investment and sales performance during distress. The 49 sample firms that are members of a keiretsu—a group of firms with product-market ties and cross-share ownership that are centered around a set of banks and financial institutions—invest and sell more during periods of financial distress. Highly concentrated bank borrowings are also associated with superior performance. For Japanese firms, close bank lending relationships and equity ownership go together. On average, the largest lender holds 23% of the firm's bank debt and 4% of its equity. The shareholdings of the top lender, however, are not statistically significant as an explanatory variable for firm performance.

The implications of the results in Hoshi et al. for U.S. firms are difficult to determine because the financial structures associated with superior performance by Japanese firms in financial distress are illegal in the United States. The Glass–Steagall Act prevents banks from holding large equity positions in firms, including the firms that borrow from them. Prowse (1990) reports that in Japan, commercial banks own 20.5% of equity securities. Japanese insurance companies own 17.7% and pension funds 5.3%. In the United States, insurance companies and pension funds own 5.2% and 14.5%, respectively. For antitrust reasons, U.S. regulations also discourage cross-share ownership within industries [Roe (1990)].

Following financial distress, U.S. firms adopt ownership structures that look more like those of Japanese firms. Gilson (1990) finds that the concentration of equity ownership by outsiders (including creditors) increases following financial distress. The holdings of all 5% and greater outside blockholders increase from an average of 12.3% one year before distress to 27.9% two years following distress. Creditors obtain an equity interest in the firm as part of the reorganization, while outsiders assemble blocks of shares through open market trading. Under Glass-Steagall, a bank working out a loan is granted a temporary exemption from the prohibition against equity ownership, although it must sell any equity position it receives in exchange for debt forgiveness within two years. In addition, the priority status of a lender can be reduced if the lender attempts to control decision-making at the borrowing firm. Gilson (1990) shows that banks take advantage of the exemption. Two years after the beginning of financial distress, banks and insurance companies own 18.7% of sample firms' equity. For 20% of Gilson's sample firms, banks receive equity as part of a private debt restructuring. In these firms, banks hold an average of 24% of the firm's equity.

The financial and ownership structures chosen by Japanese firms raise important issues for U.S. firms. If the keiretsu, as an organizational form, is superior to organizational forms allowed in the United States, and if bank equity ownership (common not only in Japan, but in Europe as well) improves firm performance, then the U.S. regulatory system imposes large costs on domestic firms and on the economy.

BENEFITS AND COSTS OF FINANCIAL DISTRESS

Previous studies of financial distress focus on the costs and ignore the possibility that distress can result in beneficial outcomes. This stems in part from a widely accepted model of the firm's capital structure decision. For example, in their textbook, Brealey and Myers (1988, p. 421) present the following simple formula for the value of a leveraged firm:

$$\textit{Value of firm = Value if all equity financed +}$$
$$\textit{PV tax shield − PV cost of financial distress,}$$

where the *PV cost of financial distress* is the probability of financial distress multiplied by the expected costs (out-of-pocket plus indirect costs). According to this formula, the firm chooses how much to borrow by balancing the tax benefits of leverage against the costs of an increased probability of financial distress. But this analysis is incomplete because it ignores both the non-tax benefits of leverage and the benefits of financial distress. Therefore, it understates the amount a firm should borrow.

Nontax Benefits of Leverage

Leverage provides discipline and monitoring not available to an all-equity firm. According to free cash flow theory it creates value by imposing a discipline on organizations that reduces agency costs [Jensen (1986)]. The value created by leverage does not necessarily come at the price of an increased probability of financial distress. A more efficiently run firm can carry a higher debt burden with an equal or reduced probability of financial distress.

Evidence on the improved operating performance of leveraged buy-out firms is consistent with this theory. Kaplan (1989a) and Smith (1990) find operating income increases by over 40% during the two to three years following a leveraged buyout. Baker and Wruck (1989) find that The O.M. Scott & Sons Company managed assets differently after its leveraged buyout than it had as an ITT subsidiary. Managers tried to increase value rather than "make budget." Production efficiency and working capital management improved. Kaplan and Stein (1990) find that asset betas fall by 40% following leveraged recapitalizations. Evidence from Wisconsin Central Ltd. Railroad's (WCL) leveraged buyout indicates that asset beta reductions result from organizational changes.[12] WCL's postbuyout strategy reduced operating leverage in a number of ways, including reducing the number of yards and cars and running a "just-in-time" railroad.

When liquidation or reorganization is the firm's highest-valued alternative, default creates value by providing an event that triggers change. Financial distress gives creditors the right to demand restructuring because their contract with the firm has been breached. They can push the firm to liquidate or reorganize. Leverage can, therefore, lead to value-maximization by triggering liquidation [Titman (1984)]. The value of a firm likely to liquidate too soon or linger too long is reduced.

Where firm value is deteriorating, high leverage leads to an earlier default, and simultaneously accomplishes two objectives. It preserves value when the alternative is a continued erosion of value, and in doing so increases the likelihood that the firm will reorganize quickly and efficiently. Figure 11–3 helps to illustrate this point. It shows two firms in the same business with the same liquidation value. One has chosen a high-leverage capital structure, while the other has chosen low leverage. Assume the debt covenants are such that the firm defaults when the net present value of the firm's cash flows falls below the face value of its obligations. The value that

FIGURE 11–3
Illustration of the Incentive for More Highly Leveraged Firms to Reorganize Privately

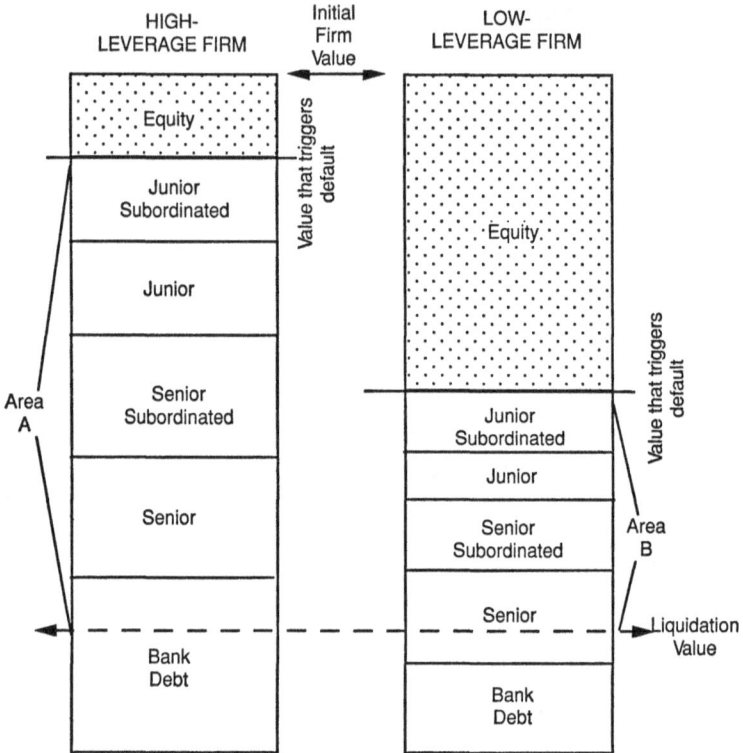

The figure presents capital structures for high- and low-leverage firms with identical initial values and liquidation values. Each firm defaults when the net present value of its cash flow falls below the face value of its obligations (firm value at default is denoted by the line labeled "value that triggers default"). The high-leverage firm defaults at a value that is much higher value than that for the low-leverage firm. Areas A and B represent the values that would be destroyed if the high- or low-leverage firms, respectively, were liquidated after default. Because liquidation and bankruptcy costs can destroy more value in the high-leverage firm (in other words because area A > area B), the high-leverage firm's claimholders have stronger incentives to reorganize quickly and outside bankruptcy court. In some situations, however, private reorganization is not a viable option. When the firm has a large number of independent and widely scattered claimants, private reorganization is extremely difficult and costly. For example, a retailer with thousands of suppliers, or a firm with product liability problems, might find private reorganization impossible. Even in this situation the incentives to resolve financial distress quickly are stronger for the high-leverage firm.

triggers default is higher for the highly leveraged firm than for the less leveraged firm.

At the time of default the claimholders of the high- and low-leverage firms face very different situations. If the high-leverage firm liquidates, the value represented by area A is destroyed. A much smaller value represented by area B is destroyed if the low-leverage firm liquidates. The larger value at risk in liquidation gives the high-leverage firm's claimholders stronger incentives to reorganize quickly, and probably privately, once default occurs.

Though the high-leverage firm has a higher trigger value, both firms could have the same value at default if an exogenous shock caused a substantial value reduction. If such exogenous shocks were the primary cause of distress, the theory that debt preserves value by triggering early default would be suspect. Not all financial distress, however, is caused by exogenous shocks. If value declines gradually as the firm's industry deteriorates, or as management wastes resources by pursuing a poor strategy, the high-leverage firm defaults at a higher value and the waste and poor strategy are more likely to be eliminated. These causes of decline in value—exogenous shocks, gradual deterioration, and poor management decision making—provide a beginning descriptive taxonomy of the causes of financial distress. The available empirical evidence on both the benefits and costs of distress, and the importance of each of these causes, is discussed below.

Benefits of Financial Distress

Changes in Management and Governance
Poor management decision making and weak governance can lead to financial distress. Incumbent managers and directors can also inhibit a firm's ability to recover if new or special skills are required to turn the firm's performance around. Gilson (1989, 1990) documents changes in top management and boards of directors following financial distress. His sample includes firms whose cumulative three-year stock return is in the bottom 5% of all firms on the NYSE and Amex. In spite of their poor performance, over half of his sample firms do not default. These firms have an average three-year stock return of –50.2%, whereas the three-year stock return for firms experiencing distress is –68.9%. The nondistressed firms have a 19% annual turnover in top management—somewhat higher than the normal turnover rate of 12% for a random sample of NYSE and Amex firms [Warner, Watts, and Wruck (1988)]. On the other hand, the distressed firms experience a

52% annual turnover of top management. These results are consistent with the idea that leverage acts as a catalyst for organizational change. Poor stock-price performance is not enough to remove incumbent managers, but financial distress provides a mechanism to initiate top-management changes.

Turnover among directors is also high following distress. Gilson finds that within four years after the onset of financial distress only 47% of old directors still hold their seats. Eight percent of the firms replace their entire board. He also finds that boards of directors are restructured following financial distress; for 60% of his sample firms, the size of the board shrinks following distress. Consistent with a loss of reputation, departing directors subsequently serve on fewer boards.

Changes in Organizational Strategy and Structure
Some firms in financial distress undergo dramatic organizational changes as part of their recovery, refocusing their strategy and undertaking restructurings. Often some assets are sold, while others are reorganized and restaffed. The U.S. steel industry is an example. Increased international competition in steel during the 1980s forced many U.S. steel firms into financial distress. Some firms, such as Wheeling-Pittsburgh, filed Chapter 11. Others, such as Inland Steel, restructured privately. These firms reduced their fixed obligations and employment, and refocused operations to produce primarily specialty steel products.

Such reorganizations illustrate how financial structure interacts with investment decisions; financial distress forces a change in the firm's economic activities and the way these activities are organized. These restructurings often create value for the firm's claimholders. The same reorganizations probably would have created value before financial distress, but the impetus for change provided by distress was absent. Financial distress can, therefore, force managers to undertake value-increasing organizational changes they would not have otherwise undertaken. For example, in its August 1990 "Preliminary Report on the Financial Condition of the Donald J. Trump Organization Post-Restructuring," the State of New Jersey Department of Law and Public Safety reported that financial distress had forced management to rethink its strategy:

> [financial distress has] created a crisis atmosphere wherein debt service payments can not now be satisfied out of the operating cash flow and has forced the Company to rethink its entire strategy and capital structure. In this case, excessive debt has acted as a powerful agent for change and, ironically, has served as a brake on management mistakes. It may very well be that the

greatest hope for preserving value lies in a quick and efficient reorganization and workout process—a privatized bankruptcy of sorts—outside the courtroom.

Without outside intervention, management often fails to change strategy, or is unaware that the company's strategy is the wrong one. Examples of situations in which financial distress forced managers to refocus, or where the absence of distress allowed managers to preside over a deteriorating firm, illustrate this point. Revco is an example of the former. Shortly after Revco's LBO, a new CEO was appointed who changed the company's strategy from one of "everyday low prices" to mini-department stores (a cash-intensive strategy change). Revco's stores began carrying television sets and small appliances. The merchandise didn't sell and the strategy was a failure. Within six months the firm defaulted and another new CEO was appointed to change its strategic direction [Wruck (1991)].

Massey Ferguson exemplifies the management of a deteriorating firm in the absence of financial distress. Baldwin and Mason (1983) report that the market value of the company's equity fell from $505 million to $100 million between 1976 and 1980. During this period management closed facilities, laid off employees, and sold assets, but made no major change in how the firm was run. Finally, in March 1979, the CEO resigned and a new manager was appointed. In late 1980 the firm began restructuring its claims through a private workout.

When firm value deteriorates as a result of poor management or when firm value is highest in liquidation and management refuses to liquidate, financial distress creates value. But the process of recovering from distress can create value even if the events leading to distress are out of management's control. For example, consider a firm pushed into financial distress by an exogenous shock. The process of recovery provides an opportunity to create value by reassessing the firm's strategy and restructuring its operations. This does not mean that the effects of the shock can be completely reversed, but rather that management can make decisions that improve the firm's depressed state.

Benefits of Chapter 11
In their analysis, Gilson et al. (1990) assume that Chapter 11 is always a worse outcome than a private renegotiation. In some special situations, however, the ability to enter Chapter 11 is a valuable alternative for securityholders. For example, trade creditors and claimants in product liability suits are numerous and have heterogeneous claims. Reaching a private

agreement with all of them is very difficult. Under Chapter 11, diffuse creditors can be dealt with as a single class, making negotiation manageable and settling protracted disputes once and for all. For example, before filing under Chapter 11, Manville Corporation faced 20,000 asbestos-related lawsuits and estimated that eventually another 32,000 would be filed. Under Chapter 11, all damage suits were stayed, and present and future asbestos claimants were put in a single class.[13] A. H. Robbins filed under Chapter 11 following liability problems with its Dalkon Shield birth control device. Other companies, such as Braniff and Eastern Airlines, have filed under Chapter 11 when faced with labor contracts that management viewed as too costly to allow the firm to survive.

Chapter 11 also allows for the issuance of new senior credit, called "debtor-in-possession financing," which can be crucial to the firm, especially in retail businesses, where trade credit is often necessary for survival. Pre-Chapter 11 trade creditors and other unsecured creditors have low priority, coming just before equityholders. Claims of creditors lending to the firm after it files under Chapter 11 are second in priority only to legal and administrative expenses. Distressed firms that require new credit have incentives to file under Chapter 11, and potential creditors have incentives to withhold credit until after the filing. Campeau, for example, was able to secure new credit quickly after it filed under Chapter 11. In less than a month, Campeau obtained a $700 million debtor-in-possession credit facility: $400 million for Federated from Citibank and $300 million for Allied from Chemical Bank.

Costs of Financial Distress

Out-of-Pocket Costs
The out-of-pocket or direct costs of financial distress are the easiest to measure. They include legal, administrative, and advisory fees paid by the company. Data on out-of-pocket costs are available for firms that restructure debt through an exchange offer, or that file for bankruptcy. Gilson, John, and Lang (1990) present the only available evidence on the direct costs of private workouts. With a sample of 18 private debt restructurings, they find that the median out-of-pocket cost of restructuring debt through an exchange offer is 0.32% of total assets measured at the fiscal year-end closest to the exchange-offer date.

A number of studies provide evidence on the direct costs of bankruptcy. The findings of four of them are summarized in Table 11–1. Warner

(1977a), Altman (1984), and Weiss (1990) all measure direct costs as a percentage of the market value of the firm one year before bankruptcy. They find that direct costs are quite small, averaging between 3% and 4.5% of market value. For firms that liquidate at the end of the bankruptcy process, Ang, Chua, and McConnell (1982) find that out-of-pocket costs are 7.5% of the liquidated value of the firm. The maximum out-of-pocket costs are 6.6% of market value in Weiss's sample and 9.8% in Warner's sample. Comparing the direct costs of private workouts with direct costs of bankruptcy suggests that out-of-pocket costs are almost ten times less when the firm is able to restructure debt privately.[14]

Indirect Costs

Indirect costs are opportunity costs imposed on the firm because financial distress affects its ability to conduct business as usual. A distressed firm is hampered on three fronts. First, it loses the right to make certain decisions

TABLE 11–1
Summary of Evidence on the Direct Costs of Bankruptcy from Four Studies Covering 1933–1986

Study	Sample Selection Criteria	Mean Cost	As a Percent of	Sample Period	Sample Size
Warner (1977a)	Railroad bankruptcies	4%	market value one year before bankruptcy	1933–55	11
Ang, Chua, and McConnell (1982)	Bankruptcies filed in the western district of Oklahoma [all eventually liquidated]	7.5%	liquidated value of firms at end of bankruptcy process	1963–78	55
Altman (1984)	11 retail and 7 industrial firms	4.3%	market value one year before bankruptcy	1970–78	18
Weiss (1990)	Bankruptcies filed in: Central CA, Southern FL, NY, Northern IL, MI, OH, District of MA	3.1%	market value at end of fiscal year before bankruptcy	1980–86	31

without legal approval. For example, a firm in Chapter 11 cannot spend money or sell assets without court approval.

Second, financial distress can reduce demand for the firm's product and increase its production costs. Demand falls if the value of the product to consumers depends on the firm's future performance and financial distress threatens the firm's ability to survive. Production costs increase if financial distress affects the firm's ability to negotiate favorable input prices or credit terms. Worried about the distressed firm's ability to pay its debts, suppliers often charge a risk premium through increased prices, tightened credit terms, or poorer service. In addition, it may be difficult to negotiate favorable terms, prices, and service if suppliers begin to view their relationship with the firm as a short-term one. The time that elapses between the first indication of distress and its resolution—a little over a year for private negotiations and a little under two and a half years for bankruptcies [Gilson, John, and Lang (1990) and Weiss (1990)]—indicates these issues can be persistent.

Third, management spends considerable time resolving financial distress. The value of this time is generally considered an indirect cost, but not all the time is lost. When management is engaged in productive restructuring and in implementing strategic change it is using its time to increase firm value. Unless the time could have been spent more productively elsewhere, its value should not be considered an indirect cost.

Estimating the indirect costs of financial distress is difficult because the costs represent lost opportunities. Available evidence is mixed. Altman (1984) estimates the unexpected loss in profits for three years before a Chapter 11 filing for 11 retailing and 5 industrial firms and uses this loss as a measure of the indirect costs of financial distress. This interpretation is problematic because it is impossible to tell whether the loss in profits is fact caused by financial distress or whether financial distress is caused by the loss in profits. He finds the sum of direct and indirect costs (loss in profits) averages 8.7% of market value one year before bankruptcy for the retailing firms and 15.0% for the industrial firms. It is not surprising that the loss in profits should be smaller for retailing firms. Industrial firms are more likely to be selling products for which the future availability of service, guarantees, warranties, parts, and support is very important. In contrast to Altman, Kaplan (1989) finds that Campeau's sales were unharmed by its Chapter 11 filing. He concludes the the indirect costs of distress for this retailer were small.

Cutler and Summers (1988) estimate the indirect costs of Texaco's April 1987 bankruptcy filing using bond and stock price data. Texaco acquired all of Getty Oil's common stock during a period when Getty had agreed to allow Pennzoil to acquire about 43% of its common stock at a lower price. Because Texaco had agreed to indemnify Getty against all lawsuits, it was liable for damages when Pennzoil sued Getty for breach of contract. The litigation resulted in a court order that Texaco pay Pennzoil $12 billion in damages. After the damages were upheld in appeals court, Texaco filed a Chapter 11 petition. The companies attempted to agree on a settlement amount, but failed until Carl Icahn purchased stock in both companies and helped bring about a final settlement of $3 billion.

The loss in the combined market values of Texaco and Pennzoil across all litigation and settlement events is the sum of the direct and indirect costs of financial distress. Cutler and Summers estimate the abnormal change in market value of debt and equity to be $2.1 billion. (Before Icahn's involvement in the settlement, combined losses in market value were over $3 billion.) Subtracting total legal costs provides an estimate of the indirect costs of financial distress for Texaco. Cutler and Summers estimate the after-tax legal costs for both firms to be $525 million. Subtracting the direct costs from the total loss in value provides an estimate of $1.575 billion in indirect costs. Texaco's market value was approximately $17 billion before the litigation (book value of debt plus market value of equity). Therefore, the indirect costs implied by stock price changes amount to about 9% of firm value.

Enforcement of Absolute Priority Under Bankruptcy Law

According to the absolute priority rule, Chapter 11 reorganization plans must satisfy senior claimants completely before more junior claimants receive anything. The extent to which absolute priority is enforced by bankruptcy courts has implications for the costs of financial distress as well as the pricing of securities; the value of contractually specified priority is negligible if the court does not systematically enforce it. Studies of reorganization plans consistently reveal, however, that absolute priority is not enforced. Warner (1977a, 1977b) studies a sample of railroad bankruptcies between 1926 and 1955. He finds that absolute priority is not enforced, and that this fact is reflected in the market prices of the firm's debt securities. In studying how the court determines whether a creditor's claim is satisfied, he finds that accounting face values, not market values, are the basis for comparing old and new securities.

More recent reorganization plans for industrial companies are studied by Franks and Torous (1989) and Weiss (1990). Franks and Torous (1989) study the reorganization plans of 27 firms emerging from bankruptcy between 1971 and 1986. The Bankruptcy Reform Act went into effect in October 1979, so some of their sample firms reorganized under the old Chapter 10 and others under the new Chapter 11. They find that of the 27 plans, 78% (21) show deviations from priority, and that in 67% (18), shareholders receive some consideration when more senior claimants are not paid in full.

Evidence on the enforcement of absolute priority under Chapter 11 is presented in Weiss (1990). He studies the reorganization plans of 37 firms filing under Chapter 11 between 1980 and 1986. Each plan states the claims of each creditor class, what each class receives under the plan, and whether a class is "impaired" or "unimpaired." A class of creditors is impaired if its claims are not satisfied in full. If a plan describes a class as unimpaired and the class disagrees it can protest to the judge who makes the final decision. No rules specify acceptable valuation methods, but in general accounting and not market values are the standard.

To study the violation of priority, Weiss divides claimants into three classes—secured creditors, unsecured creditors, and equityholders—and studies whether absolute priority is enforced by noting which classes are impaired. If a class of claimants is impaired and a more junior class receives any value on its claims, priority is violated. Weiss finds that absolute priority is enforced only 22% of the time. Seventy-eight percent of the reorganization plans violate absolute priority, 70% by giving a valuable claim to equityholders when unsecured creditors are impaired, and 8% by giving a valuable claim to equityholders when both secured and unsecured creditors are impaired. The detail on individual firms in Weiss's study shows some surprising outcomes. For example, he finds that the reorganization plans of Imperial Industries and Richton International allowed equityholders to retain 100% of the firm's common stock even though Imperial Industries' unsecured creditors received only 37% of their claims and Richton International's only 60%.

Weiss demonstrates that absolute priority is violated more frequently for relatively large firms and for firms filing in the Southern District of New York. Among the 18 sample firms filing in New York's Southern District, in only one case was absolute priority upheld. New York filings partially explain the results for large firms as well. Of the 20 firms in Weiss's sample with assets over $100 million where priority was violated, 14 filed under Chapter 11 in the Southern District of New York.

Why Deviations from Priority Arise

The rules governing bankruptcy in the United States encourage outcomes that deviate from absolute priority. Two factors are especially important in these outcomes: (i) the rights given to the firm's managers after it has filed for bankruptcy, and (ii) the reliance on a consensual voting process, rather than a market process, to reorganize the firm.

The United States is one of the few countries that leaves incumbent management in charge of a bankrupt firm.[15] Once the firm is in bankruptcy, not only do managers continue to make operating decisions, but for 120 days after the Chapter 11 filing, the managers have an exclusive right to propose a reorganization plan. The court often grants several extensions of this deadline. Management has an additional 180 days from the filing date to obtain creditor and shareholder approval. If the firm fails to propose a plan, or has had a plan rejected, creditors can propose their own plan. For creditors to propose a plan, however, they must provide proof of values for claims to be issued and assets to be retained or sold. This requires costly appraisals and hearings. Management need only obtain the judge's agreement that the values assigned under its plan are "fair and reasonable." The higher cost to creditors of proposing their own plan, in both time and money, can lead them to accept a plan that results in a lower firm value, i.e., that is inefficient, and violates priority.

U.S. bankruptcy rules allow managers to make trade-offs between firm value and their personal well-being at the expense of the firm's claimholders. For example, if liquidation is the highest-valued strategy, it is hard to imagine managers proposing it, because they would lose their jobs. In addition, it becomes difficult for claimants to fire managers because the judge must approve the decision. In light of the information and incentive problems mentioned earlier, it is clear that granting hiring and firing rights to shareholders or creditors is not a solution. A claimant class prefers managers that further its interests over managers that maximize value. It is hard to believe, however, that a bankruptcy judge is most qualified to make hiring and firing decisions.

Chapter 11's consensual reorganization process allows both impaired creditors and shareholders to vote on a plan. Because only impaired creditor classes and shareholders vote, the plan determines who votes and which claimants vote together. Acceptance of a plan generally requires approval by all impaired creditor classes and shareholders. For each impaired class, acceptance of a plan requires the approval of two thirds in amount and a majority in number of the claims voted. For equityholders, two thirds of the shares voted must favor the plan. The court can "cram down" a reorganization plan, however, even if some impaired creditor classes or shareholders refuse to approve it, if it views the plan as fair and equitable to all impaired classes. This is generally interpreted as meaning that claimholders receive at least what they would have received in liquidation [Altman (1983), pp. 13–31].

Granting shareholders the right to vote gives them power to transfer value from creditors. For example, if the firm is insolvent on a stock basis, there is no value left for shareholders after creditors are paid. The right to vote and to hold up the process allows shareholders to extract valuable claims. On the other hand, excluding shareholders from the voting implies that if the firm were insolvent on a flow basis only, creditors would be overcompensated because they would be awarded the entire value of the firm.

Information and incentive problems could be solved if a reliable third-party estimate of firm value could be obtained. Were firm value known, the court could distribute it to claimants in order of priority. As discussed earlier, creditor, shareholder, and management estimates are unreliable. Easterbrook (1990) suggests that if the market for distressed corporate assets is not too thin, auctioning the firm's assets to a third party and distributing the proceeds to claimholders would improve the efficiency of the U.S. bankruptcy process. Holding an auction that allowed the firm's claimholders to bid would quickly eliminate the opportunistic value estimates promoted by the current bankruptcy process; to back up an estimate each group would have to put its own money on the table. The winning bidder would decide whether to keep the incumbent management team. In some countries, such as Germany, bankrupt companies are auctioned routinely. The U.S. legal system, however, refuses to rely on markets to determine values. Out-of-court workouts can circumvent some of the problems with Chapter 11 but, as mentioned earlier, recent court decisions are discouraging this activity.

CONCLUSIONS

Financial distress affects more than the firm's financial structure. It triggers a process of organizational change that has the potential to create value for the firm's claimholders. The costs of financial distress must be weighed against the benefits to determine its net effect on the organization's claimholders. Direct costs of financial distress average 3.5% of market value. Estimates of indirect costs are less reliable, but evidence to date indicates they lie in the range of 9% to 15% of market value. Financial distress triggers changes in management and governance. Although the benefits of distress have not yet been quantified, turnover in top management and changes in governance indicate that corporate insiders are disciplined for poor performance. Evidence from clinical studies and case studies documents changes in strategy and organizational structure following financial distress that are consistent with a process of corporate revitalization.

The legal rules of the game in bankruptcy create conflicts of interest among claimholders. The conflicts lead to complex information and inference problems for claimholders trying to value a distressed firm. These problems can be solved by encouraging the development of a liquid market for distressed companies' assets and allowing bankrupt firms to be auctioned. Other countries, such as Germany, have successfully developed such systems. In the absence of the legal system's willingness to rely on markets, the information and incentive problems associated with Chapter 11 can be attenuated by encouraging private workouts. Creating an environment friendly to workouts helps firms avoid Chapter 11 and allows actors in financial markets to play a role in resolving distress. Unfortunately, recent court decisions suggest the United States is moving away from, rather than toward, this solution. New tax laws further damage distressed companies. The 1990 tax act imposes new taxes on troubled companies by, among other things, making it more difficult to structure nontaxable exchange offers and making debt forgiveness taxable to the firm. The result will be more bankruptcy filings.

Management can affect the difficulty of recontracting through its financing decisions. A financial structure that aligns the interests of various claimholders, for example, strip financing where creditors hold equity, reduces incentives for claimants to jockey for advantage in the event of distress. Financial structures in which creditors hold equity are common in Japan and Germany, and in both of these countries financial distress is generally resolved through private workouts.

Finally, it is important to consider whether there is a value-maximizing way to avoid distress entirely. Arbitrarily reducing leverage will succeed in avoiding distress, but is unlikely to result in value maximization. Both tax benefits and the organizational and incentive benefits of leverage would be lost. Rather the solution lies in aligning the interests of management with the interests of the firm's shareholders. The firm's financing policy, governance structure, and compensation policies can all be used to bring about this solution.

NOTES

1. Altman (1983, 1990).
2. Cheung, Bencivenga, and Fabozzi (1990).
3. This should not be confused with negative net worth in an accounting sense. The accounting balance sheet for a healthy firm can show total assets less than total liabilities. For example, Sealed Air Corporation, a New York Stock Exchange firm, completed a leveraged recapitalization in July 1989 that left it with a negative accounting net worth of over $160 million. The company has had no problems meeting debt service, and is a year ahead of schedule in paying off its debt [Wruck (1990)].
4. Altman (1983) discusses in detail the different ways insolvency is defined. He labels the flow definition of insolvency "technical insolvency," and the stock definition as "insolvency in a bankruptcy sense."
5. See "U.S. Bankruptcy Judge Rules in Favor of LTV," January 31, 1990, Reuters Newswire. The successful workout referred to above was an exchange offer completed on February 5, 1990, by SCI TV. The company, formerly owned by Storer, went private and was later taken public by KKR and George Gillett in 1987. All of SCI's banks and 95% of its publicly traded debt participated in the restructuring. Each creditor class agreed to approximately the same proportional reduction in its claims, so that in the event of Chapter 11 it would suffer the same percentage reduction in its allowable claims. (See "SCI TV Completes Exchange Offer on Notes, Debentures," February 5, 1990, Reuters Newswire.)
6. These data were obtained in private conversation with Gilson.
7. Firms sometimes liquidate privately. Hite, Owers, and Rogers's (1987) sample contains 49 NYSE and Amex firms that liquidated voluntarily and privately between 1963 and 1983. Their study does not provide evidence on the proportion of sample firms in financial distress.
8. See, for example, Altman (1968) and Beaver (1966).
9. Of course, if the value of intangible assets could be realized through a sale, this would not be true.
10. This simple example assumes a gradual deterioration of value leading to distress rather than an exogenous shock affecting both firms simultaneously and identically. If, for example, a shock instantaneously reduced the value of both firms by $90, they would both be worth $10 at the time of distress and would probably resolve distress similarly.
11. A disadvantage of using sales and investment as measures of firm performance is that they are not always positively associated with changes in value. Increased sales are not necessarily more profitable, and increased investment does not necessarily have a positive net present value. Unless systematically bad decisions are being made by sample firms, however, these performance measures should not pose a large problem.

12. See Burkhardt, Jensen, and Barry (1990).
13. See Lewin (1990). As part of Manville's reorganization plan, a trust was established to satisfy the claims of asbestos victims. The recent cash crisis in this trust calls into question the ability of Chapter 11 to resolve continuing litigation permanently, since the reorganized company might be required to contribute additional funds to the trust.
14. Evidence relating the direct costs of bankruptcy to firm size is contradictory. In his sample of railroads, Warner finds that direct costs as a percentage of market value are inversely related to size. He concludes that there are significant fixed costs of bankruptcy. Ang, Chua, and McConnell (1982) test for and find evidence supporting Warner's results in a sample of smaller firms. Weiss, however, does not find evidence of significant fixed costs. He argues that changes in the bankruptcy code, new financing techniques, and differences in samples probably explain the differing results.
15. See "Bankruptcy Law: A Sticky End," *The Economist*, February 24, 1990, pp. 77–78.

REFERENCES

Altman, Edward I., 1990, "Investing in distressed securities," *The Altman/Foothill Report on the Anatomy of Defaulted Debt and Equities*.

Altman, Edward I., 1984, "A further empirical investigation of the bankruptcy cost question," *Journal of Finance 39*, 1067–89.

Altman, Edward I., 1983, *Corporate Financial Distress*, New York: John Wiley & Sons.

Altman, Edward I., 1968, "Financial ratios, discriminant analysis and the prediction of corporate bankruptcy," *Journal of Finance 23*, 589–609.

Ang, James S.; Jess H. Chua; and John J. McConnell, 1982, "The administrative costs of corporate bankruptcy: A note," *Journal of Finance 37*, 219–26.

Baker, George P., and Karen H. Wruck, 1989, "Organizational changes and value creation in leveraged buyouts: The case of The O.M. Scott & Sons Company," *Journal of Financial Economics 24*, 163–90.

Baldwin, Carliss Y., and Scott P. Mason, 1983, "The resolution of claims in financial distress: The case of Massey Ferguson," *Journal of Finance 38*, 505–23.

"Bankruptcy law: A sticky end," *The Economist*, February 24, 1990, pp. 77–78.

Beaver, William H., 1966, "Financial ratios as predictors of failures," *Empirical Research in Accounting, Supplement to Journal of Accounting Research*, 71–111.

Beck, Susan, 1990, "Revco in ruins," *The American Lawyer*, June, pp. 56–64.

Brealey, Richard A., and Stewart C. Myers, 1988, *Principles of Corporate Finance* (3rd edition), New York: McGraw-Hill Book Company.

Burkhardt, Willy; Michael C. Jensen; and Brian Barry, "Wisconsin Central Ltd. Railroad and Berkshire Partners (A) and (B)," Harvard Business School Case

Study, 9-190-062, 9-190-070.

Cheung, Rayner; Joseph C. Bencivenga; and Frank.J. Fabozzi, 1990, "Original issue high yield bonds: Total returns and historical default experience 1977–1989," Cambridge, MA: Massachusetts Institute of Technology working paper.

Cutler, David M., and Lawrence H. Summers, 1988, "The costs of conflict resolution and financial distress: Evidence from the Texaco-Pennzoil litigation," *The Rand Journal of Economics 19*, No. 2, 157–72.

Easterbrook, Frank H., 1990, "Is corporate bankruptcy efficient?: A comment," *Journal of Financial Economics 27*, 411–17.

Franks, Julian R., and Walter N. Torous, 1989, "An empirical investigation of U.S. firms in reorganization," *Journal of Finance 44*, 747–79.

Gilson, Stuart C., 1990, "Bankruptcy, boards, banks, and blockholders," *Journal of Financial Economics 27*, 355–87.

Gilson, Stuart C., 1989, "Management turnover and financial distress," *Journal of Financial Economics 25*, 241–62.

Gilson, Stuart C.; Kose John; and Larry H. P. Lang, 1990, "Troubled debt restructurings," *Journal of Financial Economics,* forthcoming.

Harlan, Christi, "Eastern Airlines' creditors seek sales proceeds," *The Wall Street Journal,* May 18, 1990, p. B-11.

Hite, Gailen L.; James E. Owers; and Ronald C. Rogers, 1987, "The market for interfirm asset sales: Partial sell-offs and total liquidations," *Journal of Financial Economics 18*, 229–52.

Hoshi, Takeo; Anil Kashyap; and David Scharfstein, 1990, "Troubled debt restructurings," *Journal of Financial Economics 27*, 67–88.

Jensen, Michael C., 1989, "The eclipse of the public corporation," *Harvard Business Review,* September-October, pp. 61–74.

Jensen, Michael C., 1986, "Agency costs of free cash flow, corporate finance and takeovers," *American Economic Review 76*, 323–29.

Kaplan, Steven N., 1989a, "The effects of management buyouts on operating performance and value," *Journal of Financial Economics 24*, 217–54.

Kaplan, Steven N., 1989b, "Campeau's acquisition of Federated: Value added or destroyed," *Journal of Financial Economics 25*, 191–212.

Kaplan, Steven N., and Jeremy C. Stein, 1990, "How risky is the debt in highly leveraged transactions? Evidence from public recapitalizations," *Journal of Financial Economics,* forthcoming.

Lewin, Tamar, 1982, "The legal issues in Manville's move," *The New York Times,* August 27, p. D-1ff.

Morse, Dale, and Wayne Shaw, 1988, "Investing in bankrupt firms," *Journal of Finance 43*, 1193–1206.

"Preliminary Report on the Financial Condition of the Donald J. Trump Organization Post-Restructuring," public report by the State of New Jersey Department of Law and Public Safety, August, 1990.

Prowse, Stephen D., 1990, "Institutional investment patterns and corporate financial behavior in the U.S. and Japan," *Journal of Financial Economics 27*, 43–66.

Roe, Mark J., 1990, "Legal restraints on ownership and control of public companies," *Journal of Financial Economics 27*, 7–41.

Smith, Abbie, 1990, "Corporate ownership structure and performance: The case of management buyouts," *Journal of Financial Economics 27*, 143–64.

Titman, Sheridan, 1984, "The effect of capital structure on a firm's liquidation decision," *Journal of Financial Economics 13*, 137–51.

Verma, Kiran, "Inland Steel Industries, Inc.," Harvard Business School Case Study, 9-188-040.

Warner, Jerold B., 1977a, "Bankruptcy costs: Some evidence," *Journal of Finance 32*, 337–47.

Warner, Jerold B., 1977b, "Bankruptcy and the pricing of risky debt," *Journal of Financial Economics 4*, 39–276.

Warner, Jerold B.; Ross L. Watts; and Karen H. Wruck, 1988, "Stock price performance and top management changes," *Journal of Financial Economics 20*, 461–92.

Weiss, Lawrence A., 1990, "Priority of claims and ex post re-contracting in bankruptcy," *Journal of Financial Economics*, forthcoming.

White, Michelle J., 1983, "Bankruptcy costs and the new bankruptcy code," *Journal of Finance 38*, 477–504.

White, Michelle J., 1980, "Public policy toward bankruptcy: Me-first and other priority rules," *Bell Journal of Economics 11*, 550–64.

Wruck, Karen H., "Sealed Air Corporation's leveraged recapitalization," Harvard Business School Case Study, 9-391-067.

Wruck, Karen H., "What really went wrong at Revco," *Journal of Applied Corporate Finance 4*, No. 2, pp. 79–92.

CHAPTER 12

BANKRUPTCY, BOARDS, BANKS, AND BLOCKHOLDERS

Evidence on Changes in Corporate Ownership and Control When Firms Default

---

Stuart C. Gilson

INTRODUCTION

Corporate financial theory has long recognized the potential impact of bankruptcy-related costs on firms' capital structure decision and managerial incentives [Masulis (1988), Jensen (1988)]. We know little, however, about how firms actually deal with default, and what changes take place in these firms as a consequence of financial distress. For example, there has been little empirical analysis of corporate governance in financially distressed firms. Although models of bankruptcy often assume that creditors take con-

Stuart C. Gilson is Assistant Professor of Business Administration at Harvard Business School, Boston. The author acknowledges the helpful comments of Edward Altman, Keith Brown, Andrew Chen, George Gau, Ronald Masulis, Ronald Singer, Laura Starks, A. J. Senchack, Rex Thompson, Michael Vetsuypens, and Michael Weisbach. This paper is reprinted with permission from the *Journal of Financial Economics*, Vol. 27, No. 2 (October 1990). He is especially indebted to Harry DeAngelo,

Continued overleaf

trol of the bankrupt firm's assets, the actual role creditors play has not been systematically documented. Similarly, there is little evidence on how ownership of distressed companies' residual claims changes as debt is renegotiated. We also do not fully understand what determines the incentives of companies and their creditors to recontract out of default privately instead of through formal bankruptcy [Jensen (1989a, b)].

This study presents new evidence on these and related issues. The study is based on a sample of 111 publicly traded companies that experienced severe financial distress between 1979 and 1985. Sixty-one of these companies filed for bankruptcy under Chapter 11 of the U.S. Bankruptcy Code, and fifty restructured their debt privately.

Collectively, the results of this study suggest that corporate default engenders significant changes in the ownership of firms' residual claims and in the allocation of rights to manage corporate resources. In approximately three out of four firms in the sample, bank lenders and other creditors receive significant blocks of voting stock under firms' debt-restructuring and Chapter 11 reorganization plans. On average, banks receive 36% of firms' common stock. In a number of cases, banks appoint their representatives to the board of directors. Restrictive covenants in privately restructured lending agreements give banks more say in firms' investment and financing policies.

Concurrently with the banks' increased monitoring, significant internal changes take place in the board of directors. On average, only 46% of directors who sit on the board prior to financial distress, and 43% of the CEOs, are still present when their firms emerge from bankruptcy or settle privately with creditors less than two years later. The average size of the board declines, and more directors are appointed who possess some special skill or interest in managing troubled companies, including investment bankers and workout specialists. Directors who resign from these firms subsequently serve less often as directors of other companies. At the same time, the percentage of firms' common stock held by large nonmanagement blockholders rises sharply. Very few firms in the sample are involved in any sort of acquisition-related activity.

Note continued

Michael Jensen (the editor), Edward Rice (the referee), and Richard Ruback (who served as both editor and referee) for their many valuable comments and suggestions. He also benefited from discussions with seminar participants at the Harvard Business School, the University of Oregon, and Southern Methodist University. Earlier versions of the paper were presented at the 1989 Financial Management Association meetings and the 1990 Western Finance Association meetings. Kenneth Wiles and Pyung-Sig Yoon provided research assistance. The author acknowledges financial support by the Division of Research, Harvard Business School.

Evidence presented here is consistent with a general substitution of monitoring by external blockholders and creditors for monitoring by directors. Interestingly, many of the monitoring mechanisms that increase in importance for these insolvent firms have been also identified with the LBO form of organization. As Jensen (1989b) observes, a typical LBO has highly concentrated stock ownership, bank lenders that are active in making and implementing corporate policy, and a board of directors that includes investment bankers and other professionals who specialize in running highly levered companies. Such evidence, coupled with results of the current study, suggests that leverage is a potentially important determinant of how corporations are best organized and governed.

This chapter is organized as follows: the second section discusses the data and sample design, the third section presents the empirical results, and the fourth section concludes with a summary of the study's main findings.

DATA AND SAMPLE DESCRIPTION

No systematic public records are kept of firms that default on their debt or file for bankruptcy. For this study, I created a sample of such firms indirectly from a list of publicly traded companies whose common stock price dropped steeply. I assumed that such a list would contain a relatively large number of firms that were financially distressed—that is, either in default on their debt, bankrupt, or restructuring their debt to avoid bankruptcy. For each year from 1979 to 1984, I ranked all firms on the New York Stock Exchange (NYSE) and American Stock Exchange (Amex) by their three-year unadjusted common stock returns, obtained from the Center for Research in Securities Prices (CRSP) daily-returns file, and formed a stratum of firms whose returns fell in the bottom 5 percent. I then searched *The Wall Street Journal* (*WSJ*) *Index* for references to each firm in the stratum, looking at a five-year period centered on the year(s) in which the firm was sampled. A firm was retained for analysis if there was some mention of a default, bankruptcy, or attempt to restructure debt outside of bankruptcy. Additional sources used to confirm the presence or absence of these events include the *Moody's* Manuals, the *Q-file* directory of firms' 10k reports and shareholder proxy statements, Standard and Poor's *Bond Owner's Guide*, and Commerce Clearing House's *Capital Changes Reporter*. This procedure produced an initial sample of 150 financially distressed firms.

An informal debt restructuring agreement yields the same result as a formal reorganization plan in bankruptcy, in that both represent an exchange of new financial claims for the firm's previously outstanding debt contracts. There are no established legal or economic criteria, however, for determining when a debt restructuring agreement has occurred. Following Gilson (1989), I define a debt restructuring as a transaction in which the firm's debt contracts are amended on one of the following terms: (i) promised interest or principal payments on the debt are reduced; (ii) the debt's maturity is extended; or (iii) creditors are given equity securities in the firm (common stock or securities convertible into common). All debt restructurings in the sample take place in response to an actual or anticipated default, or for the purpose of avoiding bankruptcy.

The following schematic illustrates the dating convention I use to evaluate changes in board membership, stockholdings, and other variables:

$$-1 \qquad 0 \qquad +1 \qquad +2 \qquad +3 \qquad +4$$

Year

Time 0 represents the date on which a firm either files for bankruptcy or starts to restructure its debt privately. A debt restructuring is assumed to begin on the date it is first mentioned in the *WSJ*, unless an earlier date can be determined from other source documents. If a firm defaults, I assume that efforts to restructure its debt begin immediately, since creditors can generally demand immediate payment of all interest and principal after 30 days. A bankruptcy begins on the date that a firm files under Chapter 11 of the U.S. Bankruptcy Code.

Although firms can (and usually do) attempt to restructure their debt privately before filing for bankruptcy, Gilson et al. (1990) report that such attempts typically break down within one year. Failing to account for this period should not seriously bias the results of the present study, since turnover and blockholdings are reported on an annual basis. Moreover, using the firm's Chapter 11 filing identifies changes in corporate ownership and governance that are specifically attributable to the Chapter 11 process.

Board membership, stock ownership, and other variables are tracked from year −1 onward. At the end of each event year actual board membership and stock ownership are assumed to be the same as reported in the most current proxy statement or 10k report. Turnover of directors is measured by comparing board membership in adjacent years. For example, if a firm's financial distress begins in October 1982, and its proxy statements are filed every March, then turnover between event dates 0 and +1 reflects changes in board membership from March 1982 to March 1983. If no SEC filings are made in a particular year because a firm cancels its annual shareholders' meeting or obtains a filing exemption, turnover, if any, is assumed to take place on the date of the first subsequent filing that reflects the change.

For each firm, board membership and stock ownership are tracked until the firm's bankruptcy or debt restructuring is resolved. The resolution date for bankruptcy is the date on which the firm's reorganization plan is formally confirmed by the court. For debt restructurings, the resolution date is either the date on which a restructuring agreement is formally consummated, or the date of the last reference in the *WSJ* to a continuing restructuring.

This dating convention ensures that observed turnover of directors is confined to periods when firms are financially distressed. If all firms were tracked until year +4 instead, some of the turnover for firms that returned to financial health more quickly would be unrelated to either bankruptcy or debt restructuring, and the impact of default on directors' tenure would be overstated. If it is impossible to ascertain when a firm's financial distress ended, the resolution date is assumed to be year +2. This convention reflects the sample mean and median time that firms spend either in bankruptcy or privately restructuring their debt [see Table 12–2].[1]

To accommodate missing proxy statements and 10k reports, I require that enough documentation be available to determine at least one year's change in either board membership or stock ownership during a firm's financial distress. Thirty-nine firms failed to satisfy this criterion, leaving a final sample of 111 firms. The sample includes a number of large firms whose financial troubles have been the subject of much analysis and discussion in the financial press. Examples are Baldwin-United, Charter, Itel, and Wickes (bankruptcies), and Allis-Chalmers, Dome Petroleum, International Harvester, and Massey Ferguson (debt restructurings).

Table 12–1 shows when firms file for bankruptcy or start to restructure their debt privately. Clusters of both groups of firms in 1982–1984, a period of economic recession, account for 71.6% of the sample. In addition, over one-half of the sample falls into five broad industry categories, reflecting the recession's relative impact on different sectors of the economy. As defined by firms' two-digit standard industrial classification (SIC) industry codes, 18.4% of all sample firms are in mining, oil and gas extraction (SIC codes 10–14), 9.6% in real estate and financial services (60–67), 8.9% in transportation and communications (40–49), 8.8% in machinery and equipment manufacturing (35–36), and 7.9% in miscellaneous retail trades (52–59).

TABLE 12–1
Calendar Time Distribution of Starting Dates for Financial Distress[a]

| | Number of Firms | |
Year	Bankruptcy	Debt Restructuring
1979	1	3
1980	6	4
1981	8	4
1982	18	15
1983	11	15
1984	14	9
1985	3	0
Total	61	50

[a] Sample consists of 111 New York- and American Stock Exchange-listed firms that either filed for bankruptcy under Chapter 11 or privately restructured their debt to avoid bankruptcy between 1979 and 1985. The sample consists of firms that went bankrupt or restructured their debt to avoid bankruptcy in any given year, from among all firms on the CRSP daily returns tape whose cumulative three-year common stock return in any year during the 1979–1984 period fell in the lowest 5 percent of all returns for that year. Each firm's status is determined from *The Wall Street Journal,* the *Moody's* manuals, the *Q-file* directory of annual 10k reports and proxy statements, and Commerce Clearing House's *Capital Changes Reporter.* A debt restructuring is defined as an agreement between the firm and its creditors to either (i) reduce stated principal or interest payments on the debt, (ii) extend the debt's maturity, or (iii) grant creditors an equity interest in the firm (common stock or securities convertible into common stock). In addition, the purpose of the debt restructuring must be to avoid bankruptcy or default.

Table 12–2 presents selected characteristics of firms in the sample. Sampled firms are generally smaller than those analyzed in related studies. The mean and median book values of assets are $557.9 and $74.8 million, respectively. In contrast, median firm size for the sample of NYSE-listed firms analyzed by Hermalin and Weisbach (1988) is $1.2 billion. Firms in the sample could be relatively smaller because they have been consistently unprofitable, and because they may have divested a significant fraction of their assets in an attempt to remain solvent. In addition, smaller firms will be observed in disproportionately large numbers when the sampling is based on low stock returns because their returns are more volatile.

My sampled firms are highly leveraged, as measured by the ratio of total liabilities or long-term debt to total assets (all in book values), and have relatively more bank debt than publicly traded debt outstanding. These firms are also extremely unprofitable, in both absolute and relative terms. Firms' profitability is represented by two variables. The first is the annual common

TABLE 12–2
Selected Sample Characteristics[a]

	Mean	Median	Maximum	Minimum
Book value of assets ($millions)	557.9	74.8	10,208.7	6.3
Annual sales ($millions)	985.1	160.3	13,618.3	0.0
Number of shareholders	9,145	3,809	206,854	450
Number of employees	4,603	1,400	76,018	4
Leverage ratios				
Total liabilities ÷ Book value of assets	0.87	0.85	1.92	0.39
Long-term debt ÷ Book value of assets	0.52	0.51	1.22	0.01
Publicly traded debt ÷ Total liabilities	0.10	0.00	0.66	0.00
Bank debt ÷ Total liabilities	0.29	0.23	0.88	0.00
Annual common stock returns (3-year average)				
Unadjusted	−0.343[b]	−0.362[b]	0.560	−0.680
Net of market	−0.590[b]	−0.575[b]	0.005	−0.926
Net of industry	−0.523[b]	−0.544[b]	0.028	−0.883
Annual difference in earnings before interest and taxes ÷ Book value of assets (3-year average)				
Unadjusted	−0.030[b]	−0.027[b]	0.183	−0.173
Net of industry	−0.041[b]	−0.039[b]	0.174	−0.169
Length of financial distress (months)				
Bankruptcy	21.9	19.0	43.0	10.0
Debt restructuring	17.9	15.0	44.0	1.0

[a] Where applicable, variables are based on reported information that most closely predates the beginning of firms' bankruptcy or debt restructuring. Sample consists of 111 New York- and American Stock Exchange-listed firms that either filed for bankruptcy under Chapter 11 or privately restructured their debt to avoid bankruptcy between 1979 and 1985. See footnote a of Table 12–1 for a description of the sampling methodology. Income and balance-sheet data are obtained from the COMPUSTAT Annual Industrial and Research tape and the *Moody's* manuals. Stock return data are obtained from the CRSP daily returns tape. Bank debt includes debt owed to commercial banks and insurance companies. Average annual stock returns are based on returns for the three consecutive years that end with the year in which a firm files for bankruptcy or starts to restructure its debt. The market return is the corresponding CRSP equally weighted market portfolio return, and the industry return is the return on the equally weighted portfolio of all firms with the same two-digit SIC industry code. The average annual difference in earnings before interest and taxes is based on the three consecutive fiscal years that end with the fiscal year in which a firm files for bankruptcy or starts to restructure its debt. The book value of assets used to deflate the annual difference in earnings is the value at the beginning of the fiscal year. The industry benchmark for this variable is defined by analogy with industry common stock returns.
[b] Mean (median) is significantly different from zero at the 0.01 level using a one-tailed *t*-test (Wilcoxon rank-sum test).

stock return, averaged over the three years that precede the firm's bankruptcy or debt restructuring. The second is a measure of unanticipated earnings, equal to the annual difference in earnings before interest and taxes, divided by the book value of assets at the beginning of the fiscal year. Hermalin and Weisbach (1988) use the same measure of accounting performance. This variable is also a three-year average, ending with the fiscal year that overlaps the start of a firm's bankruptcy or debt restructuring. Sample means and medians are significantly negative for both stock price and accounting measures of profitability. This is true whether performance is measured in unadjusted terms, in relation to the market (for stock returns), or against the average performance of firms in the same industry (at the two-digit SIC industry level). These performance measures are also economically significant. For example, average annual unadjusted stock returns are –34.3%; corresponding market and industry-adjusted returns are –59.0% and –52.3%, respectively.

Although the foregoing sample characteristics might reasonably be expected of financially distressed firms in general, the present sample is taken from a stratum of firms with extreme negative stock returns. A priori, it is not clear how this might bias the results of the study. For example, the sample will tend to exclude defaults by firms that suffered only minor declines in their stock price (cash flows), but which were highly levered by choice before defaulting. Jensen (1989a, b) argues that an important benefit of high leverage is that poorly managed firms default sooner, thus forcing corrective changes in corporate policy to be undertaken sooner and allowing more of the firm's going-concern value to be preserved.

FINANCIAL DISTRESS AND THE MARKET FOR CORPORATE CONTROL

My main objective is to investigate changes in corporate governance that take place when firms default on their debt. Recent work by Jensen (1989a, b) suggests that leverage may be an important determinant of how decision rights in the firm are allocated among the claimholders. Because the impact of leverage (or default) on the allocation of these rights is not well understood, much of the following analysis is deliberately descriptive. Evidence is organized around changes in the importance of monitoring by the firm's creditors, the board of directors, and outside blockholders.

Monitoring by Creditors

In the standard textbook treatment of financial distress, default engenders a wholesale transfer of the firm's assets to creditors. Although this is an admitted simplification of the actual events that occur around default, evidence presented below suggests that creditors (in particular, bank lenders) exercise significant influence over resource allocation in financially distressed firms. This influence derives from two sources: (i) explicit stock ownership and representation on the board of directors, and (ii) restrictions on corporate financing and investment policy contained in the firm's debt covenants.

Creditor Control Through Stock Ownership and Board Representation

Table 12–3 documents the percentage of firms' common stock that creditors receive under debt restructuring and Chapter 11 reorganization plans. In panel A, ownership is defined as the largest percentage of common stock held by creditors in a particular class during firms' financial distress, as reported in annual proxy statements under "beneficial ownership." In panel B, ownership is defined as pro forma common stockholdings by creditors under the terms of firms' debt restructuring or reorganization plans. Sources used to determine pro forma stockholdings include 10k reports, exchange offer circulars, the *Moody's* manuals, and the *WSJ*. Ownership percentages reported in both panels are calculated under the assumption that any convertible securities held by creditors are fully converted into common stock. Ownership is presented for as many classes of creditors as the data allow. For example, stockholdings by individual bondholders in the sample are too small to be reported in proxy statements [panel A], although bondholders as a class often receive large amounts of stock [panel B]. Similarly, inconsistent reporting of restructuring and reorganization plan terms across firms necessitates presenting pro forma ownership data on a more aggregated level than data obtained from proxy statements.

Proxy statements that disclose creditor blockholdings are found for 36.0% of firms that restructure their debt privately, and 19.1% of firms that file for bankruptcy (panel A). These figures understate the actual frequency of creditor blockholdings, because many financially distressed firms do not file annual proxy statements, and because bank lenders are under legal and regulatory pressure to divest stockholdings in nonbank firms (see below). In

TABLE 12–3
Percentage Ownership of Common Stock by Creditors in Financially Distressed Firms[a]

Subsample / Creditor Class	Percentage Ownership of Common Stock				Percentage of Firms in Sub-sample
	Mean	Median	Mini-mum	Maxi-mum	

Panel A: Ownership reported in annual proxy statements

Debt restructuring					
Banks	36.1	33.3	7.8	70.4	30.0
Insurance companies	26.3	23.4	0.0	32.3	6.0
Other corporate lenders	26.7	26.7	8.2	45.1	4.0
ESOPs	7.9	7.9	7.9	7.9	2.0
All creditors	*36.1*	*35.2*	*7.8*	*70.4*	*36.0*
Bankruptcy					
Banks	14.5	9.6	6.1	46.1	14.3
Insurance companies	9.3	7.8	5.4	14.7	4.8
Other corporate lenders	17.4	17.4	5.2	29.5	3.2
ESOPs	29.4	29.4	8.8	50.0	3.2
All creditors	*21.0*	*17.8*	*5.2*	*50.0*	*19.1*

Panel B: Pro forma ownership under terms of debt restructuring or bankruptcy reorganization plan

Debt restructuring					
Banks and insurance companies	36.6	37.2	2.9	77.6	47.1
Public bondholders	33.0	26.8	3.6	86.1	43.1
All creditors	*41.9*	*45.8*	*4.9*	*86.1*	*70.6*
Bankruptcy					
All creditors	*79.2*	*88.0*	*45.0*	*97.4*	*75.0*

[a] Figures are based on a sample of 111 New York- and American Stock Exchange-listed firms that either filed for bankruptcy under Chapter 11 (61 firms), or privately restructured their debt to avoid bankruptcy (50 firms) between 1979 and 1985. In panel A, ownership is defined as the largest percentage of common stock held by creditors in a particular class while a firm is financially distressed (as reported in annual proxy statements). In panel B, ownership is defined as pro forma percentage stockholdings by creditors under the terms of a firm's debt restructuring or bankruptcy reorganization plan. Ownership percentages are calculated under the assumption that any convertible securities held or received by creditors are fully converted into common stock. Sources used to determine pro forma ownership include the *Moody's* manuals, *The Wall Street Journal,* firms' 10k reports, and exchange offer circulars. Ownership by public bondholders reflects the number of shares distributed under exchange offers net of any convertible securities surrendered by bondholders (assuming full conversion into common stock). For the subsample of bankrupt firms in panel B, ownership by all creditors equals 1.0 minus the fraction of common stock distributed to pre-petition common stockholders under a firm's Chapter 11 bankruptcy reorganization plan, and percentage of firms in subsample equals the percentage of bankrupt firms that continued to operate as independent going concerns following confirmation of their Chapter 11 reorganization plans (relative to all firms whose ultimate fate following Chapter 11 could be verified from the aforementioned sources).

panel A, creditors are allocated to four classes: banks, insurance companies, other corporate lenders, and employee stock ownership plans (ESOPs). Stock placements with ESOPs in the sample are all financed by wage concessions, and are treated as restructuring of short-term debt. In firms that restructure their debt privately, mean stock ownership by all creditors is 36.1%, with a median of 35.2%; corresponding mean and median ownership percentages in bankrupt firms are 21.0% and 17.8%. Most of this ownership can be attributed to banks, which are represented in the large majority of firms with creditor stockholdings. Weighted by the relative frequency of their holdings, banks also hold significantly larger blocks than other classes of creditors. The maximum percentage ownership by banks in the sample is 70.4%.

Evidence in panel B confirms the importance of bank stockholdings in financially distressed firms. Banks and insurance companies receive stock under 47.1% of all debt restructuring plans in the sample. Under the terms of these plans, mean pro forma percentage ownership of these lenders equals 36.6%, with a median of 37.2%. The maximum percentage of common stock they receive is 77.6%. These figures are similar to those reported for banks in panel A. Collective stock ownership of public bondholders in the sample is also substantial. Restructuring of publicly traded bonds takes place through exchange offers. On average, bondholders receive 33.0% of firms' common stock under these offers, and at the median, 26.8%. In one case, bondholders receive equity securities equivalent to 86.1% of the firm's common stock.

Finally, panel B reports the percentage of stock creditors receive under Chapter 11 reorganization plans. Of all bankruptcies in the sample for which the final outcome of Chapter 11 could be determined, 75% result in creditors holding equity in the surviving firm; the remaining firms are either liquidated (6.3%) or merged into other firms (18.7%). Collectively, creditors receive 79.2% of bankrupt firms' equity on average, and 88.0% at the median. In contrast, collective stock ownership by creditors in firms that restructure their debt privately have a sample mean and median of 41.9% and 45.8%, respectively. The reasons for these differences are not investigated here, but they could bear on the choice between alternative recontracting mechanisms [Jensen (1989a, b), Gilson et al. (1990)].

The level of bank ownership documented in Table 12–3 is influenced by a number of institutional and legal factors that prevent banks from holding large amounts of stock in nonbank firms. Such stockholdings are prohibited under Section 16 of the Glass-Steagall Act, the Bank Holding Company Act, and the Federal Reserve Board's Regulation Y. Although exceptions apply when banks obtain stock under a debt restructuring or bankruptcy reorganization plan, this stock must be divested within approximately two years. These constraints imply that blockholdings by banks, while often significant, may be shorter-lived than blocks held by nonbank entities. In addition, when banks receive equity securities under a debt restructuring plan they are more likely to be viewed as corporate insiders under bankruptcy law. As such, the banks can be forced to return any consideration received under the plan as a "voidable preference" if the firm files for bankruptcy within one year. Banks are therefore more willing to accept stock in financially distressed firms when recontracting takes place in Chapter 11.

Banks' equity ownership allows them, as shareholders, to affect the outcome of board elections. I also find evidence that banks sometimes influence board membership directly. Three firms in the sample give banks a special class of equity security that guarantees them control over a minimum number of board seats. In three other cases, bank executives join the board while the firm is attempting to restructure its debt; in one such case a former bank officer becomes the firm's chairman and CEO. In two firms that restructure their debt privately, the entire board is replaced under bank pressure. For four bankrupt firms, a minimum fraction of board seats in the reorganized firm is reserved for members of the court-appointed creditors' committee. For all twelve cases, the mean percentage of board seats controlled by banks is 38.2%, with a median of 31.7%. These results support Masulis's (1988) conjecture that corporate insolvency often leads to direct lender representation on the board of directors.

Since a nontrivial fraction of board seats in these companies continues to be held by directors elected by nonbank stockholders, it is not clear how much influence banks actually have over board decisions, particularly when the interests of banks and stockholders differ. Some insight into the constraints that banks face in their role as directors is provided by a bank chairman who was appointed to the board of Massey Ferguson during its debt restructuring (included in the current sample), who remarked: "I will certainly have the bank's interest in mind, but I also hope to represent Massey's shareholders" (*WSJ*, 13 October 1980, p. 24). A plausible motive for having made this statement is that the bank wished to reduce its legal liability to Massey's stockholders. Under lender liability laws, banks (and other creditors) can be sued if they take actions that undermine the value of the firm's other claims [Douglas-Hamilton (1975), Smith and Warner (1979)].

Bank Control Through Restrictive Covenants

Additional evidence on the monitoring role of banks is presented in Table 12–4, which provides a breakdown of the restrictive covenants included in 40 privately restructured bank lending agreements in the sample. Data on covenants were collected from firms' 10k filings, the *Moody's* manuals, and *WSJ* reports of restructurings. Examination of these covenants provides some insights into the nature of the power exercised by banks in financially distressed firms.

In general, the covenants documented in Table 12–4 grant banks property rights in the firm's assets directly. Ordinary loan agreements, in con-

TABLE 12–4
Control Exercised by Creditors Through Inclusion of Restrictive Covenants in 40 Privately Restructured Bank Lending Agreements, by General Class of Restriction[a]

Description of Covenant	Percentage
Restrictions on management activities	
Creditor approval required for changes in senior management or board of directors	2.5
Default declared if current CEO or chairman of the board leaves	2.5
Creditors permitted to attend board meetings	2.5
Restrictions on operating activities	
Maximum allowable outlay on general and administrative expenses	25.0
Increased financial reporting requirements to creditors	12.5
Creditor approval required for annual operating budget	7.5
Restrictions on new investment	
General restriction on level of capital expenditures	30.0
Restriction on permitted kinds of investment	22.5
Creditor approval required for capital expenditures	10.0
Maximum allowable cumulative investment in specified assets	5.0
Creditor approval required for mergers and other combinations	5.0
Restrictions on disposition of assets	
Creditors granted increased security interest in firm's assets	72.5
Restructured debt must be prepaid with proceeds of any divestitures[b]	55.0
General restriction on divestitures	22.5
Creditors granted ownership in assets directly	12.5
Restriction on firm's ability to collateralize assets	5.0
Creditor approval required for divestitures	7.5
Restriction on asset transfers to and from subsidiaries	10.0
Restrictions on payouts to shareholders	
General restriction on payouts[c]	37.5
Creditor approval required for dividends or share repurchases	47.5

Continued, overleaf

TABLE 12–4, concluded

Description of Covenant	Percentage
Restrictions on financing activity	
General restriction on level of borrowing	50.0
Creditor approval required for any additional borrowing	15.0
Proceeds of new financings must be used to prepay restructured debt	7.5
New common stock must be sold as condition of debt restructuring	7.5
Creditor approval required for sale of new equity	2.5
Creditor approval required for redemption of subordinated debt	2.5
Financial covenants	
Minimum required current ratio or level of working capital	45.0
Minimum required net worth	40.0
Maximum debt-to-equity ratio[d]	17.5
Minimum required profitability[e]	12.5
Minimum permitted value of assets	7.5
Minimum permitted interest coverage	2.5
Minimum permitted level of net exports	2.5

[a] Sample is based on 50 exchange-listed firms that privately restructured their debt to avoid bankruptcy between 1979 and 1985. Figures are the percentage of restructured lending agreements that contain a given covenant. Sources used to identify covenants contained in restructured lending agreements include the *Moody's* manuals, *The Wall Street Journal*, and firms' 10k reports. Covenants characterized as general restrictions include cases where it is not possible to ascertain whether the restriction is actually binding when the restructuring agreement is consummated.

[b] Includes eight cases where divestitures are required as a condition of debt restructuring.

[c] Includes two covenants that require the firm to reinvest some minimum fraction of net income.

[d] Includes one covenant that requires the firm to maintain a minimum ratio of net worth to total assets.

[e] Includes two covenants that require the firm to maintain a minimum level of net income, two that specify a minimum level of net operating cash flows, and one that specifies a minimum accounting profit margin.

trast, tend to contain only indirect restrictions on investment policy, through the operation of covenants that restrict the firm's dividend and financing policies [Smith and Warner (1979)]. Particularly striking is the number of cases in which banks are granted an explicit veto over the firm's investment and financing policies.[2] For example, banks have veto power over changes in senior management, the firm's annual operating budget, capital expenditures, mergers, divestitures, sales of new debt or equity, and the payment of dividends.

Also relatively common are agreements that grant banks increased collateral, or restrict the firm's ability to grant collateral without first obtaining banks' consent; approximately 75% of the restructured bank loan agreements contain such provisions. In 12.5% of all cases, control over physical assets is granted to creditors directly, and in 55% of all cases, the firm is required to prepay bank debt with proceeds from divestitures. In three agreements creditors are given the right to hire, fire, or otherwise monitor managers directly. Although relatively small in number, these provisions are significant in that similar restrictions are not normally observed outside of financial distress. Although only one agreement allows creditors to attend meetings of the board of directors, this probably understates the frequency of such activity, given anecdotal evidence that creditors maintain an informal presence in the firm during most loan workouts [Salamon (1982), Stein (1989)].

Although these results are based on a sample of firms that restructure their debt outside of bankruptcy, they suggest extensive bank monitoring occurs in financially distressed firms. Evidence of creditors acquiring such extensive decision-making powers is largely absent in other studies that have examined the debt contracts of relatively healthy firms [Smith and Warner (1979), Castle (1980), McDaniel (1986)]. For example, Castle (1980) surveys the covenants contained in 37 bank term loan agreements for a sample of industrial and transportation companies rated by *Moody's*. Dividend restrictions appear in 23 of these agreements, 17 of which are rated Baa or lower. Total indebtedness is limited in 21 agreements, 17 of which are rated Baa or lower. Covenants that explicitly limit capital expenditures are present in only four agreements, all rated Baa or lower. No covenants are included that limit general and administrative expenses. Covenants that limit the granting of collateral to others are common, appearing in 34 agreements. Restrictions on the sale of assets are present in 29 agreements, but 19 of these are rated Baa or lower. In no case are creditors granted a veto over any of the firm's investment or financing activities, nor is there ever any requirement that assets be divested, or that the proceeds from divestitures or new securities sales be used to prepay debt.

Another interesting comparison is provided by Baker and Wruck (1989), who document covenants in the bank loans that helped finance the 1986 leveraged buyout of O.M. Scott & Sons Company. They observe covenants quite similar to those reported in Table 12–4 for financially distressed firms. For example, the company is prohibited from paying cash dividends, divesting major assets, and engaging in transactions (for example, mergers) that would change its "corporate structure"; other covenants severely limit management's discretion over capital expenditures. Although LBOs and firms in financial distress both show high leverage

(O. M. Scott & Sons had a book debt-to-assets ratio of 0.78 immediately following its LBO, compared with a median ratio of 0.83 for the present sample of companies), factors that contribute to high leverage are obviously much different between the two sets of firms. This suggests that direct creditor control over corporate policies in general increases with the relative importance of debt in the firm's capital structure.

Given evidence that creditors obtain increased property rights in the firm when it defaults, it remains an empirical question whether any resulting reallocation of resources is consistent with maximization of firm value. Attempts by creditors to maximize the value of their fixed claims can reduce the value of the firm's residual claims and total firm value [Jensen and Meckling (1976)]. This loss of value represents a potentially significant cost of financial distress that has not been previously emphasized in the bankruptcy literature. Although creditors' incentives to engage in such behavior can be reduced by giving them equity securities in the firm, the aforementioned institutional factors effectively preclude meaningful share ownership by creditors.

Monitoring by the Board of Directors

Under normal circumstances, managers' performance is monitored more or less continuously by the board of directors. I assess how directors' roles and responsibilities change as a result of financial distress by analyzing observed changes in the membership and composition of boards when firms renegotiate their debt contracts.

Although all directors can in principle monitor managers' performance, directors' backgrounds and affiliations will in practice affect their ability to monitor effectively. In the following analysis, directors are classified as outsiders, insiders, or quasi-insiders. Inside directors are also managers of the firm. Outside directors have no continuing personal or professional relationship with the firm other than in their capacity as directors. Quasi-inside directors have such a relationship, but are not managers. Examples of quasi-insiders are retired managers of the firm, relatives of current managers, and lawyers who also serve as the firm's counsel. (A detailed description of the makeup of each class appears in Table 12–6, below.) Responsibility for monitoring management performance is commonly ascribed to the outside directors. Junior managers who are also inside directors will be reluctant to criticize senior managers on whom they depend for promotion. Quasi-inside directors who criticize management risk losing valuable business relationships with the firm. One common view is that inside and quasi-inside directors are brought onto the board for the valuable knowledge that they possess, and to advise and counsel the CEO [Mace (1986)]. In addition, inside directors can be potential candidates to succeed the CEO [Vancil (1987)].

Changes in board structure during financial distress are presented in Table 12–5. Panel A documents how many of the directors in place one year before the start of a bankruptcy or debt restructuring remain on the board once their firms' financial distress has been resolved. These results are presented graphically in Figure 12–1. As discussed in the second section above, reported turnover reflects only turnover that takes place while firms are financially distressed. For most firms in the sample, directors' tenure is tracked only until year +2, reflecting the mean time of approximately two years that these firms are financially distressed [see Table 12–2].

Of 1,006 directors who initially sit on the boards of the 111 sampled firms, only 445 (46%) retain their seats at the end of the observation period. The corresponding turnover rate is similar for all three classes of directors. Thus, more than half the board turns over on average during a typical bankruptcy or debt restructuring. For 8% of firms in the sample the board is completely replaced (not shown). For 29% of the sample, less than one-fourth of the original directors remain. There is complete turnover of outside and inside directors in 24% and 25% of all firms, respectively. Less than 25% of the original directors in each of these classes remain at the conclusion of financial distress for 35% and 38% of sampled firms.

Consistent with the results of Gilson (1989), turnover among CEOs is also substantial. Only 44% of CEOs in place at year −1 are still employed in that capacity at year +4. In contrast, 55% of CEOs, all of whom initially hold a seat on the board of directors, retain their seat at the end of the observation period. At any given date, more incumbent CEOs remain on the board than stay CEO. That the ex-CEO is not removed from the board immediately could reflect a certain amount of face saving, or facilitate a smoother transition to new senior management [Vancil (1987)].

Turnover is fairly evenly distributed over the first three years of the observation period, with about 16% of incumbent directors and CEOs leaving each year. It does not appear that directors bail out before full public disclosure of their firms' financial problems. One possible explanation is that directors could appear to be more culpable for their firms' financial problems, and increase their legal liability, if they depart from the board prematurely.

Although results are not presented for a control sample of

TABLE 12–5
Changes in the Membership and Structure of Boards of Directors During Financial Distress[a]

	Years Elapsed Relative to Start of Financial Distress					
	−1	0	+1	+2	+3	+4

Panel A: Number (mean fraction) of directors and CEOs who remain with their firms

Outside directors	517 (1.00)	427 (0.86)	334 (0.64)	270 (0.52)	243 (0.47)	237 (0.46)
Inside directors	370 (1.00)	306 (0.84)	233 (0.64)	177 (0.50)	161 (0.47)	157 (0.46)
Quasi-inside directors	119 (1.00)	108 (0.91)	76 (0.67)	63 (0.57)	54 (0.48)	51 (0.46)
All directors	1006 (1.00)	841 (0.85)	643 (0.65)	510 (0.52)	458 (0.48)	445 (0.46)
CEO (as director)	110 (1.00)	95 (0.86)	76 (0.69)	63 (0.57)	61 (0.56)	59 (0.54)
CEO (as manager)	110 (1.00)	91 (0.83)	66 (0.60)	49 (0.45)	47 (0.43)	47 (0.43)

Panel B: Mean (median) board size over time

Number of directors	9.2 (8.0)	8.6 (8.0)	7.8 (7.0)	7.6 (7.0)	7.4 (7.0)	7.3 (7.0)

Panel C: Mean (median) percentage of board seats held by different classes of directors over time

Outside directors	49.6 (50.0)	49.8 (50.0)	48.1 (50.0)	48.9 (50.0)	49.7 (52.3)	49.5 (54.6)
Inside directors	38.7 (40.0)	38.3 (40.0)	41.6 (41.4)	41.1 (40.0)	41.8 (40.0)	42.2 (40.0)
Quasi-inside directors	11.7 (9.1)	11.6 (10.0)	9.1 (0.0)	8.0 (0.0)	6.5 (0.0)	5.8 (0.0)

[a] Reported figures are based on information contained in firms' annual proxy statements and 10k reports. Sample consists of 111 New York- and American Stock Exchange-listed firms that either filed for bankruptcy under Chapter 11 or privately restructured their debt to avoid bankruptcy between 1979 and 1985. Year 0 represents the date on which a firm either files for bankruptcy or starts to restructure its debt. Reported turnover includes only resignations that take place while firms are bankrupt or restructuring their debt. Board turnover is assumed to take place on the date of the annual proxy statement that first reflects such turnover, unless a more accurate date can be established from reports of board changes in *The Wall Street Journal*. Outside directors have no other professional affiliation with the firm. Inside directors are also officers of the firm. Quasi-inside directors have some professional or family relationship with the firm, but are not insiders.

FIGURE 12–1
**Fraction of Original Directors Who Remain on the Board, Relative
to Date on Which Firm Files for Bankruptcy under Chapter 11 or
Begins to Restructure Its Debt to Avoid Bankruptcy (Year 0)[a]**

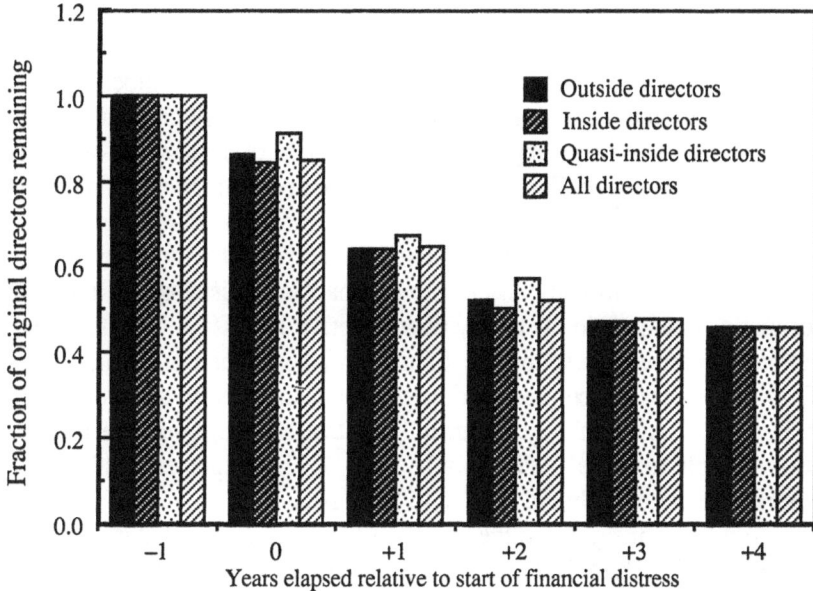

[a] Sample consists of 111 exchange-listed companies that either filed for bankruptcy (61 firms) or restructured their debt (50 firms) during 1979–1985. Outside directors have no other professional affiliation with the firm. Inside directors are also officers of the firm. Quasi-inside directors have some professional or family relationship with the firm, but are not insiders. Reported turnover includes only resignations that take place while firms are bankrupt or restructuring their debt.

nonfinancially distressed firms, reported turnover of directors and CEOs in the sample appears to be large in relation to normal turnover. By comparison, Hermalin and Weisbach (1989) report turnover of approximately one director per year for an unconditional sample of 142 NYSE-listed firms during 1971–1983. The median board size in their sample is 13 directors, implying a 7.7% probability that any one director will leave the firm in a given year. Assuming that board departures are independent across directors and over time, 79% of the board should be still in place after three years. As reported in Table 12–5 and Figure 12–1, only 52% of the original directors in the current sample remain by year +2. CEO turnover in financially distressed firms also appears to be much greater than that observed in normal situations. For example, Weisbach (1988) reports a mean annualized CEO resignation rate of 8% per firm for a sample of financially solvent NYSE firms. This implies a two-year cumulative departure rate of about 22%, compared with the observed rate of 55% for the present sample.

Panel B of Table 12–5 reports changes in total board size throughout firms' financial distress. Over the entire period, the mean number of directors on the board declines from 9.2 to 7.3, and the median number, from 8 to 7. Changes in both means and medians are statistically significant at the 1% level. Seventy-one firms, representing almost 60% of the sample, experience a decline in board size. For 36.7% of firms the decline in the total number of board seats exceeds 25%, and for 14.7% of firms, the decline is greater than 50%. Declining board size in the sample is consistent with fewer directors being required to monitor the assets of financially distressed firms, either because assets are sold off to pay down debt, or because substitute forms of monitoring arise in response to financial distress, such as monitoring by blockholders. Evidence presented below is consistent with such substitution taking place. Alternatively, financially distressed firms may be unable to attract people to serve as directors because of high expected legal and time costs associated with board service in these firms.

Additional insight into the nature of turnover is provided in panel C of Table 12–5, which indicates that fractional board representation by different classes of directors does not change significantly during the debt renegotiation process. Both the mean and median percentages of outsiders on the board stay virtually unchanged at about 50%. The mean percentage of insiders on the board rises somewhat, but the difference is not statistically significant. The median percentage of inside directors is virtually unchanged, at 40%, throughout the period. In contrast, evidence presented by Hermalin and Weisbach (1988) for a sample of mostly large, solvent firms indicates that more outsiders are added to the board following poor operating performance. They interpret this shift as reflecting demand for greater monitoring of management induced by the firm's lack of profitability. In the present sample, the appointment of new outside directors is accompanied by the departure of incumbent outside directors, leaving board composition relatively unchanged.

Analysis of Directors' Characteristics
If firms become financially distressed because directors lack certain essential skills, or if new skills are required to manage such firms, we should

expect to observe differences in the personal characteristics of departing directors and the directors who replace them. This possibility is examined in Table 12–6. As shown in panel A, departing directors are older than their replacements. The mean age of departing directors is 58.1, whereas that of newly appointed directors is 51.4; corresponding median directors' ages are 58 and 52. Both means and medians are significantly different at the 5% level. Departing directors also appear to be relatively experienced, having served on their boards for 9.5 years on average (median of 7 years) before departing. Neither departing nor newly appointed directors own very much common stock in their firms, with mean and median holdings for all types of directors of under 5%. None of the differences in stockholdings are statistically significant.

Panel B of Table 12–6 presents a detailed breakdown of board departures and replacements, according to the identity of the directors involved. A comparison of the two columns indicates that financial distress is associated with a statistically significant increase in the proportion of outside board seats held by major blockholders, investment bankers, and representatives of the firm's creditors. The role of outside blockholders and investment banks in monitoring financially distressed firms is explored more fully below. Significantly fewer board seats are held by lawyers and former managers of the company. These comparisons suggest that financial distress engenders a shift towards greater board representation by outsiders who possess some special interest or expertise in monitoring financially distressed companies, even though the total proportion of outsiders on the board is unchanged.

Identifying the Causes of Board Turnover
Evidence in Tables 12–5 and 12–6 suggests that financial distress is accompanied by significant changes in board membership. This evidence has several possible interpretations, however. Directors could be forced to resign under pressure from stockholders because they are judged to have performed poorly in monitoring the firm's management. Board resignations in financially distressed firms could also occur at the urging of creditors; Gilson (1989) finds that bank lenders frequently initiate senior management changes in financially distressed firms. Alternatively, directors could resign because they are inadequately insured against shareholder lawsuits, or because they are unable to replace an incompetent but powerful CEO, and wish to signal their dissatisfaction with current management [Mace (1986)]. In addition, directors could resign because of the personal trauma and time costs associated with serving on the board of a financially distressed firm.

TABLE 12–6
Selected Characteristics of Directors Affected by Board Turnover[a]

	Departures	Appointments
Panel A: Mean (median) sample characteristics		
Age	58.1[b] (58[b])	51.4 (52)
Years served on board	9.5 (7)	—
Percentage common stock ownership		
(i) Outside directors	1.87 (0.09)	1.08 (0.00)
(ii) Inside directors	3.22 (0.52)	1.89 (0.08)
(iii) Quasi-inside directors	0.46 (0.01)	1.43 (0.00)
(iv) All directors	1.68 (0.05)	1.55 (0.00)
Panel B: Professional affiliation of directors, in percentage		
Outside directors		
Appointed by creditors	0.0[b]	0.9
Manager in another nonfinancial firm	24.9	23.7
Manager in unaffiliated bank or insurance company	1.8	2.4
Retired manager of another company	4.1	2.4
Major blockholder in firm	8.3[b]	13.4
Investment banker	1.6[b]	3.8
Lawyer	3.7	3.8
Professor	3.7	2.4
Other	2.2	2.6
Inside directors		
Senior manager	15.9	17.2
Junior manager	20.8	20.9
Quasi-inside directors		
Lawyer affiliated with firm	4.4[b]	0.7
Investment banker affiliated with firm	0.9	1.7
Bank or insurance company lender of firm	1.2	0.7
Former manager of company	4.3[b]	0.7
Employee stock ownership plan (ESOP)	0.2	1.0
Relative of current manager	0.4	0.5
Other	1.9	1.2

[a] Turnover is identified by comparing firms' successive annual proxy statements, starting with the first proxy that predates the beginning of financial distress, and ending with the first proxy to follow the resolution of financial distress. Total turnover consists of 558 departures of directors whose incumbency predates the beginning of financial distress, and 417 appointments of new directors that follow the onset of financial distress. Sample consists of 111 New York- and American Stock Exchange-listed firms that either filed for bankruptcy under Chapter 11 or privately restructured their debt to avoid bankruptcy between 1979 and 1985. Board turnover is assumed to take place on the date of the annual proxy statement that first reflects such turnover, unless a more current date can be established from relevant stories in *The Wall Street Journal*. Outside directors have no other professional affiliation with the firm. Inside directors are also officers of the firm. Quasi-inside directors have some professional or family relationship with the firm, but are not insiders.
[b] Difference in means (medians) of departures and appointments is significantly different from zero at the 0.05 level using a two-tailed t-test (Wilcoxon rank sum test).

In the context of understanding how financial distress affects corporate governance, the evidence on board turnover raises two important issues. First, as suggested by the preceding discussion, whether board resignations in financially distressed firms reflect disciplinary action against incompetent directors is an empirical question. If insolvency leads instead to the resignation or removal of "good" directors, any resulting loss of firm value is a cost of financial distress.

The second issue concerns the possibility that board turnover in financially distressed firms is not caused by financial distress per se, but rather by the underlying decline in profitability that leaves the firm unable to service its debt. Recent evidence suggests that departures of senior managers [Warner et al. (1988), Weisbach (1988)] and directors [Hermalin and Weisbach (1988)] are more likely when firms' operating performance is poor. Although the following analysis does not control for the effects of poor performance, related evidence presented by Gilson (1989) suggests that financial distress independently engenders higher turnover among senior managers (the CEO, president, and chairman of the board). He observes a 52% annual turnover rate among senior managers for a large sample of financially distressed firms (including as a subset those analyzed here), compared with a rate of only 19% for a control sample of highly unprofitable, nonfinancially distressed firms.

The relative infrequency with which board changes are reported in the *WSJ* makes it difficult to ascertain the reasons for turnover directly. Only 19.5% of all board departures, and 37.6% of new board appointments, are reported in the *WSJ*. In addition, firms' financial performance is cited in only six articles covering a board change. In two firms a majority of outside directors resign following their companies' failure to obtain adequate directors' liability insurance. In one other case, all of the outside directors of a bankrupt company resign following the bankruptcy court examiner's recommendation that the directors be held legally liable for the company's problems.

Some indirect evidence on the reasons for board turnover is presented in Table 12–7, which documents changes in the number of outside board seats that departing directors hold in other firms over the three years that follow their departure. A decline in the number of other seats held is consistent with two explanations. If directors are held responsible for their firms' financial distress, their reputations as expert monitors will suffer, and they will be less often asked to serve on other boards. On the other hand, directors' experience with financial distress could be suffi-

TABLE 12–7
**Number of Outside Directorships Subsequently Held by
Directors Who Resign from the Boards of Companies that
File for Bankruptcy Under Chapter 11 or Privately Restructure
Their Debt to Avoid Bankruptcy**[a]

	Number of Outside Directorships Held in Years Following Resignation[b]			
	0	*1*	*2*	*3*
Outside directors				
Total	171	144	123	113
Mean	2.6	2.2	1.8	1.7
Median	1	1	1	1
All directors				
Total	350	308	270	226
Mean	2.2	1.9	1.7	1.4
Median	1	1	1	0

[a] Sample consists of 160 directors of all types (including 67 outside directors) whose incumbency predates the beginning of financial distress. All resignations occur during the 1979–1985 period. Outside board memberships are obtained from various issues of Standard and Poor's *Register of Corporations, Directors and Executives*. Totals exclude seats held on the host company's board and on boards of host-company subsidiaries. Not counted as outside directorships are seats on the boards of nonprofit organizations, professional associations, and any firm in which the director also holds a management position. Multiple directorships in affiliated firms are treated as single directorships.
[b] Time 0 corresponds to the first calendar year-end predating a director's resignation date.

ciently unpleasant to discourage them from serving on other boards subsequently.

Information on board membership is obtained from Standard and Poor's *Register of Corporations, Directors and Executives* (henceforth, the *Register*). Of the 561 board resignations in total [see Table 12–5], information on 160 directors is available in the *Register*. Only a subset of directors is represented in the *Register* because inclusion in this publication is voluntary, based on firms' response to a questionnaire. Financially troubled firms are less likely to be included if they have a lower response rate. Coverage of a particular director will continue as long as he or she sits on the board of at least one company that continues to report to the *Register*. Thus, the figures reported in Table 12–7 will not be biased down unless the 160 directors analyzed in the table systematically hold seats in other firms that also become financially distressed (and stop reporting to the *Register*). Only departing directors' subsequent board service is analyzed, because directors who continue to serve with financially distressed firms could be forced to cut back on their other board commitments by time pressures. Separate totals are reported for outside directors and the entire board, recognizing that all directors can serve as outside directors in other companies.

At the resignation date, 160 directors of all kinds jointly hold a total of 350 outside board seats, excluding seats held on the board of the original host firm and any subsidiaries. Three years later, only 226 outside directorships are held, a decline of 35.4%. The corresponding decline for outside directors is 33.9%. Although the mean number of seats held by each director is small (2.2), the mean observed three years later is significantly lower (p-value less than 5%). Almost 36% of the directors represented in the table subsequently hold fewer other outside board seats, while only 11.9% of directors hold more seats after three years. These results are not sensitive to whether departing directors are close to retirement age, although board membership is generally not restricted by age. Both the absolute and percentage decline in the number of seats held remains significantly different from zero when the sample is restricted to directors younger than 55, 60, and 65 years. The partial correlation between the decline in number of board seats and age of departing directors is negative, but statistically insignificant. Kaplan and Reishus (1988) perform a similar analysis of outside board membership for CEOs of firms that implement large dividend reductions. However, they find no significant reduction in the total number of outside directorships held by CEOs.

Results in Table 12–7 provide support for Fama and Jensen's (1983) conjecture that outside directors' principal compensation from serving on corporate boards derives from the reputation they develop as expert monitors of management performance. Fama and Jensen argue that the impact of board service on directors' wealth will be greater "when the direct payments to outside directors are small, but there is substantial devaluation of human capital when internal decision control breaks down and the costly last resort process of an outside takeover is activated [p. 315]". In the absence of this incentive, it is difficult to understand what financial incentives directors have to perform in their delegated role as monitors, since they typically own very little common stock in the companies on whose boards they serve, and are paid only a fixed, nominal fee for board service.

Table 12–8 presents additional indirect evidence on the causes of board turnover in financially distressed firms. Evidence in panel A tests the hypothesis that if directors are blamed for having failed to preempt bad man-

TABLE 12–8
Turnover of Directors in Firms with Selected Attributes[a]

Attribute	Sub-sample with Attribute	Sub-sample without Attribute	p-Value of t-Test for Difference in Means
Panel A: Mean fraction of incumbent directors who resign in a given year during firms' bankruptcy or debt restructuring			
Incumbent CEO resigns from board during the year	0.51	0.13	0.00
Incumbent CEO resigns as manager during the year	0.46	0.12	0.00
Panel B: Mean fraction of incumbent directors who resign over the course of firms' bankruptcy or debt restructuring (number of firms in parentheses)			
Incumbent CEO resigns as manager during the firm's bankruptcy or debt restructuring	0.67 (63)	0.36 (47)	0.00
Incumbent CEO is the firm's founder	0.53 (23)	0.54 (87)	0.85
Initial percentage of firm's common stock owned by managers and directors exceeds the sample median	0.60 (50)	0.43 (49)	0.01
Firm's directors are elected for staggered terms	0.51 (29)	0.55 (81)	0.58
Firm privately restructures its debt as an alternative to bankruptcy	0.49 (50)	0.57 (60)	0.16

[a] Total sample consists of 111 financially distressed New York- and American Stock Exchange-listed firms that either filed for bankruptcy under Chapter 11 or privately restructured their debt to avoid bankruptcy between 1979 and 1985. Panels A and B report the mean fraction of incumbent directors who resign from the board within a given year, and over the course of the firm's debt restructuring or bankruptcy, respectively. Stock ownership by managers and directors equals beneficial ownership of stock reported in the firm's annual proxy statement that most closely predates the start of the bankruptcy or debt restructuring.

agement decisions (that resulted in financial distress), turnover of directors should be positively correlated with turnover of the CEO. This correlation will also be positive if creditors replace both managers and directors in financially distressed firms. If directors resign for other reasons (for example, to avoid further trauma due to financial distress, or to express their displeasure with an incompetent but powerful CEO) the observed correlation should be zero or negative. Panel A shows that the mean fraction of directors who resign from the board in a given year is significantly higher in years when the CEO also resigns (in his or her capacity as either director or manager). Fifty-one percent of all directors leave in years when the CEO resigns from the board, compared with only 13% of directors in other years. As shown in panel B, 67% of incumbent directors resign over the entire course of firms' financial distress when the CEO also resigns, compared with only 36% for firms where the CEO remains. All of these differences are statistically significant at the 1% level.

Table 12–8 also presents evidence on how other firm attributes affect turnover of directors. Board turnover is unaffected by whether the CEO is the company's founder, which has been suggested as one measure of his or her power [Morck et al. (1988)]. Turnover is significantly higher when insider stock ownership exceeds the sample median, and is not significantly lower when directors' terms are staggered. These results suggest that conventional means available to managers and directors for self-entrenchment are relatively ineffective when firms are financially distressed.

Finally, board turnover appears to be lower when debt is restructured privately rather than in Chapter 11, although the difference is not statistically significant. Fifty-seven percent of directors resign in firms that file for bankruptcy, compared with 49% of directors in firms that restructure their debt privately; corresponding median percentages (not shown) are 62% and 52%. A t-test and Wilcoxon rank-sum test fail to reject the hypothesis of no difference in means and medians. Self-interest of directors would therefore not appear to be a critical factor in whether firms file for bankruptcy or attempt to settle privately with creditors. It may not be possible to generalize from such comparisons, however, because of the relatively small sample size. In addition, directors who assess a greater risk of turnover due to bankruptcy will be predisposed to settle with creditors privately (assuming that this option still exists), and their firms will be less likely to file for bankruptcy. This selection bias implies that actual turnover observed in bankrupt firms will be an underestimate of expected turnover due to bankruptcy.

Results of the univariate comparisons in Table 12–8 are confirmed when cumulative turnover rates [reported in panel A of Table 12–5] are related to these variables jointly in ordinary-least-squares regressions (not shown). Separate regressions are estimated for turnover of all directors and turnover of directors within each class (outside, inside, and quasi-inside). Cumulative turnover of all three kinds of directors is positively and significantly related to whether the firm's CEO resigns during the financial distress (p-value less than 0.01). None of the remaining coefficient estimates are statistically significant. These results are largely unchanged when measures of the firm's past profitability are included as explanatory variables, including cumulative common stock returns and unexpected annual earnings before interest and taxes (as defined in Table 12–2). For various lags, these performance variables are almost always statistically insignificant. There is weak evidence that staggered boards are associated with lower turnover when regressions include firms' unexpected annual earnings (p-value of 0.11). The multivariate results are otherwise consistent, however, with the results in Table 12–8.

Monitoring by Outside Blockholders

Concurrently with the changes in board structure, there appears to be a significant increase in large blockholdings in the sample. This is consistent with an increased monitoring role for external blockholders and other outsiders in financially distressed firms. Panel A of Table 12–9 presents mean and median percentage common stock ownership of blockholders over the same period used to measure board turnover. Changes in total blockholdings are also illustrated graphically in Figure 12–2 (panel A). Because firms depart from the sample once they emerge from bankruptcy or conclude a debt restructuring agreement, the sample size declines significantly in years +3 and +4. Because most firms are tracked at least until year +2, ownership figures for this year are potentially the most meaningful.

Exclusive of holdings by managers and directors, the mean percentage of common stock held by all blockholders—defined as those holding stakes of more than 5%—increases from 12.34% in year –1 to 27.89% in year +2, and to 28.69% in year +4. Corresponding median ownership percentages are 0.00%, 23.90%, and 26.50%. Increases in block ownership through year +3 (relative to year –1) are all statistically significant using a paired comparison t-test for means and a Wilcoxon signed-rank test for medians. These tests both make pairwise comparisons of ownership between years, to allow for

TABLE 12–9
Percentage Ownership of Common Stock in Financially Distressed
Firms, by Various Classes of Holders and by Years Relative
to the Beginning of Financial Distress[a]

Stockholder	Mean and Median Percentage Ownership in Years Elapsed Relative to Start of Financial Distress[b]					
	−1	0	+1	+2	+3	+4
Panel A: Ownership by nonmanagement blockholders						
All >5% blockholders	12.34	15.74[d]	19.76[c]	27.89[c]	21.87[e]	28.69
	0.00	5.95[d]	14.10[c]	23.90[c]	17.70[e]	26.50
Mean and median %	*5.0*	*5.0*	*7.9*	*12.5*	*3.6*	*1.2*
of board seats held	*0.0*	*0.0*	*0.0*	*0.0*	*0.0*	*0.0*
Largest >5% blockholder	9.62	12.28[d]	14.59[c]	18.23[c]	11.79	8.67
	0.00	5.60[d]	9.30[c]	14.40[c]	11.00[e]	8.65
Mean and median %	*4.4*	*4.1*	*6.0*	*10.4*	*2.2*	*0.0*
of board seats held	*0.0*	*0.0*	*0.0*	*0.0*	*0.0*	*0.0*
Panel B: Ownership by corporate insiders						
Outside directors	3.21	1.62	3.73	4.26	2.34	1.28
	0.29	0.20[d]	0.35[d]	0.17	0.04	0.34
Inside directors	16.80	16.44	11.01[d]	10.96[d]	13.18	1.10
	9.18	10.07[e]	5.00[c]	6.09[c]	2.37[d]	0.85
Quasi-inside directors	0.75	1.17	0.59	0.54	0.46	0.07
	0.01	0.01	0.00	0.00	0.00	0.05
CEO	10.52	10.09	7.53[d]	6.41[d]	6.66	0.92
	4.30	4.22	1.99[d]	1.69[c]	1.00[d]	0.54
All officers and directors	21.91	20.52	16.02[e]	16.52	16.54	2.88
	14.30	14.55[e]	11.59[c]	10.54[c]	4.95[d]	2.61
Sample size	103	92	77	75	25	4

[a] Sample consists of 111 New York- and American Stock Exchange-listed firms that either filed for bankruptcy under Chapter 11 or privately restructured their debt to avoid bankruptcy between 1979 and 1985. The sample size declines over time because of unavailability of data, and departures of firms from the sample as they complete their bankruptcy or debt restructuring before year +4. The statistical significance of the difference in mean and median ownership percentages (relative to ownership in year −1) is determined using a paired comparison t-test and a Wilcoxon signed-rank test, respectively. Ownership percentages in the table represent holdings reported in the annual proxy statement that most closely predates a given event year. Outside directors have no other professional affiliation with the firm. Inside directors are also officers of the firm. Quasi-inside directors have some professional or family relationship with the firm, but are not insiders.
[b] Year 0 represents the date on which a firm either files for bankruptcy or starts to restructure its debt.
[c] Ownership percentage is significantly different from percentage in year −1 at the 0.01 level.
[d] Ownership percentage is significantly different from percentage in year −1 at the 0.05 level.
[e] Ownership percentage is significantly different from percentage in year −1 at the 0.10 level.

FIGURE 12–2
Mean and Median Percentage of Common Stock Held by All Nonmanagement Blockholders, Relative to Year in Which Firm Files for Chapter 11 or Begins to Restructure Its Debt to Avoid Bankruptcy (Year 0)[a]

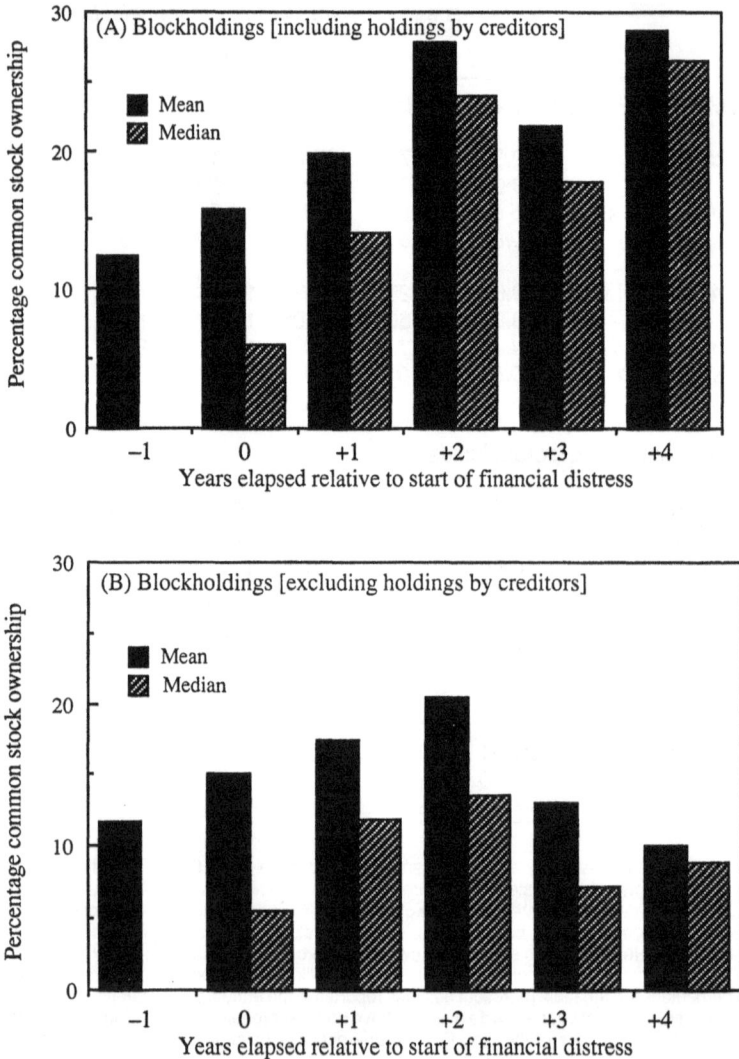

[a] Blockholders are defined as owners of more than 5% of the firm's common stock, including (A) and excluding (B) creditors. Creditors consist of banks, insurance companies, ESOPs, and other corporate lenders. Sample consists of 111 exchange-listed companies that either filed for bankruptcy (61 firms) or restructured their debt (50 firms) during 1979–1985.

the declining sample size over event time. Mean percentage holdings by the largest beneficial owner increase from 9.62% in year −1 to 18.23% in year +2, although mean holdings fall to 8.67% by year +4. A similar pattern is observed for median holdings. Mean and median ownership by the largest blockholder is significantly higher in each year through years +2 and +3, respectively. These results offer an interesting contrast to those of Loderer and Sheehan (1989), who find that percentage stock ownership by outside blockholders (and corporate insiders) changes very little over the five years that precede bankruptcy.

Increases in percentage blockholdings also appear to be accompanied by increases in board representation, although the relationship is weak. Table 12–9 indicates that blockholders on average hold 12.5% of the board seats in the companies whose stock they hold in year +2, compared with 5% of the seats in the initial year. Corresponding percentages for the largest blockholder are 10.4% and 4.4%. For both categories of holdings, however, the median percentage of seats held is zero throughout the entire interval. Thus, blockholders' ability to influence corporate policy in these firms does not appear to require majority representation on the board.

Increased ownership concentration in the sample is not simply a consequence of increased equity ownership by creditors. Panel B of Figure 12–2 graphs mean and median percentage holdings of all blockholders exclusive of holdings by creditors. Although levels of ownership are reduced by this adjustment, the same general pattern of changes in ownership concentration is observed as in panel A for the full sample of blockholdings, except for the last two years. The statistical tests described above both reject at the 5% level the hypothesis of no increase in percentage ownership for years +1 and +2. Blockholdings are noticeably less in years +3 and +4 when holdings by creditors are removed, but these declines are not statistically significant, reflecting the small sample size for these years.

A similar analysis suggests that increased blockholdings in the sample are not driven by private equity placements, but rather reflect the consolidation of blocks out of existing shares. Each firm in the sample was examined in the *WSJ Index* over the entire event period for any mention of private equity placements. This search yielded 13 such placements, but the patterns evident in Table 12–9 and Figure 12–2 do not materially change when the impact of these placements on stock ownership is excluded.

At the same time as external holdings increase in importance, stock ownership by corporate insiders, and the board of directors, declines. Data on directors' stockholdings are presented in panel B of Table 12–9, and illustrated in Figure 12–3. Holdings by outside and quasi-inside directors

FIGURE 12–3
Mean Percentage of Common Stock Held by Directors and Officers, Relative to Year in Which Firm Files for Chapter 11 or Begins to Restructure Its Debt to Avoid Bankruptcy (Year 0)[a]

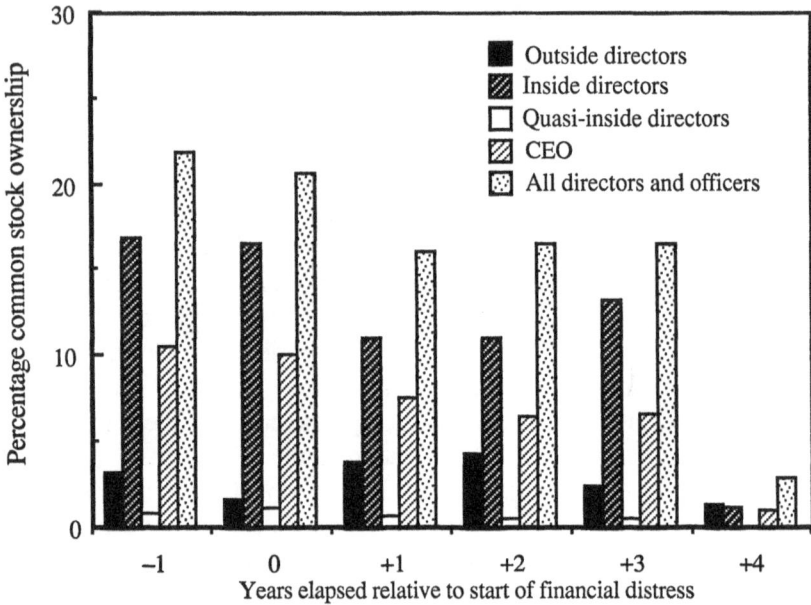

[a] Sample consists of 111 exchange-listed companies that either filed for bankruptcy (61 firms) or restructured their debt (50 firms) during 1979–1985. Outside directors have no other professional affiliation with the firm. Inside directors are also officers of the firm. Quasi-inside directors have some professional or family relationship with the firm, but are not insiders.

generally do not change significantly over the event period. Mean percentage ownership of inside directors falls from 16.80% in year −1 to 10.96% in year +2, and 1.10% in year +4; corresponding median holdings by inside directors are 9.18%, 6.09%, and 0.85%. Mean holdings by inside directors are significantly lower in years +1 and +2, and median holdings are significantly lower in each year through year +3. The same general results hold for stockholdings by all officers and directors.

This observed decline in insider ownership is somewhat puzzling, given that the incentive-related benefits of compensating managers with company stock are likely to be greatest when a firm is unprofitable [Jensen and Meckling (1976), Baker et al. (1988)]. Arguing that managers are unwilling to hold equity in these firms because of a lack of diversification does not provide a completely satisfactory explanation. Although stock-return variances are higher for financially distressed (highly levered) firms, the dollar value of stock outstanding for these firms, and thus induced changes in managers' total wealth, will be relatively small.

Evidence that blockholdings increase in importance when firms become extremely unprofitable or insolvent is consistent with the view that the discipline imposed by blockholders substitutes for monitoring by the board when the latter fails to preempt bad management decisions [Fama (1980), Fama and Jensen (1983)]. Empirical support for this view of blockholders is provided by Barclay and Holderness (1989), who find that announcements of negotiated block trades of common stock are associated with positive average abnormal stock returns of about 15%. For the present sample of financially distressed firms, larger blockholdings are more likely to be associated with greater monitoring of insiders' performance, because such blocks result largely from the consolidation of existing shares rather than private placements of new equity. Private placements, which are initiated by corporate insiders, can be structured to concentrate voting power in friendly hands, and result in less monitoring of insiders' performance [Dann and DeAngelo (1988), Wruck (1989)].

Alternatively, blockholdings in financially distressed firms may be formed for some other purpose than to facilitate increased monitoring of management or bring about substantive changes in corporate policy. For example, blocks of distressed firms' securities could be passively held by contrarian investors who believe that such securities are underpriced. Alternatively, some investors could perceive a strategic advantage to consolidating large blocks of stock (or other securities) to obtain a more generous distribution under the firm's bankruptcy or debt restructuring plan. Both forms of so-called vulture investing have lately received extensive coverage in the financial press [Sandler (1989)]. Finally, incentives exist to consolidate securities of financially distressed firms into blocks to conserve on transactions costs of renegotiating the firm's debt, if such costs are an increasing function of the number of claimholders [Gilson et al. (1990)].

One way of assessing the motives for blockholdings is to consider the identity of the blockholders. Table 12–10 reports the identity of major blockholders in the sample, as shown in firms' proxy statements. Figures in the table are the percentages of firms in the sample for which the largest blockholder falls in a particular class.[3] Over event time there is a statistically significant increase in the percentage of blockholdings owned by bank or insurance-company lenders and nonfinancial corporations. Bank and insurance company lenders are major blockholders in 3.0% of firms in year –1, and in 18.7% of firms in year +2.Corresponding percentages for nonfinancial corporations are 10.8% and 22.7%. Unfortunately, it is impossible

TABLE 12–10
Changes in the Identity of Blockholders During Financial Distress[a]

Blockholder	Percentqage of Firms Whose Largest Blocks Are Held by Various Classes of Holders in Years Elapsed Relative to Start of Financial Distress [b]					
	–1	0	+1	+2	+3	+4
Bank or insurance company	3.0	2.2	7.8	18.7[c]	28.0[d]	25.0
Nonfinancial corporation	10.8	17.6	20.8[e]	22.7[d]	24.0	0.0[c]
Other creditors	3.0	2.2	0.0[e]	2.7	4.0	0.0[e]
Investment bank	1.0	0.0	2.6	4.0	4.0	0.0
Mutual fund or investment company	8.8	8.8	10.4	5.3[d]	0.0[d]	25.0[d]
Pension fund	0.0	0.0	1.3	0.0	0.0	0.0
Employee stock ownership plan	2.0	3.3	3.9	1.3	4.0	0.0
Individual investor	2.9	4.4	3.9	6.7	4.0	0.0[d]
Nominee ("street") holder	5.9	4.4	5.2	4.0	0.0[d]	0.0[d]
U.S. government	0.0	0.0	1.3	0.0	0.0	0.0
Subsidiary of company	1.0	1.1	1.3	1.3	0.0	0.0
Estates and family trusts	9.9	12.1	7.8	6.7	0.0[d]	0.0[d]
Unknown	52.0	44.0	32.5[c]	26.6[c]	32.0[d]	50.0

[a] Sample consists of 111 financially distressed New York- and American Stock Exchange-listed firms that either filed for bankruptcy under Chapter 11 or privately restructured their debt to avoid bankruptcy between 1979 and 1985. Figures in the table are the percentage of firms in the sample whose largest outstanding blocks of common stock are held by various classes of holders. All blocks exceed 5% of a firm's outstanding shares. Sample size declines over time because of unavailability of data, and through departures of firms from the sample as they complete their bankruptcy or debt restructuring before year +4. All firms are tracked at least until year +2. The statistical significance of the difference in percentage representation of blockholders (relative to representation in year –1) is determined using a two-tailed t-test. Figures in the table are based on information contained in firms' annual 10k reports and proxy statements. "Other creditors" includes trade creditors, factoring companies, and other nonfinancial corporations.
[b] Year 0 represents the date on which a firm either files for bankruptcy or starts to restructure its debt.
[c] Percentage is significantly different from percentage in year –1 at the 0.01 level.
[d] Percentage is significantly different from percentage in year –1 at the 0.05 level.
[e] Percentage is significantly different from percentage in year –1 at the 0.10 level.

to ascertain the blockholder's identity in about 25% to 50% of all cases, since proxies must disclose the name, but not the identity, of major holders.

Monitoring by Investment Banks and Workout Specialists

Consistent with evidence on replacement directors' characteristics reported in Table 12–8, monitoring of financially distressed companies is often performed by those with expertise in managing highly levered firms or dealing with creditors. Investment banking firms are formally involved in the debt renegotiation process for 27 firms in the sample. The majority of these investment banks have acquired reputations as specialists in corporate turnarounds, including Bear Stearns (12 firms), Drexel Burnham Lambert (10 firms), Oppenheimer (2 firms), Lazard Frères (1 firm), Rothschild (1 firm), and Hambrecht and Quist (1 firm). Seven investment banks also acquire seats on the board of directors, holding a total of 21 seats on the boards of 16 companies. Eleven firms bring in new senior managers who specialize in managing financially troubled companies. Among the more notable crisis managers in the sample are Victor Palmieri, Sanford Sigoloff, and Q. T. Wiles. Another manager, William Scharffenberger, is at different times the CEO of three companies in the sample.

Corporate Takeovers

Interestingly, despite evidence that hostile takeovers are more likely to occur when firms have been performing poorly [Morck et al. (1988)], very few firms in the sample are involved in any sort of takeover-related transaction. An exhaustive search was made in the *WSJ Index* and firms' 10k reports and proxy statements for any evidence of these transactions during the event period. This search yielded only two firms that became the target of an attempted hostile takeover. Five firms were involved in proxy fights in which dissidents sought representation on the board; in two cases they won. Two additional firms adopted antitakeover amendments. In twelve cases a bankruptcy or debt restructuring concluded with the firm being acquired in a friendly merger. One possible explanation for the paucity of takeovers in the sample is that bank creditors, who are made extremely powerful by a default, can effectively block any merger that threatens to diminish their control over the firm's assets.

SUMMARY AND CONCLUSIONS

This chapter investigates changes in corporate ownership and control in firms that default on their debt. For a sample of 111 publicly traded firms that either went bankrupt or privately restructured their debt, I find evidence consistent with a shift in control over corporate resources from incumbent management and the board of directors towards nonmanagement blockholders and creditors. On average, only 46% of incumbent directors and 43% of CEOs remain with their firms at the conclusion of the bankruptcy or debt restructuring. Directors who resign from financially distressed firms subsequently serve on fewer boards of other companies. Over the period that firms are financially distressed, the percentage of common stock owned by blockholders and creditors rises. Bank lenders sometimes place their representatives on the board directly. Banks gain additional control over firms' investment and financing policies through restrictive covenants in restructured bank loans. Collectively, these results suggest that corporate default engenders significant changes in the ownership of firms' residual claims and in the allocation of rights to manage corporate resources.

NOTES

1. Even when a firm's financial distress is resolved in less than a year, it is necessary to track board membership for two years to be sure of capturing all turnover that is related to financial distress, since corporate filings are made at annual intervals. For example, suppose that a firm files for bankruptcy in June 1983 (year 0), leaves bankruptcy in April 1984, and files its proxy statement each February. Turnover that takes place in March 1984 will be first reflected in the proxy statement dated February 1985, thus falling in event year +2. As discussed later, infrequent reporting of board turnover in the *WSJ* makes it necessary to rely on proxy statements as the principal source for determining when these changes take place.
2. The language used in describing these covenants sometimes makes it difficult to distinguish cases in which a general restriction on the firm has become binding from cases in which creditors are granted an explicit veto over some aspect of the firm's investment and financing policies. When the latter situation unambiguously applies, "creditor approval" is said to be required. Covenants are classified as "general restrictions" when it is reported that the firm is "unable" to undertake some activity (such as paying a dividend), but it is not clear that this results from the exercise of a creditor veto. Also classified as general restrictions are covenants that set a ceiling or floor on some variable, such as total long-term debt.
3. Figures are based on largest, rather than total, blockholdings because I wanted reported percentages to reflect the importance of certain types of blockholders relative

to the total number of *firms* in the sample. Basing the percentages instead on the *total number* of blockholdings could potentially misrepresent the likelihood that a particular type of blockholding will arise in a financially distressed firm. For example, suppose that the sample were to consist of only two firms, that only a single blockholding existed for the first firm (held by a bank), and four blockholdings existed for the second (held by four nonfinancial corporations). Nonfinancial corporations would be holders of 80% of all blocks, but would be blockholders in only 50% of all firms.

REFERENCES

Baker, George; Michael Jensen; and Kevin Murphy, 1988, "Compensation and incentives: Practice vs. theory," *Journal of Finance 43*, 593–616.

Baker, George, and Karen Wruck, 1989, "Organizational changes and value creation in leveraged buyouts: The case of O. M. Scott & Sons Company," *Journal of Financial Economics 25*, 163–90.

Barclay, Michael, and Cliff Holderness, 1989, "Negotiated block trades and corporate control," Unpublished paper, University of Rochester, Rochester, NY.

Castle, Grover, 1980, "Term lending—A guide to negotiating term loan covenants and other financial restrictions," *Journal of Commercial Bank Lending*, November, 26–39.

Dann, Larry, and Harry DeAngelo, 1988, "Corporate financial policy and corporate control: A study of defensive adjustments in asset and ownership structure," *Journal of Financial Economics 20*, 87–127.

Douglas-Hamilton, Margaret, 1975, "Creditor liabilities resulting from improper interference with the management of a financially troubled debtor," *Business Lawyer 31*, 343–65.

Fama, Eugene, 1980, "Agency problems and the theory of the firm," *Journal of Political Economy 88*, 288–307.

Fama, Eugene, and Michael Jensen, 1983, "Separation of ownership and control," *Journal of Law and Economics 26*, 301–25.

Friend, Irwin, and Larry Lang, 1988, "An empirical test of the impact of managerial self-interest on corporate capital structure," *Journal of Finance 43*, 271–81.

Gilson, Stuart, 1989, "Management turnover and financial distress," *Journal of Financial Economics 25*, 241–62.

Gilson, Stuart; Kose John; and Larry Lang, 1990, "Troubled debt restructurings: An empirical study of private reorganization of firms in default," *Journal of Financial Economics 26*, 315–53.

Gilson, Stuart, and Michael Vetsuypens, 1991, "CEO compensation in financially distressed firms: An empirical analysis," Unpublished paper, Harvard Business School, Boston, and Southern Methodist University, Dallas.

Hermalin, Benjamin, and Michael Weisbach, 1988, "The determinants of board composition," *Rand Journal of Economics 19*, 589–606.

Jensen, Michael, 1988, "Takeovers: Their causes and consequences," *Economic Perspectives 2*, 21–48.

Jensen, Michael, 1989a, "Active investors, LBOs, and the privatization of bankruptcy," *Journal of Applied Corporate Finance 2*, 235–44.

Jensen, Michael, 1989b, "Eclipse of the public corporation," *Harvard Business Review*, September–October, 61–74.

Jensen, Michael, and William Meckling, 1976, "Theory of the firm: Managerial behavior, agency costs and ownership structure," *Journal of Financial Economics 3*, 305–60.

Kaplan, Steven, and David Reishus, 1990, "Outside directorships and corporate performance," *Journal of Financial Economics 26*.

Loderer, Claudio, and Dennis Sheehan, 1989, "Corporate bankruptcy and managers' self-serving behavior," *Journal of Finance 44*, 1059–75.

Mace, Myles, 1986, *Directors: Myth and Reality*, Boston: Harvard Business School Press.

Masulis, Ronald, 1988, *The Debt / Equity Choice,* Cambridge, MA: Ballinger Publishing Co.

McDaniel, Morey, 1986, "Bondholders and corporate governance," *Business Lawyer 41*, 413–60.

Morck, Randall; Andrei Shleifer; and Robert Vishny, 1988, "Characteristics of targets of hostile and friendly takeovers," in: Alan Auerbach (ed.), *Corporate Takeovers: Causes and Consequences,* Chicago: University of Chicago Press.

Salamon, Julie, 1982, "The workout crew: Bankers who step in if loans go bad reveal lenders' other face," *Wall Street Journal,* April 2, p. 1.

Sandler, Linda, 1989, "Todd's bondholders gird for a battle in court," *Wall Street Journal,* February 23, p. C1.

Smith, Clifford, Jr., and Jerold Warner, 1979, "On financial contracting: An analysis of bond covenants," *Journal of Financial Economics 7*, 117–61.

Stein, Sol, 1989, *A Feast for Lawyers,* New York: M. Evans and Company, Inc.

Vancil, Richard, 1987, *Passing the Baton: Managing the Process of CEO Succession*, Boston: Harvard Business School Press.

Warner, Jerold; Ross Watts; and Karen Wruck, 1988, "Stock prices and top management changes," *Journal of Financial Economics 20*, 461–92.

Weisbach, Michael, 1988, "Outside directors and CEO turnover," *Journal of Financial Economics 20*, 431–60.

Wruck, Karen, 1989, "Equity ownership concentration and firm value: Evidence from private equity financings," *Journal of Financial Economics 23*, 3–28.

CHAPTER 13

MANAGEMENT TURNOVER AND FINANCIAL DISTRESS

Stuart C. Gilson

INTRODUCTION

Several types of corporate policy decisions seem likely to be influenced by the personal costs that managers incur if their firms default on their debt. To avoid these costs, managers will rationally favor investment and financing policies that reduce the probability of financial distress.[1] They will choose more conservative levels of debt for their firms [Friend and Lang (1988), Masulis (1988)]. They will also attempt to reduce the variability of operating cash flows by favoring less risky investment projects, diversifying into new lines of business by conglomerate merger, and purchasing insurance and

Stuart C. Gilson is Assistant Professor of Business Administration at Harvard Business School, Boston.

The author would like to acknowledge the helpful comments of Ray Ball, Michael Barclay, James Brickley, Keith Brown, Linda DeAngelo, Michael Jensen, Ronald Lease, Wayne Marr, Ronald Masulis, William Schwert, Laura Starks, Seha Tinic, Michael Vetsuypens, Ralph Walkling, Ross Watts, Michael Weisbach, Kenneth Wiles, and seminar participants at Harvard Business School, Southern California, Southern Methodist, Texas at Austin, Tulane, UC at Davis, Utah, and Vanderbilt. This paper is reprinted with the permission of the *Journal of Financial Economics 25* (1989). The chapter benefited greatly from the comments and suggestions of Steven Kaplan (the referee) and Richard Ruback (the editor). The author would especially like to thank the members of his dissertation committee at the University of Rochester— Harry DeAngelo, Clifford Smith, and Jerold Warner—for their generous support. Susan Gilson provided research assistance. Financial support was received from the Social Sciences and Humanities Research Council of Canada and the Division of Research, Harvard Business School.

other financial hedges [Smith and Mayers (1982), Smith and Stulz (1985)]. Finally, they will have incentives to run their firms more efficiently to increase operating cash flows. These incentives may be an important source of the wealth gains associated with LBOs and related forms of corporate restructuring [Grossman and Hart (1982), Jensen (1988)].

The existence of managerial financial distress costs is also a critical assumption underlying capital structure models in which managers increase the firm's leverage to signal favorable information about its economic prospects [Ross (1977)]. Such signals will be credible only if managers who falsely signal suffer some personal cost when their firms default.

Despite the theoretical importance of managerial financial distress costs, we know little about whether these costs are large enough to explain observed corporate policy choices. This study presents evidence that managers' default-related losses are significant. Reductions in managers' wealth and utility due to financial distress are proxied by turnover of senior managers (the CEO, president, and chairman of the board). Results are based on a sample of 381 exchange-listed firms that experienced extreme common stock price declines during the period 1979–1984. Fifty-two percent of all sampled firms experience a senior-level management change during the period of financial distress, as evidenced by a default, bankruptcy, or debt restructuring outside bankruptcy. The corresponding turnover rate when firms are not distressed is only 19%, even though these firms are also highly unprofitable. Direct intervention by bank lenders accounts for 21% of all management changes in financially distressed firms. Although the average age of departing managers is only 52 years, none of them hold a senior management position at another exchange-listed firm during the next three years.

This chapter is organized as follows: The second section discusses the data and sample design. Evidence on management turnover is presented in the third section. The fourth section analyzes whether high turnover is specifically a consequence of firms' financial distress, or of other factors. The final section summarizes the results.

DATA AND SAMPLE SELECTION

This study analyzes a sample of firms that experience large common stock price declines. For a given year, the sample consists of the firms with three-year cumulative unadjusted stock returns in the bottom five percent of firms on the New York Stock Exchange (NYSE) and American Stock Exchange (AMEX). Stock returns are obtained from the Center for Research in Security Prices (CRSP) daily-returns file. A separate ranking is calculated for each year from 1979 through 1984, producing a total sample of 685 firm-years and 409 firms.

This approach allows me to identify firms that have suffered an unexpectedly large decline in their cash flows. The incidence of default, bankruptcy, and debt restructuring is assumed to be relatively high for these firms, facilitating a more powerful test of the relation between financial distress and turnover than would be possible with a random, albeit more general, sample. In addition, since by design all firms in the sample exhibit low stock returns, nondefaulting firms constitute a sensible experimental control; turnover is more likely when a firm's common stock has been performing poorly [Coughlan and Schmidt (1985), Warner et al. (1988), Weisbach (1988)]. Finally, sampling on a variable (stock returns) that possibly explains turnover produces an exogenous stratified sample [Manski and McFadden (1983)], which allows consistent estimation of the turnover regressions in "Multivariate Analysis of Turnover" (p. 330 below).

Management turnover is defined as any change in the group of individuals who together hold the titles of CEO, president, and chairman of the board. An exchange of titles within this group is not considered turnover. To ensure that enough information is available to identify the presence or absence of turnover, firm-years are deleted from the sample if the firm receives no mention that year in *The Wall Street Journal* (*WSJ*) or Standard and Poor's *Register of Corporations, Directors and Executives* (*Register*). (The *Register*, published annually, contains biographical information on the managers and directors of most NYSE- and AMEX-listed companies.) Firm-years are also eliminated if within a given year a firm is acquired in a merger, because it is often impossible to verify what happens to managers after their firms have been acquired. Even if they are known to retain a position in the new entity, there is no way to determine *a priori* whether they are made better or worse off by the change. Management turnover due to takeovers is analyzed by Martin and McConnell (1988).

The final sample consists of 587 firm-years, representing 381 firms. Firms appear in the sample for a mean and median of 1.7 and 1.0 years, respectively. Fifty-four percent of firms appear for only one year, and 96% for three or fewer years. The maximum number of years that any firm appears is five (for five firms).

Financial distress is defined as an inability to meet the fixed payment obligations on debt. Within a given firm-year, a firm is financially distressed if it is in default on its debt, bankrupt, or privately restructuring its debt to avoid bankruptcy. Firms are considered bankrupt when a petition is filed under either Chapter 11 or Chapter 7 of the U.S. Bankruptcy Code. Under Chapter 11, the firm's impaired debts are replaced by new financial claims, on the assumption that the firm will remain a going concern; under Chapter 7, the firm is liquidated. All bankruptcies in the sample begin as Chapter 11 filings, although two are later converted to Chapter 7 cases by the bankruptcy judge. As an alternative to the formal court-supervised bankruptcy process, firms and their creditors can privately agree to restructure troubled debt [Jensen (1989)]. Debt is considered to be privately restructured when creditors consent to reduce promised interest or principal payments, extend the debt's maturity, or accept equity securities in the firm (common stock or securities convertible into common). Firms' financial status is ascertained from the *WSJ*, the *Moody's* manuals, the *Capital Changes Reporter,* Standard and Poor's *Bond Owner's Guide,* and the *Q-File* directory of 10k reports and proxy statements.

As Table 13–1 shows, sampled firms are generally small, highly leveraged, and unprofitable. Since they were chosen on the basis of their low stock returns, their small size is not surprising. For the full sample, the mean book value of assets is $1,194 million, with a median value of $173 million; corresponding mean and median market values of common stock are $50 million and $7 million. Almost two thirds of sampled firms are listed on the AMEX, which generally lists smaller firms than the NYSE. The size distribution is highly skewed, with the largest firm (Continental Illinois) having a book value of assets of over $40 billion. Measured by book value of assets, financially distressed firms tend to be larger than the nonfinancially distressed firms in the sample.

Leverage is measured as the ratio of debt to total capital (measured by the sum of the book value of debt, the liquidating value of preferred stock, and the market value of common stock). As would be expected, leverage is significantly higher for financially distressed firms, whether debt is defined as total liabilities or long-term debt. For example, the mean ratio of total liabilities to total capital is 80.1% for financially distressed firms, and 66.0% for nonfinancially distressed firms; corresponding median ratios are 83.6% and 68.4%.

Several measures of financial performance all show that sampled firms are extremely unprofitable. Unadjusted common stock returns cumulated over three years (through the end of the current year) have a mean and

TABLE 13-1
**Selected Descriptive Mean and Median Attributes for Sample
Consisting of the Bottom 5% of New York and American Stock
Exchange-Listed Firms Ranked by Three-Year Unadjusted
Common Stock Returns for Each of the Years 1979-1984[a]**

	Mean (Median) Sample Attributes			
	Full Sample	Financially Distressed Firms	Non-financially Distressed Firms	p-Value of t-Test for Means[c]
1. Book value of assets ($ millions)	1,194	1,301	1,144	0.67
	(173)	(236)	(151)	(0.01)
2. Total market value of common	50	48	51	0.81
stock ($ millions)	(7)	(8)	(7)	(0.75)
3. Book value of long-term debt	56.4	68.6	52.9	0.00
as a percentage of total capital	(59.0)	(73.5)	(54.8)	(0.00)
4. Book value of total liabilities	69.1	80.1	66.0	0.00
as a percentage of total capital	(72.7)	(83.6)	(68.4)	(0.00)
5. 3-year common stock return (%)				
(i) Unadjusted	-56.8	-68.9	-50.2	0.00
	(-59.5)	(-73.3)	(-53.2)	(0.00)
(ii) Less market return	-161.0	-167.3	-157.6	0.00
	(-164.8)	(-172.6)	(-161.3)	(0.00)
(iii) Less industry return	-120.2	-131.2	-114.1	0.00
	(-120.0)	(-132.1)	(-115.0)	(0.00)
6. Percentage of firms that pay a				
common stock dividend	10.6	0.5	15.4	0.00
7. Percentage of firms with negative				
earnings before interest and taxes	35.5	51.0	30.3	0.00

[a] In any particular year a firm is included in the sample only if it receives some mention in that year's *Wall Street Journal*. The resulting sample consists of 587 firm-years (381 firms). Figures in the table are based on observations at the firm-year level. A firm is financially distressed if it is either in default on its debt, bankrupt, or attempting to restructure its debt to avoid bankruptcy. A debt restructuring takes place when the firm's debt contracts are amended on one of the following terms: (i) promised interest or principal payments are reduced; (ii) the debt's maturity is extended; or (iii) creditors are given equity in the firm (common stock or securities convertible into common). In addition, the purpose of the transaction must be to enable the firm to avoid bankruptcy, as determined from *The Wall Street Journal* or annual 10k reports.

[b] Income statement and balance sheet data (items 1-4 and 7) are from the *Compustat* Industrial and Research tape, and represent fiscal year-end values that most closely predate the beginning of a given firm-year. Total capital equals the sum of the book value of debt (long-term debt or total liabilities), the liquidating value of preferred stock, and the market value of common stock. Long-term debt includes long-term debt that is payable in the current year. Stock returns (item 5) are taken from the CRSP daily returns tape. The market return is the return on the CRSP equally weighted market portfolio. A firm's industry return equals the average return realized by all firms with the same two-digit SIC industry code. Item 6 is based on reported dividend payments in *The Wall Street Journal* and Standard and Poor's *Stock Owner's Guide*.

[c] Wilcoxon rank sum test for medians.

median of −56.8% and −59.5%, respectively. Firms performed poorly relative to both the market and their industry. Mean and median common stock returns measured net of the CRSP equal-weighted market return are −161.0% and −164.8%. Mean and median returns measured net of two-digit Standard Industrial Classification (SIC) industry returns are −120.2% and −120.0%. These returns are economically and statistically significant. A comparison of market- and industry-adjusted returns indicates that sampled firms tend to be in industries that performed poorly relative to the market. A large number of firms also omit their common stock dividend and report negative earnings before interest and taxes. Significance tests reported in Table 13–1 indicate a larger fraction of financially distressed firms have negative earnings than nonfinancially distressed firms. These results have important implications for interpreting evidence on management turnover in financially distressed firms [see "Multivariate Analysis of Turnover," p. 330 below].

MANAGEMENT TURNOVER AND FINANCIAL DISTRESS

Managerial turnover is more prevalent in financially distressed firms (Tables 13–2 and 13–3). In panel A of Table 13–2, turnover is defined as the number of management changes observed during a given firm-year. Unless otherwise noted, this is the sample of changes analyzed in the remainder of the study. Both the absolute number and the relative frequency of management changes are relatively stable across years. For the full sample, the mean number of changes per firm-year is 0.30. For the 190 firm-years in which firms are financially distressed—about one third of the sample—the mean number of changes per firm-year is 0.52, compared with 0.19 for years in which firms are not financially distressed. Although all sample firms are unprofitable, financially distressed firms are almost three times as likely to experience turnover as nonfinancially distressed firms.

Panel B of the table indicates that approximately 80% of the management changes in the sample are departures, and that changes involving more than one manager are relatively infrequent. On average 1.10 managers are involved in departures and 1.03 in appointments; corresponding medians (not shown) are both equal to 1. To place these figures in context, the mean number of managers in the senior management team is 1.53, with a median of 2.

TABLE 13–2
Sample Distribution of 176 Management Changes in 381 New York and American Stock Exchange-Listed Firms that Experienced Large Negative Stock Returns During the Period 1979–1984 [a]

Panel A: Number and relative frequency of management changes

Year / Subsample	Number of Firms	Number of Management Changes	Management Changes per Firm
1979	103	27	0.26
1980	99	27	0.27
1981	99	32	0.32
1982	99	26	0.26
1983	95	31	0.33
1984	92	33	0.36
Full sample	587	176	0.30
Financially distressed firms	190	99	0.52
Nonfinancially distressed firms	397	77	0.19

Panel B: Number of managers involved in senior management changes

Type of Change	Number of Management Changes	Number of Managers Involved	Number of Managers per Change
Management departures	141	155	1.10
Management appointments	35	36	1.03

[a] A firm is financially distressed if it is either in default on its debt, bankrupt, or attempting to restructure its debt to avoid bankruptcy. A management change is defined as any change in the identity of the firm's senior managers (CEO, president, and chairman of the board). A management change is deemed a departure if at least one incumbent senior manager leaves the senior management team, and an appointment if at least one new manager joins the team and no incumbent manager departs. Sample consists of the bottom five percent of New York and American Stock Exchange-listed firms ranked by three-year unadjusted common stock returns for each of the years 1979–1984. In any particular year a firm is included in the sample only if it receives some mention in that year's *Wall Street Journal*, resulting in a final sample of 587 firm-years (381 firms). Sources used to determine whether firms are financially distressed include *The Wall Street Journal*, the *Moody's* manuals, the *Q-File* directory of 10k reports and proxy statements, Standard and Poor's *Bond Owner's Guide*, and Commerce Clearing House's *Capital Changes Reporter*. Management changes are identified from *The Wall Street Journal* and Standard and Poor's *Register of Corporations, Directors and Executives*.

In Table 13–3, turnover due to financial distress is measured by track-ing the fraction of managers who retain a senior management position in their firms throughout a bankruptcy (69 firms) or debt restructuring (57 firms). Managers are tracked for four years, starting two years before the date on which a firm files for Chapter 11 or begins to restructure its debt (date "0").

For the combined sample of 126 firms, only 34% of the original managers remain at the end of the four-year period. The same survival rate obtains when managers are excluded who are within one year of assumed retirement age (65 years) at date +2. Substantially more manag-ers keep their jobs when firms recontract with creditors outside Chapter 11; the survival rate is 0.40 for firms that restructure privately, and 0.29 for firms that file for bankruptcy. Gilson (1990) reports that board turn-over is also lower when financial distress is resolved outside Chapter 11. These results suggest that corporate insiders may prefer private to legal mechanisms for resolving default, although the analysis reported in Table 13–3 does not control for other factors that affect turnover. The choice between these alternative recontracting mechanisms is discussed in Jensen (1989) and Gilson et al. (1990).

TABLE 13–3
Survival Rates of Senior Managers of Financially Distressed Firms [a]

Time (measured in years) Relative to Bankruptcy Filing Date or Start of Debt Restructuring	Fraction of Original Managers Remaining at Year-End		
	Firms that File for Bankruptcy	Firms that Restructure Privately	All Financially Distressed Firms
–2	1.00	1.00	1.00
–1	0.68	0.92	0.79
0	0.45	0.69	0.56
+1	0.36	0.50	0.42
+2	0.29	0.40	0.34

[a] Table reports the fraction of incumbent senior managers (CEO, president, and chairman of the board) who remain senior managers with their firms over the four-year period centered on date of bankruptcy filing or commencement of debt restructuring. Sample consists of 196 managers initially employed by 126 firms. Sixty-nine firms filed for bankruptcy under Chapter 11 of the U.S. Bankruptcy Code, and 57 firms privately restructured their debt to avoid bankruptcy. All bankruptcies and debt restructurings start during the period 1979–1984. Management changes are identified from *The Wall Street Journal*, the *Q-file* directory of 10k reports and proxy statements, and Standard and Poor's *Register of Corporations, Directors and Executives*.

I am aware of only two earlier studies that investigate turnover in financially distressed firms. For a sample of 11 railroad bankruptcies from 1933 to 1955, Warner (1977b) finds that CEOs are replaced at an average annual rate of 8% over the five years that follow a bankruptcy filing; for a control sample of nonbankrupt railroads the corresponding turnover rate is 9%. Ang and Chua (1981) investigate turnover of the three highest paid executives of 52 firms that filed for bankruptcy during the period 1969–1973. They find that 30% of these managers lose their jobs within two years of the bankruptcy filing date. Neither study investigates turnover in firms that privately restructure their debt outside bankruptcy, or control for other factors that affect turnover in financially distressed firms.

Turnover reported in Tables 13–2 and 13–3 is considerably higher than the norms identified by previous studies. Weisbach (1988), who defines turnover as the resignation of the CEO, reports annualized mean turnover of 0.08 per firm-year for a sample of NYSE-listed firms. Using the same definition of turnover as this study, Warner et al. (1988) report mean annual turnover of 0.12 changes per firm for a random sample of NYSE- and AMEX-listed companies. Even for the lowest decile of annual unadjusted common stock returns in their sample (with mean returns of –51.6%), the mean number of changes per firm-year is only 0.14. Although this figure is comparable to the 0.19 rate of turnover reported in Table 13–2 for nonfinancially distressed firms, it is much lower than turnover reported for financially distressed firms.

Turnover on the same scale as that reported in Tables 13–2 and 13–3 has been previously documented only for major corporate ownership shifts in the market for corporate control. DeAngelo and DeAngelo (1989) find that 38% of incumbent senior managers resign within one year of the resolution of a proxy contest, whether or not the challenge is successful. Martin and McConnell (1988) report that 42% of incumbent CEOs resign within one year when their firms are taken over through an interfirm tender offer. Barclay and Holderness (1989) document 45% turnover of CEOs within one year of a negotiated trade of a block of the firm's common stock.

Inference of Management Losses from the Nature of Turnover

Higher turnover due to financial distress will affect managerial incentives only if turnover reduces managers' wealth or welfare. Managers who are forced to resign from their firms face possible losses in income and firm-specific human capital, and in any power, prestige, and other nonpecuniary benefits they derived from managing their firms. Management changes could also adversely affect managers' reputations (and market value after leaving the firm) if turnover is viewed as a sign of incompetence. Managers' losses from turnover will be less severe if they value their leisure more highly after leaving a financially distressed firm. On the other hand, evidence on turnover will tend to understate managers' losses due to financial distress if they incur costs (for example, reductions in their compensation or decision-making authority) even when no turnover takes place [Salamon (1982), Stein (1989), Gilson and Vetsuypens (1991)].

Changes in managers' welfare due to turnover can be indirectly assessed by examining the reasons for turnover. Table 13–4 lists the principal reasons for all 176 management changes in the sample as reported in the *WSJ*. The largest category consists of 47 changes (27% of the sample) for which no reason could be determined. Such changes account for only 15% and 22%, respectively, in the more random samples examined by Warner et al. (1988) and Weisbach (1988). The relatively high incidence of unexplained changes in the present sample could occur because smaller firms receive less coverage in the financial press. Alternatively, managers and other corporate insiders may be reluctant to discuss management changes that result from dissatisfaction with managers' performance. Twenty-three changes occur for unspecified "personal reasons," which could be a euphemism for changes that discipline underperforming managers.

A significant number of changes appear to be directly related to firms' poor financial performance or insolvency. Twenty-eight changes occur in response to pressure by the board of directors. In three cases a new manager is appointed to assist in restructuring the firm's debts, and in one case management is replaced by a court-appointed bankruptcy trustee. Eleven changes are initiated by blockholders; nine of these blocks represent private placements of new equity with third-party investors. Despite extant evidence that managers are more likely to be removed through a hostile takeover or proxy contest when their firms have been unprofitable [Martin and McConnell (1988), DeAngelo and DeAngelo (1989)], the present sample contains no such changes.

Twenty management changes are initiated by bank lenders; in one additional case, banks force the CEO/chief operating officer to relinquish his latter title to one of the company's directors. The actual number of bank-initiated management changes could be much higher than the reported number, since public disclosure of such activity increases the banks' risk of being sued under lender liability laws [Douglas-Hamilton (1975)].

TABLE 13–4
Principal Reason Reported in *The Wall Street Journal* for 176 Management Changes in 381 New York and American Stock Exchange-Listed Firms that Experienced Large Negative Stock Returns during the Period 1979–1984 [a]

Reason for Management Change	Number of Changes
No reason given	47
Pressure by board of directors[b]	28
Personal reasons	23
Pressure by bank lenders[c]	20
Normal management succession	16
Retirement	12
Control change initiated by blockholders[d]	11
Death or illness	7
Policy or personality differences with directors or other managers	6
New manager appointed to restructure firm's debts	3
Bankruptcy trustee appointed	1
Other	2
Total	176

[a] A management change is defined as any change in the identity of the firm's senior managers (CEO, president, and chairman of the board).
[b] Pressure by the board of directors is assumed when *The Wall Street Journal* reports that a management change is initiated by the "company" or by "holders," when board dissatisfaction with the firm's performance is mentioned in the same article, or when board intervention is explicitly reported.
[c] Pressure by bank lenders is assumed when either *The Wall Street Journal* explicitly reports that a management change occurs at the insistence of banks, such involvement by banks is rumored, or a manager's replacement is bank-appointed.
[d] A blockholder is someone who acquires a greater than 5% stake in the firm's common stock. Includes nine blockholdings that resulted from private equity placements, and two that resulted from negotiated block purchases of existing shares.

Evidence of direct bank involvement in management changes has not been previously documented. Since earlier studies of turnover are based on samples of mostly solvent firms, it appears that banks' ability to influence corporate policy is greatest when there is significant risk of default. Banks seldom own any voting stock in these firms before forcing management changes, and exert additional influence over corporate policy through means other than the selection of new managers.[2] Gilson (1990) finds that banks also influence the selection of directors in distressed companies, and are given veto power over investment and financing policies in the covenants of restructured lending agreements. James (1987) provides complementary evidence that common stockholders realize positive abnormal returns of almost 2% when firms announce new bank loan agreements, which he attributes to the value of monitoring services that banks provide.

The sample provides no evidence that management changes are ever initiated by public bondholders, although only 33% of sampled firms have publicly traded debt.

Related evidence is presented in Table 13–5, which reports the relative frequency of certain kinds of changes in the sample. "Forced" management changes account for 0.76 of all changes. Forced changes are those that occur for any of the reasons listed in Table 13–4 except retirement, normal management succession, and death or illness. Management losses due to turnover are assumed to be greater when changes are forced; changes due to death and illness are excluded from this definition under the conservative assumption that these events are unrelated to firms' financial distress. The relative frequency of forced changes is 0.83 for financially distressed firms and 0.66 for nonfinancially distressed firms; the t-test for this difference is significant with a p-value of 0.01. By comparison, the more general samples of turnover analyzed by Warner et al. (1988) and Weisbach (1988) exhibit forced-change frequencies of only 0.28 and 0.38. The relative frequency of forced changes in the present sample will be biased upwards, however, if changes in smaller firms receive less coverage in the WSJ, resulting in a greater number of changes for which no reason is given.

Changes that result in the appointment of an outsider account for 0.43 of all changes. Outsiders are neither current managers nor directors of the firm. Firms that are unprofitable or financially distressed will bring in outsiders more often if the firm's financial condition reflects unfavorably on both junior and senior managers. The frequency of outsider appointments is 0.48 for financially distressed firms and 0.37 for nonfinancially distressed firms, but the difference is not statistically significant. For bank-initiated management changes, the frequency of such appointments is 0.55. Ten of the outsiders appointed to financially distressed firms are so-called turnaround specialists. High rates of outsider appointments have also been found for management changes that follow takeovers [Martin and McConnell (1988), frequency of 0.70] and negative earnings announcements [Bonnier and Bruner (1989), frequency of 0.50]. In contrast, the frequency of outsider appointments is only 0.20 for the random samples of changes analyzed by Warner et al. (1988) and Furtado and Rozeff (1987).

Finally, Table 13–5 shows that 0.77 of all changes in the sample involve the CEO, who is usually the lead member of the senior management

TABLE 13–5
Proportions of Senior Management Changes with Selected Characteristics[a]

Characteristic	Full Sample of Changes	Changes in Financially Distressed Firms	Changes in Non-financially Distressed Firms	p-Value of t-Test for Difference in Means of Distressed and Non-distressed Firms
		Proportion of Management Changes		
Forced management departure or appointment[b]	0.76	0.83	0.66	0.01
Outsider is appointed or incumbent manager is replaced by an outsider[c]	0.43	0.48	0.37	0.22
CEO is removed or new CEO is appointed[d]	0.77	0.81	0.73	0.61
Management departure is followed by complete turnover of incumbent management by year-end	0.46	0.47	0.45	0.89
Incumbent manager departs and is not replaced	0.25	0.26	0.23	0.66
Incumbent manager departs and is replaced	0.55	0.58	0.52	0.46
New manager is appointed and no incumbent manager departs	0.20	0.16	0.25	0.17

[a] Sample consists of 176 senior management changes in 381 New York and American Stock Exchange-listed firms that experienced large negative stock returns during the period 1979–1984. A management change is defined as any change in the identity of the firm's senior managers (CEO, president, and chairman of the board). Management changes are identified from *The Wall Street Journal*. A firm is financially distressed if it is either in default on its debt, bankrupt, or attempting to restructure its debt to avoid bankruptcy.
[b] Forced management changes include all changes except those due to retirement, death, illness, normal management succession, and other factors unrelated to firms' poor financial performance or insolvency.
[c] An outsider is someone who is not currently a manager or director of the firm. Nonmanagement blockholders (those who own more than 5% of the firm's common stock) are counted as outsiders if they have been blockholders for less than one year at the time of the management change.
[d] When no CEO title exists, this category refers to the removal or appointment of the firm's president.

team [Vancil (1987)]. In addition, almost one-half of all changes are followed by complete turnover of incumbent senior management by year-end. Both fractions are higher for the subsample of financially distressed firms, but the differences are not statistically significant.

Tables 13–4 and 13–5 provide indirect evidence that turnover in financially distressed firms generates significant personal costs for managers. A related perspective on the nature of the costs comes from the behavioral sciences. Sutton and Callahan (1987) analyze four bankrupt firms in the computer industry, and conclude that their managers suffered substantial losses in reputation and self-esteem. Consistent with their findings, one manager in the present sample committed suicide while his firm was financially distressed. In the *WSJ*, the suicide was attributed to the refusal of the firm's banks to participate in a plan to keep the firm out of "hostile hands."

Management Losses Due to Departures

Managers' losses from departures can be identified more explicitly. Table 13–6 reports descriptive attributes of 73 managers who resigned from financially distressed firms. Excluded are four managers who died, 27 who were older than 64, and 51 whose firms were not financially distressed the year they resigned [see panel B of Table 13–2]. Results are qualitatively unchanged when departures from nonfinancially distressed firms are added back to the sample.

Departing managers are relatively young, with a mean and median age of 52 and 53 years, so the earnings they potentially lose with departure are sizable. The mean salary and bonus of departing managers in the year prior to their departure is $217,000, with a median of $179,000. Their replacements are generally paid more, but the difference is not statistically significant. Given a discount rate of 10%, and assuming that managers would otherwise have been paid the same until retiring at age 65, the mean present value of managers' remaining salary and bonus is $1.3 million, with a median of $1.1 million. These estimates are biased downward by ignoring future increases in compensation.

Table 13–6 also reports the percentage of common stock owned by corporate insiders prior to managers' departure. Mean and median ownership by all officers and directors are 13.5% and 6.9%, respectively; for a random sample of NYSE- and AMEX-listed firms, Mikkelson and Partch (1989) report corresponding holdings of 19.6% and 13.9%. Thus insider holdings appear to be relatively small for the present sample. One possible

TABLE 13–6
Descriptive Attributes for 73 Managers Who Depart from Financially Distressed Firms[a]

Attribute	Mean	Median	Maxi-mum	Mini-mum
Age	51.8	53.0	64.0	34.0
Salary ($ thousands)[b]	217	179	523	44
Salary of manager's replacement ($ thousands)[c]	318	200	1,200	0
Present value of departing manager's salary ($ thousands)[d]				
Discount rate = 5%	1,723	1,604	4,817	157
Discount rate = 10%	1,293	1,102	3,464	142
Percentage of firm's common shares owned				
All officers and directors	13.5	6.9	62.2	0.3
Departing manager	2.5	0.5	31.2	0.0
Value of firm's common shares owned by departing manager ($ thousands)[e]	932	303	7,122	1

[a] Excluded are 4 managers who died, 27 managers who were at least 65 years old (assumed retirement age) in the year of their departure, and 51 managers whose firms were not financially distressed. Senior management consists of the CEO, president, and chairman of the board. A firm is financially distressed if it is either in default on its debt, bankrupt, or attempting to restructure its debt to avoid bankruptcy. Data are obtained from *The Wall Street Journal*, the *Q-file* directory of 10k reports and proxy statements, the *Moody's* manuals, and Standard and Poor's *Register of Corporations, Directors and Executives*.
[b] Salary equals the sum of all cash compensation received by the manager in the first fiscal year immediately predating his departure, including salary, fees, commissions, and bonuses.
[c] Replacement managers are identified from the first proxy filing to follow a manager's departure by at least one fiscal year. The replacement manager is the individual who fills the resulting vacancy in the top management team. Excluded are vacancies that are filled by more than one individual, or by someone who is currently a senior manager.
[d] Present-value calculations assume that departing managers (i) retire at age 65; (ii) would have received the same annual salary and bonus for the remainder of their working life as in the year they depart; (iii) are paid at year-end; and (iv) receive a full year's compensation immediately prior to leaving.
[e] Shareholdings are obtained from the proxy filing that most closely predates a manager's departure. The share price is the closing price for the month-end prior to the month of departure, obtained from Standard and Poor's *Daily Stock Price Record*.

reason for this difference is that management changes are more likely for larger firms [see "Multivariate Analysis of Turnover," p. 330 below], where insider holdings are typically smaller. Departing managers also tend to hold relatively little of their firms' common stock, with mean and median percentage holdings of only 2.5% and 0.5%, respectively.

Despite the small mean and median insider holdings in the sample, insider stock ownership is significant in a number of cases. In over 6% and

45% of all cases, respectively, holdings by departing managers and by all officers and directors exceed 10%. The maximum percentage of stock held by a departing manager is 31.2%, and by all officers and directors, 62.2%. These results suggest that large management stockholdings do not prevent control changes when firms' financial performance has deteriorated significantly. In financially distressed firms, managers' effective voting power is less than proportional to their current stockholdings because of increases in total shares incorporated in the firm's bankruptcy or debt restructuring plan.

To determine whether financial distress adversely affects managers' reputations, Table 13–7 documents departing managers' subsequent career paths. If managers are forced to resign because of perceived inadequacies, they will receive fewer job offers from other firms. Of course, such managers could voluntarily leave the labor market because they value leisure more highly after their experience with financial distress. Since managers may be less inclined to keep working if they are above official retirement age, the table analyzes only managers who are less than 65 years old when they depart. As noted in Table 13–6, the mean and median ages of these managers are 52 and 53 years.

Panel A lists managers' positions or occupations for three years after their departure, as reported in the *Register* and *Who's Who in Industry and Finance*. The *Register* obtains its information from managers' response to a questionnaire; companies are less likely to be surveyed if they have been bankrupt for an extended period. *Who's Who* uses volume of business as a selection criterion, thus possibly excluding managers of financially distressed firms. These selection criteria will not bias the results in Table 13–7 unless managers continue to serve only with financially distressed companies after leaving.

Results in panel A suggest that managers leave the labor market in large numbers following their departure from financially distressed firms. Although all managers are initially listed in the *Register*, almost two thirds are unreported in either source after they depart. Not one manager is employed by another exchange-listed firm over the entire three-year period following his departure. One year after departing, four managers are listed as senior managers with firms not listed on either major stock exchange; at the end of three years, six managers are so employed. Two managers initially stay with their firms in a junior capacity, but only one remains by the third year. Six managers remain with their firms in an honorary capacity such as "consultant" or "chairman emeritus," but only four remain after three years.

TABLE 13–7
Subsequent Career Profile of 73 Senior Managers Who Depart from Financially Distressed Firms[a]

Panel A: Position / occupation reported in Standard and Poor's or *Who's Who* directories

	Number of Managers Holding Specified Positions / Occupations		
	Years after Departure		
	1	2	3
Senior manager in another company			
NYSE- / AMEX-listed	0	0	0
Other	4	4	6
Junior manager in another company	2	2	1
Honorary position in original company[b]	6	5	4
Junior position in original company[c]	3	1	1
Holds outside directorships exclusively	7	8	6
Self-employed / private investor	4	6	6
No record of manager	47	47	49

Panel B: Intended future position / occupation reported in *The Wall Street Journal*

	Number of Managers Holding Specified Positions / Occupations
Senior manager in another company	
NYSE- / AMEX-listed	0
Other	5
Honorary position in original company[b]	31
Junior position in original company[c]	1
Self-employed / private investor	6
Other	3
No information	27

[a] Excluded are 4 managers who died, 27 managers who were at least 65 years old (assumed retirement age) in the year of their departure, and 51 managers whose firms were not financially distressed. Senior management consists of the CEO, president, and chairman of the board. Managers' occupations are determined from Standard and Poor's *Register of Corporations, Directors and Executives, Who's Who in Industry and Finance,* and *The Wall Street Journal.*

[b] Honorary positions include consultant, chairman emeritus, and vice chairman. In addition, this category includes managers who remain directors in their firms but hold no other title.

[c] Includes cases where the manager becomes a junior officer of a company subsidiary.

Panel B lists the intended future occupation of departing managers as described in the *WSJ* stories that report their departure. Only five managers intend to become senior managers in other firms, and none of these are listed on an exchange. Thirty-one managers plan to remain with their firms in an honorary capacity, but evidence in panel A suggests that these managers' subsequent association with their firms is short-lived. Six managers plan to enter private consulting or start their own businesses. No information about managers' intended future occupation is reported for 27 departures (37% of the sample).

MULTIVARIATE ANALYSIS OF TURNOVER

Evidence in Tables 13–2 and 13–3 shows that turnover is significantly higher when firms are financially distressed, and either in default or about to default on their debt. The association between turnover and financial distress could be spurious, however, if higher turnover in these firms is caused by other factors that are correlated with financial distress. For example, firms become financially distressed because they are unprofitable and have too little cash to cover their debt payments. There is evidence that less profitable firms show higher turnover, consistent with firms' poor performance being blamed on managers [Coughlan and Schmidt (1985), Warner et al. (1988), Weisbach (1988)]. If higher turnover in financially distressed firms occurs because these firms are less profitable than nonfinancially distressed firms, one cannot argue that high leverage (and the threat of bankruptcy) induces managers to make offsetting changes in their firms' investment and financing policies.

Financial distress will independently engender higher turnover if an increased probability of default conveys negative information about managerial performance beyond that conveyed by low profits. Anecdotal evidence suggests that the "stigma" of default causes considerable damage to managers' reputations [Stein (1989)].[3] Also, a default confers significant decision-making power on the firm's creditors, who can possibly further their own interests by choosing new management [see Table 13–4]. Gilson (1990) presents evidence that bank lenders wield considerable influence over financially distressed firms' investment and financing policies.

To identify the marginal impact of financial distress on turnover, I estimate logit regressions that simultaneously relate turnover to measures of financial distress and relative profitability. The dependent variable in the regressions equals one if a senior management change is observed in a particular year, and zero otherwise. Because initial sampling of firms is based on the presence of a variable that potentially causes turnover (low common stock returns), ordinary maximum likelihood yields consistent parameter estimates even though the sample contains more financially distressed firms than the general population. This represents exogenous stratified sampling [Manski and McFadden (1983)], which allows more powerful estimation of the turnover equations than would be possible using a random sample.[4]

Two variables serve as proxies for financial distress. The first is a dichotomous variable (D) that equals one for a particular firm-year if the firm is either in default on its debt, bankrupt, or restructuring its debt to avoid bankruptcy, and zero otherwise. The second proxy is the firm's leverage ratio (LVG), defined as the book value of long-term debt divided by the value of total capital. Total capital is the sum of the book value of long-term debt, the liquidating value of preferred stock, and the market value of common stock. For any particular firm-year, LVG uses data that most closely predate the beginning of the year. The predicted sign of the estimated coefficients on both D and LVG is positive, under the hypothesis that financial distress engenders higher management turnover.

The economic rationale for the variable LVG is that financial distress, by definition, occurs when firms' cash flows are low in relation to their fixed contractual obligations. Thus the numerator of LVG is defined as the *book* value of debt, while the denominator, to the extent possible, is defined in terms of *market* values. The ratio is hypothesized to be higher for firms that have more trouble meeting their fixed payment obligations to creditors. LVG is preferable to D in that it is not subject to reporting bias (firms may be unable to pay their creditors even though no default has been reported or formally declared). If, on the other hand, LVG is high because a firm has previously (and correctly) assessed a low probability of default, it will be a poor proxy for financial distress.

Following earlier studies of turnover, I use return on common stock as a proxy for firms' profitability. Regressions also include the corresponding CRSP equal-weighted market return, on the grounds that managers are less likely to be held responsible for their firms' poor performance when the market is also performing poorly. Separate returns are included for the current year and each of the two preceding years, reflecting the interval over which returns are cumulated to form the sample. Lagged returns are included because managers are more likely to be blamed when poor performance is protracted. If relative stock returns are a proxy for managers' performance, turnover will vary inversely with firm-specific returns, and directly with market returns; the predicted coefficients on these two variables are negative and positive, respectively.

Logit regression tests of the relation between turnover and financial distress could lack statistical power for several reasons. First, relative stock returns are an inherently noisy measure of managerial performance; the association between performance and returns will be weaker when returns are more volatile. Return volatility is typically higher for smaller, more highly levered firms, which make up much of the present sample. Second, the regressions test for a contemporaneous association between turnover and financial distress (within firm-years). If turnover leads or lags financial distress, no relationship will be observed. Finally, the two proxies for financial distress are correlated with unadjusted common stock returns. Pairwise correlations between D or LVG and lagged stock returns are generally negative and significant at the 5% level. This correlation makes it more difficult to assess the impact of financial distress on turnover independently of firms' stock-price performance.[5]

Logit Regression Results

Table 13–8 presents the basic logit regression results. To provide a benchmark for comparison, the first regression includes only unadjusted and market returns, exclusive of any proxy for financial distress. All three unadjusted returns have the predicted negative sign, although only current-year returns are statistically significant (p-value less than 0.01). None of the market returns is significant, and only the previous year's return has the predicted positive sign. Alternative specifications of the model, including the remaining two regressions in the table, yield qualitatively similar results. Turnover in these firms thus appears to increase rapidly in response to extremely poor stock price performance. Warner et al. (1988) obtain similar results for a random sample of firms. They report significant negative coefficients for unadjusted returns in the current and the previous year, and a significant positive coefficient for current-year market returns. Market returns are insignificant, however, when they estimate their regressions for smaller firms, which is consistent with results in Table 13–8.

Results for the second and third regressions are consistent with turnover's being significantly higher in financially distressed firms, even after differences in relative profitability are controlled for. In the second

TABLE 13–8
Logit Regressions Relating Senior Management Changes to
Variables that Are Proxies for Corporate Financial Distress
and Relative Annual Stock Price Performance [a]

	Coefficient estimates		
Explanatory variables[b]	(1)	(2)	(3)
Intercept	-1.07^d	-1.76^c	-1.77^d
	(0.09)	(0.01)	(0.05)
D	—	1.21^c	—
		(0.00)	
LVG	—	—	0.90^d
			(0.06)
Return	-1.51^c	-1.09^c	-1.57^c
	(0.00)	(0.00)	(0.00)
$Return_{-1}$	-0.35	-0.12	-0.56
	(0.25)	(0.69)	(0.14)
$Return_{-2}$	-0.15	-0.00	-0.07
	(0.23)	(0.99)	(0.61)
Market return	-0.44	0.25	-0.98
	(0.57)	(0.76)	(0.34)
$Market\ return_{-1}$	0.03	0.34	0.82
	(0.97)	(0.70)	(0.47)
$Market\ return_{-2}$	-1.60	-1.13	-1.56
	(0.11)	(0.27)	(0.21)
Model p-value	0.0002	0.0000	0.0002

[a] The dependent variable equals 1 when a senior management change takes place in a given firm-year, and 0 otherwise. A management change is defined as any change in the identity of a firm's senior managers (CEO, president, and chairman of the board). A firm is financially distressed if it is in default on its debt, bankrupt, or attempting to restructure its debt to avoid bankruptcy. Regressions are based on a sample of 587 firm-years, representing 381 New York and American Stock Exchange-listed firms that experienced large negative stock returns during the period 1979–1984. Asymptotic p-values are shown in parentheses. Sample consists of the bottom five percent of New York and American Stock Exchange-listed firms ranked by three-year unadjusted common stock returns for each of the years 1979–1984. In any particular year a firm is included in the sample only if it receives some mention that year in *The Wall Street Journal*.
[b] *D* is a dummy intercept variable that equals 1 if a firm is financially distressed within a given firm-year, and 0 otherwise. Sources used to determine whether firms are financially distressed include *The Wall Street Journal*, the *Moody's* manuals, the *Q-file* directory of annual proxy statements and 10k reports, and Commerce Clearing House's *Capital Changes Reporter*. *LVG* is the book value of long-term debt (including such debt payable in the current year) divided by the value of total capital (defined as the sum of the book value of long-term debt, the liquidating value of preferred stock, and the market value of common stock based on the previous year-end closing price). All variables used in calculating *LVG* are those that most closely predate the start of the year. The variable *return* is the unadjusted rate of return on a firm's common stock for the current calendar year. The *market return* is the corresponding rate of return on the CRSP equally weighted market portfolio. Subscripts on these variables refer to returns in prior years. If a firm's stock stops trading before year-end, returns are cumulated up to the time of delisting.
[c] p-value less than 0.05.
[d] p-value less than 0.10.

regression, financial distress is represented by the dichotomous variable D. The estimated coefficient on this variable is positive, as predicted, and highly significant (p-value less than 0.01). In comparison with the first regression, the addition of this variable increases the overall explanatory power of the model, based on reported model p-values. In the third regression, financial distress is represented by the firm's leverage ratio, LVG. The estimated coefficient on this variable is also positive and significant (p-value of 0.06). Compared with the first regression, estimated coefficients on the stock return variables are relatively stable with the addition of either D or LVG. The stability of the coefficients, as well as the results of several additional tests for collinearity (not reported), suggest that correlation between D or LVG and stock returns does not affect the interpretation of the coefficient estimates.

Evidence from the logit regressions is qualitatively unchanged with alternative definitions of the variables. Alternative definitions of turnover include management departures, CEO changes, and forced management changes (as defined in "Management Turnover and Financial Distress," p. 318 above). Financial distress is alternatively represented by the ratio of total liabilities to total capital, the ratio of long-term debt that matures within five years to total capital, and the interest-coverage ratio. Industry stock returns are used as an alternative performance benchmark to market returns. Finally, an industry-adjusted accounting profit rate, defined as the difference in annual earnings before interest and taxes divided by the beginning-of-year book value of assets, is used in place of relative stock returns; the same variable is used by Weisbach (1988), with similar results.

The regression results also hold up when other explanatory variables are added. Industry dummy variables based on firms' two-digit SIC codes are added to test whether unconditional turnover is systematically higher in certain industries. Given observed regularities in industry leverage ratios [Myers (1984), Masulis (1988)], the relationship between turnover and LVG could be spurious; however, none of the industry dummies is significant. Two proxies for firm size (the book value of assets and a dummy variable that equals one for NYSE-listed firms) have positive and significant coefficients when added to the regressions, although the other coefficients are qualitatively unchanged. Turnover could be higher in larger firms because such firms have larger internal labor markets, and therefore find it less costly to replace managers [Furtado and Rozeff (1987)]. Also, wealth-constrained managers will own a smaller fraction of company stock in larger firms, and therefore be less able to resist pressures for their removal [Stulz (1988)].

Finally, turnover is higher when more of the firm's directors have no other professional or business relationship with the firm. The probability of turnover is found to increase with the fraction of outsiders on the board, consistent with the results of Weisbach (1988).

SUMMARY AND CONCLUSIONS

This chapter investigates turnover of senior managers in financially distressed firms. For a sample of 381 exchange-listed firms, evidence is consistent with managers incurring significant personal costs when their firms become financially distressed. In any given year, 52% of sampled firms experience a senior management change if they are either in default on their debt, bankrupt, or privately restructuring their debt to avoid bankruptcy. For nonfinancially distressed firms in the sample, the frequency of turnover is only 19%, even though these firms are also extremely unprofitable. Almost all turnover in the sample takes place because of firms' financial distress or poor financial performance. Bank lenders are responsible for 21% of management changes in financially distressed firms. Although their average age is only 52, managers who resign from these firms are not employed by an exchange-listed firm for at least three years after their departure.

When managerial costs of financial distress are high, managers have incentives to reduce the likelihood of default by borrowing less, choosing less risky investment projects, and managing their firms more efficiently. Whether these costs are important in explaining observed corporate policy choices represents a potentially promising area for future research.

NOTES

1. Financial distress also has significant costs for *stockholders*, including both the legal and administrative costs of restructuring the firm's debt ("direct" costs), and the opportunity loss suffered when corporate resources are diverted to the debt restructuring process from more productive uses ("indirect" costs). The role of these costs in capital structure theory is reviewed by Masulis (1988) and Myers (1984). Attempts to measure these costs have been made by Warner (1977b), Ang et al. (1982), Altman (1984), and Weiss (1990).
2. For example, following his resignation as president and CEO of Federal Resources Corp. (included in the present sample), Joseph C. Bennett observed:
   It's apparent that we're unable to make deals where the shareholders will end up with anything. The directors and management don't have control of the company.

We can't make any expenditures without the banks approving it. We can't make any deal without the banks approving it. We're in a position where the people who are supposed to be the stewards of the company aren't in a position to manage [*WSJ,* August 2, 1982, p. 20].

3. Following the resignation of Jesse I. Aweida as chairman and CEO of Storage Technology (included in the current sample), the *WSJ* reported: "[Mr. Aweida] said he knew his days with Storage Technology were numbered once the company entered bankruptcy-law proceedings. 'Obviously you can't do anything right after that,' he said. 'People have short memories' " [*WSJ,* August 2, 1982, p. 20].

4. If causation between the sampling variable (stock returns) and the dependent variable (turnover) runs in the opposite direction—say, because stock returns reflect the probability of a future management change—then ordinary maximum likelihood estimates of the slope coefficients will be consistent, although the estimated intercept will be asymptotically biased [Manski and McFadden (1983)].

5. Pairwise correlations between D and the unadjusted annual return variables *Return*, *Return*$_{-1}$, and *Return*$_{-2}$ [see Table 13–8] are, respectively, –0.10, –0.11, and –0.19. Corresponding correlations between LVG and unadjusted returns are 0.11, –0.11, and –0.29. The correlation between D and cumulative three-year unadjusted returns (used in forming the sample) is –0.32, and the correlation between LVG and cumulative returns is –0.13.

REFERENCES

Altman, Edward, 1984, "A further empirical investigation of the bankruptcy cost question," *Journal of Finance 39,* 1067–89.

Ang, James, and Jess Chua, 1981, "Corporate bankruptcy and job losses among top level managers," *Financial Management,* Winter, 70–74.

Ang, James; Jess Chua; and John McConnell, 1982, "The administrative costs of bankruptcy: A note," *Journal of Finance 37,* 219–26.

Barclay, Michael, and Cliff Holderness, 1989, "Negotiated block trades and corporate control," Unpublished paper, University of Rochester, Rochester, NY.

Bonnier, Karl-Adam, and Robert Bruner, 1989, "An analysis of stock price reaction to management change in distressed firms," *Journal of Accounting and Economics 11,* 95–106.

Coughlan, Anne, and Ronald Schmidt, 1985, "Executive compensation, management turnover, and firm performance: An empirical investigation," *Journal of Accounting and Economics 7,* 43–66.

Dann, Larry, and Harry DeAngelo, 1988, "Corporate financial policy and corporate control: A study of defensive adjustments in asset and ownership structure," *Journal of Financial Economics 20,* 87–127.

DeAngelo, Harry, and Linda DeAngelo, 1989, "Proxy contests and the governance of publicly held corporations," *Journal of Financial Economics 23,* 29–59.

Douglas-Hamilton, Margaret, 1975, "Creditor liabilities resulting from improper interference with the management of a financially troubled debtor," *Business Lawyer 31*, 343–65.

Friend, Irwin, and Larry Lang, 1988, "An empirical test of the impact of managerial self-interest on corporate capital structure," *Journal of Finance 43*, 271–81.

Furtado, Eugene, and Michael Rozeff, 1987, "The wealth effects of company initiated management changes," *Journal of Financial Economics 18*, 147–60.

Gibbons, Robert, and Kevin Murphy, 1990, "Relative performance evaluation for chief executive officers," *Industrial and Labor Relations Review 43*, 3F–51F.

Gilson, Stuart, 1990, "Bankruptcy, boards, banks, and blockholders: Evidence on changes in corporate ownership and control when firms default," *Journal of Financial Economics 26*. [See also Chapter 14, this volume.]

Gilson, Stuart; Kose John; and Larry Lang, 1990, "Troubled debt restructurings: An empirical study of private reorganization of firms in default," *Journal of Financial Economics 26*.

Gilson, Stuart, and Michael Vetsuypens, 1991, "CEO compensation in financially distressed firms: An empirical analysis," Unpublished paper, Harvard Business School, Boston, and Southern Methodist University, Dallas.

Grossman, Sanford, and Oliver Hart, 1982, "Corporate financial structure and managerial incentives," in: J. McCall (ed.), *The Economics of Information and Uncertainty*, Chicago: University of Chicago Press.

James, Christopher, 1987, "Some evidence on the uniqueness of bank loans," *Journal of Financial Economics 19*, 217–35.

Jensen, Michael, 1988, "Takeovers: Their causes and consequences," *Economic Perspectives 2*, 21–48.

Jensen, Michael, 1989, "Active investors, LBOs, and the privatization of bankruptcy," *Journal of Applied Corporate Finance 2*, 35–44.

Jensen, Michael, and William Meckling, 1976, "Theory of the firm: Managerial behavior, agency costs and ownership structure," *Journal of Financial Economics 3*, 305–60.

Kaplan, Steven, and David Reishus, 1990, "Outside directorships and corporate performance," *Journal of Financial Economics, 26*.

King, Lawrence, 1979, "Chapter 11 of the 1978 Bankruptcy Code," *American Bankruptcy Law Journal 53*, 107–31.

Manski, Charles, and Daniel McFadden, 1983, "Alternative estimators and sample designs for discrete choice analysis," in C. F. Manski and D. McFadden (eds.), *Structural Analysis of Discrete Data with Econometric Applications*, Boston: MIT Press.

Martin, Kenneth, and John McConnell, 1988, "Corporate performance, corporate takeovers and management turnover," Unpublished paper, Purdue University, West Lafayette, IN.

Masulis, Ronald, 1988, *The Debt / Equity Choice*, Cambridge, MA: Ballinger

Publishing Co.

Mikkelson, Wayne, and Megan Partch, 1989, "Managers' voting rights and corporate control," *Journal of Financial Economics 25.*

Myers, Stewart, 1984, "The capital structure puzzle," *Journal of Finance 39*, 575–92.

Ross, Stephen, 1977, "The determination of financial structure: The incentive signalling approach," *Bell Journal of Economics 8*, 23–40.

Salamon, Julie, 1982, "The workout crew: Bankers who step in if loans go bad reveal lenders' other face," *The Wall Street Journal*, April 2, 1.

Smith, Clifford, and David Mayers, 1982, "On the corporate demand for insurance," *Journal of Business 55*, 281–96.

Smith, Clifford, and Rene Stulz, 1985, "The determinants of firms' hedging policies," *Journal of Financial and Quantitative Analysis 20*, 391–405.

Stein, Sol, 1989, *A Feast for Lawyers*, New York: M. Evans and Company, Inc.

Stulz, Rene, 1988, "Managerial control of voting rights: Financing policies and the market for corporate control," *Journal of Financial Economics 20*, 25–54.

Sutton, Robert, and Anita Callahan, 1987, "The stigma of bankruptcy: Spoiled organizational image and its management," *Academy of Management Journal 30*, 405–36.

Vancil, Richard, 1987, *Passing the Baton: Managing the Process of CEO Succession*, Boston: Harvard Business School Press.

Warner, Jerold, 1977a, "Bankruptcy, absolute priority and the pricing of risky debt claims," *Journal of Financial Economics 4*, 239–76.

Warner, Jerold, 1977b, "Bankruptcy costs: Some evidence," *Journal of Finance 32*, 337–47.

Warner, Jerold; Ross Watts; and Karen Wruck, 1988, "Stock prices and top management changes," *Journal of Financial Economics 20*, 461–92.

Weisbach, Michael, 1988, "Outside directors and CEO turnover," *Journal of Financial Economics 20*, 431–60.

Weiss, Lawrence, 1990, "Bankruptcy resolution: Direct costs and violation of priority of claims," *Journal of Financial Economics 26.*

CHAPTER 14

EQUITY VALUATION AND THE RESOLUTION OF CLAIMS IN BANKRUPTCY

Allan C. Eberhart
William T. Moore
Rodney L. Roenfeldt

INTRODUCTION

The absolute priority rule (hereafter APR) states that a bankrupt firm's value is to be distributed to suppliers of capital such that senior creditors are fully satisfied before any distributions are made to junior creditors, and junior creditors are paid in full before common shareholders. Bankruptcy reorganization proceedings, however, are leaving shareholders and junior creditors with valuable assets, even when senior claimants receive only partial settlements. As Barrett and Sullivan (1988, p. 1) note:

Allan C. Eberhart is Assistant Professor of Finance at the School of Business Administration, Georgetown University, Washington, DC.

William T. Moore is Professor of Finance at the College of Business Administration, University of South Carolina at Columbia.

Rodney L. Roenfeldt is Professor of Finance at the College of Business Administration, University of South Carolina at Columbia.

This chapter is a revised version of the authors' article entitled "Security Pricing and Deviations from the Absolute Priority Rule in Bankruptcy Proceedings," that was published in the *Journal of Finance* (December 1990).

Traditionally, shareholders have been last in line. Their claims on a troubled company's assets have had the lowest priority and their impact on the course of bankruptcy-code proceedings generally has been next to nil. But lately the balance of power has been shifting.

Warner (1977) provides one of the early discussions of the implications of deviations from the APR. Baldwin and Mason (1983, pp. 510–11) examine the resolution of claims in the Massey Ferguson reorganization and provide no support for "the hypothesis that the market believes absolute priority rules will be enforced if the firm defaults on its financial obligations." Franks and Torous (1989) analyze a sample of bankruptcies that occurred during the period 1970 through 1984, and find that 21 of 27 sample cases exhibit departures from the APR. More recently, Weiss (1990) examines 37 firms that filed for bankruptcy between 1980 and 1986 and reports that 29 of the cases involved APR violations.

The high frequency and large magnitude of deviations from the APR imply that they should be reflected in security prices. The main purpose of this study is to measure the proportions of firm value given to shareholders in violation of the APR and to determine whether these deviations are priced in the equity market.

The Bankruptcy Reform Act of 1978 (hereafter the Act) provides an environment conducive to deviations from the APR. Considerable power is conferred upon incumbent management during the reorganization period, informational asymmetry is clearly in management's favor, and creditors face an uphill battle in having recalcitrant managers removed [Franks and Torous (1989), Brown (1989)]. Consequently, we focus our analysis on cases filed subsequent to the effective date of the Act. For each case, the amount paid to shareholders in excess of that due under strict adherence to the APR is measured, and this amount is on average 7.6 percent of the total value paid to all claimants. The excess amount received by shareholders varies from zero to 35.71 percent of total value paid, and 23 of the 30 cases examined result in violations of the APR.

Firms' equity values measured subsequent to the announcement of bankruptcy reflect both the amounts paid in adherence to the APR and the amounts paid in violation of the rule. This finding is consistent with that of Clark and Weinstein (1983), who report that the average announcement-period abnormal return for shares that ultimately retain value is higher than the average abnormal return for those that end up valueless.

Franks and Torous (1989) portray shareholders' ability to delay reorganization as a call option. By agreeing to a reorganization plan sooner rather than later, shareholders can expect to be paid for the forfeiture of their option and the payment takes the form of value distributed in violation of the APR. We offer preliminary evidence in support of this argument; our measure of the time delay is lower for cases where deviations from the rule in favor of shareholders are greater.

In the first section below, we summarize those features of the Act that are conducive to deviations from the APR. The sample of bankruptcy cases is described and deviations from the APR are reported in second section. In the third, we test the relationship between equity values after the announcement of bankruptcy and the amounts ultimately received by shareholders in reorganization. The final section concludes with a summary of the findings and their implications.

REASONS FOR DEVIATIONS FROM ABSOLUTE PRIORITY

Chapter 11 of the Bankruptcy Act of 1978 (hereafter, the Act) specifies the procedures for reorganization. In this section, we highlight certain aspects of Chapter 11 that are conducive to deviations from the APR.[1] The process is characterized by uneven distribution of power among disputants, informational asymmetry, and agency conflicts, all of which lead inevitably to deviations from the APR.

Chapter 11 does not require that the APR be followed in reorganizations under the Act. A reorganization plan is deemed acceptable as long as two criteria are met: (1) a simple majority of those voting in each class vote in favor, and (2) votes representing two thirds of the amount owed to those voting in each class are in favor.[2] It is important to emphasize that the acceptability of the plan is determined by the actual number of votes cast, not the total number of potential votes. For instance, if there are 100 creditors in a given class and only 10 votes are cast, the simple majority criterion is met as long as at least six of the ten votes are for approval.

Provisions of the Act confer considerable power upon incumbent management, particularly in the crucial early stages of the process. With rare exceptions, management has the exclusive right to file a reorganization plan during the first 120 days following the petition. As proposer of the plan, management has some discretion over the priority levels assigned to certain classes of claimants. The threat of downgrading a claimant's priority may be used to convince certain creditors to accede to lower payments.

The Act does not ensure that complete information be evenly distributed. It specifies that "adequate information" be disseminated to claimants, but this is usually interpreted to mean only financial statements. Management is not required to inform claimants of other possible or competing plans. Management should have more precise knowledge of asset values than outsiders, and this may be exploited in the bargaining process. This is illustrated by the colorful statement made by the head of a creditor committee in the Wickes Company bankruptcy, 1982–1985: "For a long time we didn't know what the hell was going on. They hired the best professional talent available, kept control of the data and the timing, and very deliberately set creditor against creditor" [Sansweet (1985, p. 1)]. The result was that even though the equityholder committees were described as weak, shareholders retained their shares and received warrants for a total payout worth over $56 million in violation of the APR.

Although management's power is not totally unbridled, the checks and balances provided under the Act may be ineffective. Creditors may demand that certain managers be replaced, or that the firm be directed by a trustee appointed by the court, but the Act specifies that management should be replaced "for cause" only; e.g., "fraud, dishonesty, incompetence, or gross mismanagement" (Section 1104(a)(1), U.S. Code).[3] Even if creditors succeed in having management replaced by a trustee, their cause may not be well served:

> The bankruptcy trustee, as an agent of the court, has the authority to operate the firm. It is not clear that this agency relationship gives the trustee any incentive to run the firm efficiently and make decisions which are in fact value maximizing. [Warner (1977, p. 339)]

Impaired claimants, including shareholders, may block acceptance of a plan and force a "cramdown," whereby a plan is confirmed by the court over the objections of dissenting claimants [see Klee (1979)]. The procedure requires that the APR be followed. However, the cram-down procedure usually results in the court demanding a costly valuation hearing and added transaction costs reduce total value available for distribution to creditors and owners. Impaired claimants may receive less by forcing the cram-down procedure than from accepting a plan that deviates from the APR.

Thus, the Act awards considerable power to management, and management in turn is likely to exploit its power to transfer value from creditors to owners. The natural monopoly in information enjoyed by management can be expected to magnify the resulting deviations from the APR. Replacement of management by a trustee is difficult to do and it is not clear that a trustee will distribute value according to the desires of creditors.

EVIDENCE OF DEVIATIONS FROM ABSOLUTE PRIORITY

Sample Selection and Description

An initial sample of 190 firms was compiled from *The Wall Street Journal Index,* and the samples listed in Altman (1986), Altman and Nammacher (1985), and Johnson (1989). The sample was then purged of cases in which petitions were filed before October 1, 1979 (the effective date of the Act), and those cases in which reorganization plans had not yet been confirmed.

The most restrictive screen was the requirement of complete information needed to assess values of assets distributed to various classes of claimants. Articles published in *The Wall Street Journal* (*WSJ*) often provided details of the amounts distributed to various classes. *Moody's Manuals* and the *Capital Changes Reporter* were consulted for information confirming and supplementing that in the *WSJ* articles. Requests were also sent to firms for copies of the confirmed reorganization plans (eight responded). Since many classes of claimants were paid at least partially in marketable securities, market values were sought in *Barron's, The Wall Street Journal,* the *Capital Changes Reporter,* the *Commercial and Financial Chronicle,* and the Standard & Poor's *Daily Stock Price Record.*

The final sample consists of 30 cases. Table 14–1 contains the names of the firms, bankruptcy announcement dates, reorganization confirmation dates, and the market value of equity before and after the bankruptcy announcement.[4] The *WSJ* bankruptcy announcement date provided in column (1) is the publication date of the filing announcement in the *WSJ*. At least one announcement occurred in each of the years from 1979–1986, and 27 of the announcements occurred during 1980–1984. The confirmation date (column (2)) is the date the bankruptcy court confirmed the reorganization plan. Confirmation came within ten months for Inforex, but took over six years for Seatrain Lines. The average length of time between petition and confirmation was 2.1 years for the 29 firms with known confirmation dates.[5]

The market values of equity before the bankruptcy announcements are provided for the 30 firms in column (3) of Table 14–1 and are based on the closing prices of common stock immediately before the announcement

TABLE 14–1
Bankruptcy Announcement Dates, Reorganization Confirmation Dates, and Pre- and Postannouncement Equity Values for 30 Firms Filing Under Chapter 11 During 1979–1986

Firm	(1) WSJ Bankruptcy Announcement Date	(2) Reorganization Confirmation Date	(3) Preannouncement Market Value of Equity (in millions)[a]	(4) Postannouncement Market Value of Equity (in millions)[a]
Allied Technology	031980	083181	$ 2.216	$2.217
AM International	041582	091384	14.081	11.521
Baldwin-United	092783	092086	94.694	68.390
Bobbie Brooks	011882	021683	9.811	5.194
Braniff International	051482	090283	42.540	17.517
Charter Company	042384	040187	57.971	45.548
Colonial Commercial	120181	010683	1.910	1.528
Computer Communications	111080	052984	17.475	8.854
Continental Airlines	092683	070186	89.622	75.618
Evans Products	031385	070386	31.070	25.892
Global Marine	012886	020289	40.811	28.568
HRT Industries	112482	021384	15.822	9.669
Inforex	102579	082880	16.958	7.267
KDT	080682	033084	11.010	6.881
Kenilworth Systems	090182	012784	8.197	3.643
Leisure Dynamics	011483	120683	1.484	1.250
Lionel Corp.	022282	091385	55.490	15.215
J. W. Mays	012682	021484	8.441	4.901
Omni Exploration	030183	020384	5.365	4.471
Partners Oil	041383	101084	13.069	5.419
Penn-Dixie Industries	040880	030482	12.588	7.288

Revere Copper & Brass	102882	080185	$ 57.130	$29.993
Richton International	031980	082881	2.233	2.233
Saxon Industries	041682	032285	22.028	13.217
Seatrain Lines	021281	040187	21.719	12.669
Steelmet	022383	041085[b]	9.095	4.815
Storage Technology	110184	061987	136.854	98.364
Threshold Technology	111282	041384	13.707	7.044
Victor Technologies	020884	012885	17.303	18.321
Wickes Companies	042682	092484	53.438	33.844

[a] Preannouncement Market Value of Equity is calculated as the number of shares outstanding as of the end of the month before the bankruptcy announcement multiplied by the most recently observable share price immediately before announcement. Postannouncement Market Value of Equity is calculated similarly using the closing price on the announcement date.

[b] A confirmation date was not available for Steelmet; thus the effective date of the reorganization is provided instead.

dates. The equity values range from a low of $1.484 million for Leisure Dynamics to a high of $136.854 million for Storage Technology and the average is $29.471 million (median $16.390 million). The equity values subsequent to the bankruptcy announcements are contained in column (4) and are based on closing prices on the *WSJ* announcement dates. The average for the post-announcement equity values is $19.245 million (median $9.262 million), ranging from $1.250 million for Leisure Dynamics to $98.364 million for Storage Technology.

The decline of $38.489 million in the equity value of Storage Technology around the bankruptcy announcement date suggests that a substantial amount of information is conveyed by these announcements. This example is further supported by the market model prediction errors reported in Table 14–2. The cumulative average prediction error is –35.78 percent (Z = –32.09) for the two days –1 and 0 relative to the *WSJ* bankruptcy announcement.[6] Twenty-eight of the 30 prediction errors are negative. These results are consistent with those reported by Clark and Weinstein (1983) for bankruptcy petitions filed before the 1978 Bankruptcy Reform Act. The finding that bankruptcy announcements subsequent to the Act convey about the same amount of information as the announcements did in the era before the 1978 Act is consistent with the observation made by Morse and Shaw (1988).

Values Distributed to Claimants

The values distributed to creditors and shareholders in accordance with the reorganization plans were obtained from the sources cited in the section immediately above. Claimants were paid in various combinations of cash and securities, the values of which were determined in the manner described below.

1. *Common Shareholders*   The amounts awarded to common shareholders are in all cases based on market values of common shares and/or warrants distributed to them under the respective plans. These values were determined by multiplying the number of shares (or warrants) issued or retained under each plan by the market price per common share (warrant) on the date of distribution. These values are reported for each firm in column (1) of Table 14–3. In the Wickes Companies case, for example, common shareholders received 14,385,000 common shares in the new company, along with 2,877,088 common stock warrants, in exchange for their old

TABLE 14–2
Two-Day Prediction Errors for 30 Firms with Chapter 11 Filing
Announcements During 1979–1986

Firm	Prediction Error	Z-Value
Allied Technology	7.41%	(0.77)
AM International	−17.89	(−2.48)[b]
Baldwin-United	−24.35	(−2.77)[a]
Bobbie Brooks	−52.13	(−10.04)[a]
Braniff International	−65.20	(−8.38)[a]
Charter Company	−24.65	(−5.58)[a]
Colonial Commercial	−20.08	(−0.86)
Computer Communications	−51.29	(−8.07)[a]
Continental Airlines	−11.58	(−1.61)
Evans Products	−15.68	(−2.65)[a]
Global Marine	−29.78	(−3.93)[a]
HRT Industries	−39.27	(−9.03)[a, c]
Inforex	−43.07	(−8.58)[a]
KDT	−35.58	(−3.44)[a]
Kenilworth Systems	−66.63	(−6.00)[a]
Leisure Dynamics	−17.04	(−1.82)
Lionel Corp.	−93.65	(−19.55)[a]
J. W. Mays	−46.72	(−6.92)[a]
Omni Exploration	−24.00	(−2.51)[a]
Partners Oil	−61.98	(−13.03)[a]
Penn-Dixie Industries	−41.92	(−7.65)[a, c]
Revere Copper & Brass	−47.81	(−11.47)[a, e]
Richton International	−0.66	(−0.08)[c]
Saxon Industries	−40.37	(−10.89)[a, c]
Seatrain Lines	−41.85	(−5.13)[a]
Steelmet	−47.78	(−4.97)[a, e]
Storage Technology	−24.58	(−5.14)[a]
Threshold Technology	−49.31	(−6.27)[a]
Victor Technologies	5.43	(0.60)
Wickes Companies	−35.14	(−8.30)[a, d]
Average	−35.78	(−32.09)[a]

[a] Significant at the .01 level.
[b] Significant at the .05 level.
[c] The security did not trade on day $t = -1$; thus the prediction error is for day $t = 0$ only.
[d] The security did not trade on day $t = 0$, and the prediction error is for days $t = -1$ and $t = +1$.
[e] The security did not trade on day $t = -1$ or 0; thus the prediction error is for day $t = +1$.

TABLE 14–3

Amount Paid to Common Shareholders, Creditor Deficit, Total Value Distributed, and Percentage Deviation from Absolute Priority Rule (APR) Based on Reorganization Plans of 30 Firms Filing for Bankruptcy Protection Under Chapter 11 During 1979–1986

Firm	(1) Percentage Amount Paid to Common Shareholders (in millions)	(2) Creditor Deficit (in millions)[a]	(3) Total Value Distributed (in millions)	(4) Deviation From APR (δ)[b]
Allied Technology	$ 0.025	$ 5.397	$ 5.753	0.43%
AM International	37.088	36.863	295.450	12.48
Baldwin-United	15.609	152.885	355.850	4.39
Bobbie Brooks	15.005	0.000	31.505	0.00
Braniff International	3.316	91.467	483.520	0.69c
Charter Company	91.097	376.100	571.867	15.93
Colonial Commercial	4.202	11.007	19.196	21.89
Computer Communications	12.116	0.780	22.116	3.53
Continental Airlines	322.078	0.000	1,247.078	0.00
Evans Products	0.000	136.395	513.105	0.00
Global Marine	6.629	818.867	458.075	1.45
HRT Industries	5.933	17.217	123.616	4.80c
Inforex	4.441	9.458	53.984	8.23
KDT	1.306	0.000	28.347	0.00c
Kenilworth Systems	19.734	0.000	23.718	0.00
Leisure Dynamics	2.500	2.431	10.149	23.96c
Lionel Corp.	46.316	8.563	173.754	4.93
J. W. Mays	21.511	0.000	47.711	0.00
Omni Exploration	3.129	3.993	25.269	12.38
Partners Oil	3.028	6.216	37.813	8.01

Penn-Dixie Industries	11.097	11.097	72.194	15.37%
Revere Copper & Brass	79.982	15.500	364.482	4.25
Richton International	4.465	7.600	18.303	24.39[c]
Saxon Industries	8.988	167.762	152.238	5.90
Seatrain Lines	0.452	268.651	31.802	1.42
Steelmet	0.107	4.700	11.907	0.90
Storage Technology	124.024	0.000	1,307.049	0.00
Threshold Technology	3.427	0.525	4.367	12.02
Victor Technologies	10.000	56.362	28.000	35.71
Wickes Companies	56.821	246.197	1,419.315	4.00

[a] In the cases of Braniff International, HRT Industries, KDT, Leisure Dynamics, and Richton International, the precise amount owed to creditors or the amount actually paid could not be determined. We were able to identify an upper and a lower bound in each of the cases, and the amounts reported are those which yield the more conservative estimates of the magnitudes of deviation from the absolute priority rule.

[b] The percentage deviation from APR (δ) is defined as the amount ultimately paid to common shareholders in violation of the absolute priority rule divided by the total amount paid to all claimants upon confirmation of the reorganization plan.

[c] The δ values reported are conservative estimates of the deviations (see note a). The upper bound estimates are 1.01% (Braniff), 5.88% (HRT), 4.61% (KDT), 24.63% (Leisure Dynamics), and 28.14% (Richton).

shares. On the distribution date, the stock price was $3.625 and the warrant price was $1.625, implying a total market value of $56.821 million.

2. *Creditors*   The amounts paid to creditors included combinations of cash and securities. Security values were determined by market prices exclusively in 12 of the 30 cases. In the remaining 18 cases, combinations of face and market values were used.[7] To the extent that face values overstate true market values, the amounts paid to creditors are biased upward.

To illustrate the method for calculating amounts paid to creditors, we return to the Wickes Companies case. Creditors received $600,000,000 in cash in addition to the following securities: (1) extendable, two-year 12% notes, $173,000,000 face value (market value = 97% of face value); (2) nine-year, 12% debentures, $246,000,000 face value (market value = 85.75% of face value); (3) 20-year debentures, $150,000,000 face value (market value = 50% of face value); (4) 79,117,500 shares of common stock (market price $3.625 per share), and (5) 8,151,749 common stock warrants (market price $1.625 per warrant). The market values of the securities plus the cash paid sum to $1,353,802,530.

In cases where the amount distributed to creditors is less than they were owed, the difference is defined as the creditor deficit. These amounts are presented in column (2) of Table 14–3 and, for the Wickes Companies example, the creditor deficit is the amount owed to creditors ($1,600,000,000) less the amount paid to creditors ($1,353,802,530), or $246.197 million. The average creditor deficit for the firms in the sample is $81.868 million and ranges from zero for six firms to $818.867 million for Global Marine.

3. *Preferred Shareholders*   Several firms in the sample had preferred stock outstanding, representing in each case a small percentage of firm value. The amounts paid to preferred shareholders were valued as previously discussed. As an example, the preferred shareholders of Wickes Companies were awarded 2,397,574 new common shares priced at $3.625 per share for a value of $8,691,206.

The total value distributed to all claimants, column (3) in Table 14–3, is the sum of the amounts paid to common shareholders, creditors, and preferred shareholders. For the Wickes Companies, the total value distributed is $1,419.315 million ($56.821 + $1,353.803 + $8.691). The total value distributed ranges from $4.367 million in the case of Threshold Technology to $1.419 billion for Wickes Companies and averages $264.584 million.

Relative Deviations from the APR

A measure of the deviation from the APR that allows comparisons to be made across firms is defined as the amount ultimately paid to common shareholders in violation of the APR, divided by the total value distributed to all claimants upon confirmation of the reorganization plan. These values, denoted as δ, are reported in column (4) of Table 14-3.[8] Generally, deviation from the APR includes the difference between what creditors and preferred shareholders were owed and what they received. For our sample, however, in every case where preferred shareholders were not fully compensated, the creditor deficit exceeded the amount paid to common shareholders. Thus, deviations from APR can be determined directly by comparing the creditor deficit with the amount paid to common shareholders. For example, in cases where the creditor deficit is zero, preferred shareholders were also fully compensated and the amounts paid to common shareholders are not in violation of the APR, hence δ is zero. In the case of Continental Airlines, the creditors were paid in full and though common shareholders received $322.078 million, none of this amount was in excess of that to which they were entitled under the APR.

In six cases the creditor deficit was positive but less than the amount paid to common shareholders. In these cases, the deviation from the APR was not the total amount paid to shareholders but only the amount of the creditor deficit. As an example, δ for AM International is calculated as the creditor deficit ($36.863 million) divided by the total amount distributed ($295.450 million), or 12.48 percent.

In cases where the creditor deficit exceeded the amount paid to shareholders, the entire shareholder payment was in violation of the APR. In the case of Charter Company, for example, shareholders received $91.097 million in the face of a creditor deficit of $376.100 million. The amount received by shareholders represents 15.93 percent of the total $571.867 million distributed to all claimants.

The values of δ in Table 14-3 range from zero to 35.71 percent, with an average of 7.57 percent. For 24 cases the creditor deficit is positive. In 23 of these cases shareholders received payments in violation of the rule and δ averages 9.87 percent. Because the deviations are widespread and economically significant, one would expect security prices to reflect the market's expectation of payments in violation of the APR.

EQUITY VALUES AND DEVIATIONS FROM ABSOLUTE PRIORITY

Pricing Deviations from the APR

The post-announcement equity values presented in column (4) of Table 14–1 should reflect the amount shareholders expect to receive upon reorganization, discounted to account for the expected delay in payment, and adjusted for risk. The amount expected to be received in each case should be the sum of (1) the amount expected if the APR is enforced and (2) the amount expected to be paid in violation of the rule. Both amounts should be reflected in a firm's share price upon announcement of bankruptcy. For example, AM International common shareholders received \$37.088 million upon reorganization [column (1), Table 14–2] despite a creditor deficit of \$36.863 million [column (2), Table 14–2]. Of the total paid to shareholders, only \$225,000 would have been distributed under the strict APR (\$37.088 – \$36.863), thus \$36.863 million was paid in violation of the rule.

Using the values ultimately paid to shareholders as proxies for expected receipts, we test whether post-announcement equity values reflect the present values of the amounts paid by estimating the following linear model:

$$\text{VALUE}_i = \beta_0 + \beta_1 \text{APR}_i + \beta_2 \text{VIOLATE}_i + \epsilon_i \qquad (14.1)$$

where the postannouncement market value of equity [column (4), Table 14–1] is denoted as VALUE. The total amount distributed to common shareholders [column (1), Table 14–3] is composed of the amount distributed under strict application of the APR, and the amount distributed in violation of the rule. We discount each of these amounts at the Treasury Bill rate prevalent at the time of the filing, for the number of months between the filing date and reorganization confirmation.[9] The discounted amount paid under the APR is denoted as APR in equation 14.1, and the discounted amount paid in violation of the rule is denoted as VIOLATE.

The coefficients β_1 and β_2 in equation 14.1 are hypothesized to be positive and less than 1.0 to reflect the certainty equivalent. The model is estimated by ordinary least squares and the results are in equation 14.2.

$$\text{VALUE}_i = 9{,}877.0 + .318\ \text{APR}_i + .533\ \text{VIOLATE}_i \qquad (14.2)$$
$$(2.61) \qquad (4.99) \qquad (2.46)$$

The values in parentheses are t-statistics for the respective coefficient estimates. The estimated coefficient for the present value of the amount paid under strict adherence to the rule is .318, positive and significant ($t = 4.99$). The coefficient estimate for the amount paid in violation of the rule is .533, also positive and significant ($t = 2.46$).[10] Because the two variables, APR and VIOLATE, are significantly different from zero and account for over half the variability in VALUE ($R^2 = .51$), we conclude that share values upon bankruptcy announcement reflect significant proportions of those amounts ultimately paid in adherence to the rule and in violation of the rule.[11] This finding is consistent with that reported by Clark and Weinstein (1983), which indicates that share price reactions to bankruptcy announcements are conditioned on whether the shares are ultimately valueless. Similarly, Gilson, John, and Long (1990) find that negative stock price reactions to debt restructuring announcements are more severe for firms whose restructuring attempts ultimately fail. More recently, Eberhart and Sweeney (1991) report some results consistent with the hypothesis that bankruptcy announcement date bond prices represent unbiased forecasts of the amounts ultimately paid to bondholders.

Deviation from the APR and the Option to Delay

Payments to common shareholders in excess of what they would receive under the APR can be viewed as the purchase by creditors of the shareholders' option to delay reorganization [Franks and Torous (1989)]. The option to delay reorganization is an American-type call created by federal bankruptcy law. The payment to shareholders to forfeit the option and accept a reorganization plan may include the fair value of the option and, in addition, a premium to "avoid future legal and administrative costs" that would otherwise be suffered by creditors [Franks and Torous (1989, p. 766)]. In exchange for giving up the option sooner rather than later, shareholders can expect to receive a greater amount in violation of the rule. This argument implies a negative relation between the length of the proceedings and the deviation (δ) from the APR.

In this section, we offer the results of a test of the relation between length of proceedings and δ. A complication arises in that the duration of the proceedings, apart from the delaying tactics of common shareholders, depends on the complexity of the firm's claims. Franks and Torous (1989) posit that the total reorganization period consists of a component that reflects the complexity of the case and a component that represents the length of the delay exercised by shareholders. Since only the total duration of the process is observable, however, the component due to complexity is estimated indirectly by assuming that it is a function of firm size. Thus, the component due to delay by shareholders is estimated residually from the following linear model.

$$\text{TIME}_i = \alpha_0 + \alpha_1 \text{SIZE}_i + \alpha_2 \text{DELAY}_i + \epsilon_i \tag{14.3}$$

In equation 14.3, TIME is the number of months from bankruptcy filing to final acceptance of a reorganization plan. The total value of claims distributed under the plan is denoted as SIZE and represents our proxy for complexity.[12] The variable, DELAY, is the time spent in reorganization beyond that needed to adjudicate claims and administer the bankruptcy in the normal course of reorganization. We cannot observe DELAY, but the residual (ϵ_i) from the estimation of equation 14.4 serves as a noisy estimate of the DELAY component.

$$\text{TIME}_i = \alpha_0 + \alpha_1 \text{SIZE}_i + \epsilon_i \tag{14.4}$$

A negative relation between the measure of deviation from the rule (δ) and the residual from 14.4 would be consistent with the argument of Franks and Torous (1989). The residual from 14.4 is denoted as DELAY* in the linear model 14.5 below.

$$\text{DELAY}_i^* = \beta_0 + \beta_1 \delta_i + \epsilon_i^* \tag{14.5}$$

$$\phantom{\text{DELAY}_i^* =}\ \ 3.086 \quad -.408$$
$$\phantom{\text{DELAY}_i^* =}\ \ (1.00) \quad (-1.56)$$

Coefficient estimates using ordinary least squares appear immediately below the respective coefficients and t-statistics are in parentheses. The estimate for the δ coefficient (β_1) is negative and significant at the 7 percent level under the one-sided alternative.[13] The estimate is inefficient due to errors in measurement of DELAY*; thus the statistical significance of the estimate may be understated.[14] We interpret the findings as modest support for the notion that shareholders are paid more for forfeiting their delay option early.

SUMMARY AND CONCLUSIONS

Deviations from the absolute priority rule (APR) in bankruptcy proceedings have become a commonplace occurrence. For 30 bankruptcy cases filed subsequent to the effective date of the 1978 Bankruptcy Reform Act, 24 cases resulted in a creditor deficit. In 23 of these 24 cases, shareholders received payments in violation of the APR. The percentage of total value received by shareholders in these 23 cases averaged 9.87 percent, ranging from 0.43 to 35.71 percent. The deviations are widespread and economically significant and are consistent with the findings of Franks and Torous (1989).

Deviations from the APR may be the result of any of several influences on the reorganization plan adopted. For example, management enjoys a powerful bargaining position because they generally are given exclusive right to file the initial reorganization plan. Creditors also may lack adequate information about firm value, or they may be willing to compromise because of the potential cost of lengthy reorganizations and cram-down procedures.

We find that share values subsequent to the bankruptcy announcement are found to impound the present value of both the amount paid in adherence to the APR and the amount paid in violation of the rule. Over half of the cross-sectional variation in equity value immediately after bankruptcy announcement is explained by these amounts ultimately received. We also find weak evidence that payments to shareholders in violation of the APR may be viewed as compensation for forfeiting their option to delay reorganization proceedings. The length of the delay in the bankruptcy proceedings is negatively related to the proportion of the total distribution that shareholders are given in violation of the APR.

NOTES

1. Other sources of information on Chapter 11 include Blum (1980), Brown (1989), Franks and Torous (1989), Giammarino (1989), Hagedorn (1980), Jackson (1986), Klein (1979), Morrison (1985), Treister et al. (1988), and White (1984, 1989).
2. A reorganization plan does not impair a claim if it leaves "unaltered the legal, equitable, and contractual rights" of a class of creditors or owners, or reinstates the obligation, or fully compensates the creditors or owners in cash at the effective date of the plan (§1124(1), U.S. Code). Unimpaired claimants are presumed to be satisfied with the plan, thus their votes are not required for confirmation.
3. Of the 30 cases examined by Franks and Torous (1989), two resulted in managers being replaced by other managers.

4. The cases of Johns Manville, A. H. Robbins, and Texaco, Inc. were excluded due to their unique legal circumstances.
5. The average time in reorganization is 2.6 years for the 15 firms in the Franks and Torous (1989) sample that filed after October 1, 1979.
6. These results are based on market model prediction errors using test statistics shown in Mikkelson and Partch (1988). A brief description is given in the Appendix. The mean-adjusted returns model based on Ryngaert (1988) yields similar results.
7. In some of these cases, the information available on the plans was not sufficiently detailed to determine the extent to which face values were included in the amounts reported. For instance, in the Evans Products case, *The Wall Street Journal* reports only that creditors would receive 79 percent of $649,500,000 in allowable claims.
8. The deviation measure (d) differs from that calculated by Franks and Torous (1989). Their index of deviation focuses on the creditor deficit. Our measure captures the proportion of firm value distributed to all claimants that is paid to shareholders in excess of that which they would have received under the APR.
9. The sign and significance reported below for the estimated β_1 and β_2 coefficients in equation (14.1) are robust with respect to the discount rate used. Using two different discount rates, 10 and 12 percent, applied uniformly to all payments to shareholders and using nondiscounted values, the estimation results are nearly the same as those provided below.
10. Actual amounts paid and the actual time in reorganization are used to calculate APR and VIOLATE in equation (14.2), whereas the market's (unobservable) expectations of those amounts are the values that should be reflected in equity prices. Thus, equation (14.2) exhibits an errors-in-variables problem. If the true values of APR and VIOLATE are uncorrelated, however, the coefficient estimates for APR and VIO-LATE will be biased toward zero.

    The coefficient estimates of β_1 and β_2 are not significantly different from each other at the 10 percent level.
11. The equity values of the firms in the sample vary greatly. Equation 14.1 was estimated using weighted least squares, where the weight is the firm's equity value before the bankruptcy announcement. The estimated coefficients and t-statistics (in parentheses) are similar to those obtained by ordinary least squares:

$$\text{VALUE}_i = 1{,}045.5 + .284 \text{ APR}_i + .394 \text{ VIOLATE}_i$$
$$\quad\quad (1.86) \quad\quad (2.89) \quad\quad\quad (2.57)$$

$R^2 = .63$

12. The results reported below are not materially affected by the use of alternative measures of SIZE; i.e., equity value before filing and equity value upon announcement.
13. As noted recently by Brown and Klein (1986, p. 151), the traditional 5 percent significance level is "too low" for small samples and "too high" for large samples when compared to the (Bayesian) posterior odds ratio criterion. We compare the hypothesis (H_1) that $\beta_1 < 0$ with the hypothesis (H_2) that $\beta_1 > 0$ in equation (14.5) under the assumption that the error (ϵ_i^*) is normal and that prior information is diffuse. Zellner (1984, pp. 280–82) derives the posterior odds ratio of H_1 versus H_2 for this case

as:

$$Pr(t > -\hat{\beta}_1/S\,\hat{\beta}_1 D) \,/\, Pr(t < -\beta_1\,\hat{\beta}_1/S\,\hat{\beta}_1 | D),$$

where $S\,\hat{\beta}_1$ is the standard error estimate for β_1 and D denotes the sample information. The odds ratio for our sample is $.935/.065 = 14.38$. The odds are over 14 to 1 in favor of $\beta_1 < 0$; the proportion (δ) of firm value awarded to common stockholders appears to be greater in those cases where delays are shorter.

14. As an alternative to equation (14.5), we estimate the relationship between δ and TIME directly as follows.

$$\delta_i = \begin{array}{cc} \beta_0 & + \ \beta_1\text{TIME}_i + \varepsilon_i \\ 13.01 & -.229 \\ (3.90) & (-1.91) \end{array} \qquad R^2 = .11$$

This formulation does not avoid the errors-in-variables problem because TIME overstates the delay component and the confounding effects of size (complexity) are not isolated. We also estimate the relationship with SIZE as a control and get the following result.

$$\delta_i = \begin{array}{cccc} \beta_0 & + \ \beta_1\text{TIME}_i & + \ \beta_2\text{SIZE}_i & + \varepsilon_i \\ 13.83 & -.195 & -.00005 \\ (4.06) & (-1.60) & (-1.24) \end{array} \qquad R^2 = .16$$

APPENDIX TO CHAPTER 14

DESCRIPTION OF METHOD FOR ASSESSING MARKET MODEL PREDICTION ERRORS

The market model is assumed as the return generating process and deviations from its predictions are prediction errors (*PE*) as calculated in equation 14.1A.

$$PE_{it} = R_{it} - \alpha_i - \beta_i R_{mt} \qquad (14.1A)$$

where R_{it} is the return on security i on day t, R_{mt} is the return on the equally weighted CRSP index, and α_i and β_i are parameters estimated from the market model. The market model is estimated over days -220 to -30 relative to the announcement date (day 0) in *The Wall Street Journal.*[*] The cumulative prediction error for security i over an arbitrary interval from $t = a$ to $t = b$ is given by equation 14.2A.

$$CPE_{i,a,b} = \sum_{t=a}^{b} PE_{it} \qquad (14.2A)$$

Under the assumption that PE_{it} is multivariate normal and that PE_{it} is independent of PE_{jt}, $i \neq j$, the following statistic is normally distributed with mean zero under the null hypothesis.

$$Z = \frac{1}{\sqrt{N}} \sum_{i=1}^{N} \left[\sum_{t=a}^{b} PE_{it}/S_{i,a,b} \right] \qquad (14.3A)$$

where N is the number of observations in the sample and S_i is the root mean square error of the market model estimated over ED days and $\bar{R}_m$ is the mean market return from the estimation period. The variable $S_{i,a,b}$ is the square root of the variance of the cumulated prediction error of firm i. This variable is defined to be:

$$S_{i,a,b} = S_i \left[(b-a+1) + \frac{(b-a+1)^2}{ED} + (\sum_{t=a}^{b} R_{mt} - (b-a+1)R_m)^2 \right.$$

$$\div \left. \sum_{j=1}^{ED} (R_{mj} - \bar{R}_m)^2 \right]^{1/2} \qquad (14.4A)$$

The test statistic (Z) is used to test hypotheses regarding the average cumulative prediction error (*ACPE*) for the sample.

$$ACPE_{a,b} = \sum_{i=1}^{N} \sum_{t=a}^{b} PE_{it}/N \qquad (14.5A)$$

---

[*]The market model was also estimated using days -320 to -100 and the results were similar.

REFERENCES

Altman, Edward I., 1986, "Bankruptcy and reorganization," in Edward I. Altman (ed.), *Handbook of Corporate Finance*, New York: John Wiley & Sons.

Altman, Edward I., and Scott A. Nammacher, 1985, "The default rate experience on high yield corporate debt," *Financial Analysts Journal 41*, No. 4, pp. 25-38.

Baldwin, Carliss Y., and Scott P. Mason, 1983, "The resolution of claims in financial distress: The case of Massey Ferguson," *The Journal of Finance 38*, 505–16.

Barrett, Paul, and Allanna Sullivan, 1988, "New Activists: Usually last in line, holders become vocal in bankruptcy actions," *The Wall Street Journal*, January 21, p. 1.

Blum, Walter J., 1980, "The 'fair and equitable' standard for confirming reorganizations under the new bankruptcy code," *American Bankruptcy Law Journal 54*, 165–72.

Brown, David T., 1989, "Claimholder incentive conflicts in reorganization: The role of bankruptcy law," *Review of Financial Studies 2*, 109–23.

Brown, Stephen J., and Roger W. Klein, 1986, "Model selection in the federal courts: An application of the posterior odds ratio criterion," in P. Goel and A. Zellner (eds.), *Bayesian Inference and Decision Techniques*, Amsterdam: Elsevier Science Publishers B.V.

Clark, Truman A., and Mark I. Weinstein, 1983, "The behavior of the common stock of bankrupt firms," *The Journal of Finance 38*, 489–504.

Eberhart, Allan C., and Richard J. Sweeney, 1991, "Does the bond market predict bankruptcy settlements?" unpublished manuscript, Georgetown University.

Franks, Julian R., and Walter N. Torous, 1989, "An empirical investigation of U.S. firms in reorganization," *The Journal of Finance 44*, 747–69.

Giammarino, Ronald M., 1989, "The resolution of financial distress," *Review of Financial Studies 2*, 25–47.

Gilson, Stuart C.; Kose John; and Larry H. P. Lang, 1990, "Troubled debt restructurings: An empirical study of private reorganization of firms in default," *Journal of Financial Economics 27*, 355–87.

Hagedorn, Richard B., 1980, "The survival and enforcement of the secured claim under the Bankruptcy Reform Act of 1978," *American Bankruptcy Law Journal 54*, 1–28.

Jackson, Thomas H., 1986, *The Logic and Limits of Bankruptcy Law*, Cambridge, MA: Harvard University Press.

Johnson, Dana J., 1989, "The risk behavior of equity of firms approaching bankruptcy," *Journal of Financial Research 12*, 33–50.

Klee, K., 1979, "All you ever wanted to know about cram-down under Chapter 11 of the new bankruptcy code," *American Bankruptcy Law Journal 53*, 133–71.

Klein, Martin I., 1979, "The Bankruptcy Reform Act of 1978," *American Bankruptcy Law Journal 53*, 1–33.

Mikkelson, Wayne, and M. Megan Partch, 1988, "Withdrawn security offerings," *Journal of Financial and Quantitative Analysis 23*, 119–33.

Morrison, Rees W., 1985, *Business Opportunities from Corporate Bankruptcies*, New York: John Wiley & Sons.

Morse, Dale, and Wayne Shaw, 1988, "Investing in bankrupt firms," *The Journal of Finance 43*, 1193–1206.

Ryngaert, Michael, 1988, "The effect of poison pill securities on shareholder wealth," *Journal of Financial Economics 20*, 377–417.

Sansweet, Stephen J., 1985, "Salvage operation: How team at Wickes schemed and cajoled to restore its health," *The Wall Street Journal*, August 2, pp. 1–5.

Treister, George M.; J. Ronald Trost; Leon S. Forman; Kenneth N. Klee; and Richard B. Levin, 1988, *Fundamentals of Bankruptcy Law* (2nd ed.), Philadelphia: American Law Institute.

Warner, Jerold B., 1977, "Bankruptcy, absolute priority, and the pricing of risky debt claims," *Journal of Financial Economics 4*, 239–76.

Weiss, Lawrence A., 1990, "Bankruptcy resolution: direct costs and violation of priority of claims," *Journal of Financial Economics 27*, 285–314.

White, Michelle J., 1984, "Bankruptcy, liquidation and reorganization," in Dennis Logue (ed.), *Handbook of Modern Finance*, Boston: Warren Gorham & Lamont.

White, Michelle J., 1989, "The corporate bankruptcy decision," *Journal of Economic Perspectives 3*, 129–51.

Zellner, Arnold, 1984, *Basic Issues in Econometrics*, Chicago: The University of Chicago Press.

CHAPTER 15

AN EMPIRICAL INVESTIGATION OF U.S. FIRMS IN REORGANIZATION

Julian R. Franks
Walter N. Torous

The purpose of this chapter is to understand the institutional features of Chapter 11 from an empirical examination of 30 firms that have emerged from Chapter 11 proceedings. This permits us to characterize more realistically investment and financing decisions, whose value is affected by the probability of default.

The 1978 Bankruptcy Act affords the debtor substantial protection against creditors through Chapter 11. It is widely accepted that this protection is much greater than that prevailing prior to the Act [see Boyes and Faith (1986)]. The very large increase in the number of firms seeking protection would seem to confirm this view. In 1987, for example, 17,142 companies filed for Chapter 11 compared with only 6,298 in 1980. One important feature is that when the firm enters reorganization all repayments of capital and interest are postponed until the reorganization is complete.

Julian R. Franks and Walter N. Torous are professors at London Business School and Anderson School of Management, UCLA, respectively. The authors thank Laura Quinn for collecting some of the data. They wish to thank members of the legal fraternity who have given valuable advice on Chapter 11 proceedings, including Judge Samuel Bufford, Professor R. Jordan (School of Law, UCLA), Ken Klee, Professor T. Jackson (School of Law, University of Virginia), and Leo Hertzel (Mayer, Brown and Platt). They would also like to thank Mr. W. A. Mallory (Chief Financial Officer, Wickes) for giving us his insights on the reorganization process of Wickes Group. They are grateful to David Hirshleifer and Ted Anderson for valuable discussions. Reprinted with permission from *The Journal of Finance* (July 1989).

From an analysis of our sample of thirty firms the average period spent in reorganization is nearly four years. The delay in repayment of capital may be viewed as the exercise of an option purchased by the borrower from the creditor when the bond contract is originally completed. A second feature of the Chapter 11 process is that any reorganization plan, prior to court approval, must be agreed to by a majority of creditors (including the stockholders). The committee structure and non-unanimity requirements for creditors give rise to a protracted bargaining process. In certain circumstances, stockholders may exercise an important influence on the reorganization plan that in large part stems from their managerial representatives remaining in control of the business and their exclusive albeit temporary right to propose a reorganization plan. As a result senior claimholders may be encouraged to give up some of the value of their claims to stockholders. Such a reduction in claims is referred to as a deviation from absolute priority. Absolute priority denies any claimholder a stake in the securities of the reorganized firm, until more senior claims have been totally satisfied [see Warner (1977) for an early discussion and White (1983)]. Deviations from absolute priority are not unusual in our sample. These deviations may be viewed as an ex post change in the priorities of creditors.

Given the length of the proceedings in Chapter 11 it should not be surprising that the legal and administrative costs may be high. It is an interesting question why these firms perceived that the recontracting process of Chapter 11 was the least costly form of reorganization. It may be because equityholders bear little or no costs of the reorganization but possess the prerogative to enter and protract the reorganization process while their managerial representatives retain control of the firm. Also, some creditors may obtain some value from a period in Chapter 11 insofar as the judicial process reveals the "true" value of creditors' and debtors' claims. Notwithstanding, after some period the costs may provide creditors with an important incentive to purchase (prior to expiration) the stockholders' option to remain in reorganization. The purchase takes the form of writing down creditors' claims and writing up those of stockholders, thereby giving rise to deviations from absolute priority.

We examine two applications of the Chapter 11 process to investment and financing decisions. First we consider Myers's (1977) underinvestment problem in light of the recontracting process that takes place. Second, we examine how the pricing of risky debt is affected by the option to delay repayment of capital and interest. We compare the risk premia on debt incorporating these provisions with the risk premia calculated by Merton

(1974) who assumed an absence of Chapter 11 and that the rule of strict absolute priority prevailed. A number of the parameter values in these simulations are based on the empirical evidence in our sample of firms that have emerged from Chapter 11. To the extent that this is ignored, the premium on risky debt may be biased significantly downwards.

A DESCRIPTION OF THE BANKRUPTCY PROCESS IN CHAPTER 11

Chapter 11 of the 1978 Bankruptcy Code protects a company from its creditors while it works out a plan for reorganization.[1] In the majority of cases the firm is liquidated in Chapter 11, and in a minority it emerges as an operating concern, but with new financial claims replacing the old. The larger companies tend to be in this minority, since they are better able to obtain the administrative skills required to cope with the complexities of the reorganization process. The emerging company is usually smaller than its pre-Chapter 11 size, although there are some notable exceptions; for example, Trans American Natural Gas Company grew in reorganization to be second only to Exxon Corporation as the largest of the Texas natural gas producers.

The main purpose of Chapter 11 is to preserve the company as an operating concern while a plan for reorganization is worked out among creditors.[2] To achieve this end, substantial rights are given to the company (referred to as the debtor-in-possession) seeking protection under the Code. In Table 15–1 some of those rights are listed. We discuss those rights and their limitations below.

Although a company may seek protection in Chapter 11, the creditors may petition for its liquidation or for that protection to be denied. The latter is extremely rare and will only be granted if the debtor's action is viewed as frivolous; and a liquidation will not be agreed to by the judge in bankruptcy if the company is expected to have a positive cash flow excluding financing charges.[3]

Recently, the reasons for seeking protection have broadened. Some firms are not insolvent but seek protection against large uncertain legal liabilities. For example, Manville and A. H. Robbins have used it as an "escape hatch" from litigation in product liability suits. Texaco has used it as a result of an expensive legal claim made against it by Pennzoil. Also, Chicago Central Pacific Railroads claimed to be solvent with assets exceed-

TABLE 15–1
Rights of Debtor-in-Possession and Creditors

Rights of Debtor-in-Possession	Rights of Creditors
1. Can seek protection under Chapter 11.	Propose immediate liquidation.
2. Debtor retains control of business	Creditors' committees set up to oversee running of the business.
	Rights of discovery.
	Trustee can be appointed by court if evidence of wrongdoing.
	Creditors may demand change in management.
	Creditor may object to any payment made to a third party.
3. Debtor has exclusive right to propose reorganization plan in first 120 days. Court can renew exclusivity.	Creditors can oppose extension of exclusivity.
4. Debtor can obtain extensions to Chapter 11 proceedings.	Oppose extension. Propose reorganization plan.
5. Approval of plan requires strict majority in each and every class by number and two thirds by book value.	Creditor must obtain at least that which would have accrued in liquidation (with absolute priority rules). Creditor who votes against plan, but is outvoted, may appeal.
6. The proposer of the reorganization plan (debtor-in-possession or creditor) can propose cram-down.	

ing liabilities. It had sought protection because one creditor changed the terms of a loan, significantly affecting the company's interest and posing a challenge to the company's operations. In another filing Chas. A. Stevens cited "cash flow problems which have been exacerbated by the general downturn in the woman's apparel industry. The company is not insolvent, and it is working very hard for a substantial settlement with its creditors" (*The Wall Street Journal*, June 2, 1988). Several senior executives involved in reorganization and a judge in bankruptcy have referred to Chapter 11 as an important strategy in a company's armory when the going gets tough, rather than when the company is insolvent.

During Chapter 11 the debtor-in-possession retains control of the business, although the court can appoint a trustee if inappropriate conduct is suspected. However, creditors can and frequently do obtain a change of management.[4]

Initially, the debtor-in-possession has the exclusive right to propose a plan of reorganization within 120 days of entering Chapter 11, although extensions are frequently granted. Creditors may oppose extensions, for example, on the basis that the debtor-in-possession is unable or unwilling to propose a realistic plan that will be confirmed by the judge or creditors. Creditors were successful in their petition to terminate exclusivity in Sharon Steel, but Pennzoil's petition failed in the Texaco reorganization.

The period spent in Chapter 11 (or the old Chapter X) varies enormously; in our current sample of 30 firms the period varies from 37 days to 13.3 years with an average of about 4 years. The length of time may depend upon the size of the company, the number of creditors, the complexity of the financial claims, and, in general, the bargaining process. In the case of Wickes there were approximately 250,000 creditors, all of whom had to be contacted in order for their claims to be processed and agreed before a reorganization plan could be prepared. Those proceedings can be greatly lengthened if the financial records of the company are inadequate and if creditors seek to take advantage of the proceedings by claiming higher payments than are actually due. In one case 25 percent of creditors' claims were the subject of serious dispute.

The process may be lengthened if the debtor-in-possession is prepared to be litigious. In the case of Trans America Natural Gas Company delays resulted from lawsuits against creditors, defying court orders, missing or abruptly ending creditors' meetings, shuffling assets between companies (thereby causing more lawsuits and greater delays), and numerous objections to amounts claimed by creditors. In the Hunt reorganization case *The Wall Street Journal* (July 23, 1987) writes, "Bank attorneys say the essence of the Hunt reorganization is to buy time. They are saying sue us in perpetuity and we'll go on running our business." The incentives to lengthen the proceedings are, however, limited: legal fees rise with the period spent in Chapter 11,[5] and creditors can (with the court's permission) propose their own plan of reorganization.[6] Moreover creditors can use rights of discovery to demand information and interrogate management, with the objective of enlightenment or harassment. They may also object to particular expenditures made by the debtor-in-possession. For example, A. H. Robbins was cited for contempt for making unauthorized payments, and LTV was prevented by creditors from hiring lobbyists to plead its case.

The proposer of the plan allocates creditors to a particular class. The rules for allocation are based upon Section 1122 of the 1978 Act. Two clear rules emerge. You cannot place a significantly dissimilar claim in a class, unless the holder so agrees. Thus, secured and unsecured creditors will be in different classes. In addition claims with different collateral may be further classified according to the nature of the collateral. Stockholders are usually placed in their own class. The second rule permits a separate class to be established for small claims which can be paid off in full by the debtor. Given the broad nature of these rules, the power by the proposer to allocate a creditor to a particular class rather than another (a form of "gerrymandering") may be important in gaining consent to a plan.

For the reorganization plan to be approved unanimity is not required. Within each class, a strict majority of creditors by number and two thirds by value are necessary for confirmation of the plan. Should a plan fail to gain the agreement of each class, an amended plan may be proposed; for example, Seatrain Lines formally proposed a total of four plans. If agreement still cannot be reached, the creditors may request the judge to decide the disposition of funds among the claimholders (as in A. H. Robbins). Alternatively, the proposer of the ill-fated plan may decide on "cram-down" which requires that claims made by objecting creditors are treated according to the rule of absolute priority (see Klee, 1979). Under a cram-down, a creditor's claim is treated as though all the more senior claims have been paid in full. The use of cram-down will require a hearing to produce a valuation for the firm's assets, a lengthy and costly process. Cram-down is rarely used, but the threat may be important if senior creditors prove recalcitrant since if the hearing produced a higher valuation than the "true value" the market value of the securities issued (equity or debt) could be below their nominal value (see Brown, 1986). Legal opinion suggests that the threat of cram-down works in favour of stockholders if a valuation of assets is required. According to Klee (1979), "The threat of valuation gives negotiating leverage to the class of ownership interests. Since a valuation of the business must be made if the shareholders dissent, often seniors will give up value to shareholders to obtain their consent to the plan. If the shareholders consent, a costly valuation may be avoided" (page 145). Given the rules for approval of the plan, which includes the consent of the judge, some protection is afforded for those who vote against an approved plan through an appeals procedure.

For example stockholders in Manville appealed on the basis that they were inadequately represented in their creditors' committee. Another grounds for appeal may be that the value of the claims allowed to a particular set of securities is smaller than that which would be obtained in a liquidation.

The general picture of Chapter 11 is that substantial rights are afforded to the debtor-in-possession, especially if it can impose costs on creditors by protracting the reorganization process. We conjecture that shareholders obtain some share of the reorganized firm even when creditors' claims have not been satisfied in full. In the next section, we analyze our sample of firms to determine the extent of deviations from strict absolute priority.

DATA AND ANALYSIS

The Sample

A sample of thirty firms which emerged from Chapter 11 (or the equivalent Chapter X prior to 1978) is examined. This sample is largely taken from Altman and Nammacher (1985), who listed 125 firms (65 of which had public debt) that had defaulted on bonds outstanding during 1970 through 1984, as reported by Standard and Poor's *Bond Guide* and Moody's *Bond Record*. The sample is biased towards large publicly traded firms. Not all of Altman and Mannacher's list of companies is included, because either the company had not yet emerged from reorganization, or it had been liquidated, or details were not in our main information source, *The Capital Changes Reporter*.

The names of the firms are listed in Table 15–2 with the dates when the company entered and emerged from reorganization. The average period spent in reorganization is 3.67 years, although the range is large, from 37 days to over 13 years (standard deviation is 2.88 years). The railroads spent the longest periods in Chapter 11, perhaps because of the regulatory nature of the industry. Some companies which filed for bankruptcy under Chapter X (prior to 1978) subsequently switched to Chapter 11 after 1978.

From *The Capital Changes Reporter* we obtained a list of securities that were outstanding prior to reorganization and the new financial claims (type, amount, and usually price) that were exchanged for the old claims. If more than one reorganization plan was formally proposed, the details of each were recorded.

The list of securities outstanding prior to reorganization as recorded by

TABLE 15–2
List of Firms Reorganized with Dates of Entry and Exit
from Chapter 11[a]

Name of Firm	Entry Date	Exit Date	Number of Years in Reorganization
Boston & Main Corp.[b]	3/12/70	6/30/83	13.3
Elcor	7/20/71	8/08/71	0.10
Reading[b]	11/23/71	12/31/80	9.13
Bohack (Key International Manuf.)	7/30/74	11/11/79	5.34
Daylin	2/26/75	10/20/76	1.65
Chicago Rock Island and Pacific Railway[b]	3/17/75	6/01/84	9.25
Continental Mortgages	3/03/76	3/31/83	7.06
GAC Corp	6/07/76	10/01/80	4.33
Permaneer	6/25/76	11/15/78	2.40
Duplan	8/31/76	6/04/81	4.76
Allied Supermarkets	11/06/76	10/14/81	4.94
Interstate Stores (Toys 'R' Us)	3/11/77	4/04/78	1.07
Metroplex	12/30/77	10/15/79	1.80
Commonwealth Oil Refining Co.	3/02/78	7/24/81	3.40
Food Fair	10/03/78	7/17/81	2.83
Inforex	10/24/79	9/26/80	.93
Penn-Dixie Ins. (Continental Steel Corp.)	4/07/80	3/15/82	1.90
White Motor (NE Ohio Axle)	9/04/80	11/28/83	3.24
Itel Corp.	1/19/81	9/19/83	2.67
Seatrain Lines[b]	2/11/81	4/10/87	6.16
Sambo's	11/27/81	7/30/84	2.67
Morton Shoe	1/07/82	8/01/83	1.56
Bobbie Brooks	1/15/82	2/16/83	1.08
A. M. International	4/14/82	9/25/84	2.45
Saxon	4/15/82	3/22/85	2.94
Wickes	4/24/82	1/26/85	2.76
Braniff	5/13/82	12/15/83	1.60
Revere Copper	10/27/82	8/12/85	2.80
Continental Air	9/24/83	9/02/86	2.92
Anglo Energy	11/04/83	8/28/86	2.92

Mean = 3.67 years
Standard deviation = 2.88 years

[a] Names in parentheses are names of reorganized firms, if different.
[b] Railroad.

The Capital Changes Reporter included preferred (convertible or otherwise), convertible debt, straight debt (including some mortgages), and notes (including income notes). In a small number of cases, we have been able to obtain (from the reorganization documents) details of some nontraded claims.

Value and Type of Securities Issued on Reorganization

In Table 15–3 we detail the market value of the new securities given in exchange for the old securities. For each security we provide the adjusted face value in brackets and the market value of the securities issued in exchange immediately above. The face values have been adjusted to include accrued interest. The latter either is obtained from *The Capital Changes Reporter*, or has been calculated using the coupon rate on the security. In some cases this adjustment does not appear to be correct. In the case of CRIP, a mortgage bond received $63.095 million in exchange for an adjusted face value of $42.535 million. In this case the coupon was very low (2⅞ percent) and the debt was contracted to mature prior to reorganization. If we assume a market rate of interest is applied after the stated redemption date (the reorganization date) to accrue interest the adjusted face value very closely approximates the market value of the securities issued.

For particular securities, there is no face value or one is not given; as a result it is not possible to know what amount they should obtain in liquidation. In this case, a deviation from absolute priority cannot be established.

Reorganizations which show deviations from absolute priority are indicated by a superscript *a* in Table 15–3. To calculate such deviations the priority of securities in liquidation must be known. For some securities including equities, preference shares, convertibles, mortgages, debentures, and income notes, the seniority is usually clear. However, in other cases the seniority is less clear. For example, in the case of CRIP two mortgage notes are outstanding and one is not designated as senior to the other. In these cases we have amalgamated the two securities for the purposes of calculating deviations from absolute priority. It should be noted that the maturities of the bonds are different and this may have raised issues as to seniority.

Of the 27 firms described in Table 15–3, 21 exhibit deviations from absolute priority. Of these 21, stockholders in 18 actually receive some consideration. It does appear that deviations from absolute priority are the rule rather than the exception. There are some striking deviations. In the case of Bohack Corporation stockholders received more than $0.57 million

TABLE 15–3
Market Value (in Millions of Dollars) of New Securities Given to Each Type of Security Outstanding Prior to Reorganization and Their Respective Adjusted Face Values (in Parentheses)

| | All Securities on | | | | MV of Claims to: | | | |
Firm	Reorganization	Equity	Preferred	Convertible Preferred	Convertible Debt	Debt	Notes	Other
B & M[a]	48.847	0	0			18.249 (mort) (21.632)	30.598 (inc) (33.641)	
Elcor	9.061				9.061 (12.566)			
Reading[a]	258.88	98.08				70.56 (1st mort) (71.62) 90.24 (Gen mort) (193.30)		
Bohack[a]	.573	.559			.014 (6.354)			
Daylin[a]	29.414				.796 (3.746)	28.618 (59.277)		
CRIP	222.91	42.357				63.095 (SHmort) (42.535) 28.524 (LGmort) (24.263)	88.934 (inc) (75.585)	
Continental Mortgages	101.802	0			101.802 (124.041)			
GAC[a]	139.548	0	0		6.807 (SH) (11.908) 38.467 (LG) (68.475)	49.136 (SH) (70.589) 45.138 (LG) (68.589)		
Permaneer[a]	3.963	1.297				1.350 (SH) (8.744)		

Company							
Duplan	.2102			.2102 (2.565)	1.316 (LG) (5.921)		
Allied Supermarkets[a]	15.746	7.175					
Interstate	40.170	39.692			8.570 (23.816)		
Metroplex[a]	18.849	.888		.477 (.458)	17.960 (22.575)		
CORCO[a]	77.85	52.50	7.36 (32.00)	17.99 (20.74)			
Food Fair[a]	68.978	41.093				6.21 (SH) (11.59) 21.675 (LG) (39.342) 17.071 (SH) (17.673) 19.449 (LG) (20.160)	
Inforex[a]	38.266	1.746					
Penn-Dixie[a]	20.216	11.365		8.851 (9.887)			
White Motor[a]	94.351	81.865		1.918 (16.244)	5.878 (SH) (10.900) .804 (LG 11%) (8.089) 3.886 (LG 12%) (8.186) 175.878 (298.851)		
Itel Corp[a]	183.447	7.569					
Bobbie Brooks[b]	38.75	13.596				9.810 (SH) (11.247) 10.816 (LG) (12.184)	4.527 (CL) (4.170)

Table concluded, overleaf

TABLE 15–3, concluded

			MV of Claims to:					
Firm	All Securities on Reorganization	Equity	Preferred	Convertible Preferred	Convertible Debt	Debt	Notes	Other
A. M. International[a,b]	218.8	40.41			40.51 (12.38)	137.88 (46.85)		
Saxon[a]	23.623	8.988			4.183 (S) (14.735) 6.762 (J) (23.487)	3.690 (13.090)		
Wickes[a]	463.81	55.157	5.926 (22.500)	2.592 (18.167)	16.025 (34.346)	167.73 (190.896)	216.380 (425.280)	
Braniff[a]	85.533	3.316				39.587 (S) (57.120) 2.064 (J) (27.333)	40.566 (S) (58.209)	
Revere[a]	104.390	81.052				23.338 (26.491)		
Continental Air	372.745	322.072			27.095 (27.095)	23.578 (23.735)		
Anglo Energy[b]	238.05	28.125				182.738 (S) (189.679) 26.888 (J) (23.826)		.3 (A/P) (3.084)

[a] Indicates deviations from absolute priority. **SH** = short, **LG** = long, **S** = senior, **J** = junior, **A/P** = accounts payable, **CL** = capital lease, **inc** = income note, **mort** = mortgage.
[b] The debt settlement was given per $100 of "allowable claim." Since we could not determine what proportion of the debt claim was allowable we assumed 100%.

even though convertible debtholders received only $14,000 (where the adjusted face value was $6.354 million).[7] Other features include:

(i) For Anglo, holders of accounts payable (A/P) received $.3 million which constituted less than 10 percent of its face value (without any accrued interest). In contrast, short and long bonds were virtually repaid in full (including accrued interest).

(ii) For Bobbie Brooks, the holder of the capital lease received full repayment including accrued interest, whereas noteholders did not receive full repayment. We suspect the lease was secured on property whose value equalled or exceeded the full amount owed.

(iii) For White Motor, the short debentures and the 12 percent long-term debt received 54 percent and 47 percent, respectively, of what was owed but the 11 percent long-term debt received only 10 percent. Possibly this was the result of differences in seniority (and security).

(iv) For GAC all four debt securities outstanding received between 51 and 70 percent of their adjusted face value whereas the equity received nothing. In contrast, for Food Fair the debt securities received between 54 and 55 percent of face value, whereas the equity received almost 60 percent of the total proceeds available.

(v) For Braniff the senior debt received about 69 percent of face value, the junior debt received only 13 percent, and the equity received in dollar terms more than the junior.

These results suggest that unsecured creditors receive only a small fraction of what secured creditors obtain, and that there are large deviations from absolute priority. Such a pattern of deviations may not present difficulties for some legal scholars such as Baird and Jackson (1988), who suggest they reflect a recontracting process between stockholders and senior creditors:

> The problem (of deviations from absolute priority) is presented most starkly when the firm is worth less than what the most senior creditor is owed and the senior creditor has reason to recombine with the old shareholder. The effect of the recombination would be to freeze out an intermediate creditor.... From this baseline, then, one can argue that intermediate creditors have lost nothing when the senior creditor exercises those rights and then decides to share the assets it thereby acquires with the old shareholder.... Under this view, the senior creditor, having the exclusive right to a firm's assets following foreclosure, should be able to convey an interest in them to anyone it pleases. (pp. 3 and 4).

There are, however, limitations on the extent to which deviations from absolute priority will be sanctioned by the court. In *Northern Pacific Railway* vs. *Boyd*, the Supreme Court struck down a transaction that froze out an intermediate class of owners while granting some ownership rights to former shareholders. It is an interesting question the extent to which observed deviations from absolute priority reflect wealth transfers from one class of security holders to another class of securityholders, when the former does not initiate the reorganization plan.

There are three other explanations of deviations from absolute priority to that provided by Baird and Jackson. One is that the deviations are caused simply by the bargaining powers to the debtor-in-possession. The ability to remain in Chapter 11 when the costs are borne by the firm, and therefore in most part by creditors, may encourage the latter to give something to the equity holder. By contrast, in Baird and Jackson's framework this recontracting reflects more management's unique ability to preserve firm value rather than the bargaining powers conferred by law. The third explanation is based on misrepresentation. Managers usually know more than creditors about firm value. They overstate values so that new equity (or quasi-equity) securities are worth less than that anticipated by creditors and judges. The deviations reflect these differences in value when the truth is revealed.[8] Finally, some deviations from absolute priority may reflect bankruptcy proceedings using (imputed) market values rather than book values for liabilities.

We formally calculate deviations from absolute priority as follows. To begin with, assume there is only one security in each creditor class, and that each security has a face value, then the amount P_j a creditor should have obtained under absolute priority for a security j is

$$P_j = \min(D_j, F - \sum_{J=j+1}^{n} S_J) \tag{15.1}$$

where

   D_j = face value of claim j adjusted for interest in Chapter 11 at the coupon rate on the security

   F = total market value of all securities distributed at reorganization

   S_J = market proceeds to all the more senior claimholders J where $J = j+1, j+2, ..., n$ assuming absolute priority prevails

When there is more than one security in each class equation (15.1) becomes

$$P_j = \frac{D_j}{\sum_{i=1}^{m} D_i} \min(\sum_{i=1}^{m} D_i, F - \sum_{l=i+1}^{N} S_l) \qquad (15.2)$$

where $\sum_{i=1}^{m} D_i$ is the adjusted face value of all securities in a particular class i. A deviation from absolute priority, X_j, for security j is measured by

$$X_j = A_j - P_j \qquad (15.3)$$

where A_j is the market value of the securities actually received by security j. We can express the deviation X_j as a proportion of the aggregate proceeds of reorganization. The sum of the deviations as a proportion of the total value of the claims given is simply $\sum_j X_j / F$. For each company in reorganization we calculate this deviation from absolute priority. This measure is based upon the assumption that judges in bankruptcy base liabilities on the face value of financial claims rather than their market value.

In order to compare deviations from absolute priority across companies an index of deviations for each company has been constructed. For each individual firm the deviations for each security are squared and then summed. To normalize, the sum of the square is divided by 2, to obtain an index with bounds of [0,1]. The construction of such an index is inevitably arbitrary. For example, the value of the index declines as the number of securities increases.

We conjecture that as the market value of securities at reorganization increases as a proportion of the adjusted face value of all securities, so the deviations from absolute priority decrease. Thus, as F/D_j increases, $\sum_j X_j / F$ diminishes. Given that there are deviations from absolute priority in our sample, it is interesting to determine which types of securities bear the costs of the greatest deviations, and how the size of proceeds received by stockholders compares with the proceeds received by those security holders who have given up some priority of payment. We also conjecture from the provisions of the 1978 code and from conversations with lawyers and a bankruptcy judge that deviations from absolute priority have increased as a result of the 1978 Act.[9] It may also be that the deviations are different depending upon the proposer of the plan (old management, new management, or creditors).

Our results are tabulated in Table 15–4. As expected, for some firms these deviations are large; for example, Bohack, Saxon, Allied Supermarkets, Food Fair, Permaneer, and Reading Corporation.

TABLE 15–4
An Index of Deviations from Absolute Priority for each Reorganized Firm

Firm	Index of Deviations	Equity	Preferred	Convertible Preferred	Convertible Debt	Debt	Notes	Other
B & M	.005	0				-.0693	.0693	
Elcor	.000	.00			.00			
Reading	.142	.379				-.004 (1st mort) -.375 (Gen mort)		
Bohack	.96	.98			-.98			
Daylin	.0003				.027	-.027		
CRIP	.000	0				0	0	
Cont. Mort.	.000	.00			.00			
GAC	.103	.0	.0		.322	-.322		
Permaneer	.107	.327				-.327		
Duplan	.000	.00			.00			
Allied Supermarkets	.207	.455				-.455		
Interstate	.000	.00			.00			
Metroplex	.002	.0472			-.0472			
CORCO	.113	.352	-.317		-.035			
Food Fair	.112	.334				-.334		
Inforex	.0011	.0343				-.0343		
Penn-Dixie	.003	.051				-.051		

White Motor	.082	.328		-.152	-.176		
Itel	.002	.041			-.041		
Bobbie Brooks	.009	.0634				-.0724	.009 (CL)
A. M. International[a]	.243	-.545		.129	.416		
Saxon	.180	.380		-.160 (SH) .177 (LG)	-.398		
Wickes	.033	.119	.013	.035	-.050	-.122	
Braniff	.002	.0188	.006		-.0629 (S) .0241 (J)		
Revere	.0011	.03		-.03			
Continental Air	.000	0	0	0			
Anglo	.0011	.0278			-.029 (S) .0129 (J)		-.0117 (A/P)

[a] The debt settlement was given per $100 of "allowable claim." Since we could not determine what proportion of the debt claim was allowable we assumed 100%.

In Table 15–5 the type and value of new securities issued in exchange for the old securities are described. Existing holders of equity always receive new equity in exchange. In contrast other creditors may receive varying combinations of equity, cash, debt, and notes. An interesting question arises as to what determines the type of new instruments issued. It seems likely that the greater the uncertainty surrounding the value of the emerging enterprise the greater the role for equity-like instruments.

THE EFFECT OF CHAPTER 11 ON A FIRM'S INVESTMENT AND FINANCING DECISIONS

The treatment of default is crucial to the firm's capital structure decision and the pricing of risky debt. It is commonly assumed that, when the firm defaults on its debt, the firm is taken over by the bondholders and the proceeds from liquidation shared out between creditors according to the rules of absolute priority [see, for example, Merton (1974), Titman (1984), and Myers (1977)]. For the purposes of illustration, we examine how the recontracting process of Chapter 11 will affect the underinvestment problem discussed by Myers and the pricing of risky debt modelled by Merton.

Myers's Underinvestment Problem

In Myers's (1977) model, if the firm financed the purchase of future investment opportunities (i.e., "growth" opportunities) with debt finance, managers acting in stockholders' interest had an incentive in some states of the world not to invest in positive NPV projects. Myers assumed the value of growth opportunities was unique to the firm, and that the debt matured after the decision to invest. In the light of the description and evidence of the Chapter 11 process the underinvestment problem should be ameliorated if not eliminated. An example will illustrate the point. Assume the following balance sheet for the firm:

Assets in Place	70	Equity	0
NPV of growth opportunities	15	Debt (face value = 100)	85
	85		85

The growth opportunities require an investment of $35 and have a present value of $50. In this case there is no incentive for a stockholder-oriented

TABLE 15–5
The Type and Value of New Securities Issued in Exchange for the Old Securities

Firm	Old Security	Equity	Cash	Preferred	Convertible Preferred	Liquid Preferred	Debt	Convertible Debt	Notes	War- anties
B & M	bonds (mort)		18.249							
	notes (inc)		30.598							
Elcor	conv. debt	9.061								
Reading	equity	98.08								
	first mortg		3.87				66.69			
	gen mortg		77.46				12.78			
Bohack	equity	.559								
	conv. debt	.014								
Daylin	debt	16.312	4.579				5.151		2.576	
	conv. debt						.634		.162	
CRIP	equity	42.357								
	bonds (SHmort)	42.57				20.52				
	bonds (LGmort)	22.67				5.85				
	notes (inc)	51.95				36.98				
Cont. Mort	conv. debt		38.074	47.542			16.186			
GAC	debt (SH)	20.052	15.338				13.746			
	debt (LG)	18.859	13.393				12.886			
	conv. debt (SH)	2.800	2.127				1.880			
	conv. debt (LG)	15.830	11.988				10.649			
Permaneer	equity	1.297								
	debt (SH)	1.350								
	debt (LG)	1.316								
Duplan	conv. debt	.0121	.1981							
Allied	equity	7.175								
Superm.	debt	5.870	2.700							
Interstate	equity	39.692								
	conv. debt	.477								

Table continued, overleaf

TABLE 15-5, concluded

Firm	Old Security	Equity	Cash	Preferred	Convertible Preferred	Liquid Preferred	Debt	Convertible Debt	Notes	Warranties
Metroplex	equity	.888								
	debt	17.96								
Corco	equity	52.50								
	pref.	7.36								
	conv. debt		.13				17.86			
Food Fair	equity	41.093								
	debt (SH)	4.508	.529	.931		.254				
	debt (LG)		14.352	5.938		1.386				
Inforex	equity	1.746							16.113	
	debt (SH)	.958							18.351	
	debt (LG)	1.092								
Penn-Dixie	equity	11.365								
	conv. debt	.301	8.550							
White Motor	equity	81.865								
	debt (SH)	1.575	4.303							
	debt (LG11%)		.804							
	debt (LG12%)	1.078	2.808							
	conv. debt		1.918							
Itel	equity	7.569								
	debt	25.854	100.250	5.804					43.970	
Bobbie Brooks	equity	13.596								
	notes (LG)	.875	9.941							
	notes (SH)	.793	9.017							
	leases	.366	4.161							
A. M. Intern	equity	40.41	98.74							
	debt	39.14	29.01							
	conv. debt	11.50								
Saxon	equity	8.988								
	debt		2.915	.775						
	conv. debt (S)		5.342	1.420						
	conv. debt (J)		3.305	.878						

		1	2	3	4	5	6	7
Wickes	equity	50.800						
	pref	5.926						
	conv. pref	2.592						4.357
	debt	56.36	28.18	58.71				
	conv. debt	14.631	1.394				24.48	
	notes	75.29	45.21	68.06			19.07	8.75
Braniff	equity	3.316						
	debt (S)	1.314	35.419					1.049
	debt (J)	36.202	.750			3.119		
	notes (S)					3.312		1.052
Revere	equity	81.052						
	debt	9.452						
Continental Air	equity	322.027		3.664	10.222			
	debt		6.015	17.563				
	conv. debt		2.597	24.498				
Anglo	equity	28.125						
	debt (S)	73.688	42.30	66.75				
	debt (J)	10.688	1.20	15.00				
	A/P	.30						

management to raise equity and invest since the total NPV will accrue to creditors. The equity would be worth $20 after investment compared with the initial investment required of $35. As a result, the NPV of the growth opportunities would disappear, the firm would be worth $70, and the debt would have a value of $70.

The recontracting process in Chapter 11 could overcome this underinvestment problem. The deviations from absolute priority are consistent with debtholders reducing the face value of their financial claims and thereby increasing the value of equity holders' claims. One purpose could be to provide incentives for a stockholder-oriented management to increase firm value. Using our prior example, if debtholders agreed to write down the face value of their claims from $100 to $75, the incentives to invest in the growth opportunities would be restored. The balance sheet after investment would be:

Assets in place	70	Equity	45
Present value of growth opportunities	_50_	Debt (face value = 75)	_75_
	120		120

The value of the equity is $45 after the investment of $35. If debtholders did not agree to write down their claims the market value of their claims would only be $70, compared with the current value of $75.

Valuation of Risky Debt

In his seminal analysis of the pricing of risky debt, Merton (1974) assumes absolute priority in the event of default. However, subsequent empirical analysis has shown that, for reasonable parameter values, spreads between risky and default-free interest rates based on absolute priority are significantly less than observed spreads. In this section we provide a framework for valuing risky debt which incorporates a number of the essential features of Chapter 11.

We assume informational symmetry. That is, the true value of the firm is known by all, including management, creditors, and the courts.

Without loss of generality, we assume that B dollars of pure discount debt is due at time T. Management, acting in the best interests of equityholders, has the exclusive right to declare Chapter 11. That is, if on the maturity date T the firm cannot pay off its debt, it can exercise its option to delay until time $T^* > T$. If the firm is not reorganized at T^*, we assume the judge imposes absolute priority via the cram-down procedure. The total value of equity, $E(T)$, is given by

$$E(T) = \max [C(T), e(T)], \tag{15.4}$$

where
  $e(T) \equiv$ value of equity at time T in the absence of Chapter 11,
  $C(T) \equiv$ value of the option to pay the face value of the debt (adjusted for accrued interest) at any time through T^*.

It should be noted that the option to delay is an American option. That is, once in Chapter 11, management has the right to fulfill its contractual obligations at any point in time through the option's expiration date, T^*. Furthermore, interest is assumed to accrue at the prevailing risk-free rate of interest; this is a simplification. As a result, the exercise price of the option increases deterministically with time. The longer management takes to exercise its option, the larger the amount of accrued interest due.

The direct administrative and legal costs of Chapter 11 are financed by the future cash flows of the firm. Management does not issue additional equity to finance these costs. We assume that costs, proportional to the value of the firm, are incurred continuously throughout the Chapter 11 process. This assumption, as opposed to a fixed cost paid upon entry, more accurately reflects how costs are incurred in reorganization.

The ability to avoid future legal and administrative costs may provide an incentive for creditors to purchase the debtor-in-possession's option to continue in Chapter 11. To make the point, assume that just prior to cram-down it is known that the debtor-in-possession's claim will be worthless at T^*. Both creditors and the debtor-in-possession can be made better off by creditors simply writing down their claims by a fraction α, $0 \leq \alpha \leq 1$, of the costs saved and giving this amount to the debtor-in-possession. Bargaining between creditors and the debtor-in-possession will determine α which is assumed exogenously specified. As a result deviations from absolute priority reflect not only the fair value of the option to delay but also a premium reflecting future administrative and legal costs saved.

We assume that an initial period of time t ($0 \leq t \leq T^*$) is required to resolve the more serious conflicts among creditors through the acquisition of information, or entry into Chapter 11 is required to make threats credible [as in strikes, see Hayes (1984)]. If $t = 0$ there is as incentive for a firm not to enter Chapter 11 and reorganize outside. We assume t is exogenously specified. Beginning at time t creditors are assumed to have an incentive to purchase the option to delay. When the option is purchased, the financial claims of creditors will be written down and those of the stockholders written up. Such changes appear as deviations from absolute priority.

We now compare Merton risky debt prices with risky debt prices which reflect the preceding modelling of the Chapter 11 process. For reasonable parameter values, risk premia in the presence of Chapter 11 can be significantly larger than risk premia in the absence of Chapter 11.

The value of the firm is assumed to be log-normally distributed with variance s^2. We assume the firm's volatility is not altered by its entry into Chapter 11. A flat term structure of risk-free interest rates at 10% is assumed throughout. We use the binomial algorithm to solve the relevant partial differential equation subject to the appropriate boundary conditions characterizing the particular default assumption.

In Table 15–6 we consider the pricing of a risky pure discount bond with an original term to maturity of $T - t = 15$ years. It is assumed that costs C equal 5% of the value of the firm and are paid continuously in Chapter 11. In the bargaining between debtor-in-possession and creditors the proportion of total costs paid as a premium to equityholders is 50 percent ($\alpha = .50$). For a given $T^* - T$, t, s^2, and d (Merton's quasi-debt to firm value ratio) we tabulate both the differences in risk premia measured in basis points (Δ) and the corresponding relative differences ($\%\Delta$). Notice that these differences can be substantial. For example, for $T^* - T = 3$, $t = 2$, $d = 1.0$, and $s^2 = .10$, the difference in risk premia is 109 basis points. Also a number of interesting patterns emerge.

Given d, $T^* - T$ and t, we can conclude that Δ and $\%\Delta$ increase with volatility s^2. For example, for $T^* - T = 2$, $t = 1$, $d = 1.0$, and $s^2 = .03$, the difference in risk premium in the two models is 61 basis points, compared with 88 basis points when volatility increases to .20. The larger the volatility the more valuable the option to delay and therefore the greater the risk-adjusted rate of interest.

Given s^2 and d, we can conclude that Δ and $\%\Delta$ increase with $T^* - T$ for given t. For example, for $s^2 = .10$ and $d = 1.0$, $D = 109$ basis points for $T^* - T = 3$ and $\tau = 2$; $\Delta = 134$ basis points for $T^* - T = 4$ and $t = 2$; and $\Delta = 157$ basis points for $T^* - T = 5$ and $\tau = 2$. The longer in Chapter 11 the more valuable the call option to equityholders, and hence the greater risk-adjusted interest rate required on debt.

TABLE 15-6
Comparison of Risk Adjusted Interest Rates with and without Chapter 11

s²	d	T*-T=5 τ=2 Δ	%Δ	T*-T=4 τ=2 Δ	%Δ	T*-T=3 τ=2 Δ	%Δ	T*-T=2 τ=1 Δ	%Δ	T*-T=1 τ=1/3 Δ	%Δ
.03	0.2	5	0.5	4	0.4	4	0.4	2	0.2	1	0.1
	0.5	52	4.9	44	4.2	36	3.5	24	2.3	12	1.2
	1.0	139	11.6	117	9.8	95	7.9	61	5.1	30	2.5
	1.5	193	14.1	162	11.9	129	9.5	83	6.0	40	3.0
	3.0	255	14.6	212	12.1	167	9.6	105	6.0	50	2.9
.10	0.2	63	5.9	43	4.0	35	3.3	24	2.3	13	1.2
	0.5	124	10.2	89	7.3	73	6.0	49	4.1	26	2.1
	1.0	157	11.2	134	9.5	109	7.7	72	5.1	36	2.6
	1.5	202	13.0	154	9.9	124	7.9	89	5.7	41	2.6
	3.0	226	12.1	190	10.2	152	8.1	97	5.2	48	2.6
.20	0.2	115	9.4	100	8.1	83	6.7	57	4.6	30	2.4
	0.5	173	12.2	126	8.8	103	7.2	81	5.7	37	2.6
	1.0	191	11.7	163	10.0	133	8.2	88	5.4	46	2.8
	1.5	223	12.6	190	10.7	153	8.6	102	5.7	51	2.8
	3.0	255	12.4	197	9.5	158	7.7	103	5.0	52	2.5

$(T - t) = 15$ $\alpha = .50$ $C = .05$

Δ = differences in risk-adjusted rates expressed in basis points
%Δ = percentage differences in risk adjusted rates
$T - t$ = original maturity of debt
α = proportion of costs saved paid to equityholders

C = costs of bankruptcy as a proportion of the value of the firm
$T^* - T$ = maximum period to be spent in Chapter 11
τ = end of year in which creditors buy out option to remain in Chapter 11

CONCLUSION

In this chapter, we have described the rights of the debtor-in-possession in Chapter 11. Chapter 11 provides the debtor-in-possession with a valuable option, and we have shown how that option may be priced into risky debt. Using simulation, we have compared the risk-adjusted rates of interest with the option to enter Chapter 11 with the risk adjusted rates without that option. The differences can be substantial.

We investigated a sample of thirty firms to determine the period spent in reorganization. In addition, we determined the market values of new securities each security holder obtained on reorganization and compared them with the amounts owed. We observed that substantial deviations from absolute priority frequently occurred in our sample in favour of stockholders. One explanation for these deviations is the bargaining framework of Chapter 11. The essential features of this framework are that a stockholder-oriented management remains in control of the firm, it can protract the proceedings especially when it retains the exclusive right to propose a reorganization plan, and the costs of reorganization are paid out of the firm's cash flows and therefore are borne (in large part) by creditors. As a result, creditors may have an incentive to buy the stockholders' Chapter 11 option prior to expiration to avoid some of those costs. A deviation from absolute priority reflects the purchase of the option. An alternative explanation is that put forward by Baird and Jackson—that deviations reflect a recontracting process between stockholders and other creditors which recognizes the ability of a stockholder-oriented management to preserve value. An example of the value of such recontracting is a cure for the underinvestment problem described by Myers.

Many questions raised in this paper remain unanswered. For example, how efficient is the reorganization process in Chapter 11 compared with alternatives? (See Bebchuk (1988) for a contingent claims approach). The U.K. system reflects one alternative which has been far more creditor-oriented and has led to much shorter periods spent in reorganization. However, critics of the U.K. system point out that businesses are often prematurely liquidated. A second question is, how have lenders responded to the Chapter 11 process? For example, in leveraged buyouts have lenders demanded higher risk premiums or have they formed coalitions with other lenders who will cooperate in any subsequent reorganization? A third question is, how has the firm's capital structure altered as a result of the reorganization process? It may be that because of adverse selection problems risky debt cannot be efficiently priced so that debt markets become more incomplete. For example, secured debt seems less susceptible to problems of recontracting and misrepresentation than unsecured debt. Answers to these questions are left to another paper.

NOTES

1. Chapter 11 supersedes Chapters X, XI, and XII of the 1898 Bankruptcy Act as amended by the Chandler Act of 1938 [11 USC §§ 1101–74 (Supp. V 1981)].
2. Such reorganization plans could be worked out outside Chapter 11, and many are. For example, Wickes made efforts to reorganize outside Chapter 11, but gave up because the multiplicity of creditors (approximately 250,000) and subsequent lawsuits made agreement difficult; creditors' actions may be compared to those of depositors in bank "runs." This market failure is surely one justification for bankruptcy legislation.
3. In rare cases, creditors may seek to file an involuntary Ch. 11 petition against the company. For example, in 1987 a group of creditors filed such a petition against Rooney, Pace Group Inc. Also, in 1987 creditors filed a similar petition against Radice Corporation (see *The Wall Street Journal*, November 26, 1987).
4. For example, in the Wickes reorganization (one of the largest on record) Mr. Sigoloff and his management team replaced the pre-Chapter 11 management. Also, in A. H. Robbins, two top officers of the company were ousted because of protests by creditors that they had substantial conflicts of interest. It is an interesting question as to the extent to which creditors can get appointed a new board that is compliant with their interests. Some obstacles stand in their way—the fact that appointments may be recommended by nonexecutive directors who may side with stockholders' interests. Moreover the bankruptcy judge may find it inequitable if the managerial representatives of stockholder interests were interfered with by creditors.

   It is interesting to compare this approach with U.K. insolvency legislation. Until 1986, existing management was always removed and a receiver (or liquidator) appointed whose interests were primarily the repayment of creditors' claims. The new 1986 Insolvency Act has amended this approach by permitting in some cases an "administrator" to be appointed. The latter must act in interests of both creditors and owners (see Webb, 1988).
5. In the Wickes case administrative and legal costs of the reorganization totalled $250 million of which between $75 and $120 million are estimated to be incremental to Chapter 11. Those costs constitute between 16 and 26 percent of the value of securities distributed via the reorganization plan to former holders of publicly traded securities. These estimates are based on numbers provided to the SEC in registration documents and amended after discussions with Wickes management. In the case of Texaco, legal fees are estimated at $55 million for the 9-month period of reorganization and $31.5 million for the expenses of the creditor committees [see Cutler and Summers (1988)]. See Haugen and Senbet (1978) for a theoretical discussion of costs of bankruptcy.
6. The length of the period in Chapter 11 affects some creditors more than others.

Unsecured creditors may not be paid interest for the period in Chapter 11, whereas secured creditors accrue interest providing principal and interest does not exceed the value of their collateral.

7. Conversations with a judge in bankruptcy disclosed little surprise in such an outcome. The convertible debtholders are unsecured creditors and this class often fares particularly badly in reorganization. It is possible they would not have obtained more in a "cram-down" (i.e., under absolute priority). An interesting question raised by the convertible is whether the courts took account of the conversion feature. If so, the face value would not necessarily provide the correct benchmark for measuring deviations. An alternative explanation, given by Richard Roll, is that the convertible debt may be held by other more senior claimholders, and that they influence how the proceeds of the reorganized firm are paid. For example, it may be more tax efficient to be repaid in one form of claim than another or to have one claim repaid in full and another only partially repaid. In the case of Wickes, a group of income notes obtained less than 55 percent of their face value (excluding any accrued interest) on reorganization, whereas all of the other notes were paid virtually their face value. Those other notes were not income notes, but the differences remain stark. It has been suggested to us that the income note holders were widely dispersed and individually held small holdings. This may have affected their bargaining power in committee.

8. Misrepresentation may arise as a result of deviations from absolute priority. Say the face value of the debt is 100 and the true value of the firm $V = 101$. Given the bargaining process in Chapter 11 say stockholders obtain $.1V$ if $V \geq 90$, then stockholders will wish to misrepresent the firm as being below its true value so the firm can enter Chapter 11. Alternatively, if the true value of $V = 60$ and shareholders obtain $.05V$ if $60 \leq V < 90$ then there will be an incentive to misrepresent the firm value as being 90 or above. These incentives to misrepresent can only be effective if quasi-equity type are given in exchange for old securities. Such misrepresentation may give rise to a bargaining framework [see Giammarino (1987) and Aumann and Maschler (1985)].

9. Morse and Shaw (1988) conclude from an event study using share price data that firms entering reorganization did not obtain, on average, greater gains as a result of the 1978 Act.

REFERENCES

Altman, E. J., and S. A. Nammacher, 1985, "The default rate experience on high yield corporate debt," *Financial Analysts Journal*, 25–38.

Aumann, R. J., and M. Maschler, 1985, "Game theoretic analysis of a bankruptcy problem from the Talmud," *Journal of Economic Theory 36*, 195–213.

Baird, D. G., and T. H. Jackson, 1988, "Bargaining after the fall and the contours of the absolute priority rule," *University of Chicago Law Review 55*, 738–89.

Bebchuk, Lucian A., 1988, "A new approach to corporate reorganization," *Harvard Law Review 101*, 775–804.

Boyes, William J., and R. L. Faith, 1986, "Some effects of the Bankruptcy Reform

Act of 1978," *Journal of Law and Economics 39*, 139–49.

Brown, D., 1989, "Claimholder incentive conflicts in reorganization: The role of bankruptcy law," *Review of Financial Studies.*

Cutler, D., and L. Summers, 1988, "The costs of conflict resolution and financial distress: Evidence from Texaco-Pennzoil litigation," *Rand Journal of Economics 19*, 157–72.

Giammarino, R.M., 1989, "The resolution of financial distress," *The Review of Financial Studies 2,* 25–47.

Haugen, R. A., and L. W. Senbet, 1987, "The significance of bankruptcy costs to the theory of optimal capital structure," *Journal of Finance 70*, 383–93.

Hayes, Beth, 1984, "Unions and strikes with asymmetric information," *Journal of Labor Economics 2*, 57–83.

Klee, K. W., 1979, "All you ever wanted to know about cram down under the new bankruptcy code," *American Bankruptcy Law Journal,* 133–71.

Merton, R. C., 1974, "On the pricing of corporate debt: The risk structure of interest rates," *Journal of Finance 29*, 449–69.

Morse, D., and W. Shaw, 1988, "Investing in bankrupt firms," *Journal of Finance 45*, 1193–1206.

Myers, Stewart C., 1977, "Determinants of corporate borrowing," *Journal of Financial Economics 5*, 147–76.

Titman, Sheridan, 1984, "The effects of capital structure on a firm's liquidation decision," *Journal of Financial Economics 13*, 137–51.

Warner, J. B., 1977, "Bankruptcy, absolute priority, and the pricing of risky debt claims," *Journal of Financial Economics 4*, 239–76.

Webb, David C., 1988, "Does the 1986 Insolvency Act satisfy the creditors' bargain," London School of Economics unpublished paper.

White, M., 1983, "Bankruptcy costs and the new bankruptcy code," *Journal of Finance 38*, 477–88.

CHAPTER 16

ARE STOCKHOLDERS BETTER OFF WHEN DEBT IS RESTRUCTURED PRIVATELY?

Brian L. Betker
Julian R. Franks
Walter N. Torous

INTRODUCTION

Gilson, John, and Lang [1990, hereafter GJL] provide statistical evidence consistent with stockholders being systematically better off if their firm's debt is restructured privately as opposed to the firm reorganizing in Chapter 11. In particular, they show that cumulative stock returns are significantly higher when firms successfully restructure their debt outside Chapter 11.

This result has a number of important implications. For example, stockholders have an incentive to avoid the formal bankruptcy process and settle their financial difficulties out of court. As such, troubled firms are likely to find informal alternatives to bankruptcy increasingly attractive in dealing with financial distress [Jensen (1989)]. Furthermore, GJL's results suggest that the stock market is able to forecast a priori which firms will successfully work out their financial difficulties.

This chapter re-examines the statistical behavior of stockholder returns

Brian L. Betker, Julian R. Franks, and Walter N. Torous are affiliated with Ohio State University, London Business School, and the University of California, Los Angeles, respectively.

surrounding formal versus informal reorganizations. In contrast to GJL, we analyze a more recent sample of firms in financial distress with the additional requirement that these firms have publicly traded debt outstanding. While GJL find significantly higher abnormal stockholder returns for firms which complete workouts, our results show no difference in abnormal stockholder returns prior to the resolution of the workout attempt (i.e., successful workout or filing for Chapter 11). As a result, we find that the stock market has little *predictive* ability as to which of our firms will be able to avoid the Chapter 11 process. However, once the result of the workout attempt is known, we do find that returns to shareholders are greater for firms which successfully complete a workout, than for firms which fail and file for Chapter 11.

While previous authors have recognized the costs of formal reorganization, few have acknowledged the benefits of the Chapter 11 process. Accordingly, the second section of the chapter summarizes the advantages of formal reorganization. Stockholders may indeed be made better off in bankruptcy if management, acting in stockholders' best interests, chooses to enter Chapter 11 to take advantage of these benefits. The third section details our data while the fourth section provides evidence that stockholders are unable to predict which workout attempts will succeed and which will fail. The final section concludes the paper with a summary.

THE ADVANTAGES OF THE CHAPTER 11 PROCESS

Workouts are typically less costly than Chapter 11 reorganizations.[1] The costs of formal bankruptcy include direct costs such as legal fees and court costs as well as indirect costs including lost investment opportunities and the possible loss of customer and supplier relationships (Titman [1984]).

An interesting question is why firms enter Chapter 11. Given the costly nature of Chapter 11 and since a large number of insolvent firms do resort to formal reorganization, there must be benefits to Chapter 11 that cannot always be captured by the workout process. If some of these benefits accrue to stockholders, it is not a priori clear why stockholders will be made better off if debt is restructured outside Chapter 11.

First, there are non-unanimity requirements in Chapter 11. That is, the plan of reorganization requires acceptance by only a strict majority in each creditor class by number and two thirds in amount of allowed claims (Section 1126(c)).[2] The proposer of the plan may bind minority holdouts within a particular class subject to a best interests test which ensures that these creditors receive at least as much as they would have received in a Chapter 7 liquidation [Section 1129(a)(7)]. Furthermore, under certain circumstances, the proposer of the plan may use cram-down procedures to bind class hold-outs by forcing the nonassenting class to accept proceeds from a hypothetical liquidation according to the rules of absolute priority [Section 1129(b)].[3] The non-unanimity requirements of Chapter 11 provide a solution to the free rider problem inherent in workouts [Roe (1987)]. By the Trust Indenture Act of 1937, changing the principal amount, interest rate or maturity date of a publicly held bond requires approval of 100 percent of the bondholders. The free rider problem arises when certain creditors do not agree to renegotiate their claims in the hope of benefiting from other creditors' actions.

Second, filing for protection under Chapter 11 provides an automatic stay against creditor collection activity [Section 362(a)] thereby restraining further action against the debtor-in-possession. The orderly settlement of creditors' claims is further facilitated by the fact that Chapter 11 condemns the preferential treatment of any creditor within a particular class.

Third, Chapter 11 provides inducements to extend financing to the debtor-in-possession during the firm's formal reorganization. For example, a postpetition unsecured credit transaction in the debtor's ordinary course of business automatically has priority over all prepetition unsecured creditors [Section 364(a)]. In addition, to facilitate the funding of the reorganization, new securities issued in Chapter 11 are exempt from state and federal registration requirements [Section 1145(a)(1)]. A creditor's resale of a security received in a Chapter 11 reorganization is also exempt from state and federal registration requirements (Section 1145(b)).

Fourth, as a result of the Tax Reform Act of 1986, a change in ownership (defined to be when the old equity holders own less than 50% of any new equity issued) resulting from a workout severely restricts the use of net operating losses (NOLs) for tax purposes. By contrast, Chapter 11 is far less restrictive in terms of NOL preservation. The bankruptcy exception of the Internal Revenue Code, Section 382, sets out the guidelines under which NOLs may be preserved in the event of an ownership change. Also, any forgiveness of indebtedness in Chapter 11 is not a taxable event (Section 108 of the Internal Revenue Code), in contrast to workouts where it is fully taxable.[4]

Chapter 11 provides further advantages, including the ability to reject leases and executory contracts (Section 365), as well as collective bargaining contracts.[5] Chapter 11 also allows a firm to renegotiate potentially burdensome litigation judgments.

Some firms have sought to obtain the flexibility and cost savings of a workout with these advantages of Chapter 11. Such a combination is known as a prepackaged Chapter 11 in which the debtor-in-possession and major creditors agree informally to the firm's reorganization and then enter Chapter 11 to gain approval of the proposed plan. For example, this approach would be advantageous if large NOLs are available but a change in ownership is required as part of the restructuring; in this case a workout will put the NOLs at risk. A prepackaged Chapter 11 could also be used to overcome the free rider problem inherent in workouts.

In summary, there are distinct benefits to formal reorganization.[6] Since management, to a large extent, controls the reorganization process, it may be that the firm would enter Chapter 11 only if it were in the stockholders best interests.

DATA

The sample for this study consists of 120 firms which completed distressed restructurings during the period 1982–1990. Completion of a distressed restructuring is defined as an exchange of securities in an out-of-court workout, or emergence from a Chapter 11 bankruptcy proceeding.

Distressed firms are identified from Standard and Poor's *Creditwatch*, which reports changes in firms' debt ratings. Firms which had their S&P debt rating reduced to CCC ("vulnerable to default") or lower, or NR (not rated), were identified. *The Wall Street Journal Index* and the *Capital Changes Reporter* were reviewed to determine the status of these firms. An additional list of firms which completed Chapter 11 reorganizations was obtained from the *Bankruptcy DataSource*. There are 46 firms which completed out of court workouts and 74 firms which completed Chapter 11 reorganizations in the sample.

Monthly stock price data were obtained from the stock price tapes of the Center for Research in Security Prices (CRSP) of the University of Chicago. The CRSP tapes contain data for NYSE, AMEX, and NASDAQ firms. If a firm was delisted from these exchanges, additional stock prices were obtained from the Bank and Quotation Record and the Bankruptcy DataSource. Stock price data were collected starting 24 months prior to the first default on any debt, until the completion of the restructuring. A debt default is defined as a missed interest payment, a violation of a loan covenant, or an announcement that the firm intends to miss an upcoming interest payment. The completion of the restructuring is either an exchange of securities in a workout, or emergence from Chapter 11 bankruptcy.

RESULTS

The main results of this paper are contained in Tables 16–1 and 16–2. In these tables we present cumulative returns to the stocks of the sample firms over two intervals. In Table 16–1, returns are computed for the period from 24 months prior to the first default, up until one month prior to resolution of the workout attempt. The resolution of a workout attempt is defined as either an exchange of securities in an out-of-court workout or the filing of a petition for Chapter 11 bankruptcy. In Table 16–2, returns are computed from the month of default, until one month prior to the resolution of the workout attempt. Since we are interested in the stock market's ability to *predict* successful and unsuccessful workouts, we do not include the month of resolution in these return calculations.

Previous research [e.g., Aharony, Jones, and Swary (1980)] has found negative returns for bankrupt firms as far back as five years before the bankruptcy filing. By examining returns starting two years before the default we can gauge whether the market's ability to discriminate between successful and failed workouts begins well before a clear signal of financial distress such as a debt default. Tables 16–1 and 16–2 present the mean raw cumulative return, as well as the median, minimum, and maximum returns. A standard t-test tests whether the mean cumulative return is significantly different from zero, and whether the mean return for the workout firms is significantly different from the mean return for the Chapter 11 firms. A nonparametric Wilcoxon rank-sum test is also used to test whether the distribution of workout returns is significantly different from the Chapter 11 returns. Finally, market-adjusted returns are presented where the return on the stock is measured net of the return on the S&P 500.[7]

Turning first to Table 16–1, we examine summary statistics for the distributions of the cumulative returns from 24 months prior to the default, until one month before resolution of the workout attempt. The distributions for the workout and Chapter 11 firms are remarkably similar. The mean (*median*) return over this time span is –69.9 (*–85.1*) percent for failed workouts and –68.1 (*–80.6*) percent for successful workouts. Both the t-test and

TABLE 16–1

Cumulative Monthly Returns on Common Stock in the Period from 24 Months before the First Default on Any Debt Instrument by the Firm until One Month Prior to Resolution of the Workout Attempt[a]

	Cumulative Returns in (default–24, resolution–1)		
	Workouts	Chapter 11	t-test for difference in means (Wilcoxon rank-sum test)
N	46	74	
Mean Raw Return	−0.6811	−0.6986	$t = -0.27$
			$(Z = 0.33)$
Standard Deviation	0.2993	0.3983	
t	−15.43[b]	−15.09[b]	
Median	−0.8056	−0.8505	
Minimum	−0.9907	−0.9952	
Maximum	1.0766	1.1799	
Mean Market-Adjusted Return[d]	−1.2243	−1.0096	$t = -2.47$[c]
			$(Z = 2.53$[c]$)$
Standard Deviation	0.4277	0.4061	
t	−19.20[b]	−15.43[b]	
Median	−1.2670	−1.0639	
Minimum	−2.1302	−2.1150	
Maximum	1.0293	1.0552	

[a] Resolution is defined as either filing for Chapter 11 or exchanging securities in a workout. The sample is 120 firms which completed reorganizations between 1982 and 1990.
[b] p-value less than 0.01.
[c] p-value less than 0.05.
[d] Market-adjusted return is the return on the stock, minus the return on the S&P 500 index.

Source: Stock return data are obtained from the CRSP daily returns file, the *Bank and Quotation Record,* and the *Bankruptcy DataSource.*

the rank-sum test cannot reject the null hypothesis that the means and medians are the same. The standard deviations, minimums, and maximums are also very similar.

When considering market-adjusted returns, the mean return for Chapter 11 firms is actually significantly greater than the mean for workout firms, and the rank-sum test also rejects the hypothesis that the distribution of returns is the same.

Stockholders do not seem to be able to predict which firms will suc-

TABLE 16–2
Cumulative Monthly Returns on Common Stock in the Period from the First Default on Any Debt Instrument by the Firm until One Month Prior to Resolution of the Workout Attempt[a]

	Cumulative Returns in (default, resolution–1)		
	Workouts	Chapter 11	t-test for difference in means (Wilcoxon rank-sum test)
N	46	74	
Mean Raw Return	−0.3314	−0.2380	$t = 0.32$ $(Z = -1.91^d)$
Standard Deviation	0.5534	0.3781	
t	−4.06[b]	−5.30[b]	
Median	−0.5000	−0.2500	
Minimum	−0.9712	−0.9022	
Maximum	1.4284	1.0000	
Mean Market- Adjusted Return[e]	−0.5417	−0.2798	$t = 2.51^c$ $(Z = -3.00^b)$
Standard Deviation	0.6154	0.4339	
t	−5.97[b]	−5.43[b]	
Median	−0.5885	−0.2070	
Minimum	−1.6550	−1.6177	
Maximum	1.1797	0.9596	

[a] Resolution is defined as either filing for Chapter 11 or exchanging securities in a workout. The sample is 120 firms which completed reorganizations between 1982 and 1990.
[b] p-value less than 0.01.
[c] p-value less than 0.05.
[d] p-value less than 0.10.
[e] Market-adjusted return is the return on the stock, minus the return on the S&P 500 index.

Source: Stock return data are obtained from the CRSP daily returns file, the *Bank and Quotation Record,* and the *Bankruptcy DataSource.*

cessfully work out their financial difficulties, if returns are measured starting two years prior to the firm's default. Perhaps once the firm defaults, the market's predictive ability will improve. To investigate this, Table 16–2 presents cumulative returns measured from the month of default, up until one month prior to the resolution of the workout attempt.

Results from Table 16–2 indicate that shareholders are not able to predict which sample firms will succeed in their workout attempts, even after the firms default on their debt. Mean raw returns are not significantly different, and the rank-sum test indicates that the Chapter 11 firms have marginally higher raw returns over this time period. When market-adjusted returns are considered, both tests indicate that the returns of Chapter 11 firms are actually higher than those of the workout firms.

It is not until the month of resolution of the workout attempt that significant differences are seen in returns on the sample securities. In the month of resolution, firms which fail to complete a workout and instead file for Chapter 11 have a mean stock return of –36.4 percent, while the mean return for firms which successfully complete workouts is 4.9 percent, and the difference is statistically significant with a p-value of less than 0.0001. This is consistent with shareholders being better off on average if debt can be restructured outside of formal bankruptcy.

The ability of shareholders to identify firms which will succeed in workouts is markedly different in our sample of firms compared with GJL. An explanation for the difference in results may be sample selection procedures. GJL select their sample by looking at the firms with the lowest stock price performance over the previous three years. They report that 54 percent of their firms have no publicly traded debt. In contrast the sample selection procedure used here ensures that all the sample firms have publicly traded debt. When senior debt is restructured and there are no junior debt holders, any benefits of the restructuring would be captured by the shareholders. However, when there is junior debt, shareholders may be forced to share, or even concede, any benefits gained from the workout to the bondholders. An interesting question for further study would be to compare stock returns, as well as the terms of the reorganization, for distressed firms with and without publicly traded debt.

SUMMARY

We re-examine the ability of shareholders to predict which financially distressed firms will succeed in an out-of-court workout attempt, and which will fail and file for Chapter 11 bankruptcy. We find that cumulative returns as far as two years prior to the resolution of the workout attempt do not differ between the two sets of firms, indicating that the market cannot differentiate between them *a priori*. Returns in the month of resolution are significantly greater for successful workouts, however, indicating that shareholders are on average better off if debt can be restructured privately.

NOTES

1. See, for example, Warner (1977), Weiss (1990), and McMillan, Nachtmann, and Phillips-Patrick (1991).
2. Unless otherwise noted, references are to the Bankruptcy Reform Act of 1978, as amended in 1984.
3. See Klee (1979, 1990) for discussions of cram-down procedures in Chapter 11.
4. However, writedowns of debt in Chapter 11 are offset for tax purposes by any current or past operating losses. See McQueen and Crestol (1990) for a comprehensive discussion of the tax treatment of net operating losses of reorganized firms.
5. The Supreme Court in 1984 affirmed the right of a debtor to unilaterally reject a collective bargaining agreement. Congress responded by amending the Bankruptcy Code in 1984. Section 1113 of the Bankruptcy Amendments and Federal Judgeship Act of 1984 now allows the court to approve modification of collective bargaining contracts in Chapter 11 if the debtor makes a proposal to modify the agreement, the union rejects the proposal, and the "balance of equities" favors the modification.
6. There may be some benefits for creditors in filing for Chapter 11 as well. Giammarino (1989) argues that asymmetry of information between managers and creditors may cause a workout to fail. If the debtholders are uncertain about the firm's true value, then it may be optimal for them to obtain better information about the firm through a costly bankruptcy proceeding, rather than to accept the firm's initial workout offer.
7. Measuring abnormal returns for financially distressed firms using the market model is complicated by the lack of a suitable benchmark period for measuring "normal" returns. Clark and Weinstein (1983) and Morse and Shaw (1988) also use market-adjusted returns to analyze the behavior of bankrupt stocks.

REFERENCES

Aharony, Joseph; Charles P. Jones; and Itzhak Swary, 1980, "An analysis of risk and return characteristics of corporate bankruptcy using capital market data," *Journal of Finance 35*, 1001–16.

Clark, Truman A., and Mark I. Weinstein, 1983, "The behavior of the common stock of bankrupt firms," *Journal of Finance 38*, 489–504.

Franks, Julian R., and Walter N. Torous, 1989, "An empirical investigation of U.S. firms in reorganization," *Journal of Finance 44*, 747–69.

Giammarino, Ronald, 1989, "The resolution of financial distress," *Review of Financial Studies 2*, 25–48.

Gilson, Stuart C.; Kose John; and Larry H. P. Lang, 1990, "Troubled debt restructurings: An empirical study of private reorganization of firms in default," *Journal of Financial Economics 27*, 315–54.

Jensen, Michael C., 1989, "Active investors, LBOs, and the privatization of bankruptcy," *Journal of Applied Corporate Finance 2*, 235–44.

Klee, Kenneth N., 1979, "All you ever wanted to know about cram down under the new bankruptcy code," *American Bankruptcy Law Journal 53*, 133–71.

Klee, Kenneth N., 1990, "Cram down II," *American Bankruptcy Law Journal 64*, 229–44.

McMillan, Henry; Robert Nachtmann; and Fred Phillips-Patrick, 1991, "Costs of reorganizing under Chapter 11: Some evidence from the 1980s," U.S. Securities and Exchange Commission unpublished paper.

McQueen, C. Richard, and Jack Crestol, 1990, *Federal tax aspects of bankruptcy,* New York: McGraw-Hill.

Morse, Dale, and Wayne Shaw, 1988, "Investing in bankrupt firms," *Journal of Finance 43*, 1193–1206.

Roe, Mark J., 1987, "The voting prohibition in bond workouts," *The Yale Law Journal 97*, 232–79.

Titman, Sheridan, 1984, "The effect of capital structure on a firm's liquidation decision," *Journal of Financial Economics 13*, 137–52.

Warner, Jerold B., 1977, "Bankruptcy, absolute priority, and the pricing of risky debt claims," *Journal of Financial Economics 4*, 239–76.

Weiss, Lawrence A., 1990, "Bankruptcy resolution: Direct costs and violation of priority of claims," *Journal of Financial Economics 27*, 285–314.

CHAPTER 17

EMERGING TRENDS IN BANKRUPTCY REORGANIZATION

Edward I. Altman

The bankruptcy "game" is a big, complex business in the United States as we progress into the 1990s. As the legal-political-economic system concentrates more resources into the rehabilitation of ailing firms, it is not surprising to observe increased creativity and innovation within the evolving confines of bankruptcy law and its practice. This chapter will examine several major trends in the distressed firm arena which have either evolved into high-stakes issues and/or have been created to deal with the complexities of the multistakeholder Chapter 11 process. We will explore three major evolving trends:

- Fraudulent conveyance,
- Debtor-in-possession (DIP) financing, and
- Prepackaged Chapter 11s.

The first two are not new but have found new dimensions and importance in the aftermath of the leverage restructuring movement of the late 1980s and the attendant bankruptcies of very large entities. And the third new dimension, the prepackaged Chapter 11, is the direct result of attempts

Edward I. Altman is the Max L. Heine Professor of Finance and Professor of Finance, Leonard N. Stern School of Business, New York University, and Managing Director of Fixed Income and Credit Markets, NYU Salomon Center.

to expedite the rehabilitation of entities in the face of complex capital structures and contentious negotiation.

FRAUDULENT CONVEYANCE

The risk of increased corporate distress and possibly bankruptcy was always apparent in the high-stakes efforts to "buy out" companies by borrowing large amounts of funds in the private (bank-debt primarily) and public markets (high yield "junk" bonds primarily). These corporate restructurings involved small and medium-sized firms in the 1970s and early 1980s and were motivated by managements' efforts to become owners—called management buyouts (MBOs). As the target firms grew and the prices paid to buy out the entities increased in the mid and late 1980s, management usually teamed up with third-party "investment" or LBO (leverage-buyout) firms in order to purchase all of the public firm's stock, retire the stock, and bring the firm to "private" status. In some cases the bidding to buy the large firm was so competitive that the senior management found itself locked in a battle with an essentially outside-the-firm bidder, e.g., the $25 billion RJR Nabisco buyout won by the LBO firm Kohlberg, Kravis and Roberts over the existing senior management's bid.

All of this competition led to extremely high buyout prices or costly defensive strategies to thwart the takeover. And higher prices meant larger and more costly borrowings to pay for the transaction. What was not anticipated by the parties involved is that the transaction itself could create a situation where a "fraudulent conveyance" (FC) is created with huge potential liabilities for a number of the key players involved. This was labeled the "LBO Nightmare" by Michel and Shaked (1990) and has become increasingly a major issue in several court cases in the early 1990s.

FC: Roots and Central Concepts

The Bankruptcy Code clearly deals with the power to recover preferential transfers and to redistribute a bankrupt debtor's proceeds from one class of creditor to another. It does not solve the problem of some or all creditors' being prejudiced by a transfer of the debtor's property to a noncreditor. Transfers that are ruled fraudulent, however, are recoverable based on a law that was passed in England in 1571 under the statute of Elizabeth (13 Eliz., c. 5). This law carried over to the United States and held that transfers of property (e.g., a firm's assets) with the "intent" to hinder, delay, or defraud creditors are avoidable. Since the individuals that transfer their property (e.g., the old owners) will not admit that their actual intent was to defraud others, the courts must establish this event.

Two types of fraud are relevant, intentional or constructive, either one of which appears necessary to be demonstrated in a fraudulent conveyance case. *Intentional* fraud involves the Elizabethan law where willful intent is clearly shown. A modern day example of this is when an insolvent corporation transfers assets to other parties, e.g., old shareholders, prior to defaulting on its obligations and declaring bankruptcy, in order to hinder, delay, or defraud creditors. The transaction can then be considered void.

The second type of fraud involves *constructive* actions and applies to transfers of assets that unfairly harm creditors, regardless of whether the debtor intended to delay, hinder, or defraud. An unfair transfer will result if shareholders receive compensation prior to and to the detriment of creditors when a firm becomes insolvent. And that is precisely the case if the LBO transaction results in an insolvent entity—the old shareholders (and other parties) were paid off but certain debt holders lose all or part of their investment. [A particularly lucid discussion of fraudulent conveyance law in highly leveraged transactions can be found in Luehrman and Hirt (1991).] Losses may be incurred by the existing creditors from prior to the buyout or by the new creditors, particularly those that are unsecured. Indeed, we often find that one class of new creditor is a plaintiff in a fraudulent conveyance case, e.g., unsecured public debtholder, and another class is one of the defendants, e.g., the senior bank creditor. The latter is often involved in an LBO based on funds it provided as a "bridge-loan," enabling the transaction to take place between the time (the bridge) of the acceptance of the buyout offer and the raising of sufficient long-term capital, usually from the public debt markets. The argument against the banks is that the bridge loan was made to earn interest and fees in the months following the buyout without concern for the long-term viability of the new entity.

Was There a Fraudulent Conveyance?

In order to rule that an FC took place under a constructive fraud ruling, the courts must establish both that (1) there was not "equivalent value" or "fair consideration" given to the firm when the LBO took place and (2) the LBO transaction resulted either in the firm's "insolvency," its resulting "inadequate capitalization" to survive, or where the transfer was made with the likelihood that it would incur debts beyond its ability to pay. These conditions are specified under section 548(a)(2) of the Bankruptcy Code. "Equivalent value" terminology is found under the Code as well as in most state laws which have adopted the Uniform Fraudulent Transfers Act (UFTA) or the Uniform Fraudulent Conveyance Act (UFCA). While all three "Acts" are similar in content, one important difference is the statute of limitations. The Bankruptcy Code requires that a Chapter 11 filing be made within one year of the highly leveraged transaction (e.g., the LBO) in order for an FC action to be bought, while the UFTA has a four year limit; under the UFCA, states establish their own time limitation. For example, in New York the limit is six years. And section 544 of the Bankruptcy Code enables a plaintiff to bring an FC action under applicable state law, effectively lengthening the Code's statute of limitations to the longer state law period.

First, the question of whether the debtor received "reasonably equivalent value" is addressed. Both Luehrman and Hirt (1991) and Michel and Shaked (1990) persuasively argue that almost all LBOs will fail the equivalent value test since the law is interested only in how existing creditors fare from the transaction compared to what they would have realized if the LBO had not taken place. Since most of the FC suits involve defaults to these creditors, it is quite obvious that they were made worse off by the leveraged transaction. The courts are not interested in whether intangible values were created by the LBO, i.e., where more efficient firm operation created values greater than the out-of-pocket LBO fees incurred. While these values created by the LBO may be important, as long as they do not go to the debtor they are not considered relevant in an LBO FC defense. Indeed, in a typical LBO, the only tangible value received by the debtor relates to the repayment of any prior existing debt or an increase in cash. Since these amounts are almost always less than the increase in debt incurred after the LBO, the transaction will fail the "equivalent value" test.

The more difficult test relates to the firm's post-LBO financial condition. Insolvency or inadequate capitalization requires a valuation of assets and liabilities at the time of the LBO. While the various statutes give some guidance as to what is an insolvent condition, valid methodologies of valuation are not established. Under the UFCA, solvency is defined as when the present value of assets received in a "reasonably prompt sale" is greater than the amount that will be required to pay its probable liability on all existing debts. These debts include all liabilities, not just those found on the balance sheet, i.e., contingent claims, off-balance sheet liabilities, etc.

Courts have differed on whether assets should be valued on a liquidation or a going-concern basis. While the proceeds from a hypothetical distressed sale of assets at the time of the LBO have generally been deemed inappropriate, the adoption of a single valuation standard has not emerged. As is well known, valuation is an art and not a science, and apparently "true art" is in the eyes of the beholder (the court). Various authors have pointed out that valuations done in a number of related FC cases have utilized different criteria. For example, in the Gleneagles case (*U.S.* v. *Gleneagles Investment Company*, 565 F.Supp. 556 [Pa, 1983]), the court ruled that an FC did take place based on fraudulent intent and value was based on that amount that can be received from a reasonably prompt liquidation based on an arm's-length transaction in an existing and not a theoretical market. On the other hand, in *Vadnais Lumber Supply* v. *Byrne*, No. 88-4056 (Bankruptcy D. Mass., 1989), the court held that going-concern value is proper unless the business is very close to being discontinued. In other cases, the question of liquid versus illiquid assets has been debated. Luehrman and Hirt conclude that what may emerge is the use of several different approaches in order to make a decision. They cite the Revco case examiner's use of three different approaches to estimate going-concern value [see *In Re Revco D.S. Inc. et al. Final Report of Examiner Professor Barry Zaretsky*, 3 (Dec. 17, 1990) and *In Re Revco D.S. Inc.*, 118 B.R. 468 (Bankr. W. D. Ohio, 1990)].

Most academic and many consulting practitioner works on valuation [e.g., Copeland, et al., (1990) and Stewart, (1991)] recommend the use of a discounted present value approach. If the plaintiff–litigant, e.g., unsecured creditors, can prove that the secured lender or other defendants should have recognized the firm's insolvent condition, an FC will be deemed to have occurred. The asset values will then be deemed as inadequate to cover all the claims, including those of the unsecured creditors. In the event of a subsequent failure, a typical argument will be that appropriate financial analysis was not applied at the time of the LBO. It has been and will be alleged that a prudent or responsible analysis would have shown that the enormous new debt burden was not supportable.

Who Is at Risk in a Fraudulent Conveyance?

As MacEwen and Wilkens (1991) discuss, from a social viewpoint, there are two primary goals in assessing penalties to those found at fault in an FC case—restitution and deterrence. Restitution transfers wealth from the initial beneficiaries of the highly leveraged transaction to the relevant losing-creditor classes. Deterrence seeks to provide adequate disincentives for abusive behavior. The primary parties potentially at risk in an FC proceeding are

- Banks and other secured or senior lenders
- Pre-HLT insiders, e.g., management and directors
- Selling shareholders
- Professional advisors

The unsecured creditors can seek reparation from the senior and secured creditor and an "equitable-subordination" could be the result. This is where the court rules that unsecured creditors are given priority to collect their debts. In a case involving the Meritor Savings Bank of Philadelphia, a U.S. Bankruptcy Judge ruled, in Boston on May 21, 1991, that $8 million in bank loans, which provided funding for the 1987 buyout of O'Day Corporation, a manufacturer of Fiberglass sailboats, constituted a fraudulent conveyance because the bank had reason to know that the transaction would leave the company insolvent. The case is now under appeal. O'Day, a subsidiary of Lear Siegler, went into bankruptcy less than two years after the buyout via an involuntary petition of the same unsecured creditors. The involuntary petition came after the bank sought to foreclose on the company's assets.

It is interesting to note that in the O'Day case, the judge ruled that the bank knew that the financial projections for O'Day's performance were inaccurate and that while fraud was not the bank's intention, the course of action taken by the bank was to improve its own position at the cost of other creditors.

Advisor Liability

The O'Day decision is of interest for another reason—that of the role and liability of the financial advisor to the debtor/seller of the firm at the time of a highly leveraged transaction. Two current FC or potential FC cases involve the direct role of the advisor. In the Interco Corp. bankruptcy, the court appointed examiner found that the advisor, Wasserstein-Perrella, despite its poor performance in the ill-fated leveraged recapitalization, was not at fault since it was given inaccurate information to make forecasts of asset sales and earnings by the firm's management and thereby should not be held accountable. The Mayerson finding in the matter of *Interco Inc., et al.*, Case # 91-4-00442-172, U.S. Bankruptcy Court, Eastern District of Missouri, Report of Examiner Sandra E. Mayerson, October 23, 1991, although not legally binding, specifically addresses advisor liability.

In the case of the Revco D.S. Inc. 1986 LBO and subsequent bankruptcy, the advisor, Salomon Brothers, agreed on October 20, 1991, to pay nearly $30 million to settle a class action suit on the part of unsecured bond holders and a preferred stock issue. Salomon had been accused of failing to do "due diligence" in assessing the overly optimistic projections of management. Salomon denied these allegations but settled to avoid the expense of further litigation.

The Interco and O'Day cases are somewhat at variance in their implications for advisor liability. Clearly the advisor is now deemed to be clearly subject to claims in a resulting bankruptcy. But while the Interco case seems to exonerate the advisor for basing its judgment and forecasts on faulty data supplied by insiders, the O'Day case did not exonerate the defendant bank although the data supplied to it also were inaccurate. Perhaps there is a distinction between a bank and an outside advisor, but both should have the resources to evaluate the firm's prospects and not solely rely on management. The Interco case had the added ingredient that an asset appraisal firm was used by the advisor to assist in its determination of the fair value of the assets at time of the transaction. And the examiner did find that the appraiser was indeed at fault.

Conclusions

It is clear that some, perhaps many, highly leveraged transactions will be attacked on the basis of an FC, where the operative fraud bias will be "constructive" rather than "with intent." The most important result will be liabilities of certain parties, primarily the selling shareholders and senior lenders and to a lesser extent the various advisors to the transaction. Clearly this will make these transactions more costly and fewer will get done. This will, in the long run, reduce the bankruptcy rate due to excessive leverage. One cannot conclude, however, that the economy will be better off since fewer value-creating deals will also take place.

The short-term outlook is for increased FC claims materializing as a result of the ill-fated deals of the late 1980s. Once the system is flushed of these events, however, the longer term outlook is for fewer FC claims. This will be the result of fewer and more soundly financial leveraged deals and the more careful analysis done at the time of the transaction by those parties at risk. Luehrman and Hirt (1991) made the point that the senior creditors are in the best position to see that the unsecured creditors do not find themselves in a position where they must sue to reclaim part or all of their investment. By withholding their financing resources in the case of questionable analysis done by the other principals in a leveraged deal, the senior lender will act as an "enforcer" to ensure careful, conservative analysis.

While we agree with this observation, we also note that the pendulum may swing, in the short run, too far to the side of ultra-careful and conservative criteria—thereby stifling legitimate economic activities and national growth.

DEBTOR-IN-POSSESSION LENDING

The second emerging trend involves a recently enlarged financing mechanism whereby loans are made to companies that have become debtors-in-possession (DIP) under Chapter 11 of the Bankruptcy Code. DIP loans are generally made to provide working capital to companies which became distressed due to capital structures that are overleveraged relative to the firm's earning power and resulting cash flow coverage. As such, firms which qualify for such loans are judged to be operationally sound but find it necessary to reorganize under the protective provisions of the Bankruptcy Code. Such DIP financing is covered under section 364 of the Code and is usually secured by the firm's inventories. This section of the Code simply provides a framework for financing firms in bankruptcy but does not guarantee repayment. In its desire to rehabilitate ailing companies, the courts give preferential treatment to lenders who are willing to provide postpetition funds. These funds are oftentimes critical for the company to continue to operate during reorganization. This has never been clearer and more important than for the recent spate of large, retail bankruptcies where the ability to continually stock shelves is imperative to continuing operation.

The history of DIP financing is not as long or steeped in legal precedent as the FC event, discussed above, but it has been in existence for several decades. Indeed, a few banks, insurance, and finance companies, such as Sterling National Bank in New York, have included DIP loans as an important part of its business strategy for many years. Only recently, with the proliferation of bankruptcy filings of large, highly leveraged companies, has the DIP market expanded with lending institutions such as Chemical, General Electric Credit (GECC), Wells Fargo, Bankers Trust, and Citicorp now proudly trumpeting their activity and expertise. The reason for this new-found enthusiasm is simple, although not new. It is the ability to be granted a super-priority status in the hierarchy of creditors and at the same time realize large interest margins over the banks' cost of funds and also other fee-generating activities.

The DIP market has grown to such an extent, and with demonstrated attractive features to all parties involved, that several of the nation's rating agencies are now providing investment grade ratings to these mainly private financings. Both Fitch (March 25, 1991) and Standard & Poor's (May 1991) have put out special reports on DIP financing and have designated personnel and resources to cover the emerging market.

Since DIP financing is another form of a private placement, no comprehensive data base exists. Estimates of the size of the market are over $2 billion in 1990 and over $3 billion in 1991 (see Exhibit 17–1 for a partial list of recent DIP financings). The market has grown to include syndicated DIP loans as well as single lender-borrower relationships. In addition to the obvious loan-spread profit potential, banks attempt to acquire DIP clients who will be a source of lending activity after emerging from bankruptcy-reorganization and to obtain entry for its restructuring group to assist the firm and earn fees while in reorganization. These attractions have made the market far more competitive and margins are already beginning to fall despite the increased demand for these funds.

Fees and Spreads

The DIP business not only has attractive risk priority aspects, it also involves considerable profit potential. The following list of items constitute revenues to the lender:

- *Upfront fee*—usually 2–4 percent of the amount borrowed
- *Interest on loan*—1–3 percent over the prime rate on the amount borrowed except lower where the borrower was also a prepetition debtor of the same lender.
- *Unused line fee*—50 basis points (0.5 percent) on unused part of the DIP line of credit
- *Administrative fee*—$12,000–$20,000 per month to monitor the collateral, etc., on the loan
- *Letter of credit fee*—2–3 percent on the LC (if applicable)

Most DIP loans are made for one or two years. If only for one year, the lender may also collect points (upfront fee) for an extension. Due to these relatively high profit opportunities, competition among lenders is likely to increase and there were already signs to this effect as the early growing

EXHIBIT 17–1
DIP Financings for Major Chapter 11 Companies

Debtor	Date Filed	DIP Amount ($ Mil.)	Agent
Allied Stores Corp.	1/90	$ 300	Chemical
Allied Stores Credit Corp.	1/90	721	Chemical
Allegheny International	2/88	175	Chemical
Ames Department Stores Inc.	4/90	250	Chemical
Best Products Co.	1/91	250	Chemical
CHH Receivables Inc.	2/91	550	Chemical
C. R. Anthony	2/91	50	GECC
Carter Hawley Hale, Inc.	2/91	800	Chemical
Channel Home Centers Inc.	1/91	145	GECC
Columbia Gas System	/91	275	Chemical
Columbia Transmission	/91	80	Chemical
Federated Department Stores	1/90	400	Citibank
Greyhound Lines Inc.	6/90	10	Toronto-Dominion
Hills Stores Co.	2/91	250	Chemical
Insilco Corp.	1/91	57	Wells Fargo
Interco Inc.	1/91	185	Bank of NY
L. J. Hooker	8/89	50	GECC
Macy's	1/92	600	Chemical/Bankers
McCrory Corp.	2/92	100	CIT/Business Credit
National Gypsum Co.	10/90	105	GECC
P. A. Bagner	/91	425	Chemical
Pan Am World Airways	1/91	150	Bankers Trust
Paul Harris Stores	/91	10	Chemical
Revco D.S. Inc.	7/88	145	Wells Fargo
Rexene Chemical	11/91	25	GECC
Seaman's Furniture	1/92	25	GECC
Southland	10/90	400	Bankers Trust
Tracor Inc.	2/91	25	Continental
U.S. Home	4/91	75	GECC
Zale Corp.	1/92	510	Chemical

Sources: Fitch Investors Service, Inc., New York, *Special Debtor-In-Possession Loans Report,* March 25, 1991, and discussions with market major participants.

stage of the market stabilized at the end of 1991.

Rating Criteria

The three most important factors in determining whether a DIP issue receives a relatively high investment grade rating are (1) the super-priority status of the loan, (2) the assessment as to whether the firm will emerge as a going concern from the Chapter 11 process and (3) the lien over tangible property should the firm have to liquidate. The automatic-stay provision on prepetition borrowings and the priority status accorded postpetition DIP loans over the earlier creditors, as well as a super-priority status over other postpetition financings are keys to the market's presence and attractiveness. Since the main purposes of the DIP loan are both to finance operations and to demonstrate a company's viability, the success of the Chapter 11 process is fundamental. Finally, should there be a liquidation, the fact that the lender can look to specific assets for repayment reduces the overall risk even further.

The court can provide DIP loan priorities over other postpetition priority administrative expenses, tax authorities, prepetition unsecured creditors, and even secured creditors (as long as the latter is adequately protected). It is no wonder then that a properly constructed DIP loan with the appropriate court sanctions can and does receive an investment grade rating from the rating agencies.

Almost all ratings have heretofore been given to nonpublic issues although the firm (debtor) pays for the rating just like a public issue. The fees charged by the rating agencies vary but have been in the $35,000–$50,000 range. A high grade rating not only facilitates the DIP loan's acquisition but also sends a strong signal to suppliers, customers, and the economy in general that the borrower is a viable entity.

The first *rated* public DIP financing was a $250 million loan to Hills Department Stores from Chemical Bank in February 1991. The issue received an A rating from Fitch Investors Service. One of the primary reasons for the public rating was to demonstrate that Hills was a viable entity. An additional reason for a public rating is to help syndicate loans, particularly to foreign investors who rely on the rating services. It is somewhat surprising that there have not been more publicly rated DIP loan issues since debtors are always looking for credibility and the ratings will likely be investment grade. Perhaps the private DIP market is reasonably well promoted and the public rating is not valued as an important marginal benefit.

Most of the other credit criteria used to determine a rating are fairly standard and similar to those of public bond issues. They include an assessment of (1) business analysis, (2) industry position, (3) financial structure, and (4) management. In addition, specialized legal and loan servicing criteria are blended into the rating process. Once a rating is given and the loan made, a periodic review process is carried out. Fitch claims this review is done at a minimum on a semiannual basis and usually also when some important event occurs that affects the Chapter 11 process for the borrower.

PREPACKAGED BANKRUPTCIES

In the last few years a new type of bankruptcy has emerged that attempts to combine the time and cost saving attributes of an out-of-court distressed restructuring with the more lenient voting conditions of a formal Chapter 11 proceeding. The key element in the process is the elimination of the minority holdout problem in that only two thirds of the voting creditors in amount and more than 50 percent in number need to sanction a reorganization plan while a successful distressed restructuring prior to bankruptcy requires at least 85–90 percent of the creditors to vote for amendments to the indenture and other important charges. This is not to minimize the necessity in a prepackaged Chapter 11 to still reach an informal consensus from a reasonable amount of creditors.

Section 11 U.S.C. 1126(b) of the Bankruptcy Code permits a debtor to negotiate with creditors prior to a filing and accepts prepetition votes with proper disclosure. If no such law applies, then a plan can still be sanctioned as accepted or rejected if "adequate information" to all creditors and owners was disclosed under 11 U.S.C. 1125(a). The latter section now includes a substantial body of law as to what constitutes "adequate information." These include requirements of the SEC Act of 1934 for public securities and the receipt by all impaired stakeholders of the information in a reasonable time frame for analysis, discussion, and vote. In substantial asset cases, confirmation orders usually take at least 60 days and as much as 180 days, so reasonable time is not usually an issue. The confirmation period also ensures selection of a representative creditors' committee before the Chapter 11 commences. Appeals for additional members are still possible, however. While it may not be possible to assemble all creditors in a prebankruptcy meeting, it is often possible to locate the major creditors or their trustees to work up a plan and submit a disclosure statement.

A debtor who negotiates a prepackaged Chapter 11 has the advantage of a clearly defined exit strategy from the bankruptcy and has dramatically increased its chances of emerging as a going concern. A recent study estimated that only 10–12 percent of all Chapter 11 bankruptcies, during 1979–1986, actually successfully emerged from Chapter 11. And, while it still may take many months to emerge even after a prefiling plan is agreed upon, the average time in bankruptcy of these cases is far less than the two years plus average of all Chapter 11s under the new Bankruptcy Code.

Necessary Ingredients

According to Salerno and Hansen (1991), there are four essential ingredients to a successful prepackaged reorganization:
1. Foresight of the debtor to realistically assess the magnitude of its financial problems.
2. Willingness and ability to incur professional fees necessary to implement the prepackaged strategy.
3. Formulation of a viable exit strategy and a going forward business plan.
4. A creditor group(s) that is willing to negotiate the prepackaged plan and which finds the business plan and exit strategy, i.e., new capital structure, acceptable.

While the last ingredient is necessary, the first three are prerequisites to the plan's acceptance. In our opinion, an additional key ingredient to a successful large firm prepackaged deal reflects the debtor's ability to raise new equity capital. New equity is important even when there is a viable core business and the main problem appears to be too much debt. This was critical in the Southland Corporation case. (This case involved an unsuccessful first effort to prepackage a deal and it took six months to finally conclude a plan. Its final confirmation was mainly based on the new equity's role.) New equity infusion by existing or new investors signals the market that real economic value exists in the firm's assets. While capital can also be raised via DIP financings, the super-priority status of these investors is not as clear of a signal as the willingness for investors to contribute equity—the lowest priority type of capital.

Prepackaged Plan Risks and Costs

A prepackaged plan is not without its disadvantages and costs. Again, Salerno and Hansen list these as:
1. Requiring cash to pay the necessary fees.
2. Informing the business community of the firm's problems.
3. Providing creditors time to undertake collection efforts in anticipation of a bankruptcy.

The first requirement is obvious since there is little chance that an advisor will work toward a prepackaged filing unless there is sufficient cash set aside to cover the newly incurred costs. The second item is probably not too important since the debtor's problems are probably already known to the industry. While the third item is likely refutable through voidable preference payments, the process of dealing with panicked and difficult creditors is unpleasant at best and certainly costly in time as well as resources spent.

In addition, there is always the possibility that what was thought to be a successfully negotiated prepetition plan will prove to be rejected once the Chapter 11 confirmation process begins. This can be caused by a change in the business outlook for the debtor and/or a recalcitrant major creditor who changes its mind. A prominent example of a misfired prepackage that took much longer than planned to accomplish in Chapter 11 is Resorts International.

Other Legal and Tax Issues Motivating Prepackaged Deals

Changes in the tax laws now favor Chapter 11 filings over out-of-court distressed restructurings. The Tax Reform Act of 1986 changed the tax treatment of net-operating-loss (NOL) carryovers and the circumstances when they can be used. In rewriting section 382 of the Internal Revenue Code, the new provisions established limitations where there have been ownership changes of more than 50 percent of the company's stock within a specified period. If the ownership change is more than 50 percent over the previous three years, the availability of NOLs to offset income will be reduced to an annual limitation. If the company is in bankruptcy, however, section 352 may not apply if the prepetition stockholders *and* creditors own at least 50 percent of the vote and value of the new, restructured company. The key point is that the old creditors are included. While the technical facts in preserving NOLs are quite complex, the essence here is that a prepackaged Chapter 11 has the ability to save the restructured firm substantial tax payments and the private out-of-court distressed exchange does not.

The Budget and Reconciliation Act of 1990 discourages an exchange of one type of debt for another if the value of the new package is considerably less than the par value of the old, as is typical in most distressed situations. The debtor is liable for the difference in value and must report it as income. This is also true of debt for preferred stock exchanges. The benchmark for the amount of income reported is the trading value of both the new and old securities or just the old security if the original one is publicly traded and the new package is not. This increased "income" is not taxable under a formal Chapter 11.

What's more, the recent LTV decision by the U.S. Southern District Court in New York required that investor-creditors who accept a distress restructuring plan retain a claim, if and when a bankruptcy occurs in the future, of only the trading value of the old securities at the time of the plan's acceptance and not the par value of the old securities. In essence, the difference in values is treated as an original-issue discount. Hence, a distressed investor who purchases a debt issue at 50 percent of par value is not likely to be favorably disposed to accept an out-of-court plan when these securities are trading at a lower or even slightly higher value.

This so-called LTV decision has been vigorously opposed by many investors, bankruptcy analysts, and lawyers but appears to be the "de facto" doctrine although not yet enshrined in law. Since creditors who do not accept the prepetition restructuring are not bound by it, there is now little incentive for most creditors to accept and the likelihood of a Chapter 11 filing is considerably heightened. In a Chapter 11, however, dissenting minority creditors will, in many cases, have the plan "crammed down" and made binding to all classes of creditors and owners. Still, it is likely that a heavily impaired class, e.g., common stockholders, will be better off in a plan crafted out-of-court than one that is based on a long drawn out bankrupt proceeding. Indeed, Gilson, John and Lang (1990) provide evidence that stockholders fare better when debt is restructured privately and we hypothesize that they will also do better in a prepackaged deal.

Since not one creditor can ever be forced to give up its rights to cash interest or principal repayment, outside of a Chapter 11 case or similar state proceeding, this has caused many large company voluntary exchange offers to fail, e.g., Coleco, Petro-Lewis, Public Service of New Hampshire, and Western Union to name a few prominent ones.

Successful Prepackaged Deals

Since the October 1986 Crystal Oil bankruptcy, which was concluded in less than three months, prepackaged plans have emerged and continue to grow in number. Still, the incidence of even this seemingly new better setup has not been as prominent as one might think.

In addition to Crystal Oil's (1986—three months) and Southland's (1989—six months) results, successful prepackaged Chapter 11s include Republic Health (1989—four months), La Salle Energy (1990—three months), Circle Express (1990—two months), JPS Textile (1991—three months), TIE Communications (1991—two and one half months), Edgell Communications (1991—one month), Kroy Inc. (1990—three months), Arizona Biltmore Hotel (1990—one month), Anglo Energy (1990—three months), and 14 Wall Street Associates (1990—two months).

Most prepackaged plans in major cases involve highly leveraged debtors whose primary creditors include publicly held subordinate bonds as well as some senior bank debt and trade debt. The latter tend to be relatively small but sufficiently crucial to the going forward business plan that the proposal usually leaves them unimpaired. Sophisticated distressed investors know this likelihood and may seek trade debt purchases from creditors who are unwilling to wait even for a relatively quick Chapter 11 confirmation.

Concluding Comments

A number of economists, including Jensen's (1991) privatization of bankruptcy discussion, have argued for the benefits of out-of-court restructurings, especially their ability to significantly reduce certain bankruptcy costs. While I believe that distressed costs can still be sizeable even for the firm that successfully avoids long, drawn-out formal bankruptcy proceedings, it is undeniable that time and cost savings occur if the firm's problems are addressed earlier in the "deterioration chain." The prepackaged Chapter 11 phenomenon is a variation on the privatization theme and as such retains much of the same benefits of the private agreements that seemed to be gaining acceptance prior to recent court decisions and tax enactments.

REFERENCES

Baird, J., and T. Jackson, 1985, "Fraudulent Conveyance Law and Its Proper Domain," *Vanderbilt Law Review 38,* 829.

Cook, M. L., et al., February 1991, "Fraudulent Transfers," Skadden, Arps, Slate, Meagher & Flom, New York.

Fitch Research, March 25, 1991, "Debtor-in-Possession Loan Rating Criteria," Fitch Investor Services, Inc., New York.

Jensen, Michael, Summer 1991, "Corporate Control and the Politics of Finance," *Journal of Applied Corporate Finance.*

Leeb, Fred, and Robert Scheuring, July 15, 1991, "Prepackaged Plans: A Useful

Tool for Management," *Surveyor Crisis Management, Turnaround & Workouts.*

Liss, K. J., 1987, "Fraudulent Conveyance Law and Leveraged Buyouts," *Columbia Law Review 87*, 1491.

Luehrman, Timothy, and Lance Hirt, July 1991, "Highly Leveraged Transactions and Fraudulent Conveyance Law," Harvard Business School working paper.

McConnell, John, and Henri Servaes, Summer 1991, "The Economics of Prepackaged Bankruptcy," *Journal of Applied Corporate Finance.*

Michel, Allen, and Israel Shaked, March/April 1990, "The LBO Nightmare: Fraudulent Conveyance Risk," *Financial Analysts Journal.*

Murdoch, D.; L. Sartin; and R. Zudek, November 1987, "Fraudulent Conveyances and Leveraged Buyouts," *The Business Lawyer.*

Salerno, Thomas, and Craig Hansen, January/February 1991, "A Prepackaged Bankruptcy Strategy," *Journal of Business Strategy.*

Standard & Poor's Creditweek, May 13, 1991, "Criteria for Debtor-in-Possession Loans," New York: Standard & Poor's Corp.

Wilkens, Odette, and Bruce MacEwen, May 1991, "LBOs & Fraudulent Conveyance Doctrine: Threat or Menace," New York University working paper.